Semantic Web for Effective Healthcare

Scrivener Publishing
100 Cummings Center, Suite 541J
Beverly MA, 01915-6106

Machine Learning in Biomedical Science and Healthcare Informatics

Series Editors: Vishal Jain and Jyotir Moy Chatterjee

In this series, the focus centers on the various applications of machine learning in the biomedical engineering and healthcare fields, with a special emphasis on the most representative learning techniques, namely deep learning-based approaches. Machine learning tasks typically classified into two broad categories depending on whether there is a learning "label" or "feedback" available to a learning system: supervised learning and unsupervised learning. This series also introduces various types of machine learning tasks in the biomedical engineering field from classification (supervised learning) to clustering (unsupervised learning). The objective of the series is to compile all aspects of biomedical science and healthcare informatics, from fundamental principles to current advanced concepts.

Submission to the series: Please send book proposals to **drvishaljain83@gmail.com** and/or **jyotirchatterjee@gmail.com**

Publishers at Scrivener
Martin Scrivener (martin@scrivenerpublishing.com)
Phillip Carmical (pcarmical@scrivenerpublishing.com)

Semantic Web for Effective Healthcare

Edited by
Vishal Jain
Sharda University, India
Jyotir Moy Chatterjee
Lord Buddha Education Foundation, Nepal
Ankita Bansal
Netaji Subhas University of Technology, India
and
Abha Jain
Shaheed Rajguru College of Applied Sciences for Women, Delhi University, India

Scrivener Publishing

WILEY

This edition first published 2022 by John Wiley & Sons, Inc., 111 River Street, Hoboken, NJ 07030, USA and Scrivener Publishing LLC, 100 Cummings Center, Suite 541J, Beverly, MA 01915, USA

For more information about Scrivener publications please visit www.scrivenerpublishing.com.

Wiley Global Headquarters
111 River Street, Hoboken, NJ 07030, USA

For details of our global editorial offices, customer services, and more information about Wiley products visit us at www.wiley.com.

Library of Congress Cataloging-in-Publication Data

ISBN 978-1-119-76229-4

Cover image: Pixabay.Com
Cover design by Russell Richardson

Set in size of 11pt and Minion Pro by Manila Typesetting Company, Makati, Philippines

Contents

Preface

The tremendous amount of data being generated on a daily basis in hospitals and other medical institutions needs to be properly harnessed and analyzed in order to gain useful insights. In other words, the health-related data needs to be explored in order to uncover valuable information that could lead to improved healthcare practices and the development of better biomedical products. However, there are many challenges, which need to be addressed before this goal is reached. One of the major challenges is interoperability of health and medical data. The data generated not only comes from different sources but also has inconsistencies in naming, structure, and format. An important requirement is to capture relevant data and also make it widely available for others to use. In addition to the data integration problem, user interaction with the data is another challenge. The difficulty lies in search handling, data navigation and data presentation. Finally, another challenge is how to use this huge amount of data to find valuable new patterns and transform such data into valuable knowledge, leading to potential improvement of resource utilization and patient health, and the development of biomedical products. There is a vast potential for data mining and data analytics tools in healthcare that could lead to useful information for decision making. In recent years, the Semantic Web has been gaining ground in addressing these challenges. The aim of this book is to analyze the current status on how the Semantic Web can be used to solve various challenges and enlighten readers with key advances in ontology-based information retrieval techniques in the healthcare domain. The following is a brief summary of the wide range of subjects covered throughout the book.

- Chapter 1 discusses various information extraction techniques used to model the documents product/service reviews. The advantages of using the Semantic Web to ease communication between businesses and improve processes are also discussed.

- Chapter 2 explores the impact of Semantic Web technologies and the challenges associated with their use in effective healthcare systems and also proposes solutions, which can be achieved with the present technology. In addition to this, some algorithms, frameworks, and real-time database systems realized with the help of artificial intelligence and web technology-based solutions are also discussed.
- Chapter 3 focuses on the importance of an ontology-based system for a patient monitoring system. A domain ontology has been constructed to preserve the details of patient health issues. With the support of ontology, a patient monitoring system is constructed wherein data concerning every detail about the patient and their health is stored.
- Chapter 4 highlights the role of Semantic Web technologies in improving services provided by healthcare systems. It elaborates on the search techniques used by researchers in the field to find the desired information. The role of semantics, how they are beneficial in the search process, and domain-specific resources are presented in detail. The latest technological advancements and resources from the biomedical field are also discussed.
- Chapter 5 discusses what actionable content should look like in practice and how it can become more efficient by aiding in clinical decision-making and administrative capability. The chapter renders various definitions of actionable content, and also focuses on the stages of health analytics and how ontology can be used for prescriptive health analytics.
- Chapter 6 depicts the retrieval of ontology-based information from the medical literature database MEDLINE. The main focus of the chapter is to enhance the retrieval of information from the medical literature database and conduct the search with more clarity. The approach discussed to achieve this is the preliminary design and execution of an ontology-based intelligent agent system that applies Semantic Web language, which benefits efficient systematic retrieval of medical information.
- Chapter 7 presents a historical analysis of an ontology-based system for robotic surgery and documents the most significant interventions of robots in medical surgery. The chapter discusses how the academic field has embraced this new discipline and how inclusive research on a worldwide scale

has honed the design and method of robotic procedures, all while maintaining an impeccable metric.

- Chapter 8 presents the applications of IoT in healthcare and how these applications can be used with the help of various sensors. It discusses the established strategies used by IoT-based devices to deal with patients, doctors, and hospitals in order to provide smarter and faster services. The authors propose an IoT-based architecture for monitoring the health of patients remotely.
- Chapter 9 discusses the use of precision medicine in the context of ontology. It explains ontologies and their application in computational reasoning to promote an accurate classification of patients' diagnoses and managing care, and for translational research.
- Chapter 10 discusses the use of knowledge graphs for knowledge representation. A model for such a knowledgebase is proposed that makes use of open information extraction systems to capture relevant knowledge from medical literature and curate it in the knowledgebase of the clinical decision support system.
- Chapter 11 covers all aspects related to the successful customization of data semantics, ontologies, clinical jobs, and free learning, and depicts the Unified Medical Language System (UMLS) framework used inside AQ21 rule learning programming. Ontologies are the quality systems for expressive genuine variables in clinical and flourishing fields.
- Chapter 12 provides information on rare diseases and explores the relationship between rare diseases, diagnoses, and information retrieval. In particular, it illustrates the history, characteristics, types, and classification along with databases of rare disease information. It also explores the challenges faced by researchers in rare disease information retrieval and how they can be resolved by search query optimization.
- Chapter 13 reviews the recent advances in medical terminology tools and application strategies currently in use for semantic reasoning and interoperability in healthcare. Common terminology standards used in health information and technology, such as SNOMED CT, RxNorm, LOINC, ICD-x-CM, and UCUM, are discussed. Also discussed are the current reference terminology mapping solutions that

enable semantic interoperability of data between health systems.
- Chapter 14 builds upon the existing AI-based model in order to discover a new model to improve healthcare facilities for the faster recovery of COVID-19 patients. The chapter discusses different AI-related solutions for the healthcare industry.

In conclusion, we are grateful to all those who directly and indirectly contributed to this book. We are also grateful to the publisher for giving us the opportunity to publish it.

Vishal Jain
Jyotir Moy Chatterjee
Ankita Bansal
Abha Jain
September 2021

Acknowledgment

I would like to acknowledge the most important people in my life—my late grandfather Shri Gopal Chatterjee, my late grandmother Smt. Subhankori Chatterjee, my late mother Nomita Chatterjee, my uncle Shri. Moni Moy Chatterjee, and my father Shri. Aloke Moy Chatterjee. The book has been my long-cherished dream, which would not have become a reality without the support and love of these amazing people. They continued to encourage me despite my failing to give them the proper time and attention. I am also grateful to my friends, who have encouraged and blessed this work with their unconditional love and patience.

Jyotir Moy Chatterjee
Department of IT
Lord Buddha Education Foundation
(Asia Pacific University of Technology & Innovation)
Kathmandu, Nepal

1

An Ontology-Based Contextual Data Modeling for Process Improvement in Healthcare

A. M. Abirami[1]* and A. Askarunisa[2]

[1]Department of Information Technology, Thiagarajar College of Engineering, Madurai, Tamil Nadu, India
[2]Department of Computer Science and Engineering, KLN College of Information Technology, Madurai, Tamil Nadu, India

Abstract
The internet world contains large volume of text data. The integration of web sources is required to derive needed information. Human annotation is much difficult and tedious. Automated processing is necessary to make these data readable by machines. But mostly they are available in unstructured format, and they need to be formatted into structured form. Structured information is retrieved from unstructured or semi-structured text which is defined as text analytics. There are many Information Extraction (IE) techniques available to model the documents (product/service reviews). Vector space model uses only the content but not the contextual representation. This complexity is resolved by Semantic web, the initiative of WWW Consortium. The advantage of the use of Semantic web enables the ease of communication between Businesses and in process improvement.

Keywords: Ontology, semantic-web, decision making, healthcare, service, reviews

1.1 Introduction

Text analysis is defined as deriving structured data from unstructured text. Additional information like customer insight about the product or service can be retrieved from the unstructured data sources using text

**Corresponding author*: abiramiam@tce.edu

Vishal Jain, Jyotir Moy Chatterjee, Ankita Bansal and Abha Jain (eds.) Semantic Web for Effective Healthcare, (1–38) © 2022 Scrivener Publishing LLC

analytics techniques. Its techniques have different applications such as insurance claims assessment, competitor analysis, sentiment analysis and the like. Many industries use text analytics for their business improvement. Social media impacts different industries like product business [1, 2], tourism [3, 4], and healthcare service [5] with the tremendous changes in the recent past years.

Retrieving and summarizing web data, which are dispersed in different web pages, are difficult and complex processes; also, they consume most of the manual effort and time. No standard data model exists for web documents. This increases the necessity of annotating the huge number of text documents that exist in the World Wide Web (WWW). Extracting and collating the information from these text is a complex task. Unlike numerical dataset, text documents contain more number of features. The amount of resources required to represent big dataset may be improved by representing the text documents with most needed and non-redundant features. Classification or clustering algorithms may be used for identifying the features from the text documents. The documents are analyzed, modeled and then used in the process of business improvement or for personal interest. Thus, the annotated text improves automated decision-making process, which in turn reduces the manual effort and time required for text analysis.

The report from British Columbia Safety and Quality Council says when patients and healthcare service entities are engaged in online platform, then there would be greater improvement in offering healthcare services. Improvement in healthcare services is visible when insights from the experience of patients are analyzed [5]. Hence, it becomes necessary to consolidate the opinions from the customers or clients so as to improve business, decision-making and increase revenue. Figure 1.1 gives the overview of decision-making process from the online product/service reviews, using different information extraction and text analysis techniques.

There exist many challenges while analyzing the social media text or user-generated content. In languages like English, the same word has multiple meaning (polysemy), and different words have same meaning (synonymy). People show "variety" and use heterogeneous words while expressing their views. It often leads to complication in processing the textual data. Most of the feature extraction techniques do not consider the semantic relationships between the terms. Subjectivity that exists in text processing techniques adds complexity to the process, which in turn impacts the evaluation of results. Also, the rare availability of gold-standard or annotated text data for different domains add more challenges to text analysis [6]. Hence, the identification and application of suitable Natural Language

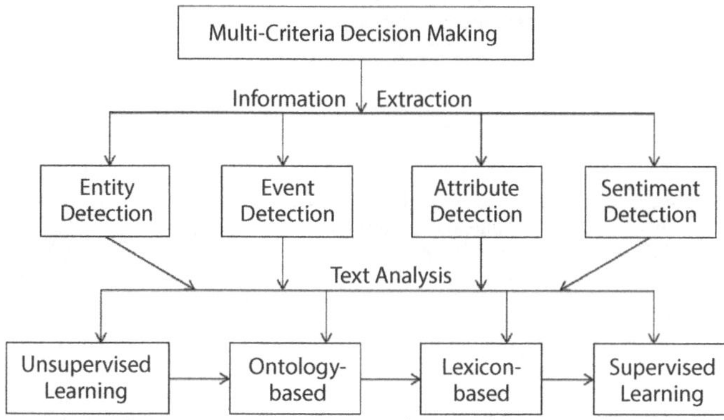

Figure 1.1 Decision-making process from social media reviews.

Processing (NLP) techniques are the main research focus in text data analysis.

Text analytics supports the context matching between the reader and the writer. This challenge can be managed if different vocabularies of features and their relationship are well represented in the data model. For example, content based contextual user feedback analysis enables the users to buy new products or avail any service by highlighting the best features of products or services. Challenges and issues in information retrieval problems are overcome if Ontology representation and topic modelling techniques are used for modeling the text documents. The chapter focuses on extracting relevant features from the set of documents and building domain ontology for them. The Ontology helps in building the predictive or sentiment analysis model by using suitable information retrieval (IR) techniques and contextual representation of data, so as to enable automated decision-making process, before buying a new product or availing a new service, as shown in Figure 1.2.

1.1.1 Ontology-Based Information Extraction

Ontology describes a domain of classes. It is defined as a conceptual model of knowledge representation. The concepts of the domain (classes), their attributes, their properties and their relationships are well described by the Ontology model. It also explains the meanings of the terms applicable to the domain. Ontology is one of the key components of semantic web technology. The semantic web technologies like Ontology, RDF and Sparql are

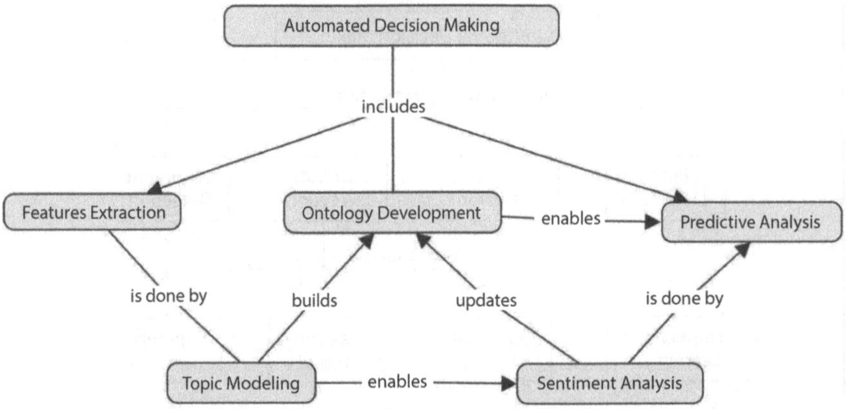

Figure 1.2 User-generated content analysis (UCA) model.

used in describing different words and their dependencies by modeling the textual data. Components of Ontology include:

- Concepts are also known as Classes. It is a unit of knowledge, shared among identified group of persons for the concept's domain. There exists relationship among concepts.
- Instances are individuals of concepts. They represent specific elements attached to the domain ontology. Instances are the "thing" represented by a concept.

Information Extraction (IE) and Ontology are related with one another like: Ontology is used in information extraction as part of understanding process of the domain; on the other hand, IE is used to design and enrich Ontology [7]. Common vocabulary and shared understanding among different people are enabled by Ontology. The contextual representation of data semantics is well described by the Ontology [8]. The UML diagrams along with Ontology support the biologists by classifying the entities and interactions between proteins and genes [9]. The terms (vocabularies) and the concepts (classes) in the source Ontology are used in term matching, thereby used in tagging the text documents. Thus the Ontology and their specifications are used in the information extraction process.

1.1.2 Ontology-Based Knowledge Representation

Knowledge is data that represents the outcome of computer-based cognitive processes such as perception, learning, association, and reasoning, or the translation of knowledge acquired by human [10]. It is the language by which human express their understanding about the concept. The concepts and the instances of a particular domain are expressed in the knowledge base also referred as the semantic knowledge dictionary. It is one of the most important techniques to represent the knowledge for a domain. Domain Ontology is developed to formally define the concepts, relationships, and rules so as to include the semantic content of the domain. The semantic approach uses the concepts in the documents to establish the contextual relationship rather than the terms. Issues like synonymy and polysemy may not be resolved if terms are used as indices while modelling the text documents. Various semantic-based information extraction approaches like Latent Semantic Indexing [11] and Latent Dirichlet Allocation [12, 13] techniques are used for building the relationship among the indexed terms, so as to represent the contexts between the concepts. This chapter focuses on developing domain Ontology to represent the features and their related terms mentioned in the product/service reviews generated in social media web sites.

1.2 Related Work

Ontology facilitates the shared understanding among the people by formalizing the conceptualization of a specific domain. The contextual representation of data semantics is well described by the Ontology [8]. Ontology defines concepts (domain) by using the common vocabulary and describes attributes, behavior, relationships and constraints. The UML diagrams along with The interactions between proteins and genes are well explained by Ontology representation which would support the biologists for classification [9]. Reviews on hotels and movies are classified using the rule-based systems and Ontology [14–16]. Document annotation and rules were used to create knowledge base of web documents from the extraction of semantic data like named entities [14, 17, 18]. Ontology learning and RDF repositories were used for building the knowledge and information management which in turn enabled the automatic annotation and retrieval of documents [19]. Wordnet Ontology was used in extracting the sentiments based on lexicon dictionaries [20, 21].

Information extraction process uses Ontology for understanding the domain and for extracting the relevant information. Its complexity is reduced as it is domain specific. IE techniques are then used for populating and enhancing the Ontology. These Ontologies can be enriched from the useful sources of knowledge [7]. SVM classification along with

SentiWordNet enabled the building of sentiment dictionary for positive and negative categorization of text documents [23]. Opinion extraction techniques along with entropy-based classification techniques are used for building structured Ontology for the datasets Digital Camera [24]. Classification of products and their attributes based on their hierarchy was done using the hierarchical learning sentiment ontology tree (HL-SOT) algorithm which in turn used for opinion mining of products and their features [25].

Knowledge base refers the dictionary for the vocabulary used to represent concepts of a specific domain. The Ontology provides the semantic knowledge for class instances like a dictionary. The meaning of the documents may be extracted using the semantic-based approach by establishing the suitable context within the document, instead of using terms present in the document. Related terms were extracted and categorized using the semantic-based approaches like LSI [11] and LDA [13] techniques. Ontology-based sentiment analysis model was developed for mining product features from customer reviews [1]. Ontology along with Genetic Algorithm, a hybrid-model, was used for automatic grouping of Chinese proposals into different clusters resulted in >90% F-measure value [26]. Sentiment lexicons of emotional categories were derived from the twitter posts of mobile products by using Ontology learning and the lexicon-based techniques [27]. Ontology and vector analysis method was used in feature selection and sentiment analysis of movie reviews [22]. Ontology-based sentiment analysis model along with rule-based classification was used in the postal services of United States and Canada [28]. Sentiment grabber model was developed using Ontology, probabilistic LDA and text annotations [13]. Hotel reviews were automatically classified by using SVM and fuzzy domain ontology [29].

Research on user-generated content was also focused on the lexicon-based or linguistic-based approach. Named entity recognition, feature extraction, reliability of content, language used are some of the challenges exist for text analysis. Information Retrieval (IR) techniques like Vector Space Modelling, Latent Semantic Indexing (LSI) and Latent Dirichlet Allocation (LDA) were used for transforming unstructured free text into structured format. Words which do not represent entities were removed from consumer product reviews by using PMI measure, to improve the precision of feature extraction method [30]. In the lexicon-based approach, positive and negative words were extracted from the opinions [31–34], and overall sentiment aggregation was determined for the documents. Words or phrases in the presence of conjuncts and connectives were considered to build word dependencies. Sentiment analysis was then done using Naive

Bayes classification algorithm [31, 34]. Opinion observer was built using NLP techniques for detecting the polarity of opinions and by using the opinion aggregation function [35]. Automatic extraction of adjectives related to sentiments from blogs and reviews was proposed and used association rule mining for building the dictionary [32], which resulted in the accuracy of more than 70% for positive adjectives and more than 60% for negative adjectives. Similarly, sentiment dictionaries were created using naive Bayes algorithm and NLP techniques for developing opinion mining model for film reviews [36]. Poirier *et al.* concluded that machine learning algorithms were suitable for larger data set, whereas linguistic methods were suitable for smaller data set.

Double propagation method was proposed for the retrieval of new sentiments from sentences and positive or negative polarity was assigned for them [33]. Product's features were extracted using unsupervised learning techniques [11] from the review documents, and words belong to the same concept are grouped using Latent Semantic Association (LaSA) model. Text analysis and statistical techniques were used to rank the product quality from their websites [31]. NLP techniques were used to identify the most frequently used positive and negative sentiment words for the classification of movie documents [37]. Non-negative matrix factorization and clustering techniques were used for retrieving suitable answers for the given query as a text summarization technique [38]. Lexicon-based NLP techniques were used to extract conjunctions, connectives, modals and conditionals for sentiment polarity detection of tweets [34]. Basiri *et al.* [39] used Dempster–Shafer theory for sentiment aggregation at document level using the mass function. The probabilistic based Latent Dirichlet Allocation (LDA) was used for annotation of semantics in text documents [13].

The user-generated content, which are in unstructured or semi-structured format, can be converted into structured format using NLP and machine learning techniques, and is made available for decision-making purposes. Multi-Criteria Decision Making (MCDM) techniques are used in different sectors like in fast food restaurants for measuring service quality [40], for ranking universities [41] and in different simple and complex industrial applications [42–45]. Customer lifetime value and their loyalty were evaluated based on the hybrid approach by combining Analytic Hierarchy Process (AHP) and association rule mining [46]. The best alternative for oil project fields was evaluated using AHP for weights identification and fuzzy TOPSIS for ranking process [44] and as the service quality indicators for tourism industry in Iran [47]. Different MCDM techniques along with statistical techniques were applied in different sectors like healthcare sector [48], movie recommender systems [49] for its performance measurement so as to improve its quality of services. MCDM technique like VIKOR was used for the measurement of customer satisfaction and ranking of mobile services [50] and for ranking the suppliers [51].

Ontology learning includes extraction of domain terms from the sources, modelling of data through Ontology development and easy retrieval while querying. Manual building of Ontology takes greater effort and it is complex and challenging. This motivates the researchers to automatically generate Ontology for the domain specific terms present in the social media reviews written for a product/service. The Ontology-based Semantic Indexing (OnSI) method tags concepts and attributes, into the Ontology using the contextually related words. It enables query processing and further information retrieval processing easier in subsequent steps. This semantic-based approach of indexing improves higher accuracy while identifying the concepts or attributes (or features) from the contents of text documents [26, 27]. Ontology-based approach for mobile product review classification was resulted in precision 75% and in recall 40% [52], and recall more than 82% [27].

1.3 Motivation

Feature extraction from product or service review documents often includes different steps like data pre-processing, document indexing, dimension reduction, model training, testing, and evaluation. Labeled data set of document collection is used to train or learn the model. Further, the learned model is used for identifying unlabeled concept instances from the new set of documents. Document indexing is the most critical and complex task in text analysis. It decides the set of key features to represent the document. It also enhances the relevancy between the word (or feature) and the document. It needs to be very effective as it decides the storage space required and query processing time of documents.

The Ontology-based or semantic-based approach is used to retrieve the concepts from the documents by establishing the contextual relationships. In content-based approach, BagOfWords model is used for representing the text, where synonymy and polysemy cannot be resolved as they use terns as indexes. However, in context-based semantic approaches like topic modeling techniques, concepts are used to extract information and their categorization. It projects the contextual relationship among the terms present in the documents.

In order to utilize the strength of Ontology in user-generated content analysis process, this chapter proposes a domain Ontology-based Semantic Indexing (OnSI) technique for product or service reviews generated by the customers in the social media platform. The integration of topic modelling technique with the Ontology learning is explained by the OnSI method; it is generic and is applicable to any domain.

1.4 Feature Extraction

The World Wide Web has large amount of text documents and the necessity of annotating them has become vital. Customers would express their views by writing product reviews, user feedback in the descriptive format, which is mostly in unstructured. This format makes difficult for the machines to process these text documents. Hence, it becomes necessary to annotate large volume of text in order to develop business intelligence or automated solutions. These data have to be analyzed and modelled for enabling the decision-making process. The challenging task of extracting the information is made easier by adding, annotating documents, which in turn paves the way for automated solutions [53].

Feature extraction is the process of building dataset with informative and non-redundant features from the initial set of data. The subsequent methods like feature selection reduces the amount of resources required for its representation. Many machine learning algorithms like classification and clustering are used for extracting the features such as entities and attributes from the text documents using their properties which are similar. The challenges like absence of semantic relations between entities while feature selection and lack of prior knowledge in domain may be overcome by applying suitable NLP and IE techniques [54, 55].

Feature extraction from product or service review documents often includes different steps like data pre-processing, document indexing, dimension reduction, model training, testing, and evaluation. Labeled data set of document collection is used to train or learn the model. Further, the learned model is used for identifying unlabeled concept instances from the new set of documents. Document indexing is the most critical and complex task in text analysis. It decides the set of key features to represent the document. It also enhances the relevancy between the word (or feature) and the document. It needs to be very effective as it decides the storage space required and query processing time of documents.

Pre-processed data is built into Term Document (TD) matrix by using term weighing schemes, as shown in Figure 1.3. The text documents are

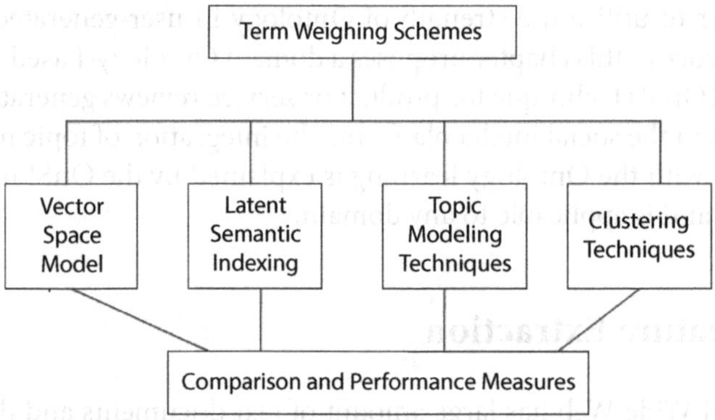

Figure 1.3 Term weighing schemes for feature extraction.

converted into numbers using Information Retrieval (IR) techniques, which vary in their weight allocation for each term.

IR like Vector Space Model (VSM), Latent Semantic Indexing (LSI), topic modeling techniques, and clustering techniques are used in the feature extraction of text documents for term weighing process. The following sub sections describe the rationales of different feature extraction techniques used in text analysis.

1.4.1 Vector Space Model

In the vector space model, the documents are represented as vectors through BagOfWords (BoW) model. It considers the set of words as "bag" but not the *order* of words present in the document. This may use *Boolean* model or *vector space* model to denote the weight of terms. Boolean model gives the weight as 1 or 0 based on the presence or absence of word in the document. Vector space model uses the term frequency as the weight of terms. Term weighting is the important factor in the document representation, which decides the efficiency of the IR system. It includes three components like Term Frequency (TF), Inverse Document Frequency (IDF) and the document length normalization. TF gives the distribution of each word in the document whereas IDF expresses the importance of each word in the document. Higher the number of occurrences of word yields lesser IDF value. Equation 1.1 determines the weight of word by using TF-IDF scheme.

$$w_{ij} = tf_{ij} * \log\left(\frac{N}{df_i}\right) \tag{1.1}$$

where tf_{ij} is the term frequency of term "i" in document "j," N is the total number of documents in the collection, df_i is the document frequency of term "i" in the collection, and w_{ij} is the weight for term "i" in document "j." Generally, the Term Document (TD) matrix of size "m x n" is built between words and documents, where "m" represents the terms (rows) and "n" represents the documents (columns), "w" represents the weight of the term.

1.4.2 Latent Semantic Indexing (LSI)

The Term Document matrix is very sparse in nature, if it is built for all words in the document collection. The terms may be unique across the documents and may not be repeated in all documents. It increases the size of matrix. The disadvantage of simple vector space model is that it cannot relate two synonymous words present in the document. In order to reduce the *sparseness* in the matrix and to address the *synonymy* issue, the vector space model can be extended and Latent Semantic Indexing (LSI) can be used for document indexing. Figure 1.4 shows the synonymy and polysemy representation of words in English language. LSI technique analyzes the text documents to determine the hidden meaning or concepts. For example, when the word "bank" comes along with other words like mortgage and loan, then it can be concluded that it is associated with a financial sector. If the word "bank" comes along with other words like fish and pond, then it is associated with the water body. This problem is solved by LSI technique by merely not comparing the words in the document space but does comparison of both words and documents in the *concept* space.

LSI uses *Singular Value Decomposition* (SVD) to reduce the dimensions of TD matrix. It reconstructs the matrix with the least possible information. It is a matrix factorization technique that factors "m x n" matrix into three matrices USV^T where matrix U represents the term matrix in concept space, matrix V^T represents the document matrix in concept space, and the S matrix is of singular values by which the number of dimensions

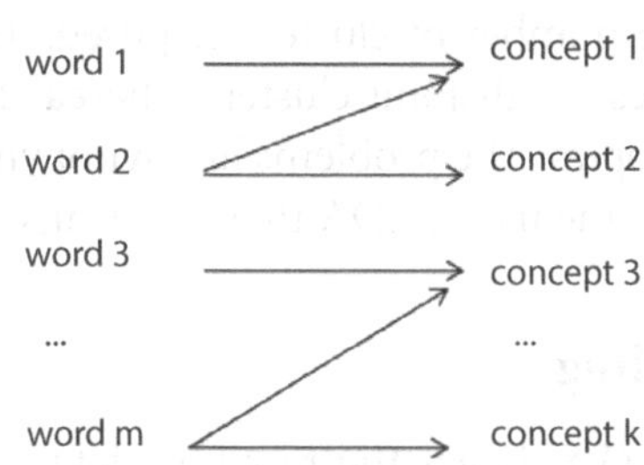

Figure 1.4 Synonymy and polysemy issues in English.

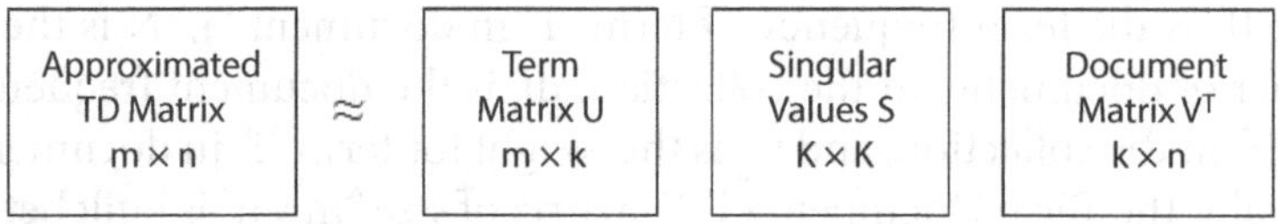

Figure 1.5 Approximated TD matrix by SVD.

or concepts can be selected. The complexity in SVD lies in figuring out how many dimensions or concepts that do exist in the document collection while approximating the matrix. The original TD matrix can be approximated to "*k*" dimensions, where *k* is much smaller than the rank of TD matrix. The value of "*k*" can be determined empirically. Usually, its value ranges between 100 and 350 for the large data collection. Figure 1.5 shows the schematic representation of truncated matrix on TD matrix.

LSI indexes words using low dimensional representation and word co-occurrence. The association of terms with documents, i.e., the semantic structure improves the relevancy of results for queries [56]. Value of "*k*" in low hundreds improves precision and recall value. LSI has its own disadvantages like more computation time and negative values in the approximated TD matrix.

1.4.3 Clustering Techniques

Clustering methods identify similar groups of data in a data set collection. Centroid model, the K-Means algorithm, is an iterative clustering algorithm groups all the data point closer to the centroid. It is important to have prior knowledge on the data set, as this algorithm takes the number of clusters as input. It partitions the "n" data points into "k" clusters in which each data point belongs to the cluster with the nearest mean. There are many variations exist in using K-Means algorithm like using Euclidian distance between centroid and the data point, fuzzy C-Means clustering and so on. Like LDA, K-Means is also an unsupervised learning algorithm where the user needs to give the number of clusters required. The only difference is that K-Means produces "k" disjoint clusters whereas LDA assigns a document to a mixture of topics. The problems like synonymy and polysemy can be better resolved with the use of LDA than K-Means algorithm technique.

1.4.4 Topic Modeling

Vector Space Models (VSM) get the raw text data and indexes the term against the documents. LSI technique shows 30% improved accuracy compared with traditional VSMs [29]. Further, the previous research carried out in IR domain with LSI technique says that LSI improves *recall* but *precision* is not comparatively improved [22, 26]. This disadvantage can be overcome by processing the raw data before applying indexing technique. Hidden concepts in the document collection can be included while indexing the terms and documents which substantially improves the accuracy [58]. Latent Dirichlet Allocation (LDA) technique [58] uncovers latent "topics" in a document collection where topics are a kind of features. It is a language model for modeling the topics of documents in a probabilistic approach. Each document may contain a mixture of different topics. Each topic may contain many occurrences of words related to it in documents. Figure 1.6 shows the framework of LDA model for topic (or feature) categorization of text documents.

For example, the Word 2 is categorized under two different topics say, "topic 1" and "topic 2." The context of this word varies and it is determined by the co-occurrence of other words. So, the word 2 with the context "topic 1" is more relevant to "Doc 1" and the same word with the context "topic 2" is more relevant to "Doc 2." Identifying latent concepts thus improves the accuracy of feature categorization.

LDA is a matrix factorization technique. It reduces TD matrix into two low dimensional matrices, M1 and M2. M1 is a document-topic matrix (NxK) and M2 is the topic-term matrix (KxM), where N is the number of documents, K is the number of topics and M is the number of terms. LDA uses sampling techniques to improve these matrices. The model assumes all word–topic mapping is correct except the current word. This technique iterates for each word "w" for each document "d" and adjusts the current topic assignment of "w" by multiplying two probabilities p_1 and p_2, where p_1 is $p(topic_t/document_d)$ and p_2 is $p(word_w/topic_t)$, the probability of assignment of topic "t" over all the documents for the word "w." Steady state is

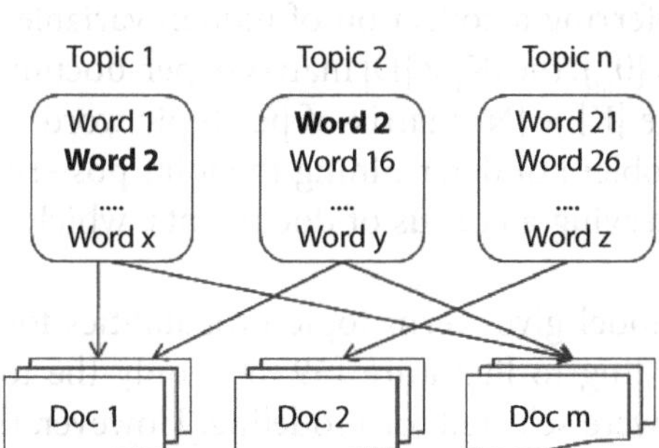

Figure 1.6 LDA framework.

reached after the number of iterations and distributions of words–topics and topics–documents may fairly be good at one instant.

For LDA model, the number of topics K has to be fixed in prior. It assumes the generative process for a document w = $(w_1, \ldots, w_N)$ of a corpus D containing N words from a vocabulary consisting of V different terms, $w \in \{1, \ldots, V\}$ for all $i = \{1, \ldots, N\}$. LDA consists of the following steps [12]

(1) For each topic *k*, draw a distribution over words $\Phi(k) \sim \mathrm{Dir}(\alpha)$.
(2) For each document *d*,
  (a) Draw a vector of topic proportions $\theta(d) \sim \mathrm{Dir}(\beta)$.
  (b) For each word *i*,
    (i) Draw a topic assignment $z_{d,i} \sim \mathrm{Mult}(\theta_d)$, $z_{d,n} \in \{1, \ldots, K\}$,
    (ii) Draw a word $w_{d,i} \sim \mathrm{Mult}(\Phi_{z\,d,i})$, $w_{d,i} \in \{1, \ldots, V\}$

where α is a Dirichlet prior on the per-document topic distribution, and β is a Dirichlet prior on the per-topic word distribution. Let θ_{td} be the probability of topic *t* for document *d*, z_{di} be the topic distribution, and let Φ_{tw} be the probability of word *w* in topic *t*. The probability of generating word *w* in document *d* is:

$$p(w \mid d) = \sum_{t=1}^{K} \theta_{td}\, \Phi_{tw} \tag{1.2}$$

Equation 1.2 gives the weighted average of the per-topic word probabilities, where the weights are the per-document topic probabilities. The resulting distribution p(w|d) varies from document to document, as the topic weights change among documents. Corpus documents are fitted into LDA model by inferring a collection of hidden variables. These variables are denoted by $\theta = \{\theta_{td}\}$, the $|K| \times |D|$ matrix of per-document topic weights, and $\Phi = \{\Phi_{tw}\}$, the $|K| \times |N|$ matrix of per-topic word weights. Inference for LDA is the problem of determining the joint posterior distribution of θ and Φ after observing a corpus of documents, which are influenced by LDA parameters.

Simple LDA model gives term-topic probabilities for all terms under each topic. According to literature [59, 60], only the top 5 or 10 terms under each topic were selected for modeling. However, the CFS_{LDA} model *(Contextual Feature Selection LDA)* selects the set of probable terms from the data set which represent the topic or concept of a domain. It builds the *contextual model using LDA and correlation technique* for selecting the list of probable and correlated terms under each topic (or feature) for the data set. The lists of terms represent the topic or concept of a domain and establish the context between the terms. The plate notation of CFS_{LDA} topic modeling is shown in Figure 1.7. The notations used in CFS_{LDA} model are:

D—number of documents
N—number of words or terms
K—number of topics
α—a Dirichlet prior on the per-document topic distribution
β—a Dirichlet prior on the per-topic word distribution
θ_{td}—probability of topic *t* for document *d*
Φ_{tw}—probability of word *w* in topic *t*
$z_{d,i}$—topic assignment of term "i"
$w_{d,i}$—word assignment of term "i"
c—correlation between the terms

LDA associates documents with a set of topics where each topic is a set of words. Using the LDA model, the next word is generated by first selecting a random topic from the set of topics T, then choosing a random word from that topic's distribution over the vocabulary W. The hidden variables θ and Φ are determined by fitting the LDA model to a set of corpus documents. CFS_{LDA} model uses Gibbs sampling for performing the topic modeling of text documents. Given values for the Gibbs settings (b, n, iter), the LDA hyper-parameters (α, β, and k), and TD matrix M, a Gibbs sampler produces "n" random observations from the inferred posterior distribution of θ and Φ [60].

Here Gibbs parameters include "*b*"—burn-in iterations, "*n*"—number of samples, and "*iter*"—number of sample intervals. Gibbs sequences

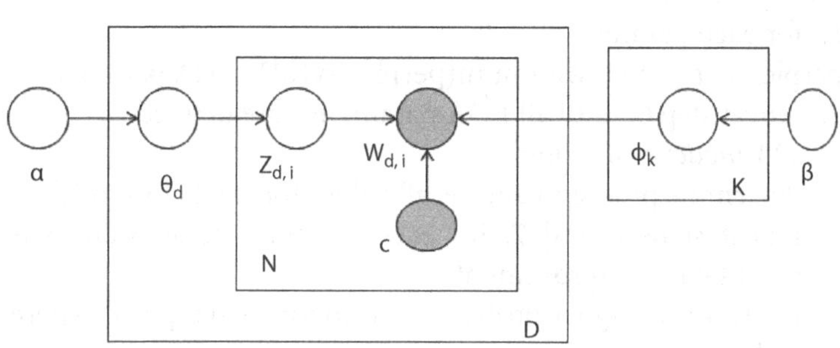

Figure 1.7 Plate notation of CFS_{LDA} model.

produce θ and Φ from the desired distribution, but only after a large number of iterations. For this reason, it is necessary to discard (or burn) the initial observations "b" [60]. The Gibbs setting "*n*" determines how many observations from the two Gibbs sequences are kept. The setting "*iter*" specifies how many iterations the Gibbs sampler runs before returning the next useful observation [60]. The procedure CFS_{LDA} model is shown:

```
CFSlda (documents d)
begin
1. for every product or service review document 'd',
   do pre-processing
   do PoS tagging
   extract nouns
2. for each document 'd',
   create TermDocument Matrix M for nouns
// LDA modeling
3. set values for LDA parameters 'params'
// Heuristic values are given for numberOfTopics 'k', α, β, and
// Gibbs' sampling parameters (b, n, iterations) initially
4. for k =2 to 100
ldaOut <- LDA(TD, params)
// ldaOut consists of matrices of term-topic probabilities,
// topic-document probabilities, topic assignment to documents
   numTopics <- maximum Harmonic mean of Marginal like-
   lihood (ldaOut)
5. repeat step 4 for each burn-in iteration value 'b' to decide the
   approximated value for 'k' and 'b'
// for each iteration, one LDA parameter is varied while all other
   parameters
// are kept constant
6. for each params
perplexity'p'<- firstMinimum(perplexity(LDA(TD, params)))
7. repeat step 6, until all LDA parameters are defined
// LDA model evaluation
8. determine precision and recall values for the LDA model
9. repeat steps 6 and 7, if necessary, until recall value has
   acceptable  improvement
10. topTerm_i <- higher probability term for each topic 'i', where
   i ∈ k
```

```
11. Let Ti include the set of terms for each topic 'i'
12. Ti <- ϕ     // Ti be initially empty
   for each term 'j' in topic 'i'
         corValueij <- correlation(topTermi, termj)
               if corValueij > 0, then
                     topicTermsi <- termj U { Ti }
13. return Ti
end
```

1.5 Ontology Development

Ontology development includes various approaches like Formal Concept Analysis (FCA) or Ontology Learning. FCA applies a user-driven step-by-step methodology for creating domain models, whereas Ontology learning refers to the task of automatically creating domain Ontology by extracting concepts and relations for the given data set [27]. This chapter focuses on building an automatic semantic indexer for online product/service reviews using Ontology. The representation of documents is semantically and contextually enriched by using the Context Feature Selection LDA (CFS_{LDA}) topic modeling technique. Search query yields improved relevant results thereby increases the recall value [26, 27].

The problem statement is simply stated as "to extract all probable relevant features from the Corpus." Given a set of terms for each feature (or topic), the objective is to construct index, which is embedded in the Ontology so as to reduce query processing time. Ontology-based Semantic Indexing (OnSI) model includes three main processes like semantic indexing, Ontology development, and evaluation, as shown in Figure 1.8.

The semantic indexing module includes topic mapping, and term indexing. Ontology development module populates Ontology with these terms and their weights (LDA weights). OnSI evaluation module evaluates the built Ontology through query processing.

1.5.1 Ontology-Based Semantic Indexing (OnSI) Model

Semantic indexing module builds indexer for the review documents with the support of CFS_{LDA} model. The topic modeling technique CFS_{LDA} is used in the feature selection process to extract the features (or topics) and their related terms. Those terms that are grouped under the same topic are selected and tagged to represent the features of domain (or concept).

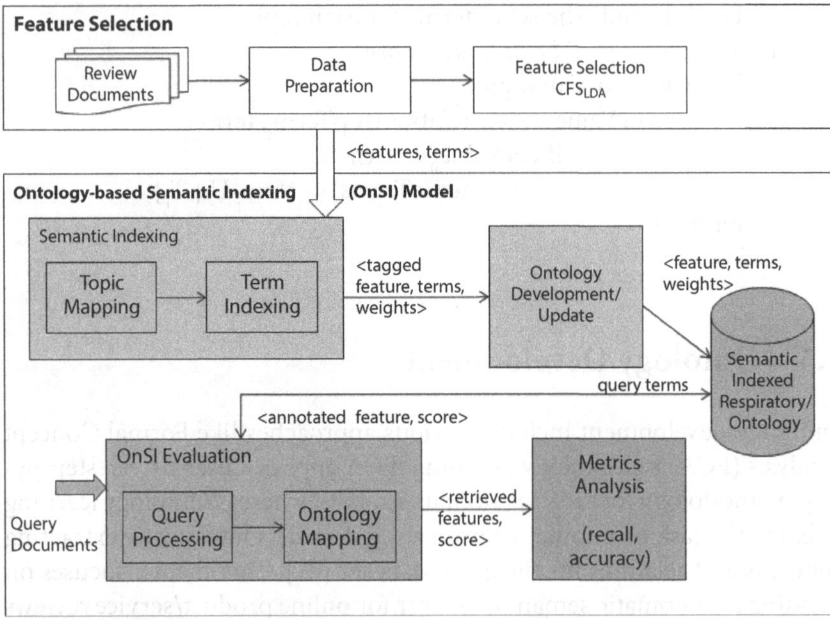

Figure 1.8 Ontology-based semantic indexing (OnSI) model.

Finally, the index is built using the keywords representing the features and feature terms with their context.

Definition 1: Context is defined as a triplet < F, T, M >. F is the set of features, T is set of terms and their LDA scores, and M is the relationship between T and F, known as Ontology mapping. In other words, T is the set of terms used to describe F features of concept. Their contextual relationship is identified by M, a mapping function between T and F using the score.

1.5.2 Ontology Development

A topic (or feature) is a duplet <F, T>, F is the set of features of the domain and T is the candidate set of terms representing F. CFSLDA model selects T = {tc | tc is correlated with tp}, where tp is the higher probable term of F selected by the model. The contextual relationship between this duplet is represented by the triplet <F, T, M>, where M represents the mapping between F and T. The Ontology development or update procedure is shown:

createOrUpdateOntology(documents)
// creates the domain Ontology for the features F, supported

```
                    // by the set of correlated terms T of features
    returned by
  // CFS_lda model along with their score
begin
        featureSet <- CFS_lda(documents)
for each feature f in featureSet, where f ∈ F
     for each term t in featureSet, where t ∈ T
       if <f, t> is a pair in featureSet, then
              domOntolgoy <- buildOntology(f, t, LDAScore_t);
end
```

Ontology tree is constructed with different levels for each <F, T> such that F forms the higher level, and T forms the next level for the corresponding F, as shown in Figure 1.9.

The LDA weight of each term is included in the Ontology representation. Ontology is used to construct the index through concept reasoning.

1.5.3 OnSI Model Evaluation

OnSI evaluation module includes query processing, tagging, and Ontology mapping for feature scoring. It retrieves the relevant feature (or topic) and its score from the built domain Ontology for the set of query terms.

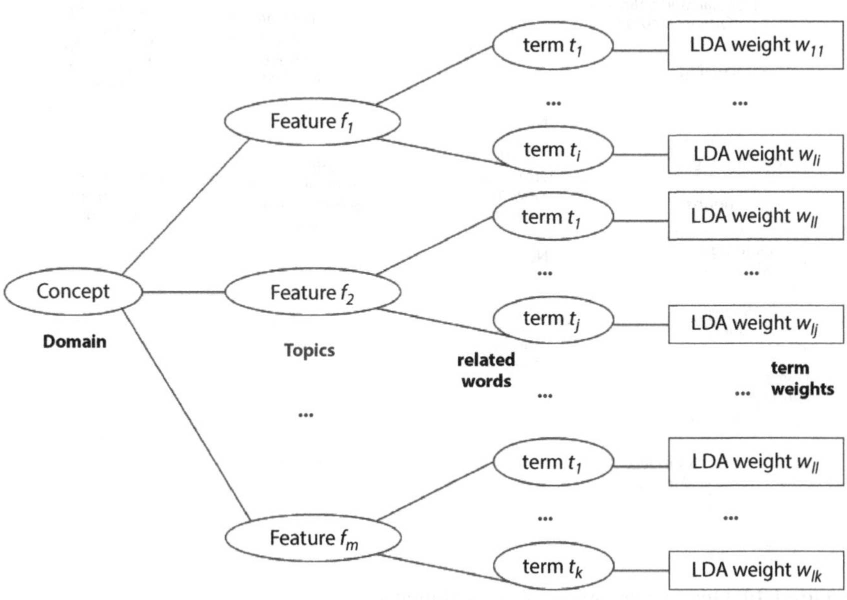

Figure 1.9 Domain ontology modeling for features.

(i) Query Processing

Searching data is made easier and speed up when they are contextually grouped along with indexing. Else searching data in relational schema is quite expensive. Each query document is pre-processed and the PoS tagged nouns are sent to Ontology.

(ii) Ontology Mapping

The resultant features from the domain Ontology are mapped to the closest feature using their feature score. It enables to retrieve the relevant feature and its score for the query documents. Sparql, a XML-based query language is used to retrieve data from the built Ontology. It is described as follows:

Let Q be the set of query documents of product/service reviews written for F features using T terms. These documents are pre-processed and the nouns are extracted from them. Each query document is represented by $q = \{t_1, t_2, \ldots, t_n\}$, where *t* is the term representing the feature *f*. The function M(*t*, *f*) maps each term $t \in T$ with the feature $f \in F$ and returns the *fScore*.

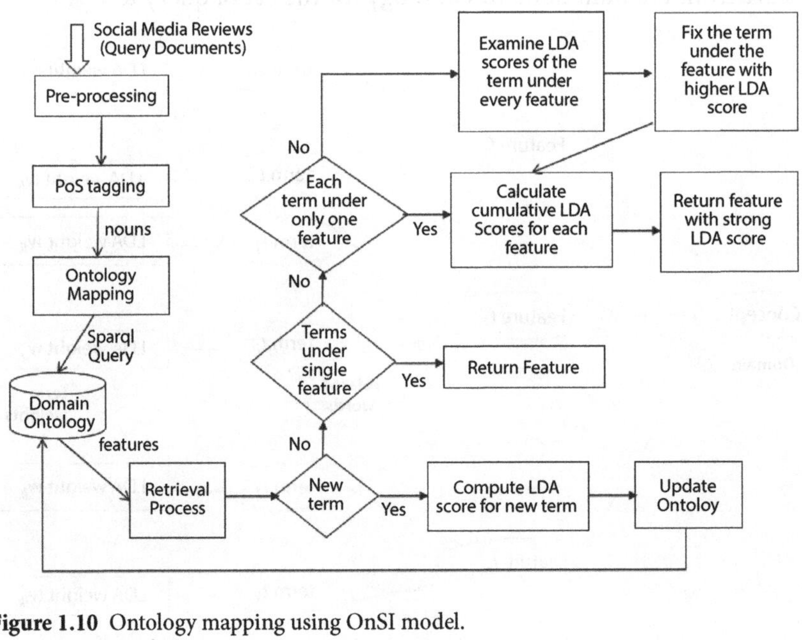

Figure 1.10 Ontology mapping using OnSI model.

This module addresses the four different types of queries, and it is shown in Figure 1.10.

(iii) Retrieval Process From Ontology

When Ontology is queried using Sparql, the query language for Ontology, there could be four different types of queries. The procedure for retrieving data from Ontology is explained:

```
<fScore> queryOntology(Q)
// Q_t is the set of terms of query documents
// search Q_t in domOntology
 begin
  for each q in Q
   for each t in q
    f_i <- ontoMap(t)
      where t ∈ Q_t , f_i ∈ F, i = 1,..., k and k is the number of fea-
      tures (or topics)
 // Type 1 Query
   if t maps to same f_i
    fScore (f_i) = Σ LDAscore(t), t ∈ Q_t
    cum_fScore (f_i) = fScore (f_i) + LDAscore(f_i)
     q(f) <- cum_fScore (f_i) // returns 'f' for query document 'q'
 // Type 2 Query
   else if {t_i}maps to f_a and {t_j}maps to f_b (f_a ≠ f_b)
    cum_fScore (f_a) = LDAscore(f_a) + Σ LDAscore(t_i), t_i ∈ Q_t
    cum_fScore (f_b) = LDAscore(f_b) + Σ LDAscore(t_j), t_j ∈ Q_t
    q(f) <- max(cum_fScore (f_a), cum_fScore (f_b) )

 // Type 3 Query
   else if t_i maps to f_a , f_b (f_a ≠ f_b)
   cum_fScore (f_a) = LDAscore(f_a) + score(nearestTerms), t_i ∈ Q_t
   cum_fScore (f_b) = LDAscore(f_b) + score(nearestTerms), t_i ∈ Q_t
   q(f) <- max( cum_fScore (f_a), cum_fScore (f_b))

 // Type 4 Query
  else 't' is a new term
     CreateOrUpdateOntology(q)
              // rebuild CFSlda model, then Ontology
 end
```

Type 1: Terms under only one feature
If all terms t_1, t_2, ..., t_n mapped to the same feature *f*, then *f* is returned as the result with the cumulative LDA scores of each term. For all i, 1 < i < n, there exists *f* such that

f <- ontoMap(t_i), where t ϵ T, and f ϵ F
fScore (*f*) = Σ LDAscore(t_i), t_i ϵ T and i = 1, ... n
cum_fScore(*f*) = LDAScore(f) + *fScore*(*f*)

For example, "treatment is good" is considered Type 1 query. Here, the word *treatment* is extracted. It comes under the feature (or topic) "Medicare," and it is returned as the feature.

Type 2: Terms under multiple features, each term under only one feature
If terms { t_i} mapped to feature +f_a ϵ F, and terms {t_j} mapped to feature f_b ϵ F, then *f* whose *fScore* is higher is returned. In this case, the cumulative *fScore* is computed for each feature *f* and the feature with higher score is selected. Cumulative *fScore* of feature *f* is determined by the sum of LDA scores of terms corresponding to the feature *f*.

f_a <- ontoMap(t_i), where *t* ϵ T, and *f* ϵ F
f_b <- ontoMap(t_j), where *t* ϵ T, and *f* ϵ F where $t_i \neq t_j$ and $f_a \neq f_b$.
cum_fScore (*f*) = Σ LDAscore(*t*), *t* ϵ T and i = 1, ... n
fScore (*f*) = max (*cum_fScore*(f_a), *cum_fScore*(f_b))

For example, "the treatment is good but the rent is costly" is considered as Type 2 query. Here, the terms *treatment* and *rent* are extracted. The term *treatment* comes under the topic "Medicare," while the terms *rent* comes under the topic "Cost."

Type 3: Terms under multiple features, one term under more than one feature
If a term t_i is mapped to feature f_a, f_b ϵ F, then nearest terms, say t_{i-1} or t_{i+1} is considered to determine the feature category of term t_i present in the document. In this case, the term is associated to a feature by comparing the *fScore* of each feature. The cumulative *fScore* is calculated for each feature *f*, and the resultant strong feature(s) is returned as the result. Cumulative *fScore* of feature *f* is determined by the sum of LDA scores of terms corresponding to the feature *f*.

f_a <- ontoMap(t), where $t \in$ T, and $f \in$ F
f_b <- ontoMap(t), where $t \in$ T, and $f \in$ F, where $f_a \neq f_b$
cum_fScore (f) = Σ LDAscore(t), $t \in i\text{-}1^{st}$, i^{th} *or* $i+1^{st}$ *terms*
fScore (f) = max (*cum_fScore*(f_a), *cum_fScore*(f_b))

For example, "the rooms are maintained neatly but the room rent is costly" is considered Type 3 query. Here, the terms *rooms*, *room*, and *rent* are extracted. The term *room* comes under both the topics "Infrastructure" and "Cost," and the term *rent* comes under the topic "cost." The term *room* needs to be fixed under a single topic (either infrastructure or cost). It is done by calculating the cumulative scores of features (or topics) under which the term occurs. Suppose, LDAscore(room, Infrastructure) = 0.17, LDAscore(room, Cost) = 0.38, and LDAscore(rent, Cost) = 0.26. Then cum_fScore(f = "Infrastructure") is 0.17, and the cum_fScore(f = "Cost") is 0.64. Since 0.64 > 0.17, the term *room* is assigned the feature as "Cost" in this context.

Type 4: Term not present in the Ontology
If given term is not present, new LDA score is computed for it and updateOntology() is used for the new term. If ontoMap(t) is *null*, where $t \in$ T, then the Ontology needs to be updated with the new term. CFS_{LDA} modeling is done again for the Ontology update. The process of querying is repeated as one of the other three types described earlier.

1.5.4 Metrics Analysis

Accuracy is measured as a performance measure for the number of terms correctly identified under the topic (or features). However, the model is further evaluated by the metrics such as precision, recall, and f-measure. Precision defines how precise the model is, and recall defines how complete the model is. It is represented as a confusion matrix, which contains information about actual and predicted results, as shown in Table 1.1.

Precision is defined as the percentage of correctly identified documents among the documents returned; whereas recall is defined as the percentage of relevant results among the correctly identified documents. Practically, high recall is achieved at the expense of precision and vice versa [61]. However, the metric f-measure is suitable when single metric is needed to compare different models. It is defined as the harmonic mean of precision

Table 1.1 Confusion matrix.

	Predicted positive	**Predicted negative**
Actual positive	TP	FN
Actual negative	FP	TN

where
TP: the number of correct classifications of the positive examples (true positive)
FN: the number of incorrect classifications of positive examples (false negative)
FP: the number of incorrect classifications of negative examples (false positive)
TN: the number of correct classifications of negative examples (true negative)

and recall. Based on the confusion matrix, the precision, the recall, and the f-measure of the positive class are defined as

$$precision = \frac{TP}{(TP+FP)} \tag{1.3}$$

$$recall = \frac{TP}{(TP+FN)} \tag{1.4}$$

$$F-measure = 2.\frac{p\,.\,r}{(p+r)} \tag{1.5}$$

$$accuracy = \frac{TP+TN}{(TP+TN+FP+FN)} \tag{1.6}$$

Ontology-based Semantic Indexing (OnSI) model is evaluated by the metrics such as precision, recall, and accuracy, as shown in Equations 1.3, 1.4, 1.5, and 1.6.

1.6 Dataset Description

Document collection like Healthcare service reviews (Dataset DS1) were collected from different social media web sites for 10 different hospitals, as detailed in Tables 1.2 and 1.3.

Table 1.2 Social media reviews for healthcare service (DS1).

Data source	Number of reviews	
	Positive	**Negative**
Twitter	1200	525
Mouthshut.com	425	110
BestHospitalAdvisor.com	200	85
Google Reviews	580	320
Total Reviews	2405	1040

Table 1.3 Number of reviews of features and hospitals (DS1).

Features	**Reviews**
Cost	663
Medicare	748
Nursing	776
Infrastructure	554
Time	704

Number of reviews			
H1	596	H6	308
H2	411	H7	313
H3	399	H8	297
H4	227	H9	281
H5	252	H10	361

Table 1.3 shows that 663 reviews were collected for the feature "cost," and 596 reviews were collected for the hospital H1. The list of features is identified from the previous work, related articles, and social media websites. For example, the document [62] clearly identified the necessary criteria for healthcare services. The expectations of patients such as cost, hospital characteristics, infrastructure facility, recommendations by other users, treatment and nursing care, and medical expertise were clearly mentioned in the article [63]. Features were also selected by referring web sites like, BestHospitalAdvisor, Mouthshut.com, webometrics, and so on. The comments given by patients or by their care takers in these websites were analyzed for different features of healthcare services of these different hospitals.

1.7 Results and Discussions

Ontology-based Semantic Indexing (OnSI) model builds domain Ontology for each product/service review documents using the selected features from the CFS_{LDA} model. Protégé software is used to build and query the Ontology model. The top five terms selected by LDA model, related to each topic for the dataset is shown in Table 1.4. Each topic is manually labeled in context with the first term in the list. It is difficult to carry out human annotation for all the terms grouped under the topic.

For example, the term "bill" is one of the top words under the topic "medicare." However, it is more related to the topics "cost" or "infrastructure" or "time." Similarly, the term "appointment" is not present in any of the list under top 5 or top 10 terms; however, it is more appropriate to the topics "time" and "medicare." In order to alleviate this problem, the CFS_{LDA} model selects the representative terms of each topic with reference to the first term *(the term which has the highest term-topic probability in each topic)* in the list, using the correlation analysis. As stated in the previous example, the term "bill" is not related to the term "doctor," and it is highly correlated with the terms "cost," "hospital," and "time." The correlation values of these terms are shown in Table 1.5. For example, the term-topic probability "Φ_{tw}" of "room" is 0.0134 and correlated value "c" with "cost" is 0.0222. As stated in another example, the term "appointment" is highly correlated with the terms "doctor" and "time," and it is grouped under the topic "medicare" and "time" as shown in Table 1.5. As an another example, the term "disease" is related with "doctor" and "hospital," and it is not related with the terms "cost," "time," and "staff," as shown in Table 1.5.

Table 1.6 shows the list of feature terms selected by the CFS_{LDA} model. Among the pre-processed and PoS tagged nouns, 68 terms are selected for the topic "cost," 110 for "medicare," 112 for "staff," 101 for "infrastructure," and 73 for "time."

Thus, the feature extraction process model, the CFS_{LDA} model, selects not only the terms with high term-topic probability value *but also the terms which are highly correlated with the topmost term under each topic,*

Table 1.4 List of top five terms by LDA model.

Topics/features of (DS1)	**Feature terms by FS_{LDA} model (DS1)**
Topic 1—Cost	cost, test, money, charge, day
Topic 2—Medicare	doctor, nurse, team, treatment, bill
Topic 3—Staff	staff, patient, child, problem, face
Topic 4—Infrastructure	hospital, people, room, experience, surgery
Topic 5—Time	time, operation, hour, service, check

Table 1.5 Sample correlated terms selected by CFS_{LDA}.

Features		Cost	Medicare	Staff	Infrastructure	Time
High probable terms		cost	doctor	Staff	Hospital	time
Term-topic probability (Φ_{tw})		0.0923	0.2132	0.2488	0.3152	0.1247
Correlated value (c)		1	1	1	1	1
Sample terms modeled by CFS_{LDA}						
Room	Φ_{tw} C	0.0134 0.0222	0.0004 0.1378	0.0005 0.2392	0.0471 0.0402	0.0134 0.0222
Disease	Φ_{tw} C	0.0004 −0.0347	0.0222 0.0547	0.0005 −0.0462	0.0004 0.0948	0.0004 −0.0408
Appointment	Φ_{tw} C	0.0134 −0.0343	0.0092 0.1802	0.0005 −0.0462	0.0004 −0.0414	0.0004 0.0477
Patient	Φ_{tw} C	0.0177 0.0042	0.0004 0.1415	0.1247 0.1429	0.0004 0.1502	0.0005 0.2238
Bill	Φ_{tw} C	0.0004 0.0468	0.0265 −0.0015	0.0001 0.1614	0.0121 0.1176	0.0005 0.2111

Table 1.6 List of correlated feature terms selected by CFS_{LDA} model.

Features of DS1	Number of terms selected by CFS_{LDA}	Correlated feature terms by CFS_{LDA} model (DS1)
Cost	68	cost, test, money, charge, day, case, department, patient, room, pay, bill, ...
Medicare	110	doctor, discharge, medicine, treatment, appointment, admission, disease, option, pain, reply, duty, test, meeting, ...
Staff	112	staff, patient, medicine, problem, report, manner, management, treatment, complaints, ...
Infrastructure	101	hospital, room, facility, meals, rate, ...
Time	73	time, service, hour, operation, day, bill, ...

which are contextually equivalent. The terms which are positively correlated with the top probable term are selected for the list. The topic name, the set of terms, and their LDA score are given to the Ontology builder tool for repository. Figure 1.11 shows the spring view of domain Ontology built for Healthcare service reviews (DS1).

Figure 1.12 shows the precision vs recall value curve and f-measure value when OnSI model is used on different query documents. It shows

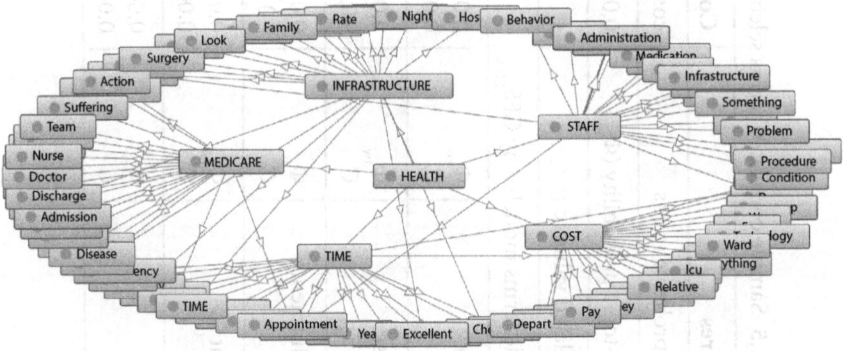

Figure 1.11 Spring view of domain ontology (DS1).

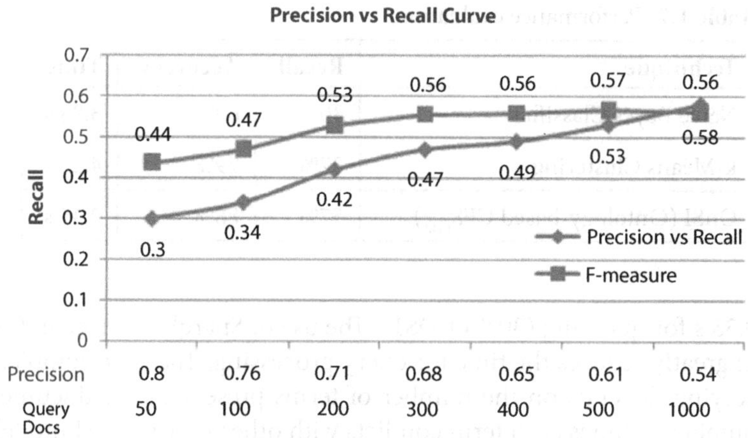

Figure 1.12 Precision vs recall curve for the Dataset DS1.

that recall improves continuously for higher number of query documents. When the document size is 500, OnSI model gives *precision 0.61*, *recall 0.53*, and *F-measure 0.57* values.

1.7.1 Discussion 1

Ontology querying involves direct extract of feature from its repository instead of doing similarity measures as other techniques like Naive Bayes algorithm do. The similarity between the terms is incorporated into the model during the CFS_{LDA} modelling technique itself rather than the querying phase. It is very much required as the lexicon-based indexing technique just uses the keywords with one-to-one mapping and it does not look for synonymous terms and contextually related terms. OnSI model retrieves these types of terms from the document collection for the features or topics, which in turn improves the recall value. 100% accuracy may not be attained sometimes, as some of the terms present in query documents may not be present in the Ontology and it may need to be updated. In the next iteration, the value gets improved.

1.7.2 Discussion 2

Time taken for modeling and querying (training and testing) text documents are measured. OnSI model takes 2.1 s for modeling (70% of DS1)

Table 1.7 Performance evaluation.

Technique	Recall	Accuracy	Time
Naive Bayes Classifier	30%	69%	3.98 s
k-Means Clustering	37%	79%	4.25 s
OnSI (Ontology-based CFS_{LDA})	57%	88%	2.45 s

and 0.35 s for querying (30% of DS1). The use of Sparql language in OnSI model greatly reduces the time for query processing. The time complexity of querying depends on the number of terms present in the documents and number of times each term conflicts with other topics. OnSI model of extracting features were compared with Naive Bayes classifier and k-Means clustering techniques, and the results are shown in Table 1.7.

1.7.3 Discussion 3

Generally, the term-document (TD) matrix is stored in .csv format which takes megabytes of storage whereas the .owl format, the Ontology file, takes only kilo bytes of storage. For example, size of .csv file was 3.5 MB (approx.) when review documents were converted into TD matrix for the dataset DS1. Each review document consumes 1 kB (approx.) storage and also it depends on the number of terms present in the dataset. However, DS1 takes only 360 kB (approx.) when .owl format is used.

This chapter focused on *building of Ontology for the contextual representation of user-generated content, i.e., the review documents.* The contextually aligned documents are represented in domain Ontology along with the semantics using the Ontology-based Semantic Indexing (OnSI) model.

It has been identified that the modeling of documents greatly impacts the query processing time and its recall value. The OnSI model improves the *recall value by 27%* and reduces the *time by 1.53 s,* when compared Naïve Bayes technique. Similarly, it improves *the recall value by 20% and reduces the time by 1.8 s,* when compared with k-means algorithm. The LDA parameters and the right choice of their values along with the correlation analysis involved in the CFS_{LDA} feature selection process improve the accuracy of model. Having the right of features in hand, the contextual feature-based sentiment analysis and predictive analytics are possible with the dataset using supervised machine learning techniques.

1.8 Applications

Much of the social media text research have been undertaken for ranking public/private sectors or products [41], for improving customer satisfaction [64], or for recommending new services of products [50]. Multi-Criteria Decision Making (MCDM) problem can be solved by using the OnSI model. Here OnSI model can be applied to extract the set of features from the given set of review documents. Ranking methods use suitable weights for each feature and the sentiment score from the sentiment analysis process. The MCDM hierarchy problem for determining the better healthcare service provider is shown in Figure 1.13.

There are many MCDM methods available like SAW (simple additive weight), TOPSIS, VIKOR and so on. This chapter focuses on applying VIKOR technique for determining the better hospital based on their features. VIKOR is one of the ranking methods for optimizing the multi-response process through compromise [42]. It compares the closeness of each criterion with the alternative and derives ranking index for each criterion. The core concept of VIKOR is that ranking the criteria from the set of different alternatives in the presence of conflicting criteria [43]. Figure 1.14 shows the ranking of features for various alternatives *(hospitals)* under consideration.

Figure 1.7 shows that the alternative H10 scored rank 1 for the features "Cost," "Medicare," and "Infrastructure," the alternative H6 for the feature "Staff" and the alternative H9 for the feature "Time." These data can be used for benchmarking by all the hospitals to improve their process.

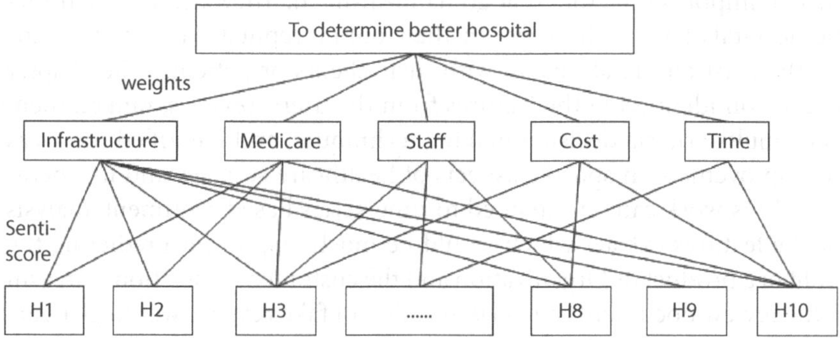

Figure 1.13 Hierarchy of MCDM problem.

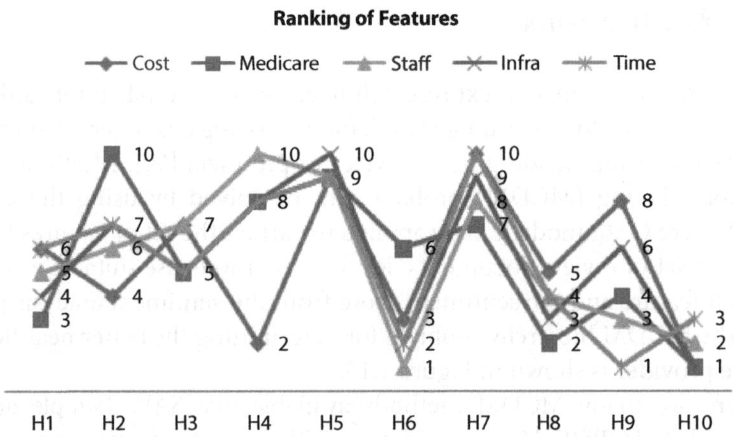

Figure 1.14 Ranking of features by VIKOR method.

1.9 Conclusion

Social media text analytics can be used in "brand experience" research. It gives the experience and strategy for building the long term customer-brand relationship. Text analytics research found that applying content analysis to user-generated content provides a rich opportunity to study users' style of writing, patterns, or preferences. Content analysis research helps all other data analysts to change their research direction to social media text analytics. The reports from different healthcare service providers recommended that the hospital status and the service quality are the two important factors that go hand-in-hand. They also reported that the hospitals have to be keen on their online reputation so as to manage the trust and relationship with their clients or patients. The chapter focused on identifying the features from the users' reviews, ranked them using multi-criteria decision making techniques, and identified the areas for improvement in specific aspects of healthcare services and its operations. This work can be extended to time-series based sentiment analysis for the features extract which would be much helpful for predicting the profit of a product or Organization and the customer satisfaction. Sarcasm in the review documents and classification of fake reviews would give further improvement in this text analytics.

1.10 Future Work

This work can be improved with complete automation in building the domain Ontology, and exploring various methods for visualizing the results, which enables the users to get more information. In this study, individuals, siblings, and concepts are the only items considered for Ontology learning. It can be further extended and modeled as "sentiment domain dictionary" with the set of positive and negative words.

However, the work can be extended to map relationship between concepts, in addition to the existing terms. It can be done by the development of multi-agent system for integration of different domain Ontology using their properties. This in turn helps to develop expert systems solution or decision support system for any decision-making problem.

References

1. Somprasertsri, G. and Lalitrojwong, P., Mining feature-opinion in online customer reviews for opinion summarization. *J. Universal Comput. Sci.*, 16, 6, 938–955, 2010.
2. Yang, J.Y., Kim, H.J., Lee, S.G., Feature-based product review summarization utilizing user score. *J. Inf. Sci. Eng.*, 26, 6, 1973–1990, 2010.
3. Jacobsen, J.S. and Munar, A.M., Motivations for sharing tourism experiences through social media. *Tourism Management*, 43, 46–54, 2014.
4. Olga, L.P. and Raj, R., Evolution of social media and consumer behaviour changes in tourism destination promotion. *Int. J. Bus. Globalisation*, 12, 3, 358–368, 2014.
5. Varanasi, P. and Tanniru, M., Seeking intelligence from Patient experience using text mining: analysis of emergency data. *Inf. Syst. Manage.*, 32, 3, 220–228, 2015.
6. Ittoo, A., Nguyen, L.M., Bosch, A., Text analytics in industry: Challenges, desiderata and trends. *Comput. Ind.*, 78, 96–107, 2016.
7. Nedellec, C. and Nazarenko, A., Ontology and information extraction: A necessary symbiosis, in: *Ontology Learning from Text: Methods, Evaluation and Applications*, P. Buitelaar, P. Cimiano, B. Magnini (Eds.), pp. 3–14, IOS Press Publications, Amsterdam, The Netherlands, 2005.
8. Maedche, A., Pekar, V., Staab, S., *Ontology learning part one—on discovering taxonomic relations from the web*, N. Zhong (Ed.), pp. 301–320, Web Intelligence, Springer, Berlin Heidelberg, 2003.
9. Rindflesch, T.C., Tanabe, L., Weinstein, J.N., Hunter, L., EDGAR: Extraction of Drugs, Genes and Relations from the Biomedical Literature, in: *Proceedings*

of Pacific Symposium on Biocomputing, Singapore, pp. 517–528, NIH Public Access, 2000.

10. Chen, M., Ebert, D., Hagen, H., Data, information, and knowledge in visualization. *J. IEEE Comput. Graphics Appl.*, 29, 1, 12–19, 2009.
11. Guo, H., Zhu, H., Guo, Z., Su, Z., Product feature categorization with multilevel latent semantic association, in: *Proceedings of the Eighteenth ACM Conference on Information and Knowledge Management CIKM '09*, Association for Computing Machinery, New York, NY, USA, pp. 1087–1096, 2009.
12. Blei, D.M. and Lafferty, J.D., A coorelated topic model of science. *Ann. Appl. Stat.*, 1, 1, 17–35, 2007.
13. Colace, F., Santo, M.D., Greco, L., Moscato, V., Picariello, A., Probabilistic approaches for sentiment analysis: Latent dirichlet allocation for ontology building and sentiment extraction, in: *Studies in Computational Intelligence: Sentiment Analysis and Ontology Engineering*, W. Pedrycz and S.-M. Chen (Eds.), vol. 639, pp. 75–91, Springer, Switzerland, 2016.
14. Maynard, D., Bontcheva, K., Cunninham, H., Towards a semantic extraction of named entities. *Recent Adv. Nat. Lang. Process.*, Bulgaria, Vol. 1, pp. 257–263, 2003.
15. Castells, P., Fernández, M., Vallet, D., An adaptation of the vector-space model for ontology-based information retrieval. *IEEE Trans. Knowl. Eng.*, 19, 2, 261–271, 2007.
16. Freitas, L.A. and Vieira, R., Ontology based feature level opinion mining for Portuguese reviews. *WWW'13 Companion Proceedings of the 22nd International Conference on World Wide Web*, Rio de Janeiro, Brazil, pp. 367–370, 2013.
17. Ciravegna, F., Dingli, A., Petrelli, D., Wilks, Y., User-system cooperation in document annotation based on information extraction', International Conference on Knowledge Engineering and Knowledge Management: Ontologies and the Semantic Web EKAW02. *Lecture Notes in Computer Series LNCS*, vol. 2473, pp. 122–137, 2002.
18. Alani, H., Kim, S., Millard, D.E., Weal, M.J., Hall, W., Lewis, P.H., Shadbolt, N.R., Automatic ontology-based knowledge extraction from web documents. *IEEE Intell. Syst.*, 18, 1, 14–21, 2003.
19. Popov, B., Kiryakov, A., Ognyanoff, D., KIM – A semantic platform for information extraction. *J. Nat. Lang. Eng.*, 10, 3–4, 375–392, 2004.
20. Kamps, J., Marx, M., Mokken, R.J., Rijke, M.D., Using wordnet to measure semantic orientation of adjectives. *Proceedings of 4th International Conference on Language Resources and Evaluation*, Lisbon, Portugal, pp. 1115–1118, 2004.
21. Taboada, M., Brooke, J., Tofiloski, M., Voll, K., Stede, M., Lexicon-based methods for sentiment analysis, in: *Computational linguistics*, vol. 37, 2, P. Merlo (Ed.), pp. 267–307, MIT Press, Cambridge, USA, 2011.

22. Penalver-Martinez, I., Garcia-Sanchez, F., Valencia-Garcia, R., Feature-based opinion mining through ontologies. *Expert Syst. Appl.*, 41, 13, 5995-6008, 2014.
23. Verma, S. and Bhattacharyya, P., Incorporating semantic knowledge for sentiment analysis', proceedings of ICON-2008. *6th International Conference on Natural Language Processing*, 2008, Macmillan Publishers, India. Available from: <https://www.cse.iitb.ac.in/~pb/papers/icon09-sa.pdf> [20-Oct-2014].
24. Lu, Y., Duan, H., Wang, H., Zhai, C.X., Exploiting structured ontology to organize scattered online opinions. *proceedings of the Twenty Third International Conference on Computational Linguistics*, Beijing, pp. 734–742, 2010.
25. Wei, W. and Gulla, J.A., Sentiment learning on product reviews via sentiment ontology tree. *proceedings of the 48th Annual Meeting of the Association for Computational Linguistics ACL 10*, Uppsala, Sweden, pp. 404–413, 2010.
26. Ma, J., Xu, W., Sun, Y., Turban, E., Wang, S., Liu, O., An ontology-based text-mining method to cluster proposals for research project selection. *IEEE Trans. Syst. Man Cybern. Part A Syst. Humans*, 42, 3, 784–790, 2012.
27. Kontopoulos, E., Berberidis, C., Dergiades, T., Bassiliades, N., Ontology-based sentiment analysis of twitter posts. *Expert Syst. Appl.*, 40 10, 4065–4074, 2013.
28. Thakor, P. and Sasi, S., Ontology-based sentiment analysis process for social media content'. *INNS Conference on Big Data 2015 Procedia Computer Science*, vol. 53, pp. 199–207, 2015.
29. Ali, F., Kwak, K.S., Kim, Y.G., Opinion mining based on fuzzy domain ontology and Support Vector Machine: A proposal to automate online review classification'. *Appl. Soft Comput.*, 47, 3, 235–250, 2016.
30. Popescu, O. and Etzioni, Extracting product features and opinions from reviews. *Proceedings of the Conference on Human Language Technology and Empirical Methods in Natural Language Processing HLT-EMNLP*, pp. 339–346, 2005.
31. McGlohon, M., Glance, N., Reiter, Z., Star quality: Aggregating reviews to rank products and merchants. *Proceedings of the Fourth International AAAI Conference on Weblogs and Social Media*, pp. 114–121, 2010.
32. Harb, A., Plantié, M., Dray, G., Roche, M., Trousset, F., Poncelet, P., Web opinion mining: How to extract opinions from blogs? *Proceedings of CSTST '08 International Conference on Soft Computing as Transdisciplinary Science and Technology*, pp. 211–217, 2008.
33. Qiu, G., Liu, B., Bu, J., Chen, C., Expanding domain sentiment lexicon through double propagation. *Comput. Ling.*, 37, 1, 9–27, 2008.
34. Chawla, K., Ramteke, A., Bhattacharyya, P., IITB-sentiment-analysts: Participation in sentiment analysis in twitter semeval 2013 task. *Proceedings of Seventh International Workshop on Semantic Evaluation*, pp. 495–500, 2013.
35. Ding, X. and Liu, B., The utility of linguistic rules in opinion mining. *Proceedings of the 30th Annual International ACM SIGIR Conference on*

Research and Development on Information Retrieval, SIGIR'07, Amsterdam, 2007.
36. Poirier, D., Bothorel, C., Neef, E.C.D., Boull'e, M., Automating opinion analysis in film reviews: The case of statistic versus Linguistic approach. *Language Resources and Evaluation Conference*, Morocco, pp. 94–101, 2008.
37. Na, J.C., Thet, T.T., Khoo, C., Comparing sentiment expression in movie reviews from four online genres. *Online Inf. Rev.*, 34, 2, 317–338, 2010.
38. Park, S., Cha, B., An, D.U., 'Automatic multi-document summarization based on clustering and nonnegative matrix factorization. *IETE Tech. Rev.*, 27, 2, 167–178, 2010.
39. Basiri, M.E., Naghsh-Nilchi, A.R., Ghasem-Aghaee, N., Sentiment prediction based on dempster-shafer theory of evidence. *Math. Prob. Eng.*, 2014, 361201, Vol. 1, pp. 1–13.
40. Chow, C.C., A strategic service quality approach using analytic hierarchy process. *Managing Service Quality*, 15, 3, 278–289, 2005.
41. Uddin, A. and Singh, V.K., A quantity–quality composite ranking of indian institutions in CS research. *IETE Tech. Rev.*, 32, 5, 273–283, 2015.
42. Opricovic, S. and Tzeng, G.H., Compromise solution by MCDM methods: A comparative analysis of TOPSIS and VIKOR approach. *Eur. J. Oper. Res.*, 156, 445–455, 2004.
43. Opricovic, S. and Tzeng, G.H., Extended VIKOR method in comparison with outranking methods'. *Eur. J. Oper. Res.*, 178, 514–529, 2007.
44. Amiri, M.P., Project selection for oil-fields development by using AHP and fuzzy TOPSIS methods. *Expert Syst. Appl.*, 37, 9, 6218–6224, 2010.
45. Velasquez, M. and Hester, P.T., An analysis of multi-criteria decision making methods. *Int. J. Oper. Res.*, 10, 2, 56–66, 2013.
46. Liu, D.R. and Shih, Y.Y., Integrating AHP and data mining for product recommendation based on customer lifetime value. *Inf. Manage.*, 42, 387–400, 2005.
47. Yazdi, A.K., Designing a mathematical model for indicators of service quality in the tourism industry based on SERVQUAL and Rembrandt methods. *Int. J. Productivity Qual. Manage.*, 15, 4, 511–527, 2015.
48. Buyukozkan, G. and Cifci, G., A combined fuzzy AHP and fuzzy TOPSIS based strategic analysis of electronic service quality in healthcare industry. *Expert Syst. Appl.*, 39, 3, 2341–2354, 2012.
49. Hdioud, F., Frikh, B., Ouhbi, B., Multi-criteria recommender systems based on multi-attribute decision making. *Proceedings of the 15th International Conference on Information Integration and Web based Application and Services IIWAS 2013*, Vienna, Austria, pp. 203–210, 2013.
50. Kang, D. and Park, Y., Review-based measurement of customer satisfaction in mobile service: Sentiment analysis and VIKOR approach. *Expert Syst. Appl.*, 41, 4, 1041–1050, 2014.

51. Sanayei, S., Mousavi, F., Yazdankhah, A., Group decision making process for supplier selection with VIKOR under fuzzy environment. *Expert Syst. Appl.*, 37, 24–30, 2010.
52. Paralic, J. and Kostial, I., A document retrieval method based on ontology associations. *J. Inf. Org. Sci.*, 27, 2, 93–99, 2003.
53. Saif, H., He, Y., Alani, H., Contextual semantics for sentiment analysis of Twitter. *Inf. Process. Manage.*, 52, 1, 5–19, 2016.
54. Liu, B., *Sentiment Analysis and Opinion Mining*, Morgan & Claypool Publishers, San Rafael, California, USA, 2012.
55. Astudillo, R.F., Amir, S.F., Ling, W., Martins, B., Silva, M., Trancoso, I., INESC-ID: A regression model for large scale twitter sentiment lexicon induction. *Association for Computational Linguistics, Proceedings of the 9th International Workshop on Semantic Evaluation (SemEval 2015)*, Colorado, pp. 613–618, 2015.
56. Zhang, W., Yoshida, T., Tang, X., A comparative study of TF_IDF, LSI and multi-words for text classification. *Expert Syst. Appl.*, 38, 2758–2765, 2011.
57. Kumar, A. and Srinivas, S., On the performance Latent Semantic Indexing-based Information Retrieval. *J. Comput. Inf. Technol.*, 3, 259–264, 2009.
58. Blei, D.M., Ng, A.Y., Jordan, M.I., Latent Dirichlet Allocation. *J. Mach. Learn. Res.*, 3, 993–1022, 2003.
59. Griffiths, T.L. and Steyvers, M., Finding scientific topics. *PNAS*, 101, 1, 5228–5235, 2004.
60. Binkley, D., Heinz, D., Lawrie, D., Overfelt, J., Understanding LDA in source code analysis. *Proceedings of 22nd International Conference on Programme Comprehension ICPC*, Hyderabad, India, vol. 14, pp. 26–36, 2014.
61. Liu, B., *Web Data Mining*, Springer, New York, USA, 2007.
62. Robert, J.D., An examination of consumer criteria for choosing hospital services, 1995. Available from: http://library3.sage.edu/archive/thesis/MGT/MGT-d255-dam-ane.pdf, pp. 1–41, January 2016.
63. Agarwal, P. and Janssens, B., Power to the patient: A new growth paradigm for Indian providers. *BCG. perspectives*, 2014. Vol. 1, pp.1–2. Available from: <https://www.bcgperspectives.com/content/articles/health_care_payers_providers_power_to_patient_new_growth_paradigm_for_indian_providers/>. [9-Nov-2015].
64. Kang, H., Yoo, S.J., Han, D., Senti-lexicon and improved Naïve Bayes algorithms for sentiment analysis of restaurant reviews. *Expert Syst. Appl.*, 39, 5, 6000–6010, 2012. Elsevier.

2

Semantic Web for Effective Healthcare Systems: Impact and Challenges

Hemendra Shankar Sharma and Ashish Sharma*

Department of Computer Engineering & Applications, GLA University, Post Ajhai, Mathura (UP), India

Abstract

The use of information technology in the healthcare industry use so many types of electronic medium to maintain and process the information for all type of patients can be single or group of patients.

Complexity heterogeneous behavior of data is also a challenge. Healthcare services dynamic demands the efficient incorporation of knowledge from various sources, pathways knowledge of the practitioner, etc. Through this, the user will facilitate to browse the information from one place but the challenge in this that the information should be verified and authentic otherwise can be proved dangerous for life.

Another point is users are not familiar with the searching terms because the language is very much different as compared to the regular keyword and also badly managed repositories of information. This condition makes information retrieval difficult. The same Security is a significant concern while managing the web well-being applications since it includes private and delicate healthcare information of the patients. Scientists and professionals need to make frameworks interoperable and incorporate them to serve all the partners including emergency clinics, clinicians, clinical care staff, and patients [1].

In this chapter, we explore the impact and challenges in healthcare in detail also discuss the solution that can be proposed by the present technology. We will discuss some algorithms, frameworks, Real-time database systems, with the help of artificial intelligence and web technology-based solution.

Keywords: Healthcare, ontology-based healthcare systems, machine learning, deep learning, medical imaging

**Corresponding author*: Ashishs.sharma@gla.ac.in

Vishal Jain, Jyotir Moy Chatterjee, Ankita Bansal and Abha Jain (eds.) Semantic Web for Effective Healthcare, (39–74) © 2022 Scrivener Publishing LLC

2.1 Introduction

Collection of the interlinked webpage on a single domain which is publicly accessible via the internet is a website which can be created by individual or group of people and also by an organization to fulfill the many types of purpose. The page (webpage) on the website includes media, images, controls, and text. The website was launched by Tim Brener lee at CERN on August 6, 1991. The web was at first envisioned and made to satisfy the requirement for automated information sharing between analysts in universities and foundations around the world but nowadays A website is meant to be in endless purpose like education, news site, forum, social media, Ecommerce, and healthcare.

The medical administration system can hardly be known as a structure. Or on the other hand, perhaps it is a confusing display of significantly decentralized divisions. Online advances offer the guarantee of an effective, improved healthcare services framework. Patients profit by expanded access to the mind, doctors are managed more prominent adaptability in care conveyance, and the wellbeing framework itself profits by lower expenses to give such mind.

The progression of electronic patient records and the frameworks organization of basic and helper thought can improve the quality and profitability of prosperity organizations. The web can similarly be used as a vehicle for prosperity examine—using on the web interviews, focus social occasions, and quantitative review strategies.

Online advancement is prepared to understand a major and important change in the nation's healthcare framework, in this the Internet playing in as a significant expert in progress. The quality report centers around on that the computerization of clinical, budgetary, regulatory interchange is basic to enhancing quality, forestalling blunders, upgrading customer faith in the healthcare Skelton, and reform the productivity [1]. That reports and others, similarly as the complete area at the highest point by William Richardson, differ the main regions in which an exchange and data advancement could contribute significantly to upgrading the human services system [1]. These probable duties combine rising the clinical dynamics by opening reliable data, developing adjustments among healthcare providers and with patients via such ways of thinking as a remote clinical proposal, collecting and conglomerating clinical information and affirmation into available data in the databases, encouraging calm access to tough flourishing information, and decrease clinical error. Regardless of the degree of areas during which correspondences and information improvement may assemble a humble oath to rising social assurance access, quality, association while decreasing costs, the exchange has been postponed to place assets into and handle such headway. Additionally, an essential subjective procedure that experiences do change in their degree of capital expends, the separations in data headway hypothesis are setting [2].

The web offers the chance of lessening disparities in healthcare—through minimal effort spread of purchaser and expert data, remote conveyance of wellbeing administrations, and evacuation of hindrances to get to. In any case, care must be taken to guarantee that differential access to innovation doesn't intensify existing disparities in wellbeing. The World Health Organization has communicated worry at the computerized partition between the developed and developing world and this has prompted activities, for example, the Health Internetwork (www.healthinternetwork.net), which intends to give free access to assets, for example, biomedical productions.

The web is an impact affecting wellbeing and social insurance. It can improve the successful and proficient conveyance of medicinal services, engage and instruct buyers, bolster dynamic, empower communication among shoppers and experts, bolster the preparation and revalidation of experts, and lessen imbalances in wellbeing. Be that as it may, there is a requirement for watchfulness concerning new and developing dangers to wellbeing presented by the web. Examination of both positive and negative wellbeing effects of this developing innovation must proceed. So far, there has been minimal thorough research on wellbeing impacts of the web. Workaround there must recognize the significance of the more extensive determinants of wellbeing: notwithstanding the more clearly direct impacts, the effect of the web on spaces, for example, the economy, business, the earth, and transport will all impact wellbeing and healthcare services.

There are so many tech agents who provide the healthcare service online based.

LiveHealth: LiveHealth, part of Creliant Software Pvt. Ltd was established in 2013 by computer science engineers Abhimanyu Bhosale and Mukund Malani, who set up the endeavor not long after moving on from college.

The company was started as a management information system (MIS) platform for healthcare providers. With the same, it also started operation as software as a service platform and growing its item contributions to people and corporations, as a major aspect of the medical advantage bundle to workers. The startup additionally offers its administrations through a versatile application accessible on both Android and iOS. For medicinal services suppliers and indicative focuses, it oversees patients, budgetary exchanges, computerizes between clinical instruments and stock. Furthermore, it gives them significant bits of knowledge to drive income and productivity and streamlines data trade with other human services suppliers, as indicated by the announcement by the organization.

For doctors, the stage gives them normalized clinical records, while patients can utilize the application to get reports, break down past health information, and screen their health utilizing health trackers, both for themselves and their family, even on a remote premise. The 5-year-old startup has additionally tied up with health specialists cope up who can gather tests at the person's doorstep.

How it worked: When a patient chooses to do some demonstrative tests with one of the 135 health suppliers the startup has tied up with, the framework does the accompanying: it enrolls the patient with the supplier; creates a novel standardized identification for the sample; tracks the status of the sample, and gathers the outcomes legitimately from medical instruments in the lab. Utilizing the barcode produced before, the test outcomes then consequently takes care of into comparing reports of patients and checked by specialists through the application itself.

Reports are anything but difficult to peruse and have the reference ranges for test results showed powerfully. Likewise, the greatest distinction between typical reports, and there is that they make specialists and pathologists give an end or analysis, which is generally not present in ordinary reports. it is anything but a stage for diagnosing or treating sicknesses; we confide in just the specialists to do it. We just assistance lessen the odds of manual blunders.

Lybrate: Lybrate is an online specialist stage that a target taking care of the issue of the Indian medicinal services conveyance framework, which is the unavailability of specialists attributable to enormous specialist deficiency issues in the nation. It has been established in the year 2013 by Saurabh Arora and Rahul Narang two proficient from Facebook and Snapdeal.

The stage permits clients to impart flawlessly and advantageously with specialists online from anyplace, whenever and makes this conceivable in a situation where the shortage of medicinal services specialists is a significant issue by increasing the nearness of specialists through innovation and grow their compass to anybody in any piece of the nation. Something inconceivable in India not many years back as specialists used to be restricted to their geological limit.

Utilizing Lybrate platform, clients can chat with more than 100,000 "trusted" specialists from more than 80 urban communities through content, voice, and video. As indicated by the organizers, Lybrate is the main stage that typifies all three types of correspondence, making it valuable for the two specialists and clients to interface easily.

The organization as of late wandered into labs and propelled India's initially incorporated social insurance arrangement Lybrate Lab. The stage empowers clients to counsel specialists on the web, complete proposed lab tests with no problems of venturing out and proceed with conference upon programmed sharing of reports with social insurance specialists, without breaking the circle of specialist discussion.

Procto: The two specialists Shashank ND, and Abhinav Lal from NIT, Suratkal found Practo Technologies Private Limited in the year 2008.

The account of the rise of the organization began when Shashank's dad required a knee medical procedure, and he needed a solid second conclusion. He explored far and wide; shortlisted the best specialists, and focused on a specific authority in the US. The specialist was prepared to see the report yet the issue was that the specialist needed to see all the clinical records before offering any of his input. Yet, there was no simple, secure, and brisk approach to get those over.

Procto is an online based help of meeting with the specialist. With the help of procto one can discover for experts subject to distinguishing strength and territory, authority name, or focus name. You can in like manner search through dependent on the zone inside the city, availability, timings, and conversation charge. In the wake of finding the right master for yourself, you can truly design a course of action from the application. It offers to bother free planning at the entire hours and ordinary access to reports and records. More than millions of customers search through million masters and make thousands of courses of action through this passage on a customary daily schedule.

The top difficulties were issues of records structure, record safety, data normalization, aggregation and moves, and administrative aptitudes ability, for instance, statistics administration. The top open doors uncovered were a quality improvement, populace the board and wellbeing, early discovery of the new illness, information fine, structure, and openness, advanced dynamic, and value decrease.

There are so many agents in healthcare but also so many issues are there when things are related to data. We will discuss some issues concerning healthcare.

Customized healthcare services, information sharing procedures, and late advancements in legislation expect patients to take part in the subtleties of their electronic clinical records regularly put away in remote and decentralized stages. Information in these stages is frequently dissipated across various associations with huge issues that gave respect to its exactness and clearness. Protection and privateness are vital for patients. Patients need to have managed who sees their statistics. Medicinal offerings professionals want to get entry to pertinent (quiet) statistics to clarify judgment. Specialists need to get entry to statistics of a huge range of patients for you to verify and enhance human services. Along those lines, social coverage applications need to be performed so that patient's safety is guaranteed and gets entry to data is controlled. There is a scope of specialized and procedural additives that intend to shield classification; limiting data get admission to permitted clients.

The information has emerged as a ubiquitous concept in our everyday lives with the normal assortment, stockpiling, preparing, and investigation of a large degree of information. This trademark is cross sartorial, walking from the distance of AI and building to monetary aspects and medication.

In the route of the maximum latest decades, there has been growing eagerness of the potential handiness of these giant amounts of information, called Big Data, in changing character consideration, clinical attention, and well-known wellbeing. The increasing accessibility of electronic scientific statistics gives the notable capability for locating qualified patients for clinical research. Notwithstanding, facts heterogeneity makes it difficult for scientific scientists to grill resources reliably. Existing preferred inquiry dialects are frequently no longer ok to question throughout assorted portrayals. Along these lines, a more elevated level location language is needed with the purpose that questions become information portrayal freethinker. To this end, we represent a clinician significant computational language for questioning whether or not patients meet qualification standards from medical preliminaries. This language is fit for executing the transient semantics required by several ECs and maybe consequently assessed on heterogeneous statistics assets. Artificial intelligence can likewise anticipate a fundamental activity to give higher outcomes at some point of retrieval off acts.

As we know there are so many agents there is need to be a universal platform through patients can have control over data and data encryption for secure data from hackers, also the system should be able to store heterogeneous data with a heavy amount. The system should be able to maintain the history of the patient and can be shared with specialists. Also, can choose the medical provider for medicine [3].

The examination results presented here are noteworthy because they provide the most recent information on leveraging data innovation to improve quality and effectiveness in the medicinal services industry. The key to this improvement is the utilization of the Internet as worldwide communications arrange. In this paper we will discuss all emerging technology to provide a solution for the issue and also how can be it very useful for all types of users.

2.2 Overview of the Website in Healthcare

2.2.1 What Is Website?

A website is an assortment of pages (for example, those that are acquired via the Internet, for example, which you are viewing now. A site page is something you type while typing on a web address. Look at the screen. Click on a connection, or you search on a web crawler through a query. A page can have any amount of data and can include content, media, design, Vividness, and sound.

Exactly whenever someone gives you the address of their website, the software named web browser connects you with their web page which is commonly home page of the website. Which provides you the interface, data with a different format, and links? You can click on links to reach different areas of the website. A site can include one page, or of an enormous number of pages, dependent upon what the site owner is endeavoring to accomplish.

2.2.2 Types of Website

2.2.2.1 Static Website

A static site is one that does not utilize any outer database and is composed totally in HTML. This implies each client who visits that site will get precisely the same data. Moreover, making updates to static sites implies going legitimately into the HTML and rolling out the improvements from that point.

Even though there is an immense measure of the site that wants to demonstrate dynamic substance to their guests, the development of static sites is on the ascent.

2.2.2.2 Dynamic Website

A unique site then again, can create content dependent on the client. Consider Facebook a model, when you login, you are welcomed by a page of updates custom fitted to you depending on your preferences, companions, and so forth. This page of substance is explicit to you as a client and will refresh progressively over the long haul.

A powerful site can likewise make it simpler for a client with no HTML information to refresh the information on the site. Numerous unique sites based on Content Management Systems (CMS) make it easy to refresh data through a simple to utilize interface. Dynamic sites likewise utilize a server side language (for example, PHP, Java, and so forth) and a database where all posts, pages, and media are put away.

2.2.3 What Is Semantic Web?

The Semantic web was originated with a very good motive to manage, process, and understand the information not only the machine but human also. Another important purpose is to create an environment where the human and machine can work together. Almost 50 years, ago it seems very adventurous to make a web with information to post semantics on a large scale and try to conclude the results. at that time even you could describe it. But now, we are seeing its advantage. We are seeing its first stirrings, and it will draw on some key bits of knowledge, instruments, and procedures that got from 50 years of AI research. Semantic web means machine understandable information [4].

The collection of information on the web is a semantic web. Information can be considered as a number, date, title, or some other information. The World Wide Web Consortium (W3C) has attempted to bring together various methodologies and the aftereffect of these endeavors is the Resource Description Framework (RDF) the current standard to ship metadata and a significant mainstay of the Semantic Web. RDF permits us to depict ideas other than a web report.

RDF gives the establishment of distributing and connecting your information. Different innovations permit you to install information in records (RDF, GRDDL) or uncover what you have in SQL databases or make it accessible as an RDF document [4].

As we understand the meaning of Semantic web we need to understand the challenge in this area. The main challenge is the extraction of heterogeneous data and creates a schema to store data. Some sources of data are shown in Figure 2.1.

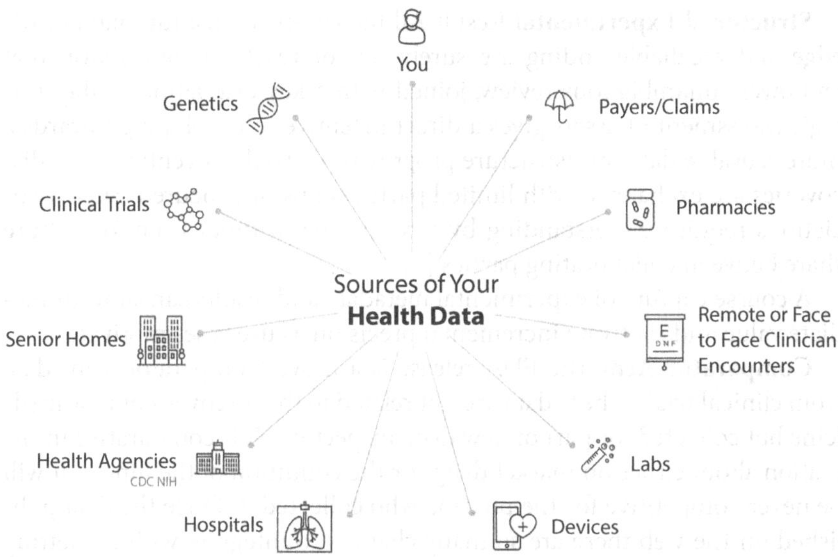

Figure 2.1 Sources of data in healthcare. Wikipedia contributors. (2021, May 11). Health data. In Wikipedia, The Free Encyclopedia. Retrieved 03:51, September 6, 2021, from https://en.wikipedia.org/w/index.php?title=Health_data&oldid=1022666417 [31].

The SW can improve the nature of care by incorporating information storehouses. As dynamic in medicinal services is frequently a synergistic procedure that requires data sharing, this capacity encourages the clinicians to gather the correct data and abstain from rehashing the revise (Figure 2.1).

2.2.4 Role of Semantic Web

The semantic web lets us use itself seamlessly integration of multidisciplinary data. It has so many use cases to discuss. Here we are going to discuss some sampling of use cases which is respective to healthcare.

Drug Discovery Semantic web architecture empowers bottomless collaboration and also connects the highly connected data and text. Synthesis, pathway, systems biology brings us to the next level of proactive drug discovery, semantic web engineering enables unlimited cooperation and interface the exceptionally associated information and text. Combination, pathway, frameworks science carries us to the following degree of proactive medication disclosure [5].

Structured Experimental Result All the complete institutional knowledge and recallable coding are surely out of reach. A description that empowers unambiguous review, joined with a key evaluation of the strategic assessment of assets gives a direct incentive to developing towards a more reusable data infrastructure progressively; trial conventions and discoveries are exchanged with limited partnerships or procured. Such associations require understanding by x`x` parties without time for culture share between collaborating parties [5].

A course capture of experimental metadata and results can show immediate value and motivate incremental precision as use cases motivate.

Comparator Arm The FDA release is a move "comparator arm" data from clinical trials. These data are not related to the discovery of new medicine but collected for part of new drug inspection. It is comparative information about either on market drugs or the condition of the illness. It will be never competitive for the pharma who collected it. Once the data published on the web there are so many chances to integrate with it. Getting the norms directly for designing, questioning, and managing it will be enormous, and the organizations that are at the table will be the best prepared to utilize the information first [5].

Patient Data Ownership Traditional health data to a cutting edge variant of health data, genomic data. Patients are progressively catching their information. The guidelines are not such acceptable to unite information over this chain into a strong, usable, and incorporated framework. On the off chance that pharma does not make a decent standard for the information then the privately owned business will dominate and will begin to give the information on lease to the individuals who need access to a huge population for clinical profiling.

Biotech Acquisition Complex coherent data business can make it accommodating for the system of due steadiness through the web gauges especially RDF/OWL/SPARQL. Projects, products, biotech associations, and each other endeavoring to get persistently by pharma. They are typically shaping organizations by methods for concurrences with each other, and by a long shot, the greater part of the essential information would be far more straightforward to facilitate at whatever point set aside in website architectures. This is work that is essentially less exploratory than the current Healthcare work, as these data positions are presently all around worked out and the best an ideal opportunity to bring down the financial basics it takes either to make a securing onto finish it is high.

Web Integration The setting up of the Semantic Web progresses the blend of the assertion framework with conventional web designing and instruments. Web norms like HTML and Path upheld by the universality of devices and empower affiliation structure information with the area of record imparting all the while in dialects languages tailored to people and machines. Web design permits end client to look and peruse result with less need or no requirement for preparing. The development of this structure to help resource associating and remarks just as a making of composed data will be the easiest change into significant data [5].

2.2.4.1 Pros and Cons of Semantic Web

Cons:
All things considered, there is an enormous number of a website owner who is not aware of the semantic web's significance. Because of this unawareness, they do not feel motivated. Since it is hard to expect them to include the metadata physically into OWL (Ontology Web Language) semantic markups.

There's likewise another substantial explanation content writer is worried about in regards to the semantic web, particularly the proprietors of those sites which rely upon advertising profit. They believe that there is less profit to create a semantic website for a specific purpose rather than a simple website or general search engine since the client will simply look through anything on the program and the outcomes, as significant dates, normal measurable data, or verifiable information may show up immediately, making an ordinary connection like indexed lists obsolete, expelling the need to opening sites by any stretch of the imagination. That way, so to support this is nearly impossible for site owners.

The utilization and the executives of individual information could turn into an issue since it will be a higher priority than at any other time to set up strong protection arrangements. Fundamentally, all that you post online could be uncovered because the ability of substance generators (or essentially everybody) will be decreased since it would be where they post the substance, which will conclude whether to share aimlessly the data or not.

Pros:
The end clients will be the ones profiting the most from this since they will see an improvement in the manner they collaborate with machines, look for data, and explore the Internet.

The user allowed communicating with the machine the way as they communicate with other users. There is no requirement to understand or utilize irrelevant words or expressions rather than we can use expressions we use regularly.

The machine can answer like the human with the End client through the visit; it would seem that that machine is talking with you and attempt to comprehend your need. If you look or ask anything it will no arrival the rundown of connections, yet it will return you the basic sign and give the data which taken structure numerous other sites. This is the base of the semantic web: list of the link would not work since you are not requesting links however you need the outcome in the basic structure on the off chance if you request something [11, 12] (g, h).

There is no uncertainty that the not so distant future will see the ascent of innovations ready to react to people's inquiries in a precise and natural manner, even though these days we want to get natural reactions. Machines will be ready to take part in a characteristic correspondence system with people more than ever. This may assist with making PCs progressively adjusted to human needs, and possibly, this all-inclusive utilization of semantic web may create another transformation in the manner we convey.

Health Level Seven (HL7) Health Level Seven International also is known as HL7 [18]. In 1996 HL7 founded the Special Interest Group on Vocabulary. In 1998 this was elevated to a Technical Committee (TC) [5–7]. The HL7 standard is not revenue driven; American National Standards Institute certified standard making association. This standard is primarily committed to providing an absolute system that is related to measures of the trade, incorporation, sharing, and collection of electronic healthcare data. That supports clinical practice and the organization, movement, and evaluation of healthcare services organizations [8].

Many different types of computer systems or software used by hospitals and healthcare providers for the different types of functionality like billing, patients' records, and tracking. These systems should communicate with one another when they like to get new information, or when they like to retrieve data, anyway not all do in that capacity.

Such huge numbers of adaptable standards, rules, and approaches specify by HL7 standard international by which healthcare systems can communicate with each other. Such guidelines or information norms are a lot of decides that allow data to be shared and handled identically and fixedly. These data checks are proposed to allow human services associations to effortlessly share clinical data [9]. The basic operation of a database management system is to store and manage data. This can be used for corporate and organizational purposes, such as hospitals, private medical centers, clinics, and offices that require effective health management system must have all the related information of its patients, medical records, departments, doctors. Theoretically, this capacity to exchange information should relive by restricting the inclination for clinical thought to be topographically detached and profoundly factor [10].

2.2.4.2 *Impact on Patient*

The outlook of patients is essentially not the same as the two heads and experts, as they are purchasers of the administration as opposed to suppliers. Since they are at the medical clinic, they are likely additionally generously increasingly restless, terrified, in torment, or any case not in their optimal state.

In Healthcare technology product innovation tools are included to support patients, devices like timetable gatherings, sitting areas, data shows, and electronic patient records. Which might be used close by specialists, at the emergency clinic, or somewhere else, either in disposition for their visit or afterward.

The fundamental devices improve the proficiency of the patient's objectives. These days, no one wants to invest the energy and time filling the form type of any way it is manual or digital. Patients need to recover their data in 5 to 10 min rapidly basically and straightforward.

Today patients do not have just data about them yet also have more information about them to bring specialists. They can get information for healthcare applicable data like the nourishment esteem they admission, food logs, rest logs, and hereditary information in such huge numbers of cases through this. They can all the more likely take care of themselves. Through the framework given by the medical clinic or any outsider, they can likewise monitor their wellbeing record, narratives, solution, and others. In any case, while numerous patients currently have this information, they are not in every case sure how to manage it, or if and how their supplier may use it.

The semantic web can support the individual patient, yet also beyond personal health, it can help by giving a boundless measure of data of the fluctuating degree of legitimacy accessible to the patient about side effects, analyze medicines. Numerous patients need to or want to have more power over their wellbeing, particularly where such huge numbers of alternatives accessible as they have more prominent huge availability into the human service space. A lot of data on patient care, instruction, and backing are accessible. Most wellbeing locales have customarily been data based and the Net (Internet) is, for instance, the most ideal approach to locate a self-improvement gathering for any sickness. It is likewise a tremendous wellspring of subtleties on singular sicknesses, regardless of how dark, and is progressively being utilized by patients as a method of finding the best emergency clinics and specialists.

2.2.4.3 Impact on Practitioner

Specialist and medical attendants are demonstrating less fervor to bring execution the innovation inside the working environment in any case. Though assessments have been changing as of late—and in light of current circumstances. For a couple of years, programming in the medicinal services district battling in ease of use and structure behind apparatuses in the purchaser space, likewise in different cases. Professionals in emergency clinics want high data thickness unlike in numerous different businesses.

Young professionals are accepting of the type of technology used in hospitals rapidly because like tools, electronic health records, as those were the part of their education and they understand the importance. Most practitioners, whether doctors, nurses or lab techs, are highly disciplined with specific, repeatable processes they have honed over the years. Maybe this is because they do the same practice regularly. For example: a radiologist inspecting XRAYS, for a few minutes and spent the time reviewing the images from a single patient before the next patient and repeat the same.

Notwithstanding their degree of experience, those specialists are individuals with solid inspiration which is required for long unpleasant working hours. So semantic web helps to plan their meeting. It likewise gives simple entry to a patient's wellbeing record.

Connections on the internet will likewise help the specialists in India, particularly those rehearsing in littler urban communities, towns, and country zones and who, in this manner, frequently feel disconnected, to stay in contact with new turns of events. They can become individuals from data gatherings and search through free data databases on the Internet. The greater part of the journals distributed in different nations set aside a long effort to arrive at remote spots in India and is additionally over the top expensive. These can be presently gotten to for an ostensible expense on the Internet with no superfluous loss of time.

Progressively, the Internet will be utilized to pass on increasingly "ongoing" data. A doctor rehearsing in a remote town would now be able to counsel a master sitting at any separation by giving him all pictures and information on the web, hence disposing of the hazard associated with and set aside the time and cash spent on movement.

2.2.4.4 Impact on Researchers

We keep confidence in the reasonable utilization of semantic web advances that can manual for quicker development of development from clinic, hospital, and research center as well. The Semantic Web approach offers a growing blend of principles, innovations, and social practices layered on the head of the best data scattering and sharing mechanical assembly in presence—the World Wide Web.

The vision of a Semantic Web accelerated examination critically relies upon the holder of logical and clinical information making that information accessible in a reusable structure. Frequently the exertion that goes into getting ready and serving this information will not straightforwardly advantage the supplier. Rather, specialists are estimated for delivering logical disclosures and expounding on them, specialists for helping wiped outpatients, and pharmaceutical organizations for creating sheltered, successful medications. There are likewise protection dangers associated with sharing individual data. Significant patient information must be procured with fitting assent and with affect ability to those protection issues. It is an open inquiry of how to structure motivations to cause these holders of significant data to believe the push to be to their greatest advantage.

If the examination network chose today that it was propelled to distribute information semantically, we do not yet have satisfactory quantities of gifted information laborers. Information demonstrating even without the expectation of interoperating is a hard educated ability, and the test is considerably amplified when the goal is to share data for unexpected employments. We have to build up and populate another control, a blend of interdisciplinary abilities that incorporate strong comprehension of bio medicine, software engineering, reasoning, and the social human studies of science and figuring.

2.3 Data and Database

Anybody can fail to detect the massive change in any piece of social healthcare delivery or arranging today regardless of whether the layout of those change, not to mention the subtleties alone, are in dispute. There is a different expansive requirement for significantly more and much better data about the utilization of healthcare services and the results of that care [13].

It is exceptionally difficult to get data from various sources. The procedure to gain information makes persistent disappointment for the individuals who endeavor for this like policymakers, scientists, wellbeing experts, buyers, patients [13].

Now the way has changed to process the healthcare data in the healthcare industry because of the digitalization. The technology in this sector is growing. Whether you can consider AI, Machine learning, or computerized records, healthcare in condition poof flux. The high volume of data to manage and analyze along with each of their patients acquire by the healthcare center. The digitalized form of medical records simplifies the many tasks for an accomplished office [13].

2.3.1 What Is Data?

The information has a ton of significance in the database. It ranges from little to a colossal amount and structures the primary hotspot for rest parts to communicate with one another. Information is ordered into further two sorts, one client information that is liable for the database. It is put away in various tables as lines and segments. Second is metadata likewise called information about information? It contains data about information, for instance, names of tables in the database, requirements of the database, essential keys and outside keys, and so forth.

2.3.2 What Is Database?

A database can be considered as a collection of information that is managed in such a way so that can be easily retrieved, managed, accessed.

Different Definitions of the Database

1. "A usually large collection of data organized especially for rapid search and retrieval (as by a computer) an online database" (Merriam-Webster)
2. "A comprehensive collection of related data organized for convenient access, generally in a computer." (dictionary)
3. "A database is an organized collection of data." (Wikipedia)

The database was developed during the 1960s began with the hierarchical database. The relational database was created by EF Codd during the 1970s while an object oriented database was designed during the 1980s. During the 1990s object oriented database rose with the development of item arranged programming languages. These days, databases with SQL and NoSQL are well known. The Evolution of database is given in Table 2.1.

2.3.3 Source of Data in the Healthcare System

In this part, we will talk about the diverse human services information sources and the essential investigation strategies that are universally

Table 2.1 Growth of data [15].

Evolution of database				
1960–1970	Files processing system	First Database system developed		
1970–1980	Hierarchical and network	DBMS commercial use	Relational model (E.F. Codd)	
1980–1990	Relational model used widely	Use of SQL		
1990–2000	Use of heterogeneous data	Use of relational and object oriented database	Use of NOSQL	Research to develop a common database
2000 & Beyond	Data mining & Distributed database	Data warehousing and data	Big data analytic	Data shearing and processing on cloud

utilized for the preparation and examination of such information. The patient information, clinical and nonclinical situations, which are presently being gathered in the different structures. The information in the clinical structures will have organized healthcare records and biomedical records images. We will likewise examine the mining of sensor information and biomedical sign analysis. Due to the progressions in genomic information customized medication has increased a ton of significance. The few measurable procedures associated with genomic information investigation will likewise be talked about. Biomedical writing, patients in unstructured medical clinic in formation will likewise be talked about [17].

2.3.3.1 Electronic Health Record (EHR)

The electronic record is known as EHR likewise is only a digitized type of the clinical history of patients. It contains the total data about patient consideration in like manner medicine, issue, lab reports, and radiology reports, doctor's perception, progress notes, and so forth. Various EHRs go past a patient's clinical or treatment history and may contain additional increasingly broad perspectives of a patient's consideration. A huge property of EHRs is that they give a convincing and gainful way for human administration providers and relationships to grant to one another. In this novel situation, EHRs are inherently planned to be ceaselessly and they can promptly be gotten to and adjusted by affirmed clients. This can be handy, similar to a hospital or in clinic and authority may get to the clinical records of the supplier. The EHR makes the work process smoother by permitting access to continuous records. It can deliver an all-out record of a patient's clinical encounter, and support other thought related activities, for instance, evidence based decision help, quality organization, and results reporting. The limit and recuperation of prosperity related data are dynamically profitable using EHRs. It helps with improving the quality and solace of patient thought, increases relentless interest in the human administration's process, improves the precision of ends and prosperity results, and improves care coordination [17].

2.3.3.2 Biomedical Image Analysis

Within the healthcare care here and now, due to its gigantic capability to provide high quality images of anatomical structures within human beings, the medical imaging system plays a vital role. Analyzing these pictures efficiently can be useful for doctors and health professionals, as it can aid in tracking illness, organizing care, and predicting.

Even so, only the initial stage of the procedure is to study these organs with the assistance of images. The ultimate aim of biomedical image analysis is to have the option of generating quantitative data and making derivations from the image which will inevitably provide further bits of information about a disease. Such examination has major cultural essentialness since it is the way to understanding biological frameworks and taking care of medical issues.

Whatever it may be, it contains various difficulties because the picture is diverse, complex, and with noisy qualities may include intermittent forms. Different general classifications of analysis problems that arise when examining pictures are object discovery, picture division, camera enlistment, and extraction highlights. When clarified, both of these difficulties will motivate the age of substantial expository figures that can fill in as contributions to the various regions of knowledge investigation of medicinal services. So this is another source of data for medical professionals and researchers [17].

2.3.3.3 Sensor Data Analysis

Sensor data is inescapable in the clinical region both for progressing and for survey assessment. A couple of kinds of clinical data arrangement instruments, for instance, an electrocardiogram (ECG), an electroencephalogram (EEG) are sensors that assemble signals from various parts of the human body. These assembled data instruments are from time to time used for audit assessment, anyway more normally for ceaseless examination Maybe; the hugest use case of the ongoing investigation is concerning concentrated consideration units (ICUs) and persistent far off checking of patients with the select disease.

The amount of the details to the treated can be relatively large in each of these situations. For example, in an ICU, having input from several sources is not uncommon for the sensor, and alarm should be triggered gradually. Of that kind applications that require the use of such big data frameworks and focused platforms for equipment. That both real-time activities and the long term analysis of different trends and treatment decisions are of huge significance in remote observing applications [17].

Although the rapid production of sensor information offers a major guarantee that it will impact medicinal services, it also poses an information overburdening problem. Subsequently, designing new knowledge forensic methods that can transform these massive quantities of information collected into meaningful and interoperable information turns out to be crucial. These analytical approaches will not only take better account of the physiological signs of patients and help to give the bedside situational focus but can also provide better insights in the areas of inefficiencies of healthcare systems that may be the key driver of flooding costs.

2.3.3.4 Genomic Data Analysis

Numerous illnesses are inherited, but the concept of causality between the genetic markers and the sicknesses has not been entirely established. For example, diabetes is well understood to be an inherited infection; in any case, the precise arrangement of hereditary markers making a person diabetes inclined is ambiguous. For example, the visual impairment caused by disease in several specific cases, the important attributes are recognized but not all possible changes have been fully detached. A better understanding of the interactions between different genetic genes, modifications, and conditions of infection has tremendous potential to help advance the various quality gene therapies to repair these conditions.

One will be commonly excited about understanding what kind of well-being related requests can be tended to through in silicon assessment of the genomic data through the regular data driven examinations. Likewise, deciphering inherited revelations into redid medicine practice is a significantly non minor task with a lot of questionable challenges [17].

For instance, the genomic scenes in complex sicknesses, such as cancer, malignant growths are overwhelmingly complicated, uncovering a high request for heterogeneity among various people. Resolving these issues will be befitting a significant bit of the riddle and it will bring the idea of personalized medication a lot nearer to the real world. Ongoing headways made in the biotechnologies have prompted the quick age of huge volumes of organic and clinical data and progressed genomic research. This has additionally prompted remarkable chances and trust in the genome scale investigation of testing issues in life science. For instance, progresses in genomic innovation made it conceivable to consider the total genomic scene of healthy people for complex infections.

Huge numbers of these exploration headings have just indicated promising outcomes as far as creating new bits of knowledge into the science of human infection and to anticipate the customized reaction of the person to a specific treatment. Likewise, hereditary information is regularly displayed either as arrangements or as systems. Consequently, the work in this field requires a decent comprehension of succession and system mining strategies. Different information examination based arrangements are being created for handling key exploration issues in medication, for example, recognizable proof of illness biomarkers and restorative targets and expectation of clinical results [17].

2.3.3.5 Clinical Text Mining

A large proportion of healthcare records are gathered as clinical notes. Such notes are typically put in an unstructured location of knowledge and are the source of quite a bit of information about healthcare facilities. This includes the clinical data from transcription transfer, direct passage by vendors, or use of applications for discourse recognition. These are possibly the most lavish wellspring of unused information. The manual encoding of this free text structure on an extensive extent of clinical information is unnecessarily costly and dreary; in any case, it is compelled to fundamental and assist ant investigations and system for charging purposes [17].

Such notes are famously testing to break down naturally because of the intricacy associated with changing over clinical content that is accessible in free text to an organized format. It turns out to be hard primarily in light of their unstructured nature, heterogeneity, diverse designs, and shifting settings across various patients and practitioners. Natural language handling (NLP) and substance extraction have a significant impact on gathering valuable information from huge volumes of clinical content to naturally encoding clinical data in an opportune way.

As a rule, information preprocessing strategies are progressively significant in these settings when contrasted with genuine mining procedures. The preparation of clinical content utilizing NLP techniques is all the more challenging when contrasted with the text of different messages because of the ungrammatical idea of short and transmitted expressions, correspondences, shorthand vocabularies, for example, shortenings and abbreviations, and frequently incorrectly spelled clinical terms. Every one of these issues will directly affect the different standard NLP errands, for example, shallow or full parsing, sentence division, text arrangement, and so forth. Along these lines making the clinical content preparing profoundly testing.

2.3.3.6 Social Media

The quick development of different internet based life assets, for example, long range informal communication locales, sites/micro blogs, discussions, question replying mail, and online networks gives an abundance of data about the popular sentiment on different parts of social insurance. Web based life information can be dug for examples and information that can be utilized to make helpful inductions about populace wellbeing and general wellbeing observing. A lot of general wellbeing data can be gathered from the contributions of different members at web based social networking locales [17].

Although most individual web based life posts and messages contain minimal enlightening worth, the accumulation of a huge number of such messages can produce significant information. Successfully dissecting these immense bits of information can altogether decrease the latency in gathering such complex data. Past exploration via web based networking media investigation for social insurance has concentrated on catching total wellbeing patterns, for example, episodes of irresistible infections, recognizing reports of unfavorable medication associations, and improving interventional capacities for wellbeing-related exercises. Malady flare-up location is frequently. Unequivocally reflected in the substance of web based life and an examination of the historical backdrop of the substance gives significant experiences about sickness episodes. Point models are much of the time utilized for significant level examination of such wellbeing related substances.An extra wellspring of data via web based networking media destinations is acquired from the online specialist and patient networks. Since ailments repeat across various people, online networks give a significant wellspring of information about different ailments. A significant test in online life investigation is that the information is regularly questionable, and in this manner, the outcomes must be deciphered with alert [17].

2.3.4 Why Are Databases Important?

Single Patients have recorded when they visit any medical center, a lot of information is collected from different practitioners, prescription diagnoses, and other reports, need to be on record for current as well as future use.

Now take an example for any single day the number of visits. In this case, a hospital needs a good design database of patient information. It will likewise help with accomplishing productivity because of the handling of information; accordingly giving the Healthcare supplier significant data with a tick of a button. To make it easier for us there is a need to perform many manipulations on data. The practitioner has a very busy schedule, needs fast and efficient access. Therefore, the information undergoes query, filtering, and retrieval using the relevant technology.

It is subsequently significant that there is work unification through things like patient recognizance, access control over healthcare data, administration service, among others. Technical Innovation is required since norms for the work process are a significant prerequisite. Advancement is essential since standards for the work procedure are a critical essential.

In the healthcare service, the healthcare database plays a key role in monitoring and improve the value of service. The healthcare provider can get the database for their medicinal practice; the data can help in quality certification and development programs for healthcare services at a nearby level. The information can offer significant responses to the methodology about issues encompassing changes in the part.

Hospitals, clinics, government organizations, health departments, etc., also are important sources of healthcare data. This type of data release is very much important to the estimation of quality. These types of appropriate data include a conclusion, strategies, length of remain, charges, among others. It helps in the quality expert for quality inspection as they use hospital data to access healthcare quality.

2.3.5 Challenges With the Database in the Healthcare System

Integrity guarantees that the information is exact and has not been changed. EHRs work as an approach to improve the patient's health safety by diminishing healthcare service mistakes, decrease healthcare differences, and improve public health in general. Be that as it may, concerns have been raised about the precision and dependability of information that went into the electronic record [16].

Misfortune or obliteration of information happens when the data is inappropriate or incorrect because this data create concern about the integrity of the database as patients thought decisions to rely upon them. These types of developing issues come under clinical data cheat. The result is the contribution of mistaken data into the record of the person in question. The person's insurance organization is charged for clinical organizations not given to the genuine policyholder and the patient's future treatment is guided by the deception that neither the patient nor the provider quickly sees [16].

The main issue with data security, as healthcare data is much important and also connected with the patient's personal life, impresses hackers to target. in this case, the healthcare industry should make sure that the patient records will stay secure. Else, you face legal action from patients if their data is compromised. Another hazard to remember is the possibility of electronic records being seized by hackers who hold the patient information prisoner, scrambled until you pay the ransom ware expense to open the data [16].

Healthcare information is especially good and it is gotten from a broad classification of sources like as sensors, media, and text in the form of biomedical writings/clinical notes, and Conventional electronic records. Because of the variety of different sources, the collection of data is heterogeneous. This leads to a challenge for processing and analysis. There is likewise a wide decent variety in the technology that is required to analyze these various patterns of information. Also, information heterogeneity normally makes different challenges like unification and data analysis. By and large, experiences can be gotten from different information types, which are in any case impractical from a vast potential of the information [16].

2.4 Big Data and Database Security and Protection

2.4.1 What Is Big Data

The term big data demonstrates the enormous volume of information. The information can be organized or unstructured. That immerses the administration on an everyday premise. In the term big data, the measure of information is not significant; however, what we do with the significant information, big data can be considered for knowledge that assists with bettering choices and vital moves [20].

A different definition of big data:

1. **Wikipedia: "Big data** is a field that treats ways to analyze, systematically extract information from, or otherwise deal with data sets that are too large or complex to be dealt with by traditional data processing application software" [19].
2. **O'Reilly Radar:** "Big data is data that exceeds the processing capacity of conventional database systems. The data is too big, moves too fast, or does not fit the strictures of your database architectures. To gain value from this data, you must choose an alternative way to process it." By Edd Dumbill.

2.4.2 Five V's of Big Data

Big data analytics can be considered as a choice in healthcare for solving the data complexity in healthcare. Let us discuss the main dimension of Big data. Some sources describe three, four, or five. We are considering all five dimensions.

1. Volume : (The term volume defines the size of data, its quantity, from terabyte to zeta byte)
2. Variety: (Variety denotes the type of data, what it is structured or unstructured or it is semistructured)
3. Velocity: (The flow of data, how data that are produced, processed, and analyzed)
4. Veracity: (The term means quality, relevance, predictive value, the meaningfulness of the data)
5. Value: (The usability of data define the value of data the value of information for decision making, developing strategy).

2.4.2.1 Volume

Volume means simply the quantity of data. This data must be used further to gain important knowledge. Healthcare, making current data digitalize, and also developing new types of data is the reason for growth. Now the data in healthcare has exponential growth. if we consider just, for example, any single patient has his data in gigabytes and it is also increasing day by day. With the same, if we consider the patient data of the hospital or city, the data will be in terabytes or petabytes. currently, the volume of the existing healthcare system includes the sources from personal medical records, radiology images, clinical trial data, FDA submissions, human genetics, and population data, genomic sequences, etc. now the modern variety of data from a source like 3D imaging, genomics, and biometric sensor readings, are also included in healthcare data. Advances in data the board, particularly virtualization and dispersed processing, are empowering the improvement of stages for the progressively convincing catch, storing, and control of immense volumes of data [21, 22].

2.4.2.2 Variety

Variety indicates the variation in healthcare data as it can be structured, semi structured, unstructured. Unstructured data is a challenge for data manipulated. Most of the data in healthcare is unstructured such as medical notes, hospital records, and prescription records. Radiograph, CT scan, MRI, and other images. Data in structured format also include in healthcare such as accounting and billings, actuarial data, (some) clinical data, (some) laboratory instrument readings. Structure data have static schema so it is easy to analyze, store, queried.

However, new data streams like fitness devices, genetics and genomics, social media research, and another source also currently included in healthcare. Relatively little of this data is manipulated and analyzed by computer for extracting information by capture, store, and organizing.

Healthcare applications particularly need progressively beneficial ways to deal with uniting and change over varieties of data, including the automatic change from structured out to unstructured data.

Many tech giant companies like s, Practice Fusion, Athena health Inc., Humedica, and One Health, etc., are also working on mange and analyze data. Let us take the example of IBM Watson. Watson, with its stand out trademark language capacities, is the basic model. In like manner, in this current paper's universe, Health Fidelity is using ordinary language planning to change over unstructured into structured data [21, 22].

2.4.2.3 Velocity

This implies the time where Big Data can be processed. A couple of activities are noteworthy and need speedy responses, which is the explanation brisk getting ready to intensify profitability. In velocity two related concepts are most preferable in healthcare: the first one is the speed at which data is generated by technological devices and the second one is the need for the process and analyzes data in real time. Let us take as an example so many sensors and devices that are designed to understand the health status of patients but they are meaningless without analyzation over data. There is a need first of all to analyze the data provided by the device and then handover to clinician's and others.

Nowadays the traditional data is quite static such as paper notes, reports. This data has a lower priority for analyzing purposes. But in another case the real time (such as blood pressure monitoring, room monitor for anesthesia, heart monitors) data analyzing is a higher priority; otherwise, it can become a question of life.

Companies related to the medical device field are working for speedy capturing and display real time data in hospitals, ICU, ambulance.

Some smaller company also focuses on the device which can be usable at home, like blood pressure monitoring, diabetes monitoring. This IoT (Internet of things) will lead to the progressive velocity of big data in healthcare [21, 22].

2.4.2.4 Veracity

Conventional data the administrators expect that warehoused data is certain, clean, and accurate. In any case, as any person who has suffered bank, credit, or insurance botches knows, data maybe once in a while uncertain, unsure, or inside and out misguided.

The data can differ as per the condition like time to time, place to place, and treatment to treatment. For example, what clinician learned during the course curriculum, during practice, by the experience? The patient can be the main factor in how they express about their health. These factors decide what to be next. Such changeability implies information must be genuinely deciphered when the consideration setting and conveyance process is taken into settings. For example, the diagnosis of CP means differently for person to person, form cardiologist or primary care physician it can be "chest pain" and for the neurologist, it can be "cerebral palsy."

While various affiliations are stressed over data quality in therapeutic administrations, they are revolved around standard IT issues, e.g., data the administrators, warehousing, consistency, audit, distortion prevention, error uncovering, and regulatory consistency. There radiates an impression of being less focused on the concealed veracity (trustworthiness, essentialness, perceptive estimation) of the data, an issue that will be of extending criticalness in understanding the vision of human administrations Big

Data examination and modified prescription. For example, Watson's ability to give exact provider decision help relies upon the finish and precision of the data it can get to [21, 22].

2.4.2.5 Value

To wrap things up, the big data must support its qualities. Implies the information ought to be precise and lead to quantifiable improvement by the day's end. On the off chance that if we are going to utilize the infrastructure need to gather and decipher information that must guarantee the precision. Companies may use comparable gadgets and progressions for the get together and analyzing the data they have available, anyway how they by then set that data to work is finally up to them [21].

2.4.3 Architectural Framework of Big Data

The standard healthcare informatics analytics and the determined big data structure adventure relative nature. The guideline differentiate is about how the taking care of executed, in the standard project, the processing should be conceivable on any business intelligence tool on a standalone system. In any case, in the processing of big data, the processing is isolated and execute on different nodes. So the as the name shows it is used for large datasets as the healthcare provider exploits their tremendous data vaults to get understanding for choosing better taught prosperity related decisions [14].

The user interface of the conventional analytical system provides ease of use as compared to big data tool as the big data tool are very much complex, programming intensive and desire the variety of skills. They emerge as an open source development tool and platforms with a lack of support that vendor proprietary tools possess.

Conceptual architecture of big data, Figure 2.2 below.

As we have already discussed previously the source of the big data can internal and external and format are also can be different and may be placed in different positions. The source data type includes social media, big transaction, biometric information, machine to machine data, human generated data, etc.

There are essentially two ways to deal with information analytics. First methodology architecture. Another is data warehousing. In the first methodology, the information will be in row state and the middleware services need to process, call, recover the information, in the second methodology information from different sources collected and prepared

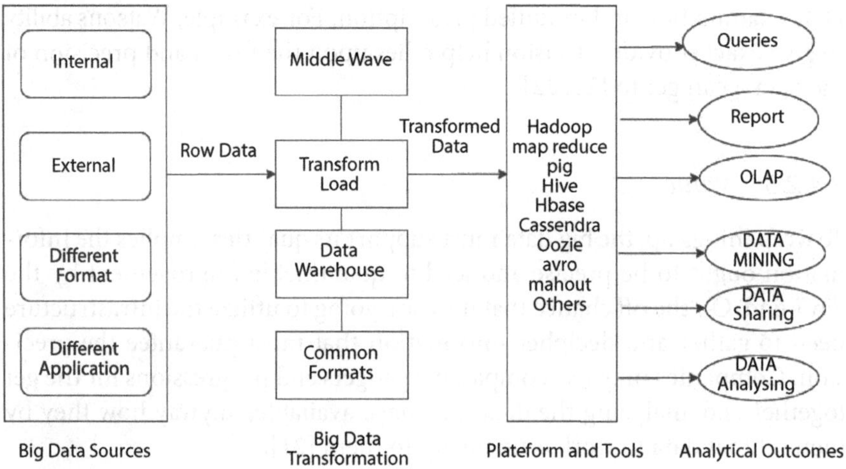

Figure 2.2 Conceptual architecture of big data.

for handling, even though the information is not accessible progressively. Using the means of concentrate, change, and burden (ETL), information from various sources is purified and prepared. Contingent upon whether the information is organized or unstructured, a few information arrangements can be a contribution to the enormous information investigation stage [14].

Numerous decisions are made in the next period of the architecture concerning the data input approach, appropriated design, tool assembly assurance, and analytical models. Finally, the four utilization of big data analytics is shown. These are requests, reports, OLAP, and data mining. Visualization is a sweeping theme over the four applications, a wide collection of techniques and head ways has been made and changed by complete, control, look at, and envision enormous data in social protection for Drawing from such fields as experiences, programming building, applied science, and economic related issues [14].

The developments in information technology in recent years computerizing many applications in various areas as a result. Now the data become very important assets for any organization, and that is why ease of data access, sharing, retrieving information, making it ease of use is the basic need [28].

Additionally, the security of data is the main concern as it containing very confidential information. For patients, privacy is very important and they want to have full control over their data [14].

2.4.4 Data Protection Versus Data Security in Healthcare

At this time, now at this time, this is very much important to understand the basic difference between both data protection and data security. Data protection means keeping data private. This can be accomplished by defining organizational measures and security rules which include user agreements policies, accessibility, and guidelines for data access. Data security related to the mechanism for data storage, data access ability for the authenticated user [25].

2.4.4.1 Phishing Attacks

Phishing attacks are becoming more common nowadays and the user must be educated on the possible threat are hiding in their inbox. It can be coming from email, text messages, or can be from web chat links. It will be looks like the general message which is deal with by users daily. It is generally a kind of link which redirect user on the suspicious website and ask from the user for the credentials [25].

These types of attacks can be failed by the smartness of the user. The hospital staff and general user as well should make sure the link is coming from an authenticated source or not. If it is not then the user should not open the link and mail or even download any attachment coming from the unknown link, mail.

2.4.4.2 Malware and Ransomware

Malware is a type of program which can enter into the system through several channels such as network, downloaded file, and utility software. They hack the access and sneak the information or can be damage the system.

Ransomware is very popular on the list because the semantic web is frequently updated and also stored much information, so they are ideal for hackers. This type of attack is dangerous because the patient can suffer in emergency conditions. There is a need to make a strong network so the hackers are not able to acquire the access which they are looking for. Additionally, IT staff should also continuously inspect the network for the possible loophole for malware [25].

2.4.4.3 Cloud Threats

Nowadays healthcare provider is moving their stuff on the cloud, in past healthcare providers don't want to adopt o cloud. But the feature of the cloud impresses them to come on the cloud. If healthcare provider usage cloud means check which information is need to upload. May healthcare providers at this time there is a need to enhance the security and privacy level because the data is globally reached. Before shifting to the cloud, a healthcare provider should know which data and assets should reside on the cloud and what data should be on its server [25, 26].

In this scenario, data encryption can play a vital role. A strong encryption technique can ensure that data is protected while it is going to migrate from a personal server to a cloud.

Cloud Access Security Broker (CASB) courses of action can in like manner go about as security and consistency procedure execution points, put between cloud pro communities and the staff to join and contribute in security approaches as the cloud based assets are gotten too. These plans can in like manner log coordinated efforts with oversaw data to support the survey necessities that are a great part of the time some bit of consistency frameworks, for instance, HIPAA [25, 26].

2.4.5 Technology in Use to Secure the Healthcare Data

Many technologies are now being used to secure the data. Some of them we are going to discuss over here.

Authentication: In the healthcare system, there is a need to be verified both information users and information providers at each point. The use of data authentication can face a special problem like man in the middle and also can help to prevent this. many cryptographic protocols also use some type of authentication to prevent these types of invasion, for example, cryptographic protocols like TLS (Transport layer security) and SSL (Secure socket layer) which mainly responsible to provide the secure communication over the Network, these protocols encrypt the fragment of the network connection at the transport layer end to end, an application like internet suffering, email, fax, messaging, and calling use widely some version of the protocol.

Additionally, another cryptography algorithm hash function SHA-256 can also implement to achieve authentication. The hashing technique and Kerberos mechanism are based on the ticket tracking service for authentication. One another technique is known as the bull eye which is used to monitoring all suspicion information in 360°. These techniques ensure information security and also maintain the connection between original data and replica. With the same, it also confirms that the user is allowed to read and write data [27].

Data Encryption: To prevent unwanted access to sensitive information encryption of data can be an effective way. Encryption is useful to dodge introduction to enters, for instance, packet-sniffing and thievery of the storage device.

The encryption technique should be able to understand a new variety of electronic forms of data and also easy enough to implement. there are so many types of encryption algorithm provided such as RSA, Rijndael, AES and RC6, DES, 3DES, RC4, IDEA, Blowfish, etc., which can be used for security purposes. Sometimes it is hard to make the decision which one should be used for the application [27].

Data Masking: Data masking or data obfuscation is another way for data security used by many healthcare providers. This s not like encryption technique but at the place of encryption, the original data will be replaced with the unidentified data. The first solution is proposed by Swaney and Samrati and is K-ANONYMITY. This is okay for the identity disclosure but fails for the attribute disclosure, another sensitive proposed, which can protect against identity disclosure and attribute disclosure both. Other methods like adding noise, swiping cells, replacing group with copies of a single representative are also available [27].

2.4.5.1 Access Control Policy

The access control policy provides control over data. It checks the user credential and the permission which allowed accessing the data when the user enters the system access will be controlled by access control policy. It checks your privileges and allows you to access what you are authorized. For example, a patient is allowed to enter/modify their information, access their information, and maintain their record but, they cannot do the same for another person however the administrator can do this because the administrator has permission for that. The most popular access control policy is Role based access control (RBAC) and another one is the attribute based access control (ABAC) [27].

2.4.6 Monitoring and Auditing

Security can be also provided by monitoring and auditing. This is not compulsory but optional can be used as a security layer. Monitoring means simply inspect the data and auditing mean is to create the log record for the activities. The security monitoring architecture is developed to detect intrusion and prevention procedures via inspecting DNS flow, IP flow, HTTP traffic, and honey pot data. It also can store the data and process in the distributed source. At this phase, three probability measurements have been determined to recognize whether domain name, data packets or stream is malicious. Contingent upon the score acquired through this figuring, an alarm happens in the discovery framework or procedure ends by the anticipation framework [27].

2.4.7 Standard for Data Protection

As the healthcare data is going to be digitalized and advance. The new types of threats are coming into knowledge for healthcare records. In starting there was no strong policy for security and privacy. Additionally, given these emerging threats, there is a need for a strong healthcare protection standard.

The United States (US) imposed several rules and regulations, which also includes privacy and security rules under HIPAA (1996) and State Alliance for eHealth (2007).

In the U.S healthcare provider strongly influenced by the HIPPA regulations. it confirms that the healthcare provider and organization are up to date and also fulfilling the latest requirement. It also ensures that the organization and healthcare basically HIPPA includes two key primary components.

Managerial, physical, and technical dealing with personal health information requires some standards which are described by security rules.

HIPAA Security Rule—HIPPA security provides security for digital health information. It protects the creation, utilization, and backing of healthcare data. This is provided by HIPPA covered organization. the main motive of this rule is to set the standard managerial, physical, and technical dealing with electronic health information [29].

HIPAA Privacy Rule—Privacy is very important for the health record because the health record contains very sensitive information. There is a need to provide the safeguard for the health record, insurance record, hospital record, lab report, and other private details. This HIPPA privacy rule protects the information from misuse by controlling the usage of information [29].

2.4.7.1 Healthcare Standard in India

Let us discuss the security and privacy policies in India as well. There are three standards for security and privacy

1. Security technical standards
2. Administrative safeguards standards
3. Physical safeguards standards

2.4.7.2 *Security Technical Standards*

The actual purpose of this standard is to secure and protect data as per technical aspects. Healthcare includes the following requirements (30).

1. Authentication
2. Automatic log off
3. Access control
4. Access Privileges
5. Audit log
6. Integrity
7. Encryption
8. Digital Certificates

2.4.7.3 *Administrative Safeguards Standards*

This Safeguard needs healthcare service providers to create and execute security the executive's procedure that incorporates arrangements and strategies that address the full scope of their security weaknesses. It includes a security management process standard, assigned security responsibility, security awareness program, information access management, security incident procedures, evaluation [30].

2.4.7.4 *Physical Safeguard Standards*

Physical safeguards standards are safety efforts to secure a healthcare service supplier's electronic data frameworks, related hardware, structures lodging the frameworks from common and natural dangers, and unapproved interruption. Medicinal services suppliers must satisfy the accompanying guidelines. These types of standards are access control standard, workstation utilizes standard, workstation security standard, gadget, and media device controls standard [30].

References

1. Institute of Medicine (US) Committee on the Health Professions Education Summit, Chapter 2, Challenges Facing the Health System and Implications for Educational Reform. Greiner, A.C. and Knebel, E. (eds), Health Professions Education: A Bridge to Quality. National Academies Press, Washington, DC, 2003. Available from: https://www.ncbi.nlm.nih.gov/books/NBK221522/

2. Ruttenberg, A. *et al.*, Advancing translational research with the Semantic Web. *BMC Bioinf.*, 8, 3, 1–16, 2007.
3. Karami, M. and Rahimi, A., Semantic web technologies for sharing clinical information in healthcare systems. *Acta Informatica Medica*, 27, 1, 4, 2019.
4. Shadbolt, N., Berners-Lee, T., Hall, W., The semantic web revisited *IEEE Intell Syst.*, 21, 3, 96–101, 2006.
5. Dolin, R.H. *et al.*, The HL7 clinical document architecture. *J. Am. Med. Inf. Assoc.*, 8, 6, 552–569, 2001.
6. Jain, V. Dr. and Singh, M., Ontology Development and Query Retrieval using Protégé Tool. *Int. J. Intell. Syst. Appl. (IJISA), Hongkong*, 5, 9, 67–75, August 2013.
7. https://www.w3.org/standards/semanticweb/, last updated on Oct 5, 2020
8. Bakken, S. *et al.*, Toward vocabulary domain specifications for Health Level 7—Coded data elements. *J. Am. Med. Inf. Assoc.*, 7, 4, 333–342, 2000.
9. Mahmudova, N., The Importance of Using Database Management Systems in Hospitals, Khazar University Periodicals Khazar Journal of Science and Technology, 3, 2, 2019.
10. Wikipedia contributors, *Health Level 7*, 2020, Wikipedia, The Free Encyclopedia. Wikipedia, The Free Encyclopedia, 1 Jun. 2020. Web. 28 Jul.
11. Yadav, U., Narula, G.S., Duhan, N., Jain, V., Murthy, B.K., Development and Visualization of Domain Specific Ontology using protégé. *Indian J. Sci. Technol.*, 9, 16, 1–7, April, 2016. having.
12. https://www.bypeople.com/semantic-web-pros-and-cons/, last updated on Oct 5, 2020.
13. Donaldson, M.S. and Lohr., K.N., Health databases and health database organizations: uses, benefits, and concerns, in: *Health Data in the information age: use, disclosure, and privacy*, National Academies Press, US, 1994 https://www.ncbi.nlm.nih.gov/books/NBK236556/.
14. https://www.ibm.com/blogs/watson-health/the-5-vs-of-big-data/, last updated on Oct 5, 2020.
15. https://towardsdatascience.com/how-to-secure-health-data-in-the-cloud-541fbdad811a, last updated on Oct 5, 2020.
16. Ozair, F.F. *et al.*, Ethical issues in electronic health records: A general overview. *Perspect. Clin. Res.*, 6, 2, 73, 2015.
17. Reddy, C.K. and Aggarwal, C.C., *Healthcare data analytics*, vol. 36, CRC Press, 2015.
18. Wikipedia contributors, *Health Level Seven International*, 2020, Wikipedia, The Free Encyclopedia. Wikipedia, The Free Encyclopedia, 8 May. 2020. Web. 28 Jul.
19. Wikipedia contributors, *Big data*, 2020, Wikipedia, The Free Encyclopedia. Wikipedia, The Free Encyclopedia, 1 Jul. 2020. Web. 28 Jul.
20. Feldman, B., Martin, E.M., Skotnes, T., Big data in healthcare hype and hope. 360, 122–125, 2012. Dr. Bonnie.

21. Hadi, H.J. *et al.*, Big data and five v's characteristics. *Int. J. Adv. Electron. Comput. Sci.*, 2, 1, 16–23, 2015.
22. Raghupathi, W. and Raghupathi, V., Big data analytics in healthcare: Promise and potential. *Health information science and systems*, 2, 1, 3, 2014.
23. Sachdeva, S., Mchome, S., Bhalla., S., Web services security issues in healthcare applications. *2010 IEEE/ACIS 9th International Conference on Computer and Information Science*, IEEE, 2x1010.
24. Yadav, D.P. *et al.*, Feature extraction based machine learning for human burn diagnosis from burn images. *IEEE J. Trans. Eng. Health Med.*, 7, 1–7, 2019.
25. Sharma, A., Sharma, A., Jalal., A.S., Distance-based facility location problem for fuzzy demand with simultaneous opening of two facilities. *Int. J. Comput. Sci. Math.*, 9, 6, 590–601, 2018.
26. https://www.beckershospitalreview.com/healthcare-information-technology/the-top-5-cybersecurity-threats-hospitals-need-to-watch-for.html, last updated on Oct 5, 2020.
27. Abouelmehdi, K., A Beni-Hessane, and Hayat Khaloufi. "Big healthcare data: preserving security and privacy. *J. Big Data*, 5, 1, 1, 2018.
28. Sharma, A. and Upadhyay, D., VDBSCAN Clustering with Map-Reduce Technique, in: *Recent Findings in Intelligent Computing Techniques*, pp. 305–314, Springer, Singapore, 2018.
29. https://digitalguardian.com/blog/healthcare-cybersecurity-tips-securing-private-health-data, last updated on Oct 5, 2020.
30. EMR Standards Committee, Recommendations on Electronic Medical Records Standards in India. Ministry of Health and Family Welfare, Government of India, New Delhi, 2013. https://mohfw. gov. in/sites/default/files/24539108839988920051EHR% 20Standards-v5% 20Apr 202013.
31. Wikipedia contributors. (2021, May 11). Health data. In Wikipedia, The Free Encyclopedia. Retrieved 03:51, September 6, 2021, from https://en.wikipedia.org/w/index.php?title=Health_data&oldid=1022666417

3

Ontology-Based System for Patient Monitoring

R. Mervin[1]*, Tintu Thomas[2] and A. Jaya[3]

[1]*Department of Information Technology, Saudi Electronic University, Riyadh, Saudi Arabia*
[2]*Department of Public Health, Saudi Electronic University, Riyadh, Saudi Arabia*
[3]*Department of Computer Applications, B.S. Abdur Rahman Crescent Institute of Science and Technology, Chennai, Tamil Nadu, India*

Abstract

In the current scenario, web sources are flooded with information and the user can search for needed information from it. The output of the search keyword may be relevant or irrelevant despite the search keyword. Since the vast majority of the web sources are finding their results syntactically than semantically. So, the machine must understand the meaning of the search keyword to give relevant search results. The responsibility of researchers is to find the solution for Patient Monitoring System, which must give an accurate result for the search keyword. There is a need to construct the Patient Monitoring System with the support of ontology. Every detail of the patient and their health information must be stored in the Ontology.

This research work focuses on the importance of ontology based system for the patient monitoring system. The domain ontology has been constructed to preserve the details of the patient health issues. This system consists of four phases includes Domain ontology construction, Pre-processing, Rule construction and Reasoning of Query. After the validity of the query, the most relevant result must be produced automatically. The correctness of the query must be validated with the support of reasoner.

**Corresponding author*: m.mary@seu.edu.sa

Vishal Jain, Jyotir Moy Chatterjee, Ankita Bansal and Abha Jain (eds.) Semantic Web for Effective Healthcare, (75–94) © 2022 Scrivener Publishing LLC

Keywords**:** Semantic web, ontology, web ontology language, description logic, semantic reasoning, semantic web rule language, patient monitoring system and patient's ontology

3.1 Introduction

Over a few decades, numerous research activities have been focused to identify with human services to screen the health issue of the patients in the clinic. Nonetheless, it is hard to characterize fixed norms that gather every patient need in those unstable conditions. Also, the medical practitioner who is involved in the healthcare system used to take decisions on the patient's health issue [4].

Ontology is the popular technique which helps represent the knowledge in semantic way. The knowledge representation is composed of the relationship between subject, object, and predicate along with its properties. The knowledge has been shared and the relationship is constructed with defined rules. The objective of ontology is to categorize the structure of the information based on their concepts and the relationship with the attributes of the objects. The semantic search identifies the key concepts and matches its attributes in an exact way. Ontology mapping plays an essential role of research area in the area of semantic web [8].

The medical practitioners, users, staff files are preserved in the ontology repository which is created with the support of OWL (Web Ontology Language) format. The Meta information about the database is preserved for the reference of the people in the record. This ontology helps to map the patient's data related to their records in an efficient manner. The benefit of storing metadata is to avoid the missing and irrelevant data which identified in the ontology construction [7].

Information Retrieval (IR) model using ontology is developed based on the for the specific research area to create the knowledge repository in the particular domain, and also, we can create ontology for any domain based on the research [27]. If the domain is specified for ontology creation, then it is called as closed domain ontology and if the ontology is not related to the particular domain, then it is called as open domain ontology. The ontologies are constructed semantically and unstructured data can be converted as structured data. It helps to find the search keyword semantically, not syntactically [21].

At the same time, the semantic web is also focused on reasoning which validates the correctness of the ontology. Resource Description Framework (RDF) is a framework for developing knowledge base in the form of triples. It is the pictorial way of representing information in knowledge base called graph. SPARQL (Simple Protocol And RDF Query Language) is a specific Query Language for used to retrieve the data in the RDF from [17].

The remaining part of the paper is prepared as follows, Section 3.1 gives the basics of ontology. Section 3.2 deals with Literature Survey, Section 3.3 describes Architectural Design, Section 3.4 discusses the Experimental Results. Finally, Section 3.5 deals with the conclusion and the eye opener of this research future directions.

3.1.1 Basics of Ontology

Ontology learning is a semantic way of knowledge representation which converts the unstructured data sources into structured data. It provides the semantic meaning of classes and gives the relationship between the attributes of the objects, which acts as the knowledge base for the domain. Ontology is the field of identifying the relationship of the data base in the entire domain.

A few scientists are moving in the direction of creating ontology based models for health recommendation system. Ontology helps to find the relationships between various classes and its individuals of selected domain. There are several uses of ontology-based systems related to information retrieval, Artificial Intelligence, machine learning applications and others [3].

The purpose of an ontology is a formal way of knowledge representation of classes called concepts, data and object properties of each class relating various features and attributes of the class. In the era Artificial-Intelligence, Ontology becomes the unavoidable knowledge repository in which group of classes and its attributes along with its relationship creates a knowledge repository. Many researchers started developing standardized ontologies in the field of medicine and used to share and annotated information. The types of ontologies are as follows

Top-level ontologies or upper-level ontologies: These kinds of ontologies describe general concepts common to most domains. These ontologies can be reused based on the different purpose of the research. Examples of ontologies are object, purpose, reason, time, space, etc.

Domain ontologies: These ontologies are developed for a specific closed domain. For example, BASEBALL is an example for domain ontology.

Task ontologies: It describes tasks or activities which involves some input, process and output. An ontology related to any specific task and also helps to make decision after completing the task.

Application ontologies: These ontologies are developed for any application which may include the ontologies of domain, task ad top level ontology. Examples are banking application or healthcare application.

3.1.2 Need of Ontology in Patient Monitoring

Recent days, the necessity of ontology is unavoidable in any domain. The need for ontology is also important in the field of medicine. The reason for developing patient monitoring system ontology is listed below [1]:

- To represent and sharing knowledge between patient and the medical practitioners.
- To retrieve information based on semantically not like syntactic search.
- To apply the reasoning mechanism to validate the correctness of the ontology.
- To define the "N" number of rules.
- To share the knowledge base and its structure of information with different people.
- To support the reusability of information.
- To create the explicit knowledge base.
- To differentiate domain knowledge base from the operational knowledge base.
- To investigate domain knowledge base.

3.2 Literature Review

The literature review provides a detailed survey of the investigations about various studies, models, methodologies and evaluation methods of patient's monitoring system. The different aspect of the patient's monitoring system was discussed by referring to the various authors. The summarization lists the definitions and discussions on the basic information related to the patient monitoring system, which is important for designing any successful system.

3.2.1 Uses of Ontology in Various Domains

Sabbah *et al.* proposed a method of the term-weighting techniques for calculating terrorism activities detection by means of textual information. This method collects the features set form different web pages and then applies the term weighting on the collected features. The dimensionality reduction of the features can be computed by UNION and Symmetric Difference combination functions [5].

Kumari *et al.* follows the traditional Term Frequency Inverse Document Frequency (TF-IDF) method and uses a dictionary of data for the specific domain. The dictionary defines the synonyms of each words and the semantic similarity between words can be calculated by TF-IDF. It is an information retrieval technique in which the weights of the relevant words of documents can be calculated [6]. Escalante *et al.* developed a framework for the study of combining the set of basic words to discriminative term weighting system [9].

Narula *et al.* developed a Multimedia Information Retrieval (MIR) Model handling different data types including text, images and video documents [10]. It uses different IR techniques Extended Boolean Approach, Bayesian Network Model, etc., which provide relevance thus satisfying user's query.

Amir Zidi and Mourad Abed described a generalized framework public transportation system using ontology which supports to retrieve information related to a public transportation system. Here the semantic information about the public transportation system extracted from different data source and mapping will be done through the ontology. The scalability is an improved version for entity based semantic indexing retrieval method. Finally, it evaluated with real world data sources and provides meaningful search results [13].

Suganyakala and Rajalaxmi developed a framework for movie related semantic search system using ontology. This framework aims to solve the limitations of traditional information retrieval and improve retrieval effectiveness. A query interface requires the user input in their natural language and movie domain-specific ontology is developed to give the output. The semantic ontology prototype proposed model improves search accuracy [15].

K. Soner *et al.* developed an ontology-based retrieval system using semantic indexing. It deals with the issues in semantic search, namely, usability, scalability, and retrieval performance and proposed to a keyword-based semantic retrieval approach [16, 24].

Turhan deals with on the importance of Description Logic reasoning for Semantic web ontologies. There are families of knowledge representation formalisms that have formal semantics. This family of logics is represented the terminological knowledge of an application domain in a structured manner [20, 29].

3.2.2 Ontology in Patient Monitoring System

The decision making process is very difficult in the field of medicine. The researcher must analyze a lot of input from the heterogeneous knowledge sources. It is also a collaborative process where the experts used to share their information about the clinical data to make the correct decision. The communication level must be semantic rather than the syntactic and also the context of the information does not affect the meaning [2].

Lee *et al.* proposed a recommendation system for patient's diet menu using ontology. Diet is considered as an important factor for all people, particularly for diabetic patients. This system gives valuable suggestions for the patient's diet menu by considering their clinical information and also it recommending a meal plan for diabetic patients [23].

Beale and Heard developed a framework for a clinical information ontology-based model. All kind of clinical information is stored based on the ontology including the number of categories of requirements, ranging from the semantic to the performance of the software at runtime. The classification clinical information is processed by Clinical Investigator Record (CIR) ontology which helps in the problem solving process [26].

Jayaweera developed a Clinics Management System (CMS) based on Patient Centered Process Ontology. It constantly created new specialties, different roles, public and private organizations in patients' health recommendation system supported in critical issues. It also provides solutions related to IT for various areas of health recommendation systems [28]. Jayaweera and Johannesson created a patient's ontology repository for information retrieval in the field of healthcare system. This system provides better recommendation on the patient's health issue. It also focused on the patient's health history and visualizations can be made based on history [30].

Kumar *et al.* implemented a clinical guidelines ontology knowledge repository in the field of healthcare system [31]. This research work gave the brief glimpses of ontology related to healthcare guidelines. This framework helps to take decision on patient's health issue by analyzing their health condition and symptoms on a particular disease.

3.3 Architectural Design

This research work focuses on the importance of ontology based system for the patient monitoring system. The domain ontology has been constructed to preserve the details of the patient health issues. This system consists of four phases includes Domain ontology construction, Pre-processing, Rule construction, and Reasoning of Query. After the validity of the query, the most relevant result must be produced automatically. The correctness of the query must be validated with the support of reasoner. Figure 3.1 shows the conceptual diagram for Patient's Monitoring System and explains the different phases of the system.

In the pre-processing, the system utilizes a Parts of Speech (POS) tagger, which helps to identify the search terms from the user input query. The stemming process must be applied to find the root word and the search has been established within the ontology. If the word is already stored in the ontology, the system will give the result for the query. Otherwise, the ontology has to be updated automatically with the new keyword. Then the parse tree has to be constructed to understand the query in a better way. From the pre-processed keyword, the similarity measure must be done with the words in the ontology. TF-IDF (Term Frequency—Inverse Document Frequency) method is used for weight calculation and distance measure between words.

The ontology system also supports rule which helps to infer new knowledge. In OWL (Web Ontology Language), rules are expressed with the help of SWRL (Semantic Web Rule Language) is the rule language of the semantic web. With the support of Description Logic, there is a necessitate writing SWRL rules for the given concept and the relationship with the classes. Reasoner is used to derive the information from the knowledge base with the help of the inference engine. Reasoners detect inconsistent ontologies. The entire searched keyword is checked for the correctness with the three reasoners, namely, Fact++, HermiT, and Pellet. Pellet is the best reasoner by comparing the other two reasoners because of its debugging feature. The inference engine supports to generate new rule on the search keyword. The correctness of the inference is validated by the reasoned. Finally, the information has been retrieved by SPARQL. SPARQL is the query language

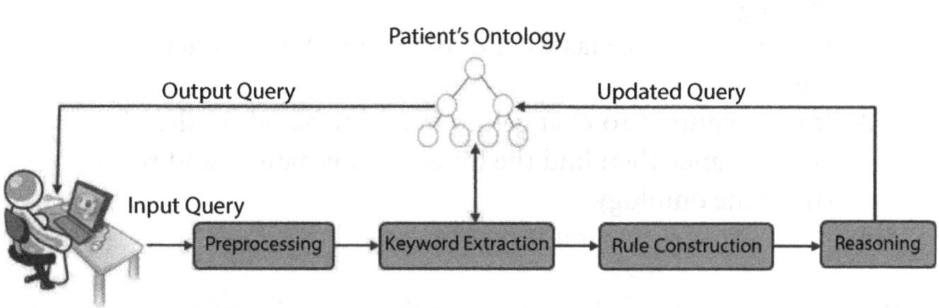

Figure 3.1 Conceptual diagram for patient's monitoring system.

used to retrieve the data in the RDF (Resource Description Framework) format.

Ontology based patient monitoring system must be helpful in the field of medical sciences. All the details of the patient history can be retrieved without any complication and also it provides opinion for the deceases. It solves the entire problem in the traditional database and gives more accurate semantic result for the query. The correctness of query is also checked with reasoner which gives a more accurate result for the query.

3.3.1 Phases of Patient Monitoring System

The ontology includes the domain classes and their relations to retrieve a new relationship among the classes. Ontology is used to extract the information from the domain knowledge, representing a relationship between classes, knowledge repository, discovering knowledge, reusing knowledge, integrating different classes based on the requirement [14].

The domain knowledge of classes is called concepts. The properties represent the different features of classes and attributes of the class is called as properties and restrictions or role restrictions are also acceptable. The Classes also classified into different kind of subclasses and super classes. For example, the gender class can be divided into male, female, and transgender subclasses.

In general, creating an ontology is an iterative process which includes defining classes, arranging the classes in a taxonomic such as subclass–superclass hierarchy, defining properties and the values for these properties, finding the values for instances. The expert's knowledge is involved for describing the attributes of the domain object, finding their relationship between the objects and classes. The iteration may go as follows

1. Select the domain and Start construction the first pass of the ontology.
2. Find the objects, classes and its relationship to redefine the ontology.
3. If it is required to change the ontology based on the given circumstance then find the different alternations and reconstruct the ontology.
4. Refine the process if it is required.

There are always viable alternatives for the selected domain. The existing ontology must be identified before creating the new ontology. The reusability property is always supported by the ontology for any kind of domain. Few basic rules in patient ontology construction are described as follows:

Step 1: Find and analyze the domain and objective of the ontology
The initial step is to find the domain and objective of the ontology. In this research, patient information is chosen as the core ontology. In the field of medicine, patient's details and their disease information is managed in the ontology. This ontology can be reused in the applications of medical filed. Naturally, the concepts describing different types of people information like their name, age, gender, address, type of disease, etc.

Step 2: Find the reusable ontology
Reusability of ontology is one of the best property in any domain. It is always required to analyze the existing ontology which is created by someone in the same domain and try to reuse the ontology in the appropriate field. For example, Ontolingua ontology library or the DAML ontology library, and some popular domain ontologies like UNSPSC, RosettaNet, DMOZ, etc.

Step 3: Identify the required classes in the ontology
It is necessary to find out all classes and its objects which are required to construct the domain ontology. The next two steps are closely knotted to each other, namely, developing the class hierarchy and defining the object and data properties of classes.

Step 4: Define the classes and the class hierarchy
The definition of class hierarchy depends on the top–down approach, bottom–up approach, and hybrid approach. In the top–down approach, the core class is identified first, and then the iteration starts by finding the subsequent classes. A bottom–up approach is defined as the characterization of the precise concepts with levels of hierarch, finally, it will reach the merging of child classes into more specific parent class. In hybrid approach is a grouping of the top–down and bottom–up approaches. It is also necessary to check the following criteria.

- Validating the defined class hierarchy is accurate
- Checking the position of the child in a class hierarchy
- Checking the Multiple inheritance

Step 5: Define the properties of classes
For selected classes, the list of properties must be defined based on the requirement of the application. The object properties can be classified as:

"intrinsic" properties such as the gender; "extrinsic" properties such as a patient's name, age, gender, etc., and "Is-a" is the relationships between individual of the class object and with other objects.

Step 6: Create instances
The next step is to build the individuals of a class object which requires 1. Select a class, 2. Create an individual instance of that class, and 3. Creating the restrictions for the class and individual. Figure 3.2 shows the ontology for the patient's monitoring system in which Patient is the root or parent class, Name, Gender, Phone_Number and AgeGroup is the child or sub-class. Again the Gender class is classified into three subclasses like Male, Female and Transgender subclass.

After constructing the ontology, the pre-processing query is started with Part-of-Speech (POS) tagging. POS Tagging is a method of classification of query that may be defined as the automatic assignment of grammatical description to query. The descriptor is called as a tag of POS which gives the semantic information of the phrase. The tag will be assigned to each word of the phrase which is called labeling. The process of tagging is to assign POS tags to words related to its syntactic category. The POS tagger will segment the word and assign the proper labeling based on the given context. Usually, words can be categorized

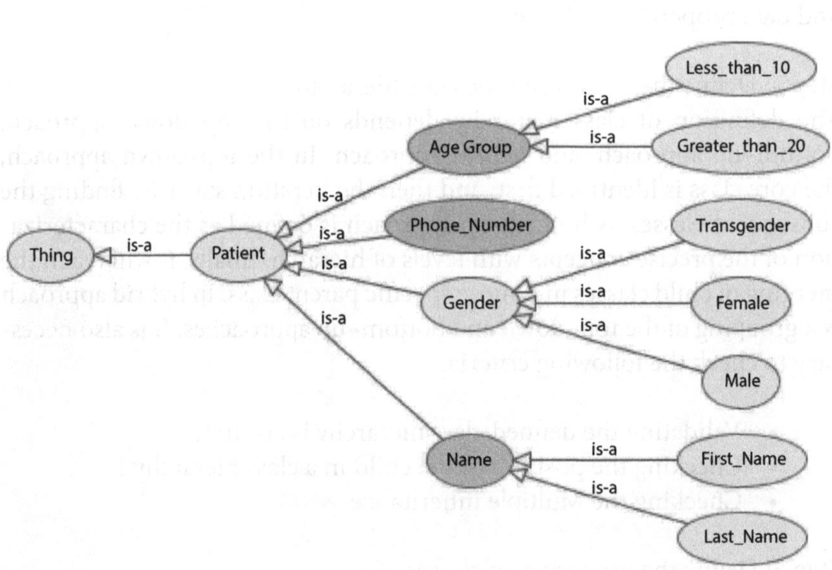

Figure 3.2 Ontology for patient's monitoring system.

into nouns, verb, adverbs, adjectives, pronouns, conjunction and their sub-categories.

- ***N(oun):*** The living or nonliving object or entity is called as noun. Examples are name, age etc. **N** is the symbol used in POS tagging to represent noun.
- ***V(erb):*** The actions of the word are called as verb. Examples of verbs are visiting, breathing, see and so on. **V** is the symbol used in POS tagging to represent verb.
- ***Adj(ective)***: Adjectives are used to describe the nouns or noun phrases. **ADJ** is the symbol used in POS tagging to represent adjective.
- ***Adv(erb):*** Adverbs are the modifiers of either nouns, adjectives, verbs, or other adverbs. **ADV** is the symbol used in POS tagging to represent adverb.

Noun POS tag can be further classified into singular nouns (NN), singular proper nouns (NNP), and plural nouns (NNS). The Patient's monitoring system utilizes, POS tagger which identifies the query and extracts the root word from the user's input query. For example, the query "Find the patient's name affected by Corona?" will be classified as follows:

[S [NP Find][DT the][VP [V patient's name affected][IN by] [NP Corona]]]

After completing the POS tagger process, built a parse tree to find the query keywords and to understand the concept quickly. This is implemented by the help of Stanford Parser. Parsing is the process of splitting the sentence into words to find out the grammatical relationship between each word in a graphical structure representation. It is a splitting process of sentence into atomic words, which helps to investigate data, the structure of the sentence and also it is meaning. The parse tree identifies the basic connection between a sentence and the grammar by giving the detail analyze of describing how the grammar was used to produce the sentence. The parsing technique includes Top–Down and Bottom–Up is used. These techniques describe the direction of the parsing process [32]. Figure 3.3 shows the example parse tree for a query.

To find out the answer for a particular query, we need to depend on search engines by computing the terms in the query [18]. After completing the pre-processing, the root word has to be extracted to retrieve the

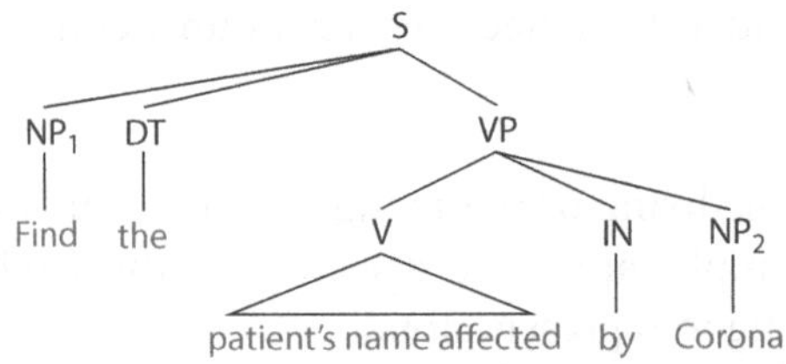

Figure 3.3 Parse tree for patient's monitoring system.

result for the query. The keyword extraction is executed by calculating the TF*IDF weight of the term. It is calculated according to the formula:

$$TF(t) = \frac{\text{(Number of times term 't' appears in a document)}}{\text{(Total number of terms in the document)}} \quad (3.1)$$

$$IDF\ (t) = log_e \frac{\text{(Total number of documents)}}{\text{Number of documents with term 't' in it}} \quad (3.2)$$

$$TF{*}IDF\ (term) = TF\ (t)\ {*}\ IDF\ (t) \quad (3.3)$$

where *TF(term)* indicates the frequency of a term in the given document, IDF indicates Inverse Document Frequency.

After the query analysis with the support of POS tagger, the extracted keyword will be used to find their results. Before extracting the results, with the support of Description Logic there is a necessitate writing SWRL rules for the given concept and the relationship with the classes. In OWL (Web Ontology Language), rules are expressed with the help of SWRL (Semantic Web Rule Language) is the rule language of the semantic web. In SWRL Rule processing, the user query has been taken as the input and process into the rule engine with the help of previous knowledge.

In SWRL the facts and rules were stored in the Rule database where facts are considered as a class or subclass and rules are used as URI reference. Depending on the user query, the rule engine checks for the rules for the given query and produces the results with the support of the inference engine which acts as the intermediate to produce the result. Figure 3.4 shows the results of SWRL rule for the Patient's Monitoring System.

Rule 1: hasName(?x, ?y) -> hasFName(?x, ?y) , hasLName(?x, ?y)
Rule 2: Patient (?x), hasName(?x, ?y), hasAge(?y) -> hasGender(?x, ?y)

Figure 3.4 SWRL for patient's monitoring system.

Rule 3: Patient (?x), hasName(?x, ?y), hasSymtoms(?y) -> hasDisease(?x, ?y)
Rule 4: hasDisease (?x, ?z) -> hasName(?x, ?y)
Rule 5: hasDisease (?x, ?z) -> select(?x), count(?z), orderByDescending(?z)

3.3.2 Reasoner in Patient Monitoring

Reasoner is used to get the data from the knowledge repository with the support of the inference engine. At the time of ontology constructions, Reasoners helps to detect inconsistent ontologies. By correcting the inconsistent ontology, the quality of ontologies is preserved [19]. The entire query is validated for the correctness with the three reasoners namely Fact++, HermiT and Pellet. Pellet is the best reasoner by comparing the other two reasoners because of its debugging feature. It is open-source software implemented in Java and it follows tableau algorithm. To handle the inconsistent ontology, Pellet follows the following guidelines.

- service clash detection is method of detecting the root inconsistency
- axiom tracing is used to find irrelevant ontology by creating more number of axioms on objects.

Reasoners are integrated with 450 significantly diverse ontologies that achieve high accuracy result for the prediction model. Such prediction models have a wide range of applications. It gives better accuracy even for the large and complex ontology [11]. FaCT++ is open-source software, which follows tableaux-based algorithm and it supports C++ language. It follows description logic on the classes. The concepts and its related instance can be represented using OWL [22, 25].

HermiT is another reasoner used to identify the inconsistent ontology and also clearly identify the relationships between classes, and its objects.

It follows novel hypertableau algorithm, which is having well-organized reasoning capacity. The pallet is having the best features comparing to other reasoners.

- Consistency checking is used to find out the contradictory ontology.
- Concept satisfiability deals with many instances for a particular class.
- Classification creates the class hierarchy for every class and its subclasss
- Realization helps to identity the individuals each class.

Jena is an open source software which includes different reasoning modules such as Assertional Box (Abox), Terminological Box (Tbox), and Knowledge Base (KB). A box describes the assertions about individuals, example type and property value. Realizing the ABox, defines the most precise concepts of each individual and the relationship with its instances. The list of axioms on the classes and subclasses can be defined in the Tbox. Any Knowledge Base can be created with the combination of an ABox and a TBox to form a complete OWL ontology.

Jena ontology API is an ontology language and Java ontology class represents OWL class, RDFS class, or DAML class. Every ontology model is bounded with a Profile [12]. The inference made by reasoners follows the inductive reasoning and gone through the more number of facts and rules. It helps the medical practitioners to take an effective decision on the patient's health issue. So that the system will act as a better recommendation system. Therefore, the patients too believe that the given information is much reliable and the accuracy is also much relevant than the system which is not undergone with the reasoners.

3.4 Experimental Results

Before executing the query, all the pre-processing, keyword extraction, rule construction and validation must be done by the reasoner. Finally, the query has been executed with SPARQL. Then the comparison has been made with the traditional database. As a result, it is proved that the result of ontology is more accurate and semantic. Whatever the problem is identified in the traditional database has been recovered.

3.4.1 SPARQL Results

Any semantic application requires semantic query language to retrieve the data. SPARQL is the query language which retrieves RDF based semantic data. This research work depends on semantic information and the database is also created with semantic meaning. The data stored in the ontology follows the semantic structure. Figure 3.5 shows the sample query.

```
PREFIX rdf: <http://www.w3.org/1999/02/22-rdf-syntax-ns#>
PREFIX owl: <http://www.w3.org/2002/07/owl#>
PREFIX rdfs: <http://www.w3.org/2000/01/rdf-schema#>
PREFIX xsd: <http://www.w3.org/2001/XMLSchema#>
PREFIX info: <http://www.patinfo.com/info#>
SELECT ?Patient ?DName
    WHERE { ?Patient info:DName ?DName }
```

3.4.2 Comparison Between Other Systems

The traditional database is having a lot of issues with missing values, redundancy and most of the system provides syntactic results than the semantic results. The better way is to solve the entire problem with the support of ontology. Figure 3.6 shows the comparison between SQL and SPARQL and the importance of semantic database has been discussed.

- Data redundancy has been reduced.
- Errors have been reduced and increased consistency.

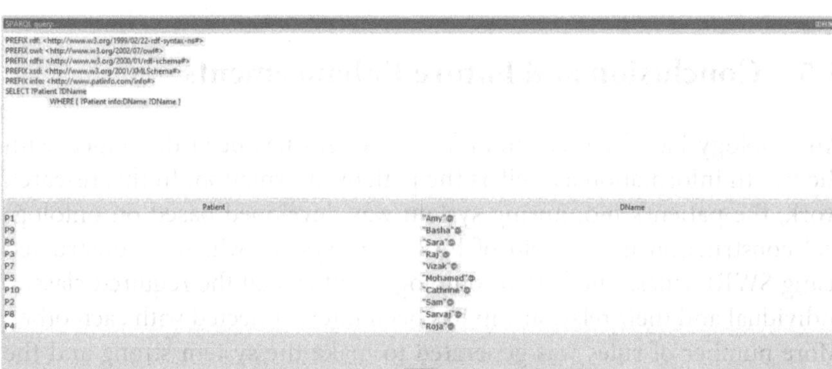

Figure 3.5 SPQRAL query for patient's monitoring system.

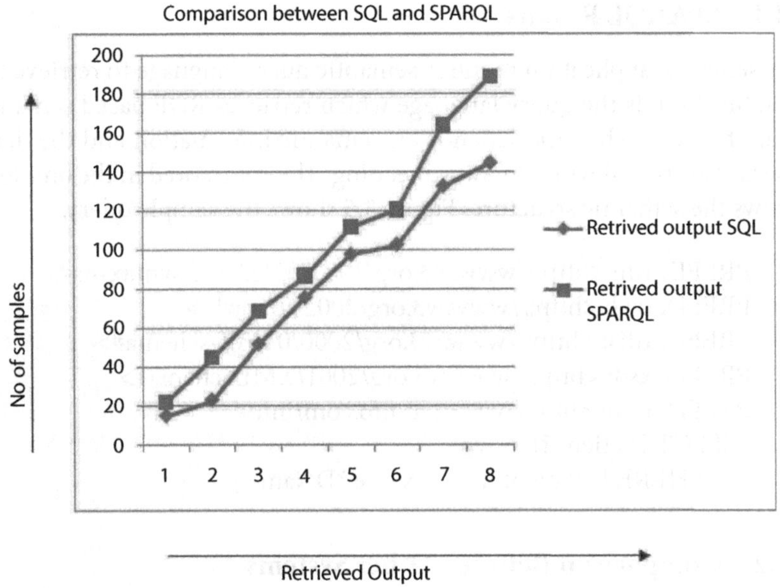

Figure 3.6 Comparison between SQL and SAPRQL.

- It supports data integrity.
- Data has been accessed easily through different query languages.
- Data security has been improved.
- Data entry, storage, and retrieval costs have been reduced.
- It also supports to develop many new applications program.

3.5 Conclusion and Future Enhancements

An ontology based patient monitoring system has been developed with the health information as well as the patient information. In this research work, the patient's monitoring system was developed based on ontological construction in the field of healthcare system which is constructed using SWRL rules. The patient ontology contains all the required classes, individual and their relationship has been interconnected with each other. More number of rules was generated to make the system strong and the correctness of the system is evaluated by the reasoners. Patient's monitoring system can be able to compare their innovation results and obtain a better understanding of their innovation context based on artificial intelligence reasoning techniques. This framework can be extended in the field of medicine, also for analyzing a different kind of disease. This initiative is open for additional international collaborations, thus providing an opportunity to establish an international network of companies and hospitals from various countries.

References

1. Moreno-Conde, A., Parra-Calderón, C.L., Sánchez-Seda, S., Escobar-Rodríguez, G.A., López-Otero, M., Cussó, L., del-Cerro-García, R., Segura-Sánchez, M., Herrero-Urigüen, L., Martí-Ras, N., Albertí-Ibarz, M., Desco, M., ITEMAS ontology for healthcare technology innovation, *Moreno-Conde et al. Health Res. Policy Syst.*, 17, 47, 1–10, 2019.
2. Karami, M. and Rahimi, A., Semantic Web Technologies for Sharing Clinical Information in Healthcare Systems. *Acta Inform Med.*, 27, 1, 4–7, 2019.
3. Chen, L., Lu, D., Zhu, M., Muzammal, M., Samuel, O.W., Huang, G., Li, W., Wu, H., OMDP: An ontology-based model for diagnosis and treatment of diabetes patients in remote healthcare systems. *Int. J. Distrib. Sens. Netw.*, 15, 5, 1–15, 2019.
4. Ajami, H. and Mcheick, H., Ontology-Based Model to Support Ubiquitous Healthcare Systems for COPD Patients. *Int. J. Electron.*, 7, 12, 1–29, 2018.
5. Sabbah, T., Selamat, A., Selamat, M.H., Ibrahim, R., Fujita, H., Hybridized term weighting method for Dark Web classification. *Neurocomputing*, 173, 1908–1926, 2016.
6. Kumari, M., Jain, A., Bhatia, A., Synonyms Based Term Weighting Scheme: An Extension to TF.IDF. *Procedia Comput. Sci.*, 89, 555–561, 2016.
7. Abinaya, Kumar, V., Swathika, Ontology based public healthcare system in Internet of Things. *Second International Symposium on Big Data and Cloud Computing*, pp. 99–102, 2015.
8. Rupali, R., Khune, Mapping of Semantic Web Ontology in User Query System. *Int. J. Comput. Appl.*, 111, 14, 0975–8887, 2015.
9. Escalante, H.J. *et al.*, Term-weighting learning via genetic programming for text classification. *Knowledge-Based Syst.*, 83, 1, 176–189, 2015.
10. Narula, G.S. and Jain, V., Improving Statistical Multimedia Information Retrieval (MIR) Model by using Ontology. *Int. J. Comput. Appl.*, 2, 35–45, May 2014.
11. Kang, Y.-B. *et al.*, How Long Will It Take? Accurate Prediction of Ontology Reasoning Performance. *Proceedings of the Twenty-Eighth AAAI Conference on Artificial Intelligence*, pp. 80–86, 2014.
12. Ameen, A., Ur Rahman Khan, K., Rani, B.P., Reasoning in Semantic Web Using Jena. *Comput. Eng. Intell. Syst.*, 5, 4, 39–47, 2014.
13. Zidi, A. and Abed, M., A Generalized Framework for Ontology-Based Information Retrieval Application to a public-transportation system. *IEEE Int. Conf. Adv. Logist. Transp.*, 1, 1–5, 2013.

14. Meraji, M., Sadoughi, F., Ahmadi, M., Kahani, M., Designing an Ontology-based Health Information System: A systematic Approach. *Life Sci. J.*, 10, 7, 735–739, 2013.
15. Suganyakala, R. and Rajalaxmi, R.R., Movie related information retrieval using ontology based semantic search. *IEEE International Conference on Information Communication and Embedded Systems (ICICES)*, pp. 1–6, 2013.
16. Soner K., K., Özgür, A., Orkunt, S., Samet, A., Nihan K., C., Ferda, N.A., An ontology-based retrieval system using semantic indexing. *Inf. Syst.*, 37, 4, 294–305, 2012.
17. Shazmeen, S.F. and Ramyasree, E., Semantic Web Mining: Benefits, Challenges and Opportunities. *Int. J. Adv. Comput. Res.*, 2, 4, 7, 2012.
18. Carpineto., C. and Romano, G., A Survey of Automatic Query Expansion in Information Retrieval. *ACM Comput. Surv.*, 44, 1, Article1, 50 pages, 2012.
19. Dentler, K., Cornet, R., ten Teije, A., de Keizer, N., Comparison of Reasoners for large Ontologies in the OWL 2 EL Profile. *Semantic Web 1 IOS Press*, 1, 1–5, 2011.
20. Turhan, A.-Y., Description Logic reasoning for Semantic web ontologies. *ACMWIMS'11*, 1, 1–5, 2011.
21. Fernández, M., Cantador, I., López, V., Vallet, D., Castells, P., Motta, E., Semantically enhanced Information Retrieval: An ontology based approach. *Web Semantic*, 9, 4, 434–452, 2011.
22. Hafizullah, A.H. and Aniza, A., The Spiral OWL Model? Towards Spiral Knowledge Engineering. *World Knowl. Eng. World Acad. Sci. Eng. Technol.*, 38, 45–52, 2010.
23. Lee, C.S., Chen, M.H., Hagras, H., A type2 fuzzy ontology and its application to personal diabetic-diet recommendation. *IEEE T Fuzzy System*, 18, 2, 374–395, 2010.
24. Saravanan, Ravindran, Raman, Improving legal information retrieval using an ontological framework. *Arti. Intell. Law*, 17, 2, 101–124, 2009.
25. Chi, and Chen, *Ontology and semantic rules in document dispatching*, vol. 27, 4 pp. 694–707, The Electronic Library, 2009.
26. Beale, T. and Heard, S., An Ontology-based Model of Clinical Information. *In Proc. MedInfo*, 1, 760–764, 2007.
27. Li, Z., Raskin, V., Ramani, K., A Methodology of Engineering Ontology Development for Information Retrieval. *International Conference on Engineering Design, ICED'07*, Paris, France, pp. 1–12, 2007.
28. Jayaweera, P., Jayasinghe, J., Wellakkage, L., Malawaraarachchi, V., Liyanage, S., Perera, P., Clinics Management System (CMS) based on Patient Centred Process Ontology. *Ruhuna J. Sci.*, 1, 1, 40–39, 2006.
29. Jun-feng, S., Wei-ming, Z., Wei-dong, X., Zhen-ning, X., Ontology-based information retrieval model for the semantic Web. *The 2005 IEEE International Conference on e-Technology, e-Commerce and e-Service*, pp. 152–155, 2005.

30. Jayaweera, P. and Johannesson, P., A Patient Centred Process Ontology for Information Visualization in Healthcare. *In Proc. Caise Workshops*, 3, 311–314, 2004.
31. Kumar, A., Smith, B., Pisanelli, D.M., Gangemi, A., Stefanelli, M., An Ontological Framework for the Implementation of Clinical Guidelines in Healthcare Organizations. *Study Health Tech. Inform.*, 102, 95–107, 2004.
32. Grune, D. and Jacobs, C., *Parsing Techniques A Practical Guide*, pp. 64–66, Ellis Horwood Limited, Prentice Hall, UK, 1990.

4

Semantic Web Solutions for Improvised Search in Healthcare Systems

Nidhi Malik[1], Aditi Sharan[1] and Sadika Verma[2]

[1]*School of Computers and Systems Sciences, JNU, New Delhi, India*
[2]*Sadika Verma, SVIET Banur, Punjab, India*

Abstract
The health sector has also grown tremendously in previous decades and digitization has a played a great role in this growth. The demand from a healthcare system is that it will be correct, interactive, prompt and accurate. To achieve these goals, semantic web technologies are proving to be of great use. A healthcare and life sciences group has been established by World Wide Web Consortium, which aims at development and support of these technologies in healthcare and related fields. In this chapter, we wish to highlight semantic web solutions, which improves the process of searching as compared to traditional approaches.

Keywords: Semantic web, search engine, ontology, vocabulary

4.1 Introduction

All aspects of life have benefitted from the use of IT technologies including the healthcare sector [1]. Healthcare services are greatly improvised in terms efficiency, effectiveness and accessibility. This has become a standard practice in many healthcare organizations to use information systems that can manage and locate important information quickly. With the democratization of web and emergence of web 3.0, lot of health related information is available in public domain. The stakeholders of this information

**Corresponding author*: nidhimalik14@gmail.com

Vishal Jain, Jyotir Moy Chatterjee, Ankita Bansal and Abha Jain (eds.) Semantic Web for Effective Healthcare, (95–114) © 2022 Scrivener Publishing LLC

include doctors, patients, researchers, etc. In spite of the availability and accessibility of health related information on the web, there are lot of issues regarding its processing and understandability. A minor issue is related to its understanding and consumption by human beings, however a major limitation is related to its interpretability by the machine itself.

This chapter highlights role of semantic web technologies in improving services provided by healthcare systems. Second section elaborates the searching techniques used by researchers in the field to find out desired information. In the third section, the role of semantics, how are they beneficial in the searching process and domain specific resources are presented in detail. Latest technology advancements and resources from the biomedical field are discussed in fourth section. Some popular and recent techniques and resources are also discussed. Section five concludes the chapter.

4.1.1 Key Benefits and Usage of Technology in Healthcare System

Due to ever growing data on the web and in context of globalization, health information technology is also much in demand [36]. Stakeholders of this information access it to share, to comparing with other alternative sources of information, transfer to others using network [2]. All developments in the health services are done with this thing in mind. So, use of technology has become must to facilitate such extensive use of information. Some of the key benefits that are crucial to health sector are:

- Almost all healthcare services have benefited from Information technology especially development of electronic medical records (EMR). Information is maintained in the form of single database. It will minimize paper work and will keep track of the medical history of patients also.
- Data management systems for keeping patient's data automatically retrieve data corresponding to a patient from the patients' requirements in terms of medical equipment, medication, etc. [3]. After doing basic summarization and restructuring, this data facilitates healthcare providers in interpreting the data.
- Decision support systems to be used in clinical setup also require tools for decision making and working of the system [3]. Clinical systems need to timely track the patient's requirements, setup notifications, alarms, reminders for the

caretakers and patients. Clinical summaries, documentation, test, reports, medications, etc., are to be managed and tools are required for all these tasks.

- Information technology act as communication medium between different stakeholders of the system [3]. To monitor the patients' health, guide the patient for further medication, discussion about the after effects, counselling, and behavior of the patient, communication is required.
- For patient monitoring, clinical data is processed. Patients need continuous monitoring in terms of medications to be given, tests to be performed, etc., Monitoring may be required in emergency rooms, operation theatre or for surveillance purposes.

4.2 Background

Internet and Web 2.0 have been instrumental in evolving most of the Information Technology (IT) applications that we are now accustomed to. Barely 20 years ago, we had not imagined the technological advancements, which are now implemented into our lives. Technological advancement, riding on the wave of disruptive technologies of the last quarter of a century, is reshaping and redefining the world's social order and norms. The medical field is part and parcel of our lives and is perhaps one that we care the most about. In the recent times, this field has undergone vast changes [5]. The medical profession today has evolved greatly since the beginning of this century. Not only the medical procedures, the medical data flow and management has also undergone considerable improvement [4]. Advance data transfer and management techniques have made improvements in disease diagnostic and have been a critical role in national health planning and efficient record keeping [5].

4.2.1 Significance of Semantics in Healthcare Systems

The web has become an inseparable object of our daily lives and the amount of online information is growing. In addition to simple texts which occupy most of the multimedia information like graphics, audio or video have become a prevalent part. The question is how to find useful information in this vast of information? It means to find what you need without much research while there is infinite information about what you are looking for. Traditional search engines will come to the limits of their powers when it comes to understanding the content of the information [6]. The use of such knowledge is at the heart of the semantic web, which promotes the use of formal statements and reasoning to deliver advanced services not available on the Web now [2]. The semantic web is an extension of the traditional web, in the sense that the information contained in the natural text is supplemented by clear semantics based on the formal representation of knowledge. It has also been conceived as an extension of the WWW that allows computers to search, combine, and intelligently process web content, based on the understanding that this content has on people [6]. To facilitate machine-readability and knowledge processing, a set of standards, query languages, and the semantic stack was proposed by the World Wide Web Consortium (W3C).

The complexity and diversity of knowledge and terminology of medical/health science needs to be tackled in order to fully utilize it. Extracting knowledge from previous practices and past medical history is also very difficult due to this diversity [6]. Moreover, information sharing is very important in this field and this is the reason for semantic web to have come into picture.

4.2.2 Scope and Benefits of Semantics in Healthcare Systems

Semantic web technologies have become a key driver for innovation and change in many domains, including eCommerce, education, eGovernment, entertainment, healthcare, social networks, and software engineering, among others. Semantic Web technologies and semantics provide us with a new approach to information management and processes, the basic principle of which is the creation and use of semantic metadata. Metadata is a data set that provides information about other data [6]. The use of semantic metadata is also crucial for integrating information from heterogeneous sources, whether within an organization or across organizations. Various schemes are used to describe and classify information, and different terminologies are used together with information. By creating different schemes, it is possible to create a unified view and achieve interaction between processes that use the information. Semantic descriptions can also be applied to processes presented as web services. When the function of an Internet service can be described semantically, then the web service can be more easily detected. When existing web services are provided with metadata describing their function and context, then new services can be automatically compiled from a combination of existing services.

4.2.3 Issues in Incorporating Semantics

Semantic Web enabled solutions can provide end-to-end solutions for information sharing among all the stakeholders and in a meaningful way [6].

Information is stored in heterogeneous distributed Health Information Systems, in different file formats which are mainly proprietary [3]. So, the systems sharing information need to be interoperability compatible so that the semantics of the shared information are preserved, and no information is lost due to semantic and syntactic differences [7]. Some of the issues that need to be considered are [8]:

- Common Standards/Guidelines: For information sharing and reuse, it is required to analyze and decide upon the rules to resolve policy-conflicts so as to ensure that the modified rule is syntactically and/or semantically valid.
- Ensuring mapping of data: Taking attributes and values from different systems and combining them often results in semantic differences, which further leads to partial mapping of data. This happens due to incompatible or non-formalized structuring of data.
- User involvement: Developing systems for users involve them to as to correctly identify all common terms and their meanings. If this is not done, it leads to undue disclosure of data.
- Domain vocabulary: creation of a vocabulary with correct identification of terms with multiple meanings that can be used to determine the semantic relationships between one attribute value and another.
- Ontology Mapping: to reach out to an optimal solution which fits in globally across the domain for mapping concepts from different ontologies. Semantics associated with them also need to be considered.

4.2.4 Existing Semantic Web Technologies

In simple words, Semantic web adds meaning to information which further enables computers and people to work in cooperation. Semantic technologies are emerging and several applications ranging from business process management to information security have demonstrated encouraging prospects of its benefits.

The Semantic Web Stack shown in [9] illustrates the architecture of the Semantic Web. The functions and relationships of the components can be summarized as follows [9].

- XML is a markup language that defines the elemental structure within documents.

- XML Schema describe the structure of XML document.
- RDF refers to objects and their relationships and provides language support to various data models.
- RDF Schema is a basic vocabulary for describing hierarchies of properties and classes.
- OWL extends vocabulary support for properties and classes.
- SPARQL is a protocol and query language for semantic web data sources.
- RIF is an XML language for enabling rule exchange that different systems can execute. It stands for the Rule Interchange Format.

4.3 Searching Techniques in Healthcare Systems

Search engines retrieve documents for a user's keywords from a large index and rank them by various criteria. While such keyword-based search is fast and powerful to retrieve single documents, it is far from the vision of answering a user's questions by "understanding" the user's query. Web is also accessed to obtain medical and health information by the general public [11]. It has been found that the most common health and medical topics searched on the Internet are about a specific disease or medical problem, certain medical treatment, diet, nutrition and vitamins, and exercise or fitness, as well as prescription drugs [11]. In particular, researchers have classified and analyzed the information needs of users to improve search engines [11]. A medicine-related information search is different from other information searches, since users often use medical terminology, disease knowledge, treatment options, and so on.

4.3.1 Keyword-Based Search

Keyword-based search will give output in response to the term entered by the user but one also need to search using synonyms and variations of the search term to make sure that you have retrieved all of the relevant records [12].

For example, if the user is looking for information on "heart attack" using a text word search, it is also needed to search using the terms "heart attacks," "myocardial infarction," "myocardial infarctions" and so on. However, keywords are often ambiguous and could have multiple meanings. For example, given a keyword 'Alzheimer', the user intent can be searching the information for this disease or for some drugs to treat it [13].

To address this problem, *semantic search* was proposed to improve search accuracy by understanding user intent and search context.

4.3.2 Controlled Vocabularies Based Search

Controlled vocabularies are also used by researchers which are standardized, hierarchical lists designated to represent the major subject concepts and conditions contained within a database [12]. They can change from database to database. The hierarchical nature of the vocabularies benefits search strategies by allowing broad concepts to be narrowed in a manner that stays consistent within that framework.

4.3.3 Improvising Searches With Semantic Web Solutions

- Dealing with heterogeneous data is the main issue in dealing with querying information. To get desired data in terms of meaning is more challenging due to diversity of vocabularies [13]. The formal representation mechanism of Ontologies enables unification by matching classes, different types of properties and instances with one another.
- The intent of semantic web allows facilitates knowledge sharing and reuse across applications and organizations. Non availability of standards for information exchange, improper syntactic and semantic rules have been a problem for Sharing of information in the medical sciences field. Semantic web technologies can be applied to tackle all these problems.
- Semantic Search improves searching precision by understanding the purpose of the search and the contextual significance of words as they appear in the searchable data space [16], whether on the web to generate more relevant result [14].
- The data model, Resource Description Framework [5] is based on graph theory and it suits the representation mechanism for biomedical data by using subject–predicate–object triples.
- For fetching information from ontology, there is language support available in terms of ontology editors such as Portege [8], ontology reasoners such as Pellet, SPARQL endpoint, etc.

- Specifically, for biological and biomedical ontologies [35], flat file format OBO is used which is a graph based representation language.

4.3.4 Health Domain-Specific Resources for Semantic Search

Having discussed about the changes made by the evolution of web, semantic web, and other technology advancements, we wish to discuss about the role of semantic web in the health domain, which is largely driven by biomedical domain. The semantic web will help in connectivity of online data, efficient searching and browsing, effective communication and human

Table 4.1 List of popular biomedical ontologies.

Ontology	Purpose
Common anatomy reference ontology	Defines interoperability between various anatomy ontologies for different species
Disease ontology	Cross maps terms of disease ontology to SNOMED OMIM, MeSH, ICD, NCI's thesaurus
Foundational model of anatomy	Knowledge representation about human anatomy
GENE ontology	Information about molecular functions, biological processes and cellular components
Ontology for biomedical investigations	Description of life-science and clinical investigations in the form of integrated ontology
Ontology for general medical science	Covers research based on the papers Toward an Ontological Treatment of Disease and Diagnosis. Also include Carcinomas and Other Pathological Entities
Vaccine ontology	Represents vaccine knowledge and supports automated reasoning also
Human phenotype ontology	Covers phenotypic abnormalities encountered in human disease
Infectious disease ontology	Set of interoperable ontologies in the domain of infectious disease

interaction. The biomedical domain is very important for the health related information and provides a rich background for interpreting and analyzing this information.

The biomedical domain has made its digital presence along ago with biomedical resources being developed for communication and interchange of biomedical information. In order to dwell into the world of biomedical domain, the awareness about rich biomedical resources, their representation, classification, usage mechanism need to be understood. Initially, to seek information from any domain was restricted to accessing journals and that too by academic people only. But with advancements in technology, it has not remained so.

Here, we are elaborating the resources from the biomedical domain which are used widely by the researchers.

4.3.4.1 Ontologies

Around the year 1988, researchers in biological and biomedical fields started using ontologies [32]. By 2007, enough interest and research was done by researchers in the field with the initiatives by Open Biomedical Ontologies (OBO) Foundry [33] or the NCBO, National Center for Biomedical Ontologies [34]. As stated by [37], some of the most usable ontologies in this field are mentioned in the Table 4.1.

4.3.4.2 Libraries

In almost all domains, there are libraries available which host different ontologies, vocabulary and other meta data. Some of the commonly used libraries used by researchers in biomedical domain are listed in Table 4.2 below:

4.3.4.3 Search Engines

Researchers from biomedical domain have worked on including semantic web aspects while searching [10]. Some of the popular search engines along with their features are discussed below [39]:

4.3.4.3.1 PUBMED

It is a Keyword based search engine that uses the Entrez search engine for keyword matches of the search term against the text in the title, abstract, and citation information of each document no full-text document

Table 4.2 List of popular biomedical libraries.

Library	Contains	Features
BioPortal	Hosts 885 ontologies having 12,045,609 classes	Browse through library of ontologies, options for advanced search are also there
OBO Foundary	Hosts more than 185 active ontologies	Well formed and scientifically accurate interoperable ontologies
OLS—Ontology Lookup Service	Repository for biomedical ontologies; 257 ontologies 6,253,863 terms	Provides cross-ontology mappings between terms from different ontologies, assist in mapping data to ontologies and tool for building ontologies from spreadsheets
Ontobee	Facilitates data sharing, visualization of data, query analysis, and integration	Applied for more than 230 ontologies
ICD—International classification of Diseases	For classification of disease, it provides diagnostic codes	Provides injury or disease specific classification of symptoms, complaints, findings, and various causes
Logical observational identifiers, names and codes	Information in the form of database for medical laboratory observations and their standards	Medical observations characterized by laboratory code, types of outcomes, and inputs about patients

(*Continued*)

Table 4.2 List of popular biomedical libraries. (*Continued*)

Library	Contains	Features
MeSH—Medical Subject Headings	Domain information in the form of hierarchy for creating index and catalog	Database from National Library of Medicine and popular MEDLINE/PubMed
RxNorm	Standardized representation for clinical drugs	Software and vocabulary need not be same when mediating messages between different systems
SNOMED-CT [24]	Medical terms with codes, different forms of terms, and their definitions	EHR nomenclature for symptoms, clinical findings, devices, organisms, substances, etc.
UMLS—Unified Medical language System	Collection of files and tools for health and biomedical vocabularies	Interoperability standards
NCBI taxonomy	Nomenclature for organisms in public sequence database	Represents 10% species of life on the planet
NDF—National Drug File	Electronic drug list used by the VHA hospitals and clinics	Manage drug interactions and send prescriptions to pharmacies

searching [22]. The search engine also matches search terms against the MeSH headings to find documents.

- **Ranking Results:** Results are not sorted based on relevance but are by default sorted by date. Further filtering can be done on the basis of author, journal or title.

4.3.4.3.2 Quertle

It relies on natural language processing techniques to match search against actual assertions made by the author, rather than simple keyword matching or proximity. It uses ontology extensively so that all the meanings, forms, aliases of the search term are applied automatically [40]. The ontology also allows sub concepts to be found; for example, a search for "rodent" will find "mice," "rats," etc.

- **Ranking Results:** Relevance of the results is decided by the number of times the document supports the assertion.

4.3.4.3.3 FACTA+

It is an index based entity search engine [41]. It is used for finding associated biomedical concepts and these concepts are presented to user along with textual evidence of associations between query item and concept. Several biomedical databases like UniProt, BioThesaurus, UMLS, KEGG, and DrugBank are used for building indexes using conceptID and their names/synonyms.

- **Ranking Results:** The ranking is done based on co-occurrence statistics. The search space that is uses is PubMed.

4.3.4.3.4 THALIA

This semantic search engine recognizes concepts occurring in biomedical abstracts [42]. Thalia stands for Highlighting, Aggregating and Linking Information in Articles. It uses text mining tool Argo to recognize the entities using various models based on dictionary matching and CRF models trained using human annotated data.

- **Ranking Results:** The search space that it uses is PubMed. Same concept is present in the query and the retrieved documents. Searching API also has options for filtering documents according to Publication Year, Journal Name, Author, Publication Type, and MeSH tag.

4.3.4.3.5 LitVar

It is an entity based search engine for linking genomic variant data. It Process entire set of articles (PUBMED abstracts and PMC-OA full-text) using advanced text mining techniques to compute and extract relationships between variants and other associated entities such as diseases and chemicals/drugs by integrating Pubmed, PMC-OA, dbSNP, and ClinVar [43].

- **Ranking Results:** The search space used by LitVar is PubMed + PMC-OA. The results are ordered by publication date. Results can be filtered on Top Journals, Publication, Year, Publication Type, and Part of publication matching the query .With entity level filters, it can focus on articles with the sentence level co-occurrence of gene, disease, chemical, variant entities.

4.3.4.3.6 CTGA

As described in [38], in this Graph based search, neural information extraction model is used to turn text into tuples. Then, these tuples of a query or document are represented as a knowledge graph of linked concept nodes and finally uses efficient graph based algorithms to return related documents asper structured knowledge. It applies *MIMO* (multi-input multi-output), a deep neural information extraction model for extraction of factual and conditional tuples from unstructured content. Then this extracted information is represented using three-layer knowledge graph.

- **Ranking Results:** The search space used by it is PubMed and mean reciprocal rank (MRR) is used to rank results.

4.3.4.3.7 GoWeb

It is a semantic search engine which uses text-mining and ontologies in semantic web. It uses filter mechanism for long list of search results which are in accordance to the categories provided by GENE ontology and medical sub headings (MeSH) [23]. The result of search operation gives summaries in text form for web documents, known as snippets. Further, entity recognition techniques are used to map concepts form background knowledge to snippets.

- **Ranking Results:** Based on keywords and concepts highlighted from background knowledge (i.e., ontologies) and uses Proxy-Based Solutions. The filtering mechanism reduces the search results substantially to small number of relevant results.

4.3.4.3.8 BioTCM

It is a semantic search engine prototype for IR of Modern biology and Traditional Chinese medicine. It builds an ontology that combines contents from different data sources and convert it into RDF format based corresponding ontology schema [15]

- **Ranking Results:** A web application is offered using which biomedical knowledge can be browsed through a single access point. SPARQL is used for execution of the user query based on semantic rule set.

4.3.4.3.9 BEST

It is Keyword based search engine that extract entities from text [44] based on a dictionary-based approach. For construction of entity dictionary, entity names from 12 different sources have been integrated. Then entities and abstracts are indexed based on document-entity list pair indexing.

- **Ranking Results:** Common search operations such as Boolean operators, proximity search and term boosting are supported. The results are based on
  - Term match score ($T_d(q)$).
  - Entity number score (N_d)
  - Reputation score (Q_d)
  - Recency score (R_d)

4.4 Emerging Technologies/Resources in Health Sector

Technology in this era is growing at very fast pace. Earlier, only academic persons used to access information from domain using published journals and reports. Now, scenario is different. With advances due to information technology, new concepts have been worked and managed upon by people ranging from evidence based medicine, clinical trials, diagnosis data, remote monitoring, remote interaction with the expert etc.

The involvement of semantics in these tasks kind of completes the interaction between the healthcare providers and health services receivers. Thousands of new articles are published every day in peer-reviewed journals [17]. The stakeholders of this information include doctors, patients, researchers, etc. Some of the emerging technologies that are being used by researchers in the health sector are discussed below:

4.4.1 Elasticsearch

"Elasticsearch is a distributed, open-source search and analytics engine built on Apache Lucene and developed in Java. It started as a scalable version of the Lucene open-source search framework then added the ability to horizontally scale Lucene indices. Elasticsearch allows you to store, search, and analyze huge volumes of data quickly and in near real-time and give back answers in milliseconds [18]. The reason that it is able to achieve responses in a fast manner is that it searches index and not the text. It uses a structure based on documents instead of tables and schemas and comes with extensive REST APIs for storing and searching the data."

The PRecIsion Medicine Robust Oncology Search Engine (PRIMROSE) for cancer patients has been proposed by [29] that retrieve scientifc articles and clinical trials based on a patient's condition, genetic profile, age and gender. This search engine utilizes Elasticsearch indexes for information storage and retrieval, and we developed a knowledge graph for query expansion in order to improve recall.

Elastic search has been used by [30] along with big data platform to process huge volumes of clinical data. A framework for social media data analytics using Elastic search has been proposed by [31]. This research emphasizes on insights on how to standardize and configure the processes of Elastic search, which result in increased analysis efficiency.

4.4.2 BioBERT

BioBERT is a pre-trained language representation model for the biomedical domain [17]. With the progress in natural language processing (NLP), extracting valuable information from biomedical literature has gained popularity among researchers, and deep learning has boosted the development of effective biomedical text mining models [17]. But it is observed to be unsatisfactory when advancements in the NLP area are applied directly for mining information in biomedical because of word distribution shift from general domain to biomedical domain [17]. BioBERT has been pre-trained on biomedical domain corpora consisting of PubMed abstracts and PMC full-text articles.

4.4.3 Knowledge Graphs

Semantic web technologies make it possible for the web to "understand" the human knowledge and provide an efficient querying and reasoning framework for the vast heterogeneous web contents by using conceptual graphs. Further, Machine Learning enables the automated construction of large graph knowledge bases. Some of the prominent examples are Google's Knowledge Graph, DBPedia, and YAGO [19].

The use of knowledge graphs is increasing in biomedicine field and with the invention of latest technologies, usage of knowledge graph will continue to grow. Artificial intelligence and machine learning techniques can be used to infer knowledge from theses graphs [20, 21].

BioGRAKN is a graph-based deductive database that combines the power of knowledge graphs and machine reasoning [27]. BioGRAKN is built upon GRAKN and provides an integrated, intelligent database in biomedical field for researchers to handle complex data [28].

PubMed Knowledge Graph (PKG) has been constructed by [21] using 29 million PubMed abstracts by extracting bio-entities from them. Data has been disambiguated by author names, integrating funding data through the National Institutes of Health (NIH) ExPORTER, ORCID has been used to find out educational history of the authors.

BioASQ

BIOASQ [25] is an EU-funded support action [1] that sets up challenge on question answering (QA) [26] and biomedical semantic indexing. Real life biomedical questions are asked in English. Biomedical repositories such as MEDLINE [45] are used to semantically index documents from them. Information is integrated from multiple heterogeneous resources such as research articles, ontologies, scientific documents to find out answers to questions [22]. Biomedical researchers face a common problem of synthesizing and filtering information from multiple, big and ever growing sources. Existing search engines only partially address this need. They take into account limited number of resources. But seeing the pace at which the biomedical data is growing, it becomes necessary to consider varied sources including specialized drug databases, repositories and ontologies.

4.5 Conclusion

Research in health domain is largely driven by the ever growing biomedical sub domain. The biomedical domain has made its digital presence along ago with biomedical resources being developed for communication and interchange of biomedical information.

The concept of semantic web was introduced in order to make the information understood and processed not only by machines but also by humans. The semantic web will help in connectivity of online data, efficient searching and browsing, effective communication and human interaction. SW technologies are tools that facilitate the management and sharing of knowledge between systems. The chapter aims to highlight the role that semantic web technologies can play in development of improved searching solutions in healthcare domain. The importance of incorporating semantics, how to utilize them, and different types of resources available have been discussed thoroughly.

References

1. Almunawar, M.N. and Anshari, M., Health Information Systems (HIS), in: *Concept and Technology*, 2012.
2. Simba, D.O. and Mwangu, M., Application of ICT in strengthening health information systems in developing countries in the wake of globalisation. *African Health Sci.*, 4, 3, 194–198, 2004.
3. Alotaibi, Y.K. and Federico, F., The impact of health information technology on patient safety. *Saudi Med. J.*, 38, 12, 1173–1180, 2017. https://doi.org/10.15537/smj.2017.12.20631.
4. Gulavani, S. and Kulkarni, R.V., Role of information technology in healthcare. *Proceedings of 4th National Conference, INDIACom-2010.*
5. Yamin, M., IT applications in healthcare management: a survey. *Int. J. Inf. Technol.*, 10, 503–509, 2018. https://doi.org/10.1007/s41870-018-0203-3.
6. Manika, P., Xhumari, E., Ktona, A., Demiri, A., Application of ontologies and semantic web technologies in the field of medicine. *International Conference of Recent Trends and Applications in Computer Sciences and Information Technology*, 2018.
7. Iroju, O., Soriyan, A., Gambo, I., Olaleke, J., Interoperability in Healthcare: Benefits, Challenges and Resolutions. *Int. J. Innovation Appl. Stud.*, 3, 1, 262–270, May 2013.
8. Bhartiya, S., Mehrotra, D., Girdhar, A., Issues in achieving complete interoperability while sharing electronic health records. *Proc. Comput. Sci.*, 78, 192–198, 2016.
9. https://en.wikipedia.org/wiki/Semantic_Web
10. Trivedi, M., A study of search engines for health sciences. *Int. J. Lib. Inf. Sci.*, 1, 5, 69–73, 2009.
11. Wang, L., Wang, J., Wang, M., Li, Y., Liang, Y., Xu, D., Using Internet Search Engines to Obtain Medical Information: A Comparative Study. *J. Med. Internet Res.*, 14, 3, e74, 2012. URL: https://www.jmir.org/2012/3/e74.

12. https://research.library.gsu.edu/c.php?g=115556&p=751704
13. Hu, W., Qiu, H., Huang, J., Dumontier, M., BioSearch: a semantic search engine for Bio2RDF. *Database*, 2017, 1-13, 2017.
14. Roy, S., Modak, A., Barik, D., Goon, S., An overview of Semantic Search Engines. *Int. J. Res. Rev.*, 6, 10, 73–85, 2019.
15. Chen, X., Chen, H., Bi, X., Gu, P., Chen, J., Wu, Z., BioTCM-SE: A Semantic Search Engine for the Information Retrieval of Modem Biology and Traditional Chinese Medicine. *Comput. Math. Methods Med.*, 2014, 1–3, 2014.
16. Gandon., F., A Survey of the First 20 Years of Research on Semantic Web and Linked Data, in: *Revue des Sciences et Technologies de l'Information - Série ISI: Ingénierie des Systèmes d'Information*, Lavoisier, (Ed.), 2018, ff10.3166/ISI.23.3-4.11-56ff. ffhal-01935898f.
17. Lee, J., Yoon, W., Kim, S., Kim, D., Kim, S., Ho So, C., Kang, J., BioBERT: A pre-trained biomedical language representation model for biomedical text mining. *Bioinformatics*, 36, 4, 1234–1240, 15, February 2020.
18. https://www.knowi.com/blog/what-is-elastic-search/
19. Nakashole, N., Theobald, M., Weikum, G., Scalable knowledge harvesting with high precision and high recall. *WSDM*, pp. 227–236, 2011, [20] Constructing knowledge graphs and their biomedical applications.
20. Xu, J., Kim, S., Song, M. *et al.*, Building a PubMed knowledge graph. *Sci. Data*, 7, 205, 2020. https://doi.org/10.1038/s41597-020-0543-2.
21. Tsatsaronis, G., Balikas, G., Malakasiotis, P. *et al.*, An overview of the BIOASQ large-scale biomedical semantic indexing and question answering competition. *BMC Bioinf.*, 16, 138, 1–28, 2015. https://doi.org/10.1186/s12859-015-0564-6.
22. https://pubmed.ncbi.nlm.nih.gov/
23. Dietze, H. and Schroeder, M., GoWeb: a semantic search engine for the life science web. *BMC Bioinf.*, 10, S7, 1–13, 2009. https://doi.org/10.1186/1471-2105-10-S10-S7.
24. http://www.snomed.org/
25. *The BioASQ Challenge, BMC Bioinformatics*, 2015, http://www.bioasq.org/
26. https://blog.grakn.ai/biograkn-accelerating-biomedical-knowledge-discovery-with-a-grakn-knowledge-graph-84706768d7d4
27. Messina, A., Pribadi, H., Stichbury, J., Bucci, M., Klarman, S., Urso, A., BioGrakn: A Knowledge Graph-Based Semantic Database for Biomedical Sciences, in: *Complex, Intelligent, and Software Intensive Systems. CISIS 2017. Advances in Intelligent Systems and Computing*, vol. 611, L. Barolli and O. Terzo (Eds.), Springer, Cham, 2018, http://doi-org-443.webvpn.fjmu.edu.cn/10.1007/978-3-319-61566-0_28.
28. Shenoi, S.J., Ly, V., Soni, S., Roberts, K., Developing a Search Engine for Precision Medicine. *AMIA Joint Summits Trans. Sci. Proc. AMIA Joint Summits Trans. Sci.*, 2020, 579–588, 2020.

29. Chen, D. *et al.*, Real-Time or Near Real-Time Persisting Daily Healthcare Data Into HDFS and ElasticSearch Index Inside a Big Data Platform, in: *IEEE Transactions on Industrial Informatics*, vol. 13, pp. 595–606, April 2017.
30. Shah, N., Willick, D., Mago, V., A framework for social media data analytics using Elasticsearch and Kibana. *Wireless Networks*, 2018, 1–9, 2018. 10.1007/s11276-018-01896-2.
31. Hoehndorf, R., Schofield, P.N., Gkoutos, G.V., The role of ontologies in biological and biomedical research: A functional perspective. *Briefings Bioinf.*, 16, 6, 1069–1080, 2015. https://doi.org/10.1093/bib/bbv011.
32. Ashburner, M., Ball, C.A., Blake, J.A. *et al.*, Gene ontology: Tool for the unification of biology. *Nat. Genet.*, 25, 25–29, 2000. [PMC free article] [PubMed] [Google Scholar].
33. Smith, B., Ashburner, M., Rosse, C. *et al.*, The OBO Foundry: Coordinated evolution of ontologies to support biomedical data integration. *Nat. Biotech.*, 25, 1251–5, 2007. [PMC free article] [PubMed] [Google Scholar].
34. Musen, M.A., Noy, N.F., Shah, N.H. *et al.*, The National Center for Biomedical Ontology. *J. Am. Med. Inform. Assoc.*, 19, 190–5, 2012. [PMC free article] [PubMed] [Google Scholar].
35. Horrocks, I., *OBO Flat File Format Syntax and Semantics and Mapping to OWL Web Ontology Language*, University of Manchester, 2007.
36. Heath, T. and Bizer, C., *Linked Data: Evolving the Web into a Global Data Space, 1st edn.*, Morgan & Claypool, San Rafael, California, USA, 2011.
37. Editor's Version, Manchester, 2007, https://guides.lib.umich.edu/ontology/ontologies
38. Jiang, T. *et al.*, CTGA: Graph-based Biomedical Literature Search. *2019 IEEE International Conference on Bioinformatics and Biomedicine (BIBM)*, San Diego, CA, USA, pp. 395–400, 2019.
39. http://www.biomedicalsearchengines.com/
40. https://quertle.com/
41. http://www.nactem.ac.uk/facta/
42. Soto, A.J., Przybyła, P., Ananiadou, S., Thalia: Semantic search engine for biomedical abstracts. *Bioinformatics*, 35, 10, 1799–1801, 15, May 2019.
43. llot, A., Peng, Y., Wei, C.H., Lee, K., Phan, L., Lu, Z., LitVar: A semantic search engine for linking genomic variant data in PubMed and PMC. *Nucleic Acids Res.*, 46, W1, W530–W536, 2018.
44. Lee, S., Kim, D., Lee, K., Choi, J., Kim, S., Jeon, M. *et al.*, BEST: Next-Generation Biomedical Entity Search Tool for Knowledge Discovery from Biomedical Literature. *PLoS ONE*, 11, 10, e0164680, 2016. https://doi.org/10.1371/journal.pone.0164680.
45. https://www.nlm.nih.gov/bsd/medline.html

5

Actionable Content Discovery for Healthcare

Ujwala Bharambe[1]* and Anuradha Srinivasaraghavan[2]†

[1]*Computer Engineering Department, Thadomal Shahani Engineering College, Mumbai, India*
[2]*Computer Engineering Department, St. Francis Institute of Technology, Mumbai, India*

Abstract

The clinical decisions are driven by all the available information of the medical and patient history. The issue currently faced is the provision of medical information that is based on evidence as soon as its requirement in delivering the best possible care at that time. This can be done by making the "evidence based actionable content" available to the healthcare professional at that time so as he can choose the best possible decision at that time. The actionable content gives clinical guidance in terms of recommendations that can be queried, link to relevant context, and actionable items. To discover actionable content in healthcare domain, health analytics needs a sequence of three types of analytics: descriptive, predictive and prescriptive. These analytics helps to retrieve coherent meaningful information that can represent actionable content. Traditional machine learning techniques help to transform descriptive analytics into predictive analytics. However, these techniques are data-hungry and in healthcare domain, data comes from multiple heterogeneous sources. These heterogeneity issues are addressed using semantic technology i.e. ontology. This chapter discusses the usability of ontology and proposed ontology-driven three layer architecture to extract actionable content from multiple heterogeneous information sources in healthcare domain.

Keywords: Analytics, descriptive analytics, predictive analytics, prescriptive analytics, ontology, actionable content

**Corresponding author*: ujwala.bharambe@thadomal.org
†*Corresponding author*: g.anuradha@sfit.ac.in

Vishal Jain, Jyotir Moy Chatterjee, Ankita Bansal and Abha Jain (eds.) Semantic Web for Effective Healthcare, (115–138) © 2022 Scrivener Publishing LLC

5.1 Introduction

Healthcare data is collected and analyzed to improve the quality of health of patients, reduce costs of treatment, and also to generate meaningful insights for patients and researchers. The clinical decisions taken by the healthcare system are driven by all the available information on the medical data and also patient history for specific kinds of illnesses. This requires validation by medical practitioners [34]. The best care can, however, be guaranteed by providing evidence-based medical information. For this Health professionals need "actionable content."

The question remains as to how the actionable content should be included in the practice and be made efficient for use by aiding in clinical decision making and administrative capability. As an example, suppose an oncologist has an appointment scheduled with a 44-year-old premenopausal woman.

After some primer examination, it was discovered that the woman has an early stage of breast cancer. It was found that it is triple-negative (ER, PR Her-2 negative), and the woman has a history of breast cancer, in her family. Although this was crucial in diagnosis, she has not gone through genetic testing for a BRCA1 or BRCA2 mutation that would affirm (or dismiss) an inclination to breast or ovarian malignancy.

At the time when the appointment between the patient and the oncologist is going on, details about the options in treatment regimens, health insurance plans for the patient, altering clinical traits to be administered to the patient should be made available, which is just at the click of a button. In other words, the workflow should be generated. The challenges in the processing are multi-fold. Not only the information should be made available, but it has to be filtered and processed for actionable content. There is a need for high-quality data and good metadata which is valid and comparable with other resources. Also, Artificial Intelligence (AI) and clinical decision making play an important role in this scenario. The AI model with ontologies will help to access information from multiple sources and transform it into a stepwise procedure. This would influence doctors or medical practitioners in the decision-making process.

"Actionable content is meaningful actions obtained by analyzing any type of raw data. They help organizations make well-informed decisions and they are obtained as a result of data analytics." Not all insights are actionable though. The goal of this chapter is to present the use of ontology in the extraction of actionable content in the healthcare domain. This can be achieved by initially providing a sketch of the emerging discipline of health analytics and put forth ontology as one of the tools for extracting actionable content.

The entire chapter is structured as follows. Section 5.2 renders the various definitions of Actionable content with its descriptions. Section 5.3 focuses on the stages of health analytics and Section 5.4 focuses specifically on how ontology can be used for prescriptive health analytics.

5.2 Actionable Content

Actionable intelligence/knowledge/Content "is not only relevant to the world of practice, but it is also the knowledge that people use to create that world" [5, 14]. There was a wide gap between the output of data mining algorithms and the effect of this output in terms of actionable output. This gap was because of the academic objectives and the business goals between identified patterns and deliverables. This entailed the requirement of active knowledge that had to be identified and delivered in the form of an action plan.

5.2.1 Actionable Content in Theory

This conceptualization of the term Actionable content started in [6] Cleveland in 2001 when a term Action plan was suggested. Then in [7, 10, 11] 2010 Cao *et al.*, presented a conventional view of Actionable Knowledge Discovery (AKD). It was elucidated from the system and decision-making perspectives. Actionable knowledge discovery was defined as a "closed optimization problem"[1]. AKD is designed to deliver business rules which are operable and seamlessly integrated with business processes and systems. The six dimensions of AKD which are described as an optimization process are as follows. This is a generic structure that is applicable in any domain. According to [8, 9] AKD is a five dimensional optimization process.

[2]AKD ::=optimization(problem, environment, model, decision, data)

[1]http://ieeexplore.ieee.org/abstract/document/5072220/

[2]O. Thonnard and M. Dacier, "Actionable Knowledge Discovery for Threats Intelligence Support Using a Multi-dimensional Data Mining Methodology," 2008 IEEE International Conference on Data Mining Workshops, Pisa, 2008, pp. 154-163, https://dl.acm.org/doi/10.1109/ICDMW.2008.78.

- Optimization: Helps in synchronizing between the model, problem, data, and environment by providing suitable optimization techniques.
- Problem: This is the knowledge discovery target, which inputs data, business protocols, and the environment and aims at contributing to corresponding knowledge discovery objectives and business analytics goals, along with evaluation and validation of knowledge discovery findings.
- Data: Features corresponding to a problem, which reflects the mapping between the business problem and the decisions. This mapping is crucial in selecting the appropriate data.
- Environment: The problem and its associated data are enclosed in a certain environment, embodied through organizational or social factors.
- Model: A model is required to transform data into proper decisions pertaining to the problem at hand within the constraints of the environment. Model if biased is not fully reflective of the problem, data environment or decision.
- Decision: a decision is the knowledge discovered and is presented in terms of identified patterns.

The knowledge identified by AKD is quantified by actionability computing. This also refers to the impact of AKD findings on direct decision-making.The general architecture of actionable knowledge discovery is shown in Figure 5.1. In this architecture, the input data is sequentially fed into the model (Figure 5.1a) or in a parallel way (Figure 5.1b). This composition is responsible for updating the generic pattern produced by different models. The final actionable pattern is the fusion obtained by taking the help of domain and meta-knowledge.

AKD supplements the data mining associated procedures by precisely including "human, domain knowledge, organizational structure and social insight, and their synthesis." This enables the end-users and managerial users to easily comprehend the results, and take actions on the discoveries.

The domain knowledge by human experts, organizational structure, and social intelligence are being exploited using the data mining techniques complemented by AKD. This warranties the understanding of outcomes by both end-users and decision-makers and also helps in taking actions on the findings.

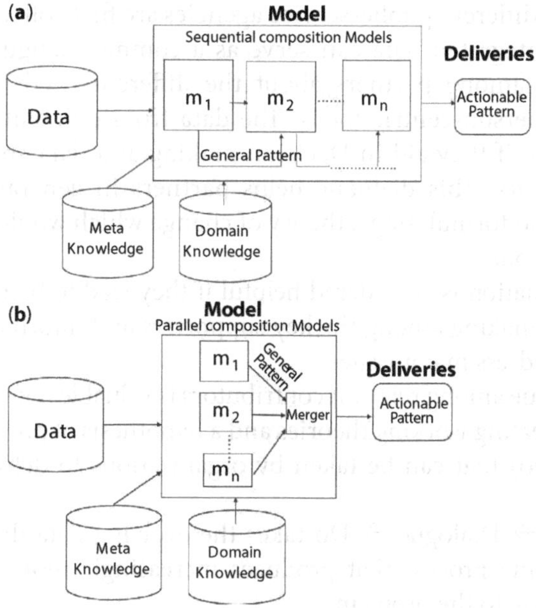

Figure 5.1 (a) Sequential composition model; (b) Parallel composition model.

In other words, it provides coherent integration of data mining outputs into the operational environment.

The contribution of this approach is that it presents a formal framework for the discovery of actionable knowledge, action ability of patterns, and deliverables. But the main limitation of this approach is that it does not consider characteristics and diversity in data. As the volume and velocity of data inflow increased last decade by many folds the heterogeneity in data in terms of syntactic, semantic have also to be considered which is not the case.

Fantuzzo *et al.* [15] have used the term actionable intelligence for actionable knowledge. The word Actionable Intelligence is involved in both data and research. It is derived from the combined contributions of various key contributors such as executive leaders, practitioners, researchers, and citizens [14]. The output of data mining is getting data with some meaning in it which would help in formulating a theory of change and is further tested. Hence the name Actionable Intelligence because of the contributions it makes in churning the intelligence from data. "It is the product of an evolving Data → Dialogue → Do cycle."

Data from different public-service agencies are first collected and integrated. The integrated data can serve as a common language to facilitate dialogue among partners about the different needs and services and keeps a person-centric focus. The data from different agencies are deemed useful if they aid in Decision making and data-sharing among key contributors. This dialogue helps partners in generating working hypotheses and formulating a theory of change which would further lead to Doable actions.

This information is considered helpful if they lead to beneficial Dialog and decision-making among the key supporters and information-sharing agencies to address major issues.

This dialogue among relevant contributors is valuable if it assists accomplices with creating working theories and a hypothesis of progress prompting action (Do) that can be taken by organizations to deliver improved results.

This Data → Dialogue → Do takes the evolving data driven iterative decision making process that produces increasingly more effective and ethical response to the problem.

To attain a detail understanding of this process, we need to identify (1) The key contributors can be executives in an organization who are in the position to make key decisions for their organization, researches, and practitioners (2). The mutual consensus among the key contributors is inherently dynamic which needs to be adhered to (3) the integrated data have a fecund dialogue leading to actionable intelligence.

Actionable content is generated when actionable intelligence supports decision making (Figure 5.3). Actionable content is the feasible action which is the end product of a data mining task which results in a product enhancement or development whereby reducing the gap between the identified patterns and the deliverables. It can be contemplated as a stepwise procedure or set of rules to perform a particular activity. And to derive this content from various diverse sources, Domain-driven data mining (D^3M) has been proposed to analyze the underlying problems by [10].

The Domain-driven in-depth pattern discovery (DDID-PD) process comprises of put four essential procedures. They are (i) loop-closed mining, (ii) human-cooperated mining, (iii) in-depth mining, and (iv) constraint mining.

The Constraints to any business problem are domain-specific, functional, non-functional, and environmental, and play significant role in discovering knowledge actionable to the business. These constraints mentioned are domain-specific and have major role in discovering knowledgeable action for the business. These constraints form the context for actionable knowledge discovery. In the relevant phases of DDID-PD must be considered to varying degrees.

In summary, the current actionable content keyword gets its root and refinement for the last two decades as shown in Figure 5.2. The word Action Plan was coined by [6] Cleveland in 2001, which then was mostly the knowledge extracted from the information churned from the data using different data mining techniques [16]. The outputs of those data mining techniques had many patterns, but they were not informative and transparent to business people because the users were not aware of the most suitable pattern satisfying the business needs. The technicalities and knowledge put forward by researchers were not being implemented as a workable project because it was failing to meet the goals of industries. A lacuna was developed which necessitated the action plan to get converted to actionable intelligence by taking into consideration the different players. However, the involvement of actionable knowledge with artificial intelligence and machine learning has only taken place in recent years as shown by the apex of the triangle in Figure 5.3.

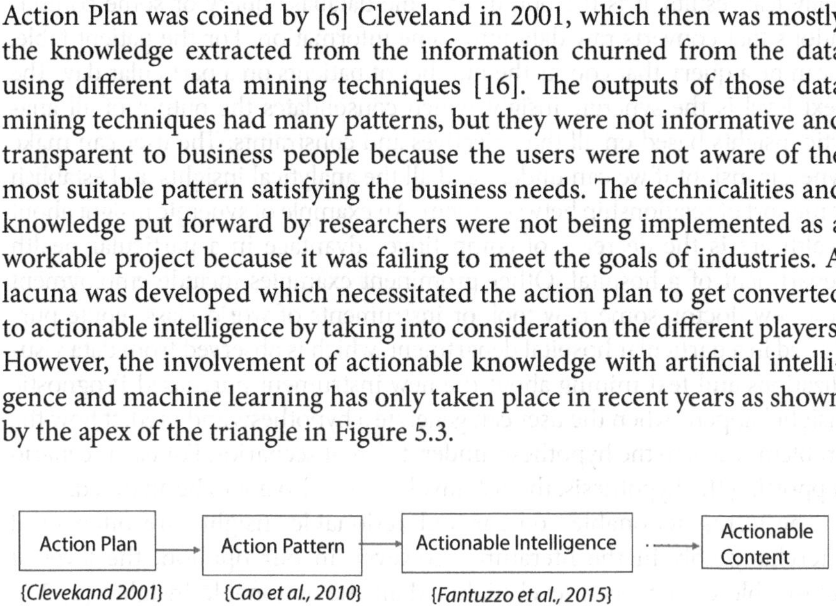

Figure 5.2 Evolution of actionable content.

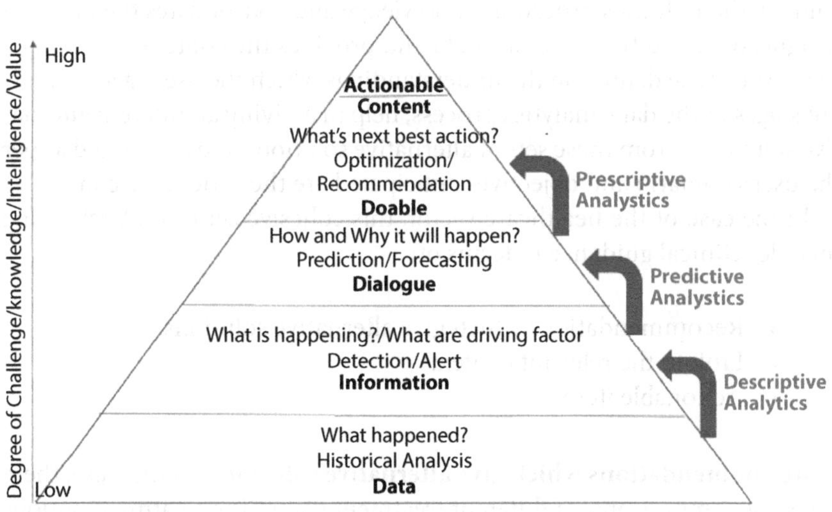

Figure 5.3 Data to actionable content triangle.

5.2.2 Actionable Content in Practice

The three major components of Actionable insight are analytic, synergic, and prognostic insights. Analytic insight concentrates on the understanding of analytical results. It is the output of some database query or some computations that converts raw data into some information. For the patient table, it can be a query that counts the number of patients on a particular day. The next level is the synergic insight which consolidates the output of all analytic insights based on all the objectives and constraints. The user can make synergic insight if we can understand all the analytical insights and establish some sort of relationship between them. An example of synergic insight about healthcare is the decrease of competitive advantage in a particular health department of a hospital. Other prominent examples include employment of a new doctor, some new tool, or instruments of world-class repute purchased in a particular hospital department, which is observed from data visualizations and text mining about the new instrument purchased Prognostic insight happens when the user can generate a hypothesis and predict how the problem reacts to the hypothesis under different scenarios. For each scenario supporting the hypothesis, the risk involved has also got to be analyzed.

The terms actionable content and actionable insights are often used interchangeably in the literature. However, in our opinion, the level of Actionable content is a level higher than the actionable insights [2, 27]. Actionable content is a verified content by aligning diverse sources and analyzing interrelation among them. However actionable insights can be the subjective interpretation of data that is useful for the end-user and has value to them. It uses procedural knowledge and consolidates the different insights obtained from the raw data and provides the content accordingly [25]. As per the definition the understandings which the users get at different stages of the data analytics process, help in arriving at different alternative solutions. From these sets of alternative solutions, the best suited as per the user's scenario and objectives anticipated are the actionable content.

In the case of the healthcare sector, this cohesive set of understanding includes clinical guidance in terms of:

- Recommendations which give alternative solutions
- Link to the relevant context
- Actionable items

Recommendations which give alternative solutions: In this case, there can exist comparisons, of different treatment plans. The treatment options can be optimized for personalized medications or treatment implantations.

Link to relevant context: This can be in the form of case studies, existing research projects, outcomes of clinical trials, longitudinal cohort studies of disease outcomes, Information from allied fields like health economic models, or/and pharma-economic models for use of personalized medicine. This might give insight into the newly developed personalized medical approaches.

Actionable items: This would improve the overall process to combat the disease. This actionable item can arrive as an output of amalgamations of standard definitions related to disease vocabulary with its sources, disease classification with explanations about the keywords used.

In the example cited above, in the oncology management, the medical oncologist would be provided with various approved systemic therapy guidelines. The validity of the suggested treatment options with the patients' insurance company and the place where it is approved will also be provided. Along with this, if the patient is eligible for any on-going clinical trial will also be provided to the oncologist.

The oncologist can access this information when sitting with the patient in his clinical consulting room. After due information of the same to the patient, he/she can finalize the treatment accepted by the patient. The treatment plan starts with the registration of patients in the oncology department, scheduling appointments for the entire course of treatment, managing the insurance claims of patients, and its referrals. All these happen as and when the oncologist after the consensus of patients clicks the Okay button [20]. This actionable content comes from a variety of sources, the most prominent among them are based on the evidence available, patients, and/or facilities available.

- Based on evidence: Guidelines provided by different healthcare sectors, clinical code for the treatment of a particular disease, studies based on published results.
- Based on patient-specific data: This can either be laboratory and other test results, which are available as Electronic Medical Records (EMR) and data collected from insurance companies or insurance-related information.
- Based on practice: This can be based on the facilities provided by hospitals for treating a specific disease and research facilities in the area and remuneration contracts with insurers actionable content provides various benefits to healthcare workers, insurers, and patients. Benefits provided to healthcare providers exhibit the best clinical knowledge, which it would give to the patients. For the insurers, it can

connect to all the stakeholders with assurance. For patients, personalized attention is provided.

But, the major challenge here is the integration of data collected from all of these sources. A syntactical integration has to be done to give a meaningful result (interoperable). With data and good analytical methodology in place, would it be possible to present the actionable content to the stakeholders in an understandable way is another point to ponder with? The above questions give a flow from integration to meaningful insight, and then to the coherent statistical methodology for good health analytics which is shown in Figure 5.1. However, it is challenging to discover actionable content in the healthcare domain.

There are three types of data analytics proposed in the literature. They are descriptive, predictive, and prescriptive analytics, which is elaborated in Section 5.3. However, currently in the healthcare domain, applications are heavily dependent only predictive analytics and prescriptive analytics is still a challenge [23].

5.3 Health Analytics

Healthcare analytics is a type of data analytics used by healthcare professionals that would improve health system management, patient diagnosis, and spending [23]. It is broadly classified into three types as shown in Figure 5.4.

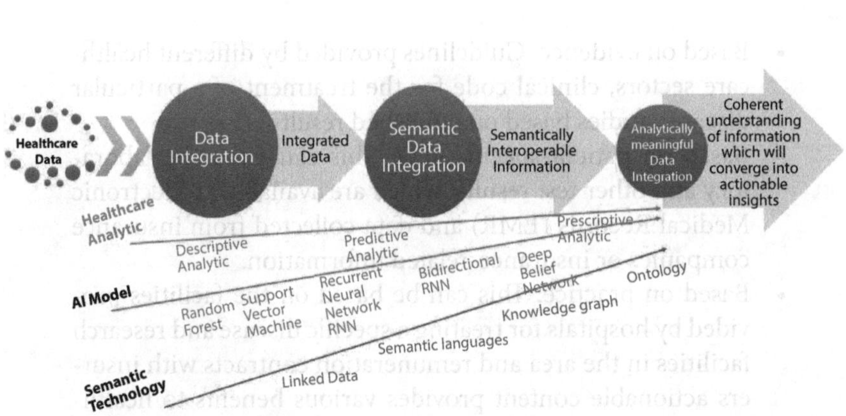

Figure 5.4 Spectrum of healthcare analytics.

Descriptive analytics as the name implies refers to the statistical inference of the data which can be used for other operations in a useful way [9]. It is more data-driven and is describes the data "as is" and hence the name. It uses a lot of visualizations. This can graphically represent details about patient's hospitalizations, physician performance, and utilization of resources to name a few. Queries about patient's count, revenue generated, identifying high-risk patients are all answered using descriptive analytics.

As evident from its name Predictive analytics makes predictions about unknown future events with reasoning using advanced analytics [9]. Predictive analytics. In the healthcare sector, Predictive analytics enables decision making allowing personalized care for each individual. To implement predictive analytics, it requires a large volume of real-time data to be generated accurately, and precise information for clinicians [12].

The blending of clinician minds and software tools yields predictive analytics whose main objective is to widen training data set beyond individual experiences and in turn, helps in giving timely and accurate treatment to patients.

Prescriptive analytics refers to the type of data analytics that recommends actions for smart decision-making [17]. It can tell a user what course of action would produce the highest likelihood of maximum benefit when a predicted event does occur. So it does provide information, not just about answers to a certain question but also the consequences of those choices.

5.3.1 Artificial Intelligence/Machine Learning-Based Predictive Analytics

Healthcare Analytics and Artificial Intelligence (AI)/Machine Learning (ML) go hand in hand to reach out to the patients without them even realizing it [18]. Machine Learning can be deployed for various pivotal applications in healthcare such as machine learning based behavior modifications, clinical trial and research, and epidemic prediction. Moreover, machine learning for image analysis is more popular in healthcare (for example, cancer cell drug sensitivity prediction drug targeted interaction strength prediction, etc.).

Currently, image-based diagnostics focus on machine learning based on deep learning and radionics. These aim to extract, structured, reproducible, quantitative, machine-readable information out of medical images, and supplement the prognosis of a medical practitioner.

However, traditional machine learning has some limitations to handle diverse, multifactorial, multi-dimension, highly interrelated healthcare data. This is primarily because

- Artificial intelligence/ML, require a lot of data. This can represent an issue in healthcare when endeavoring to apply a Deep Learning algorithm to disease processes with less predominance. This is further complemented by the fact that clinical information is not common among multiple systems.
- Absence of information sharing framework to healthcare institutions, heterogeneity and deficiency in the assortment of information, and completion between institution/organization.
- This FAIR (findable, accessible, interoperable, reusable) guideline ensures that the data is findable, by being assigned a globally unique and persistent identifier [31]. By being accessible the data with metadata should be easily available for free. Interoperable is that feature that the data must use a formal, accessible, shared form of knowledge representation.

It is not able to ensure that the clinical information is transferred and interpreted between multiple systems. Predictive analytics generally get employed by traditional AI/ML techniques.

5.3.2 Semantic Technology for Prescriptive Health Analytics

As quoted above, the traditional artificial intelligence (AI)/ML techniques do not address the issue of heterogeneity, interpretability, and sharing of information between multiple systems. However, all these issues can be addressed by semantic technologies and which will also be useful for discovering actionable content from the data. Semantic technology is a tool to establish a semantic link among the various underlined data sources, which will help meaningful ways of a coherent understanding of information that can be converted in terms of actionable information.

Semantic technologies are "meaning-centered." Semantic Technology develops its languages to express rich self-describing interrelation of the data and linking it in a form that is processable by the machine, despite it being in a long string of characters and index tons of data [32]. It also identifies the meaning and logical relationship of the data and can store manage and restrict its information.

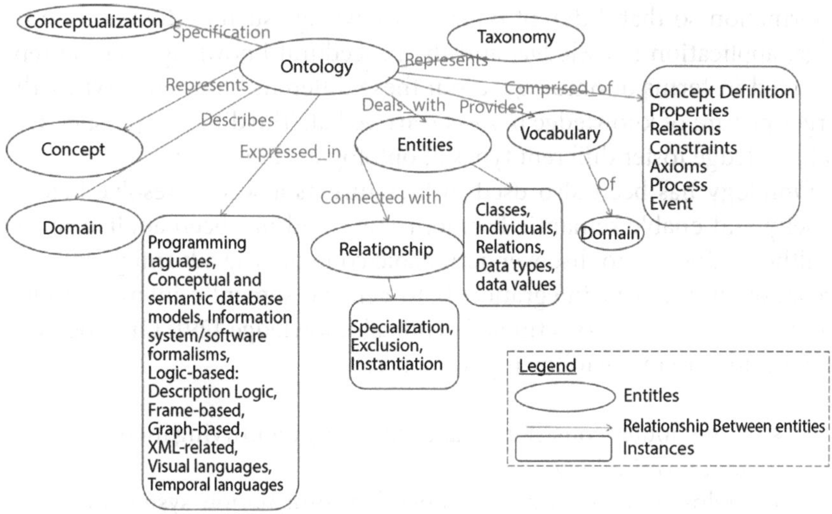

Figure 5.5 Model of ontology.

Semantic technology includes various standards/terminologies such as taxonomy, graphs (triple store), semantic query language (SPARQL), lightweight ontology (RDF, knowledge graph), and heavyweight ontology (OWL) [30].

Among these different types of standards, ontologies are the ones central to semantic technology. An ontology represents encode/decode knowledge which is formalized using descriptive logic and expressed in terms of axioms. Researchers have also used ontologies in the healthcare domain [28].

Ontologies were developed to enable knowledge sharing and reuse in the field of Artificial Intelligence. More recently, the notion of Ontology is also becoming widespread in the fields of intelligence retrieval, electronic commerce, and knowledge management. "An Ontology is a formal explicit specification of a shared conceptualization" [13]. Ontology provides a vocabulary of terms and relations to model the domain which is represented in Figure 5.5.

5.4 Ontologies and Actionable Content

Domain knowledge and meta-knowledge is an integral part of the architecture of actionable knowledge discovery. Ontologies are one of the methods of representing knowledge and correlations between different pieces of information so that different types of knowledge such as domain knowledge, application knowledge, and the procedural knowledge can be represented in terms of ontology. From these different knowledge types, the larger picture of knowledge has to be arrived at. The different perspectives of knowledge foster different types of ontologies (Figure 5.6).

Ontology has been also used in literature as a way to resolve heterogeneity and enable semantic harmonization and has been applied in the healthcare domain to discover actionable content. The advantage of using an ontology for data integration is to achieve semantic interoperability which can convert into actionable clinical knowledge [29]. Ontology can help healthcare in the following ways. It can

- Contributes consistent management by identifying inconsistent terminology.
- Helps in supporting interoperable information systems by explicating terms and vocabulary used by communicating systems.
- Facilitates the integration of information across disparate systems in healthcare.

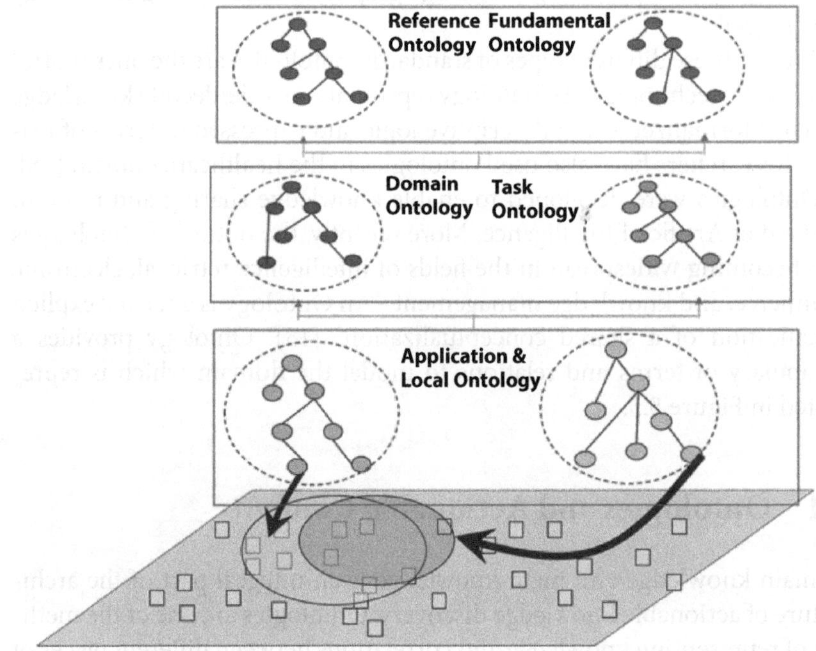

Figure 5.6 Different types of ontologies.

- Support re-use, sharing, and transmission of a patient and other health-related data.
- Support semantic enabled statistical aggregation of disparate healthcare information.
- Provide real-time correlation among test results, symptoms, and individual medical histories by cross-checking diagnosis, which is based on standard procedure and protocol.

So, ontology can be considered indispensable technology that can facilitate actionable knowledge by taking advantage of AI/ML as well.

5.4.1 Ontologies in Healthcare Domain

Healthcare data information originates from various sources, for example, electronic health records, research centers, drug stores, insurance agencies, web-based media, smartphone applications, medical images, electronic clinical records, specialist's notes, and paper archives [4].

Due to the multitude of data sources and a variety of data types the characteristics of healthcare data are also unique. To name a few characteristics,

- Much of the data is scattered
- The data is structured and unstructured
- Inconsistent/variable definitions
- The data is Complex and dynamic
- The data is Large: Healthcare data is voluminous.

Information sources in the healthcare domain often use different terms to describe the same object leading to semantic heterogeneities. This causes misrepresentation and mismanagement of the knowledge. Ontologies developed using such information sources make the meaning of the healthcare terminologies explicit and provides shared and precisely defined terms, thus enabling interoperability.

The vast diversity of ontologies in the healthcare domain necessitates the establishment of semantic mappings among the ontologies to ensure semantic interoperability [21, 22].

The semantic heterogeneities between ontologies in a healthcare domain can be resolved by creating formal relationships between the entities in those ontologies. There is a need for establishing semantic relationships across complex, heterogeneous, and highly interrelated healthcare information sources to extract actionable insights and there is a need for highly aligned and loosely coupled integration.

This can be easily employed using ontology matching techniques. The main objective of ontology matching is to harmonize the variations among the two ontologies, each designed with different perspectives and described using a different vocabulary.

Advantage of ontology matching as follows:

- Connect ontologies with the information sources described there helps to discover common semantics between two sources;
- Connect different ontologies used in an integration system thereby enabling the convergence of terminological standardization;
- Add knowledge (query concept expansion) to a user's query thereby enabling semantic retrieval.

Literature offers various proposals that use ontology and ontology matching techniques to combine ontology and deep learning techniques for the extraction of clinical intelligence. However, converting it into actionable content is still a challenge with the concerns being designing a machine learning model that can access and process the clinical knowledge abstraction provided by the ontology. The second concern is that the healthcare domain knowledge representation in a small set of axioms, i.e., ontology is a challenging process.

In the next two sections, we provide a general block diagram of actionable content discovery, and further, we will explain how ontology can be employed in healthcare analytics.

5.5 General Architecture for the Discovery of Actionable Content for Healthcare Domain

The advancement of the healthcare domain utilizing current technology lead to a lot of clinical information from various heterogeneous suppliers, for example, diagnosis, monitoring, clinical notes, medical administrations, and numerous other pertinent information sources.

There is a need to integrate patient data from all those heterogeneous systems, which is inevitable for actionable content discovery (Figure 5.7). For this, not just integration alone is required, but also semantic interoperable. Semantic interoperability is needed for a coherent understanding of information from which actionable content can be produced.

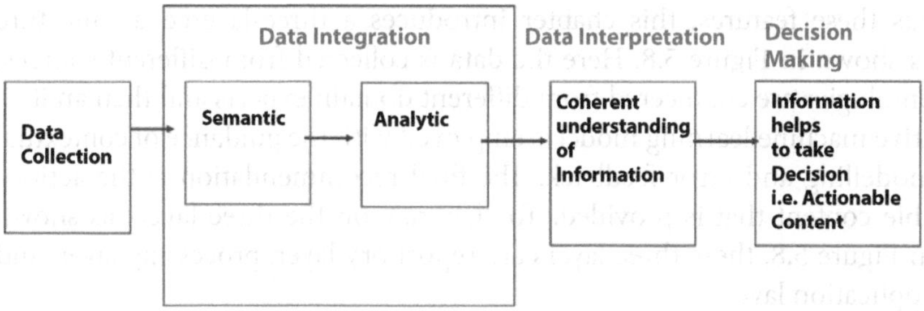

Figure 5.7 Block diagram for actionable content discovery.

The benefits of Semantic interoperability in the healthcare domain are as follows [3]:

- The organization of the patient's health records in such a manner, so that any health worker can update the patient's information effectively in a simple way.
- Aggregation of all patient's clinical data from many different sources.
- Communicating and sharing standardized information to other healthcare system
- Expedite the access of patient's medical records in any location at any time.
- Lessens medical care costs by removal of duplicate tests, decreasing paper-based medical reports, and avoiding unnecessary medical tests and imaging procedures.

5.5.1 Ontology-Driven Actionable Content Discovery in Healthcare Domain

Actionable content is a type of information that assists in providing a choice of medical solutions to patients. It may provide the procedure or conceptual theory or description to act or take a medical decision. There are six attributes for any actionable content [33] Alignment, Context, Relevance Specify, Novelty, and Clarity. To generate actionable content that has these attributes, it needs big and diverse data sources, which need to align or establish a coherent link among them. It also needs to understand the context and relevance of the information which needs to be provided.

Actionable content should be influential enough to act on. To do that it needs to be novel, clear, and specific. To discover actionable content that has these features, this chapter introduces a three-layered architecture as shown in Figure 5.8. Here the data is collected from different sources, ontologies are engineered from different domain experts and then an iterative machine learning model is employed with the guidance of contextual modelling and error feedback. The final recommendation is the actionable content that is provided. To elaborate on the three layers as shown in Figure 5.8, these three layers are repository layer, processing layer, and application layer.

1. **Repository layer:** This is the bottom-most layer. These repositories are made of the knowledge base, structured data, unstructured information, and external information.
   The healthcare domain creates enormous amounts of information from a wide range of information sources, for example, social media, principles, images, scan, XML (Extensible Markup Language), ADL (Archetypes Description Language) documents, and tabular records to give some examples [26]. These data have heterogeneous structures and semantics.
   Ontologies are used in the healthcare domain to reconcile this structure and semantics. Ontologies in healthcare are mainly concentrated on the representation and (re-)organization of medical terminologies.Ontologies are utilized in

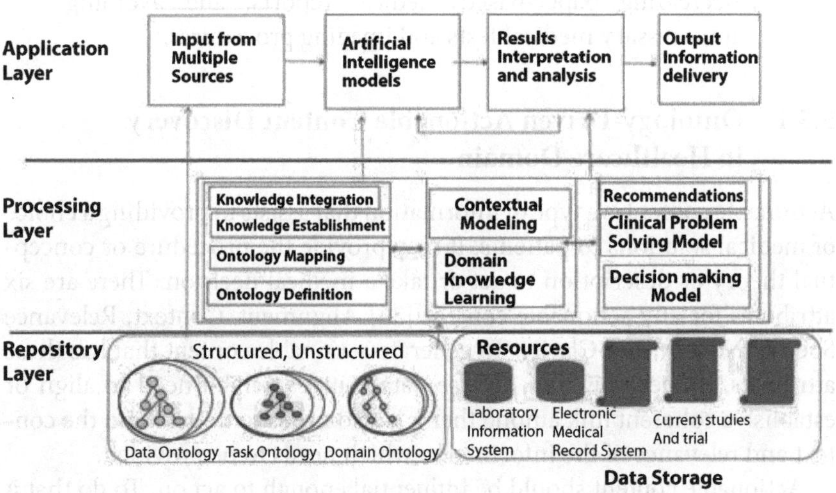

Figure 5.8 Overall architecture of ontology-driven actionable content discovery for healthcare domain.

the healthcare domain to accommodate this structure and semantics. Ontologies in healthcare are essentially centered around the representation, organization, and (re-)association of medical terminology.

Doctors/healthcare workers build up their particular languages and vocabularies to store and impart general clinical information and patient-related data proficiently. Such terminologies are described by a significant amount of implicit knowledge and optimized for human processing.

Healthcare information systems, on the other hand, need to be able to unambiguously communicate complex and detailed healthcare concepts.

It is a challenging task and requires a significant investigation of the structure and the ideas of healthcare terminologies. However, it tends to be accomplished by developing the healthcare domain ontologies for representing healthcare terminologies. Ontologies are stored in Knowledgebase.

The knowledgebase contains different ontologies from domain ontologies. These domain ontologies mostly include disease ontology, application ontologies, medical terminologies [1]. Not only these even the Task ontologies such as diagnostic and treatment ontologies are stored in the knowledge base. Structure and Unstructured information consist of information generated from the Hospital Information Systems (HIS). This can be patient-related data, his/her medical data, laboratory reports, and Electronic Medical Records (EMR). External information comprises guidelines, international and national protocol, case studies, research articles, and/or research papers.

2. **Processing Layer:** This layer is involved in main operations like knowledge integration, contextual modeling, domain learning, clinical decision making, and recommendation. Information present in the repository is diverse. (i.e. different formats, different structures, and semantic). There is a need for first integrating this information. Then the integrated information needs to be channelized in such a manner, that it can be shared and disseminated in various Artificial Intelligence Models to support predictive and prescriptive analytics. Also, this knowledge should provide various clinical guidance. This can be in terms of actionable content, which requires pattern extraction, summarization,

and optimization and multi-criteria decision-making models to be incorporated. All these would facilitate healthcare workers or medical practitioners in providing recommendations for taking better clinical decisions.

3. **Application Layer:** This layer is the one that gives the output in the form of actionable content to the end-users. This layer provides various choices to the end-users based on their existing conditions, historical data, and the knowledge-based which is processed. AI models are used and the results of such models are interpreted and the information is given to the end-users in this layer.

5.5.2 Case Study for Actionable Content Discovery in Cancer Domain

Let us see how the profiling of the patient is done electronically through the different blocks of actionable insight and the inner mechanism of the proposed architecture with an example is cited in Figure 5.9. Considering the case described above, the patient visits the oncologist with the presence of a lump in the breast and/or with associated pain in the same area. The patient provides a detailed history of its occurrence stating the time she noticed it and provides all the investigation reports she has done for the same. This investigation as suggested by the medical practitioner includes detailed

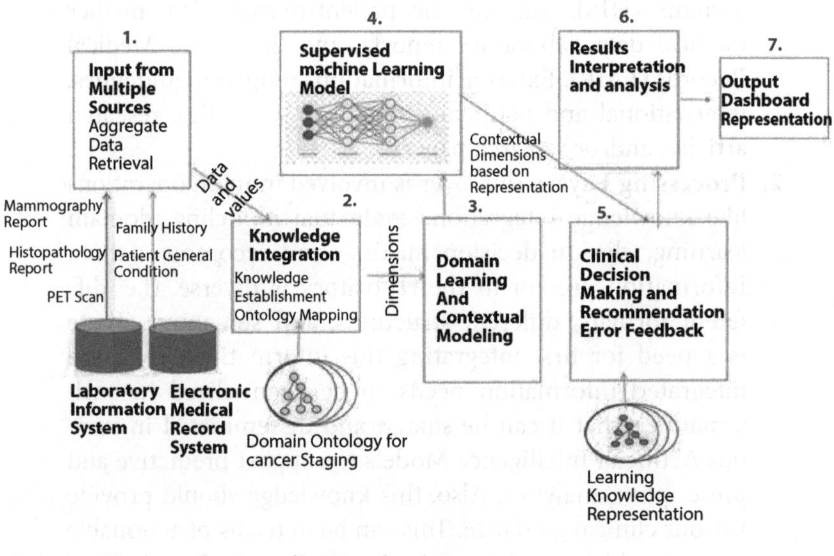

Figure 5.9 Inner mechanism of proposed architecture.

laboratory investigations of, renal function, liver function tests and complete blood counts. She also has radiology reports and images of Mammography/sonography, the biopsy reports indicating the histopathological confirmation of malignancy with the associated immunotherapy reports of estrogen/progesterone receptors along with her reports. There may be detailed radiological reports and images as well to rule out any metastatic disease. These reports are automatically stored in a Laboratory Information System (LIS).

The oncologist reviews the same by retrieving from the repository layer and after detailed medical examination records his findings. He also suggests any pending medical investigations to be done and reviewed. All the reports and findings are fed into the Hospital Information System (HIS) and the system evaluates them and provides the detailed diagnosis and staging of the patient. The system also provides the various treatment options with regards to the available treatment options of oncosurgery, medical oncology, radiation oncology, hormone therapy, and immunotherapy provided in different combinations best suitable [1]. These recommendations help the oncologist in deciding the best possible workflow of treatment and recommend it to the patient. These recommendations are discussed with the patient at length, with the results of trials supporting them. The best option is chosen by the patient with the support of the oncologist and her family. If the insurance plan is available is discussed with the accepted option and the treatment dates are arranged.

To perform all these activities, diverse information that is available in varied formats is initially aligned for AI Model. The healthcare domain has a different type of formats, for example, Mammography, PET scan image, which

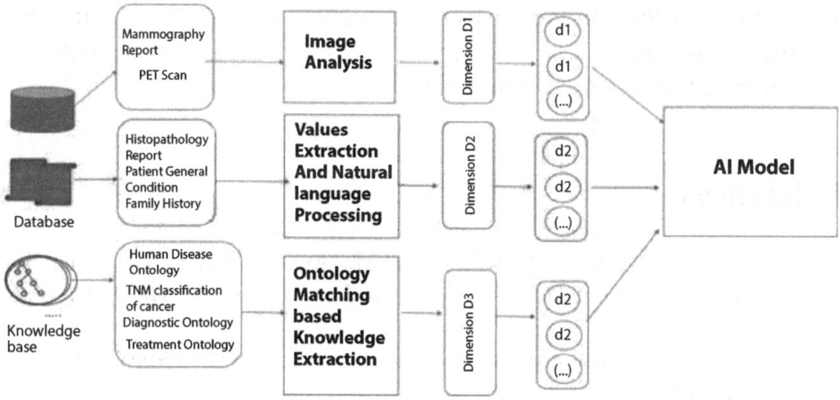

Figure 5.10 Contextual dimension modeling diagram with data coming from various data sources and processed using the image and natural language processing to create dimensions by merging context from various ontologies.

will be coupled with natural language. Pathology reports will be in terms of values. Doctors' notes will be in natural language while Domain knowledge will be in OWL format. All these formats have to be transformed into a common format that is in the form of quantitative data, which is the input to the AI model. The major challenge here is quantization to preserve the structure, context, and semantic of the input source [19]. This chapter presents the solution based on ontology to infuse structure, context, and semantics to the AI Model. The detailed mechanism is depicted in Figure 5.10.

5.6 Conclusion

There is a need for actionable content in the healthcare domain to support clinicians and medical health workers for better diagnosis, treatment, and patient care. To discover actionable content in the healthcare domain, health analytics needs a sequence of three types of analytics: descriptive, predictive, and prescriptive. These analytics helps to retrieve coherent meaningful information that can represent actionable content. Traditional machine learning techniques help to transform descriptive analytics to predictive analytics. However, these techniques are data-hungry and in the healthcare domain, data comes from multiple heterogeneous sources. Heterogeneity, especially the semantic heterogeneity among these sources is an important issue. This problem can be addressed using semantic technology, i.e., ontology. This chapter provides the usefulness of ontology in the healthcare domain to extract actionable content from multiple heterogeneous information sources. We have presented a three-layered architecture for the ontology-driven discovery of actionable content in the healthcare domain. A case study from the cancer domain is presented to demonstrate the proposed architecture.

References

1. Alfonse, M., Aref, M.M., Salem, A.B.M., An ontology-based system for cancer diseases knowledge management. *Int. J. Inf. Eng. Electron. Bus.*, 6, 6, 55–63, 2014.
2. Argyris, C., Actionable knowledge: intent versus actuality. *J. Appl. Behav. Sci.*, 32, 441–444, 1996.
3. Adel, E., El-Sappagh, S., Barakat, S., Elmogy, M., Ontology-based electronic health record semantic interoperability: A survey, in: *U-Healthcare Monitoring Systems*, pp. 315–352, Academic Press, 2019.

4. Blide, L.A., Characteristics of health data: structure and relationships. *Topics Health Inf. Manage.*, 15, 2, 80–88, 1994.
5. Guillerm, Romaric, Hamid Demmou, and Nabil Sadou. "Information model for model driven safety requirements management of complex systems." In *Complex systems design & management*, pp. 99–111. Springer, Berlin, Heidelberg, 2010.
6. Cleveland, W.S., Data science: an action plan for expanding the technical areas of the field of statistics. *Int. Stat. Rev.*, 69, 1, pp. 21–26, 2001.
7. Coles, E., Wells, M., Maxwell, M., Harris, F.M., Anderson, J., Gray, N.M., Milner, G., MacGillivray, S., The influence of contextual factors on healthcare quality improvement initiatives: what works, for whom, and in what setting? Protocol for a realist review. *Syst. Rev.*, 6, 1, 168, 2017.
8. Cao, L., Actionable knowledge discovery and delivery. *Wiley Interdisciplinary Rev. Data Mining Knowl. Discovery*, 2, 2, 149–163, 2012.
9. Cao, L., Data science: a comprehensive overview. *ACM Comput. Surv. (CSUR)*, 50, 3, pp. 1–42, 2017.
10. Cao, L. and Zhang, C., Domain-driven actionable knowledge discovery in the real world, in: *Pacific-Asia Conference on Knowledge Discovery and Data Mining*, pp. 821–830, Springer, Berlin, Heidelberg, 2006, April.
11. Cao, L., Zhao, Y., Zhang, H., Luo, D., Zhang, C., Park, E.K., Flexible frameworks for actionable knowledge discovery. *IEEE Trans. Knowl. Data Eng.*, 22, 9, 1299–1312, 2009.
12. Caron, F., Vanthienen, J., Baesens, B., Healthcare analytics: Examining the diagnosis–treatment cycle. *Procedia Technol.*, 9, 0, pp. 996–1004, 2013.
13. Gruber, T.R., Toward principles for the design of ontologies used for knowledge sharing? *Int. J. Hum. Comput. Stud.*, 43, 5–6, 907–928, 1995.
14. Fantuzzo, J. and Culhane, D.P. (Eds.), *Actionable intelligence: Using integrated data systems to achieve a more effective, efficient, and ethical government*, Springer, 2015.
15. Fantuzzo, J., *Actionable intelligence: Building and using research capacity to close the achievement gap*, Keynote address at the 13th annual Cross-University Collaborative Mentoring Conference, New York City, 2013.
16. Islam, M.S., Hasan, M.M., Wang, X., Germack, H.D., A systematic review of healthcare analytics: application and theoretical perspective of data mining, in: *Healthcare*, vol. 6, p. 54, Multidisciplinary Digital Publishing Institute, 2018 June.
17. ICPerMed, *Action plan. Actionable research and support activities identified by the International Consortium for Personalised Medicine*, vol. 2017, International Consortium, 2017. https://www.icpermed.eu/
18. Jiang, F., Jiang, Y., Zhi, H., Dong, Y., Li, H., Ma, S., Wang, Y., Dong, Q., Shen, H., Wang, Y., Artificial intelligence in healthcare: past, present, and future. *Stroke Vascular Neurol.*, 2, 4, 230–243, 2017.
19. Kursuncu, U., Gaur, M., Sheth, A., Knowledge infused learning (K-IL): Towards deep incorporation of knowledge in deep learning, in: *arXiv preprint arXiv*, 2019, 1912.00512.

20. Mitus, A.J. and Coughlin, L., The value of actionable content in a clinical setting: access to better information facilitates enhanced cancer care. *Am. Health Drug Benefits*, 6, 2, 104, 2013.
21. Pomp, A., Paulus, A., Kirmse, A., Kraus, V., Meisen, T., Applying semantics to reduce the time to analytics within complex heterogeneous infrastructures. *Technologies*, 6, 3, 86, 2018.
22. Altiner, M., Secginli, S., Mathiason, M. A., & Monsen, K. A., Method development for describing content of multitasked interventions using the Omaha System. Research and theory for nursing practice, 33(2), 147–168, 2019.
23. Raghupathi, W. and Raghupathi, V., An overview of health analytics. *J. Health Med. Informat.*, 4, 132, 2, 2013.
24. Raghupathi, W. and Raghupathi, V., Big data analytics in healthcare: promise and potential. *Health Inf. Sci. Syst.*, 2, 1, 3, 2014.
25. Rao, R., From unstructured data to actionable intelligence. *IT Professional*, 5, 6, pp. 29–35, 2003.
26. Sahoo, A.K., Mallik, S., Pradhan, C., Mishra, B.S.P., Barik, R.K., Das, H., Intelligence-based health recommendation system using big data analytics, in: *Big Data Analytics for Intelligent Healthcare Management*, pp. 227–246, Academic Press, 2019.
27. Tan, S.Y. and Chan, T., Defining and conceptualizing actionable insight: a conceptual framework for decision-centric analytics, in: *arXiv preprint arXiv*, 2016, 1606.03510.
28. Tudorache, T., Ontology engineering: Current state, challenges, and future directions, in: *Semantic Web*, pp. 1–14, 2020, (Preprint).
29. Wu, M., Wang, Z., Zhang, A., Kong, X., A research on spatial information service based on geo-ontology, in: *International Symposium on Spatial Analysis, Spatial-Temporal Data Modeling, and Data Mining*, vol. 7492, p. 74924E, International Society for Optics and Photonics, 2009, October.
30. Nandini, D., *Semantic Web, and Ontology*, Bookboon, 2014.
31. Vesteghem, Charles, *et al.* "Implementing the FAIR Data Principles in precision oncology: review of supporting initiatives." Briefings in bioinformatics 21.3 (2020): 936–945.
32. What is Semantic Technology? (2018). Ontotext.Com. https://www.ontotext.com/knowledgehub/fundamentals/semantic-web-technology/
33. Brock, Timothy R. "Performance analytics: the missing big data link between learning analytics and business analytics." Performance Improvement 56, no. 7 (2017): 6–16.
34. https://www.healthcatalyst.com/wp-content/uploads/2014/08/5-Reasons-Healthcare-Data-Is-Unique-and-Difficult-to-Measure.pdf, http://www.illuminationworksllc.com/wpcontent/uploads/2017/06/ILW-Data-Science.pdf

6

Intelligent Agent System Using Medicine Ontology

Tintu Thomas[1]* and R. Mervin[2]

[1]*Department of Public Health, Saudi Electronic University, Riyadh, Saudi Arabia*
[2]*Department of Information Technology, Saudi Electronic University, Riyadh, Saudi Arabia*

Abstract

Retrieval of accurate medical information is a big challenge in today's time due to the enormous growth of medical literature. Ontologies are used to enhance databases in different levels and can be used to eliminate vagueness in the structured query language of the database. Here we depict ontology based information of retrieval from medical literature database MEDLINE. The main focus of this article is to enhance the features of information retrieval of medical literature database and make more clarity to the search. In this research, our approach is a preliminary design and execution of ontology based intelligent agent system with application of Semantic Web language which benefits efficient systematic retrieval of medical information.

MEDLINE Ontology system will be very useful in the area of medical and health sciences. Medicine information details can be retrieved with a much easier way. It will reduce the cognitive burden of MEDLINE information search. It can be overcome difficulty faced in the traditional database and provides more accuracy level of semantic outcome for the query. To get a better accurate result, the precision of the query can be tested with the help of reasoners. The present research dealt with the application ontology based intelligence system for the semantic search in the field of medicine. The domain ontology was created and the system includes various phases namely pre-processing, rule based approach and reasoning of the user query. At the final stage, the validity was checked, the correctness of the query was identified with the help of reasoner, and most relevant result was established.

**Corresponding author*: thomas.tintu@gmail.com

Vishal Jain, Jyotir Moy Chatterjee, Ankita Bansal and Abha Jain (eds.) Semantic Web for Effective Healthcare, (139–158) © 2022 Scrivener Publishing LLC

***Keywords*:** Semantic web, ontology, web ontology language, description logic, fuzzy reasoning and semantic web rule language

6.1 Introduction to Semantic Search

Semantic search states to the query understanding, data understanding and suitable depiction of knowledge permitting meaningful retrieval. Semantic search is also referred to as search with meaning [1]. It helps to achieve the high level accuracy and pertinence by distinguishing three vital perspectives called meaning, context, and intent of the inquiry given by the user. A sort of modifiable semantic structure, in which the system can recover the information from a relational database and supports an effective ranking on bibliographic content established on the different cross reference in scientific articles [2]. A combination of semantic and statistical techniques can too be utilized to retrieve information from XML database in which weight to rank the results built on structural locations in the terms in XML files [3]. In a typical semantic web classified into two distinctive types called as ontological and instant data. In the actual data, the user is seeking for individual class effect but in the case of ontology, the knowledge domain and the relationship is designated predominantly as class relationships. Semantic search is facilitated via intensifying the query part or by interacting with the various entity features, which gives an idea of utmost recurrent entities to make narrow down the retrieved information [4].

6.1.1 What Is an Ontology in Terms of Medicine?

Ontology is an unambiguous representation, which include common concept defined in a great semantic way of characterization that is needed in a complex situation [5]. In the branch of medicine, Ontology defines the important concepts of medical terminologies and also tells the interconnections, so it is one of the possible way to share medical knowledge. However, ontology based studies were related to a risk and inaccuracies in modeling may worse the quality of result [6]. Mainly ontologies consist of Individuals, Classes, attributes, relations, function terms, restrictions, rules and axioms. The individual instance or objects which are one of the essential parts of ontology, the classes are a concept that is additionally called types, sort, category, etc. Relation which tells how classes and individuals associated. The function term referred to as a complex structure generated based on specific relations and can be replaced by a specific word. Individuals or instance contribute the essential component which makes ontology, Classes can be additionally called either type or category and kind is specified to be an extension. Objects can be categorized in ontology that was utilized in a way to compare with similar type of things particularly traits. The similar type of things are described as attributes, though it could not be dependent on each other and attributes are the possible parameters of the object. And it is represented as either class or individual. Connections indicate the relation about objects. Usually connection describes the specific relation and sort of logic by which they are classified within.

6.1.2 Needs and Benefits of Ontology in Medical Search

Ontology can offer assistance to construct more stronger and interactive system of information in healthcare. In an ontology, the formal definition denotes conventional description about common conceptualization. It implies approved or comprehensive model of a problem domain. Ontology has some benefits, that is capable of making resolution to semantic diversity, which exists in data. Ontology characterizes the link of various sorts of semantic information. It especially help to determine the aspects of inquiries and different common search approaches, as a result to enhance query items that are introduced for medical professionals. Ontology is directly understandable to the machines and human can also process it [7].

In medical practice, the patients take shift from acknowledging their doctors or specialist, now actively search the resource for information which bother their wellbeing. Major therapeutics sites like mayo clinic and Medscape were user focused and give enough information to customers viz counsel and details related to common therapeutic subjects [8]. Ontologies provide steady vocabularies and word representing vital information inside knowledge fields. The ontology alludes the knowledge and various understanding of area of interest and can merge to form the framework. This can epitomize objects, concepts, descriptions related between them [8, 9].

A lot of significant work is offered to demonstrate the therapeutically concepts that can be represented in description logic [10] and are thoroughly connected by formalism of Conceptual Graphs [11, 12]. Ontology utilizes description logic to designate content present that is available for use, for example illness conditions, anatomical features, processes, etc. Nonetheless, even though both formalism and ontology worked together, they share numerous attributes, and some contrasts specifications [12]. A guideline is a basis for the creation of the number of ontologies inside a given healthcare set-up and these ontologies can at that point to be utilized to help identify tasks and subtasks, which are needed by those implementing the instruction from a different perspective [13].

The benefit of content task ontologies is to contain contextualization of ontologies, giving ontologies tailored to a particular perspective, break difficulties that are included for generating ontology to diversified stages, providing plan using better suggestions comprised of strategies which need to incorporate with medical practice [13]. One of the important challenges in the healthcare area is to make sure the interaction among healthcare system. Ontology can assist to construct robust and more interoperable information system. It can also be a part big contribution to the essential requirement of the healthcare process for reuse, transmitting and sharing of personal data of the patient. The utilization of ontology in medicine is mostly concentrated on the representation and organization or reorganization of medical terminologies. If it is comprehensible, ontology is a critical component to several resolutions in medical terminology field [14].

6.2 Sematic Search

Semantic search help to reduce the search and offers the most relevant end result. It can be achieved through ontology which signifies the knowledge semantically. The literature review explained in a comprehensive manner towards the information of different related studies and existing methods of intelligent agent system for sematic search in the field of medicine.

6.2.1 How NLP Works in Sematic Search?

Semantic search can be explained in way that it allows meaningful search. In the case of text, the meaning stated the way of natural language. While considering the knowledge base, most meaning embedded in its configuration and it components were considered as natural language. The basic methods to identify features of meaning in the natural language elucidated with the help of different techniques. They include POS tagging, chunking, entity recognition, disambiguation, sentence parsing, and word vectors.

6.2.2 Part of Speech Tagging and Chunking

Part-of-Speech (POS) tagging, the role designated that to allocate to each word of particular sentence tag from a pre-defined form designates the word's linguistic character in that sentence. POS tagging defined in two separate subsections.

In the first case: Suppose a given a sentence s = (w1, . . . wn) and a set of accessible POS tags T, the resulting output in the form a sequence t1, t2, . . . tn that gives every single word wi a corresponding tag ti ∈ T.

Following is an example of a general POS tag

NN (noun), VB (verb), adjective (JJ), RB (adverb)

Based on the application of various situation POS tagging defer, the tags can differentiate between the types of nouns either it is singular (NN) or Plural (NNS) nous. Similarly, it also distinguishes between regular adverb (RB), comparative adverb (RBR), and superlative adverb (RBS).

Shallow parsing or chucking is one of the important problems that may be arise related to POS tagging. The role chunking can be recognize, then tag basic constituent in the sentence like nouns, verbs, adjectives, etc., based on POS tagged words.

In the second scenario: In a given sentence s = (w_1, . . . wn) and a set of accessible chunk tags C.

While chunking, the output result recognized by triples (si, ei, ci), where si considered as starting index, ei the ending index, ci ∈ C were category in chunk i.

General chunking tags can be explained in the following way,

NP is (noun phrase), VB is (verb phrase), ADJP is (adjective phrase)

In the usual cases, chunking is the preliminary stage of entity recognition and sentence parsing.

6.2.3 Sentence Parsing

The grammatical structure of a sentence can be distinguished with the help of sentence parsing. Constituent parse and the dependency parse are the two important types of commonly used representation in sentence parsing. In the case of constituent parse, the sentence is initially fragmented, then again fragmented into smaller components, and the process is repeated until the chunking is accomplished.

A constituent parse of a sentence can be narrated in a tree structure with each word represented in leaves form. And the internal nodes denote the classes present in the word orders matching in the sub tree.

An example narrated as follows

- noun phrase (NP),
- verb phrase (VP),
- Subordinate clause (SBAR), or independent clause (S).
- The root in the tree denoted as S

The dependency parse, each word of the sentence exactly based another word of sentence, it is head; the root in tree leads to the key verb in the sentence. Independency parse sentences can be represented as a tree with each word as nodes. Each node has exactly directed to one head. And the edge denoted with the grammatical connection among words.

6.2.4 Discussion About the Various Semantic Search in Medical Databases

Natural Language Processing (NLP) has the potential role to solve the issues in the biomedical field by extracting and structuring text based biomedical data, making this information accessible for current utilize and future analysis [15]. There are a few ontology and framework that have been made these days in the field of medicine. CODE is an example which is called "Cooperative Open Environment Development Project of the Medical Informatics Group at the University of Manchester" [16]. Another one is LinkBase, which is called biomedical ontology and it has a categorized pattern, coverage, operational usage, formal and linguistic connections, jointly connected to basic linguistic knowledge, makes outstanding ontology to maintain Natural Language Processing and Understanding (NLP or NLU) and information incorporation applications [17]. MedO is also a biomedical ontology established at the Institute of "Formal Ontology and Medical Information Systems, Germany." Basic Model of Anatomy is an ontology which specifies comprehensible form of unambiguous disclosed information regarding human anatomical structure. The Consortium of Ontology of Geneva which purposes to create an organized dictionary, which fits to all category of entities as knowledge though the role of genes or proteins in the cell is collecting or altering [14].

The information provided are utilized to update the anatomy based ontology, counting frame-based configurations (for example "Foundational model of Life anatomy") and description logic (e.g., GALEN, SNOMED

CT®) [18]. The gene ontology (GO) [19] is one of the greatest effective and commonly used ontology for biological data illustration. The Sequence Ontology (SO) is another sort of ontology to represent genomic features and their interrelationships. Ontology encompasses types need to update a genome with essential features and the terms required for the annotation of genomic variants [20]. Support vector machines (SVMs) techniques utilized in the classification of extracted gene ontology terms were suitable in c DNA sequence or not [21]. One of novel ontology and whale optimization support vector machine method called OWSVM, which is utilized in the selection of kernel parameters in the heart diseases data sets [22]. A smart body environment structure utilized an ontology oriented method, which recognized patients wellbeing stages and make available appropriate actions and ontology used specially in the essential health surveillance of COPD patient [23].

The search ontology generator (SONG) make complicated enquiries from excel template and once it is made, it can be used again, these characteristics look after clarity of the search and reproducibility, an permitted authority of post market surveillance of therapeutic devices [24]. Ontology for Micro RNA target (OMIT), which is used for semantic annotation, data integration and semantic search [25]. From the original search query, greatest resemblance term was selected from ontology to be integrated to the search query and semantic similarity utilized for query expansion, and it was mainly achieved by distance concepts in the ontology and hierarchy position [26]. Thought entities, language primitives, knowledge representation (KR) primitives, and query elements are a set of models, which was utilized to gain information related to mental, user system and query [27]. A search based multiple ontology can also be used to capture information retrieval effectively. It has the capability of rewrite the user query by including sematic information with the help of multiple ontologies [28].

6.2.5 Discussion About the Retrieval Tools Used in Sematic Search in Medline

Abundant biological information stored through the years is presently accessible in the online text repositories called as Medline. This information is very important for biomedical researchers in their action plan and performs new experiments and results in validation [29]. A unique structure of MEDLINE is that the records are indexed by NLM (national library of medicine) medical subject Headings (MeSH®). Medline is one of the major components of PubMed, a portion of the Entrenz Series of the database. Medline Ranker is a web server which permits an adaptable ranking in Medline for a subject of interest with limited knowledge and if the input comprises thoroughly connected abstracts, the program gives back to relevant abstracts from the latest bibliography with great accuracy [30].

For free-text and natural language query, we can utilize AskMEDLINE, which will help in exploring MEDLINE or PubMed. It takes advantage of multi round search approach. Initially parser does not include the punctuation or remove arguments present in "stop-word." Stop word data contains "PubMed stop words" or arguments based on knowledge, which was not favorable for previous analysis. Parser, a PHP script post updated request via PubMed "Entrez E-Utilities." The Extensible Markup Language (XML) file received from E-Utilities specifies required type of information [31]. MEDLINE filters were used to improve searching method, with the help of these filters clinical users easily get information without searching the entire MEDLINE database. Researchers used two important types of filters namely "Method" and "Content."

The first one recognizes the articles of great methodological precision for the therapeutic method of health problems, not dependent on any clinical discipline [32, 33]. The high performance filters are presently part of PubMed interface and which can also right to use with the help of Clinical Queries field. The second type called "content filters" were more applicable in the area of clinical practice [32] ("content" filter) [34]. BioMedLEE is a system that identifies a broad range of phenotypic information with good precision from the biomedical literature and the issues related to this were easy for resolution [15]. Researchers used domain specific knowledge for the utilization of information in the system of chromosome location and gene expression localization [29]. SciMiner is web based literature mining and functional analysis tool that explores gene and proteins with the application of context specific analysis of MEDlLINE abstract and full texts [29]. It is also particularly helpful when the situation of lack of full text bodies [35].

6.3 Structural Pattern of Semantic Search

In the general domain, the identification of semantic connections among entities utilized either statistical methods or machine learning techniques based on the form of linguistic model [36] or combined use of both methods. In the field of medicine, Relation Extraction (RE) system usually utilizes, as knowledge base, UMLS (unified Medical language system) [37]. A proposed system was used to extract a different kind of relations namely detect, treat, sign, and cure among medical entities [38].

6.3.1 Architectural Diagram

The research emphasis the features of information retrieval from medical literature database and improve the quality of the search with the help of ontology based system. The overall process consists of various phases which include the pre-processing procedure, keyword extraction construction of rules and query reasoning. In the last step include the validation technique implementation which will help to produce the net effect of most relevant and accurate result.

The primary step of this process is the knowledge extraction and followed by preprocessing. The Parts of Speech (POS) method is used in which the grammatical medical information type is assigned to each word in a text. The POS tagger used by the system search information from the user query. The search process within the ontology can be demonstrated by the stemming method, which helps to identify the root word of the medicine. The system will provide the result of the query of the existing medicine information stored in the ontology. If it is not, the ontology is updated with a novel key word. The query can be understood in a better way with the help of parse tree method. The ontological parser has two important functional elements namely lexer and a parser. The sentence lexers take a sentence and change that into a sequence of ontological entities and parser which convert the sequence of ontological entities into predicate structures.

SVM based tagger was used in Tej Bahadur *et al.* [39] study in which, it showed an efficient, portable, accessible, and trainable. Support vector machine (SVM) was introduced in supervised learning method and showed good performance and generalization ability. SVM has been effectively implemented in text classification and revealed that SVM can handle enormous features and is resist of over fitting [39]. Figures 6.1 and 6.2 represent the schematic presentation of architectural diagram and parse tree method respectively.

[S [NP List] [DT the] [NP [NP components] [IN of] [NP Tylenol]]]

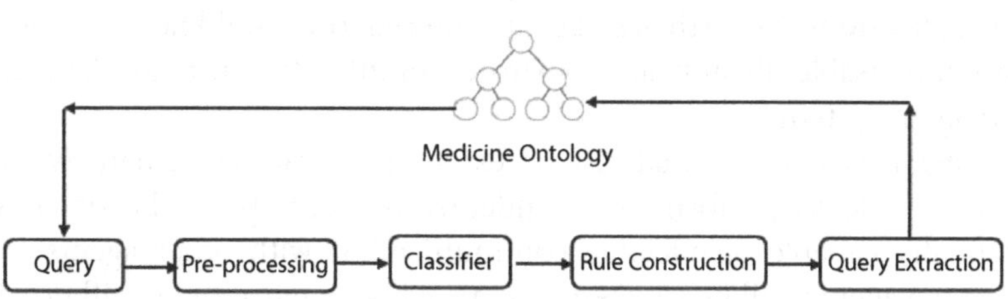

Figure 6.1 Architecture diagram.

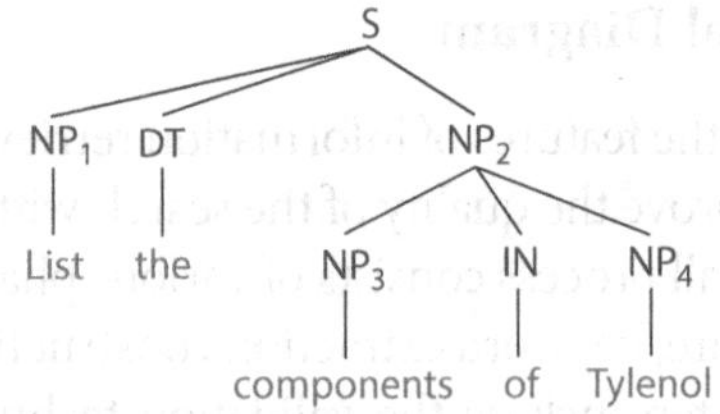

Figure 6.2 Parse tree of medicine.

6.3.2 Agent Ontology

Ontologies describe the usage of vocabulary includes the agents, their characteristics functionalities, and the operating domains. A multi-agent system allows an application developer to fragment a complex assignment into the easiest subtasks. According to its role, the individual agents will get a specific task. In the context of multi-agent system can be described by two organizations. The distribution of tasks to agents identifies the task-based organization of MAS development. Knowledge is embedded in agents is an integral part of the knowledge depends on organization. In a single agent in a MAS system, it is essential for three different sources of knowledge namely domain knowledge, agent knowledge, and computational knowledge. Agents control information related to some specific application domain and the domain knowledge can be integrated into domain ontology.

There is an essential need to the structuring of domain-based knowledge shared between various agents and use again for making multi agent system that works on same kind of domains. The agent must know the characteristic features of the interacting or connecting agents. Proper agent ontology definitely helps in the explanation of a set of common and unambiguous features to portray the various classes of agents. The semantic web offers heterogeneous, dissimilated information, permit applications to communicate user requirements and obtain data resources. Agents contribute highly and are capable to provide skills in progress of Semantic Web applications. Nevertheless, agent centered tools could not be achieved commonly usable till sufficient expansion of infrastructures availability of multi agent system [40].

An agent is a system that require essential characteristic namely environment, able to perform independently to accomplish the objectives and finally capable of effective communication with other agents [41]. Hence the agents will be situated systems where environment will provide

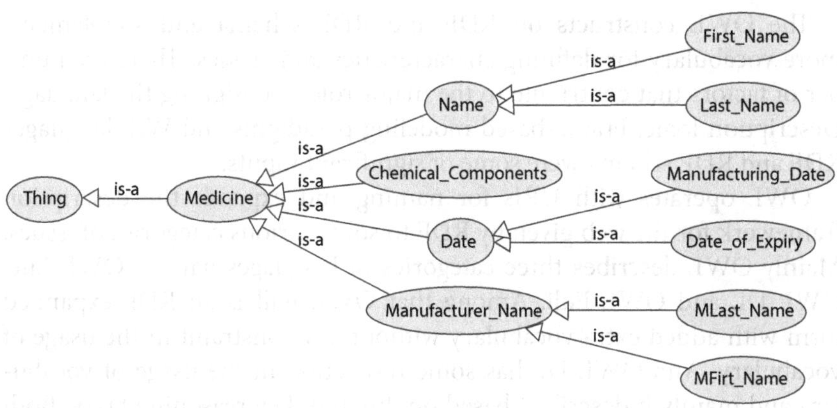

Figure 6.3 Medicine ontology.

necessary facts for agents to execute. Therefore, great sematic web will make agent oriented computations useful pattern to analyze [40, 42]. The HealthCare Agent executes medical facility supplier catalog, implementing search with a catalog centered around agents' queries. The queries can be completed with the help of keywords characterized by ontology. Agent will identify the exact service details based on request ontology [40]. An example of medicine ontology shown in Figure 6.3.

6.3.3 Rule-Based Approach

Ontology use rule based method which is written in OWL. SWRL is the semantic web rule language of Semantic web. The Web ontology Language (OWL) is a family of knowledge demonstration language and the ontologies are the explicit method to designate taxonomies and classification networks mainly it describes the structure of knowledge for different domains. Even though ontology shows similarity to class hierarchies in object-oriented programming there are many differences. The OWL languages are specified by recognized semantics. It is constructed on the world wide web consortium (W3c) XML format for an object known as Resource Description Framework (RDF). The OWL is a computational language that depends on logic and the OWL documents, called as ontologies, available or issued through the world wide web, and it can make reference from other ontologies. OWL is a component of the W3C's Semantic Web technology stack, which contains RDF, RDFS, SPARQL, etc.

The OWL constructs on RDF and RDF schema and supplements more vocabulary for defining characteristics and classes. There are number of factors that contribute to the major role in designing the language. Description logic, Frame-based modeling paradigms and Web languages RDF and RDF schema were some of significant inputs.

OWL operates with URIs for naming and expands the description framework for the web given by RDF to solve various categories of issues. Mainly OWL describes three categories of languages namely OWL Lite, OWL DL and OWL Full. Among that OWL Full is an RDF expanded form with added extra vocabulary without any constraint in the usage of vocabulary. And OWL DL has some restriction in the usage of vocabulary and mainly it described based on different key reasoning tasks. Both OWL DL and OWL Lite focused on model theoretical semantics based on Description logic and enables the utilization of DL reasoners to give reasoning support to the language.

The semantic web rule language (SWRL) utilized to show both rules as well as logic The SWRL is also known as a high-level abstract syntax for Horn like rules. And all rules were based on the terms of OWL concepts namely classes, properties, and individuals. SWRL surges the expressivity of OWL and makes it happen to model additional domain knowledge than OWL alone. The SWRL rules can be utilized in a production rule style where they used to compute outputs or the validation purpose. SWRL built-ins also give a natural way of extension mechanism whereby the modeling language can be improved with domain-specific built-ins.

Both OWL (Web Ontology Language) and SWRL (Semantic Web Rule Language) gives the path to denote information in the form of a sequence in associated terms. However, SWRL implement rule that operates on OWL. SWRL rules are built in antecedent consequent pairs denoted by rule body and head. SWRL rule and ontology model is implementing to signify the complex relationships and validation process will be done with the help of reasoner. The rules of construction schematically represented in Figure 6.4.

Rule 1: hasName(?x, ?y) ->hasFName(?x, ?y), hasLName(?x, ?y)

Rule 2: Medicine (?x), hasName(?x, ?y), hasDate(?y) ->hasMName(?x, ?y)

Rule 3: Medicine (?x), hasDate(?x, ?y), hasMDate(?y) ->hasEDate(?x, ?y)

Rule 4: hasDate (?x, ?z) ->hasMDate(?x, ?y), hasEDate(?x, ?y)

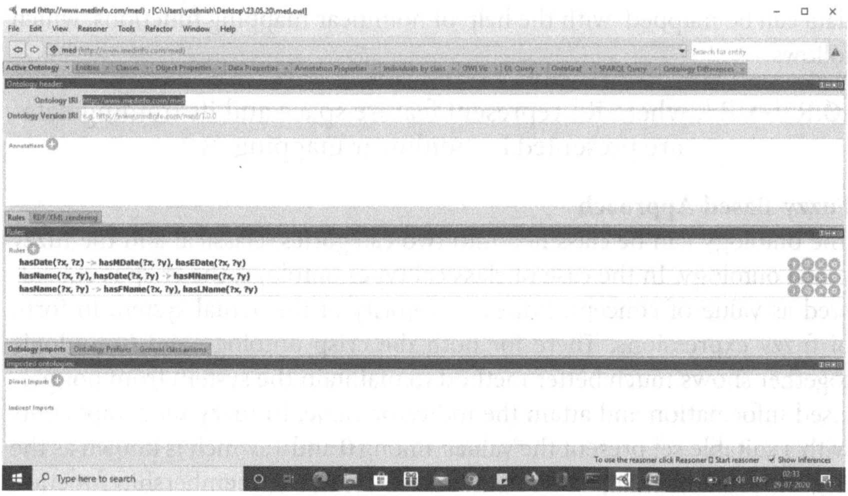

Figure 6.4 Rules of construction.

6.3.4 Reasoners-Based Approach

SVM-Based Approach

An SVM is a supervised learning method mainly used for classification purpose, and it has the capability to identify best probable boundaries to distinguish the relevant samples from irrelevant samples. One of the major goal of an SVM to identify a maximum margin hyper plane behind the training process to solve the classification problem. The first step in SVM, it makes a training data set model and works that model to reach facts for a testing data sets. Once the pre-processing process of retrieved documents done, the text categorization can do with the following procedure

$\emptyset : (DS \times CS) \rightarrow \{R, IR\}$, where DS and CS denotes sets of documents and categories, respectively

If $\emptyset : (DS \times CS) = R$, then DSi is a significant member of CSj,

And

DSi is not a relevant member of CSj, if $\emptyset : (DS \times CS) = IR$.

The algorithms were focus to categorize the text or review sentences. The SVM function offers a value of (+1) for the most significant data points, and a value of (−1) in non-significant or irrelevant cases. And the training data can be mapped with the help of nonlinear mapping functions, which follows

$$\emptyset: R^{N} \rightarrow R^{F}, \text{ where } R^{F} \text{ represent feature space and its training data are presented by nonlinear mapping } R^{N}$$

Fuzzy-Based Approach

The ontology can be classified into two categories, classical and the fuzzy based ontology. In the case of classical types ontology, the crisp is considered as value of concept, however majority of the actual system in form of fuzzy expressions. There for both the crisp ontology and fuzzy logic together shows much better method to maintain the system from not précised information and attain the indicator value. In fuzzy set components with a suitable set present the values among 0 and 1, which is known as the degree of membership. In a mathematical way, the membership function μF can be utilized to describe fuzzy set, F, and A, which states element A in the interval zero and one

$$\mu F\,(A) : A\ 0 \rightarrow [0, 1]$$

The fuzzy inference layer mainly composed of four elements; they are fuzzification, inference, defuzzification, and knowledge-and rule-based ontology. Fuzzy ontologies encompass all visited URLs, supporting words, therapeutical terms, improper expressions, and normal words. It also gives a semantic web rule language (SWRL) rule-based knowledge platform for relevant information mining and intelligent classification to automatically recognize the type of webpage or document. The use of ontology helpful to specify different category of information, which includes features and key words. The user's query for a URL is allocated to the web crawler, the content information's were retrieved, and keywords and values are then mined from the retrieved information with the help of the fuzzy ontology to compute the indicator value for the decision making system. Moreover, knowledge- and SWRL-rule-based ontology states rules (if–then) for the decision system. The fuzzy inference layer is combined with the ontology to certainly mine information and find the relevant document type.

6.4 Implementation of Reasoners

Reasoners will identify unreliable ontologies but it does not support the diagnosis and resolution of the bug. To validate and improve the correctness of the keywords based on the semantic context of the information can be done by Fuzzy Reasoning. Fuzzy ontologies were applied in diversified domains [43], namely in human behavior [44], modeling in the diabetes field especially in diet and diagnosis [45]. The application of fuzzy ontology with a rule based system is not widely used compared to another system because of its essential needs to bring together unambiguous models of domains [43].

Mainly there are five important steps involved in the reasoners based approach, they are as follows:

Step 1
Extract information from the knowledge base
Step 2
Identify any inconsistent ontology
Step 3
Perform the correctness check using fuzzy reasoner
Step 4
Generate new rule
Step 5
Accomplish the validation of the inference

6.5 Implementation and Results

In the final stage of the medicine information retrieval can be achieved SPARQL (Simple Protocol and RDF Query Language) which SPARQL agrees for a query to involve of triple patterns, conjunctions, disjunctions, and optional patterns. The medicine ontology executed with the help of SPARQL SPARQL query output displayed in Figure 6.5.

```
PREFIX rdf: <http://www.w3.org/1999/02/22-rdf-syntax-ns#>
PREFIX owl: <http://www.w3.org/2002/07/owl#>
PREFIX rdfs: <http://www.w3.org/2000/01/rdf-schema#>
PREFIX xsd: <http://www.w3.org/2001/XMLSchema#>
PREFIX med: <http://www.medinfo.com/med#>
SELECT ?Medicine ?MComp
  WHERE { ?Medicine med:MComp ?MComp}
```

6.6 Conclusion and Future Prospective

Ontology defines dependencies between entities, which permits an RDF store to enhance users' answers with relevant results not explicitly defined

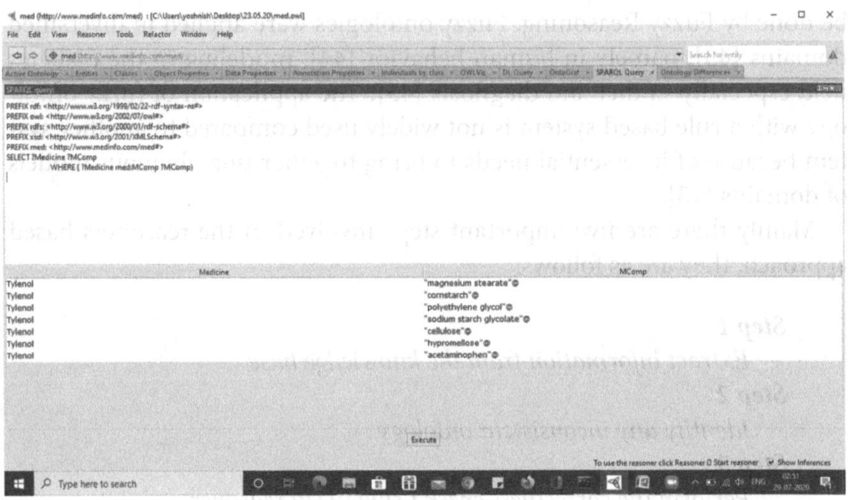

Figure 6.5 SPARQL query output.

in the data. Queries are usually expressed in SPARQL, and the key computational service of RDF stores is to assess queries over both the explicit facts and the facts implied by the background knowledge. The retrieval of queries result with respect to arbitrary OWL ontologies is often not much easily feasible in practice because of high computational complexity and an enormous amount of stored information.

Though the SWRL rule were capable to make efficient expression ability of owl based ontologies and rule based approach is one of the promising methods for giving users with favorable query services. In addition to the use of general rule based approach, look forward to implement in statistics based method in the future work. In the future research stem focus on expansion approach of SWRL probability extension techniques, which integrated with reasoning method and it will execute to handle uncertainties and make more efficient query services for active users.

References

1. Bast, H., Björn, B., Haussmann, E., Semantic search on text and knowledge bases. *Found. Trends Inf. Retrieval*, 10, 119–271, 2016.
2. Balmin, A., Hristidis, V., Papakonstantinou, Y., Object Rank: Authority-based keyword search in databases. *Proceedings of the 30th VLDB Conference*, pp. 564–575, 2004.

3. Kotsakis, E., Structured Information Retrieval in XML documents. *Proceedings of the seventeenth ACM Symposium on Applied Computing*, pp. 663–667, 2002.
4. Axel, J.S., Przybyła., P., Ananiadou., S., Thalia., Semantic search engine for biomedical abstracts. *Bioinformatics*, 35, 10, 1799–1801, 2019.
5. Feilmayr, C. and Wolfram, W., An Analysis of Ontologies and their Success Factors for Application to Business. *Data Knowl. Eng.*, 101, 1–23, 2016.
6. Aldosari., B., Alanazi., A., Househ., M., Pitfalls of ontology in medicine. *Study Health Technol. Inform.*, 238, 15–18, 2017.
7. Gomez-Perez, A. and Corcho., O., Ontology languages for the Semantic Web. *IEEE Intell. Syst.*, 17, 1, 54–60, 2002.
8. Leroy, G. and Chen, H., Meeting Medical Terminology Needs: The Ontology-enhanced Medical Concept Mapper. *IEEE Trans. Inf. Technol. BioMed.*, 5, 4, 261–270, 2001.
9. Gruber, T., A translation approach to portable ontology specifications. *Knowledge Acquisition*, 5, 199–220, 1993.
10. MacGregor, R., The evolving technology of classification-based knowledge representation systems, in: *Principles of Semantic Networks: Explorations in the representation of knowledge*, pp. 385–400, 1991.
11. Aubert, J.P., Baget, J.F., Chein, M., Simple conceptual graphs and simple concept graphs. *14th International Conference on Conceptual Structures – Proceedings*, pp. 87–101, 2006.
12. Rector, A.L., Zanstra, P.E., Solomon, W.D., Rogers, J.E., Baud, R. *et al.*, Reconciling Users' Needs and Formal Requirements: Issues in developing a Re-Usable Ontology for Medicine. *IEEE Trans. Inf. Technol. BioMed.*, 2, 4, 229–242, 1999.
13. Kumar., A., Ciccarese., P., Smith., B., Piazza., M., Context-Based Task Ontologies for Clinical Guidelines—Ontologies in Medicine. *Proc. Workshop Med. Ontol.*, V102, 81–94, 2004.
14. Manika., P., Xhumari., E., Ktona., A., Demiri., A., Application of ontologies and semantic web technologies in the field of medicine. *Proc. of the 3rd International Conference on Recent Trends and Applications in Computer Science and Technology*, v-2280, 24–30, 2018.
15. Chen, L. and Friedman, C., Extracting phenotypic information from the literature via natural language processing. *Medinfo*, 11, 2, 758–762, 2004.
16. Musen, M.A. *et al.*, The Protégé Project: A Look Back and a Look Forward. AI Matters., 1, 4, 4–12, 2015.
17. van Gurp., M., Decoene., M., Holvoet., M., Casella dos, M., LinKBase a Philosophically-inspired Ontology for NLP/NLU Applications. *Proceedings of the Second International Workshop on Formal Biomedical Knowledge Representation*, pp. 67–75, 2006.
18. Zhang, S. and Bodenreider, O., Experience in Aligning Anatomical Ontologies. *Int. J. Semant Web Inf. Syst.*, 3, 2, 1–26, 2007.

19. Ashburner, M., Ball, C., Blake, J., Botstein, D., Butler, H., Cherry, J., Davis, A., Dolinski, K., Dwight, S., Eppig, J., Harris, M., Hill, D., Issel-Tarver, L., Kasarskis, A., Lewis, S., Matese, J., Richardson, J., Ringwald, M., Rubin, G., Sherlock, G., Gene ontology: Tool for the unification of biology -The gene ontology consortium. *Nat. Genet.*, 25, 1, 25–9, 20002000.
20. Eilbeck, K., Lewis, S., Mungall, C., Yandell, M., Stein, L., Durbin, R., Ashburner, M., The Sequence Ontology: a tool for the unification of genome annotations. *Genome Biol.*, 6, R44, 1–12, 2005.
21. Vinayagam., A., König., R., Moormann., J., Schubert., F., Eils., R., Glatting, K.-H., Suhai., S., Applying Support Vector Machines for Gene ontology based gene function prediction. *BMC Bioinformatics*, 5, 116, 1–14, 2004.
22. Karlekar., N.P. and Gomathi, N., OW-SVM: Ontology and whale optimization-based support vector machine for privacy-preserved medical data classification in cloud. *Int J. Commun. Syst.*, 31, 12, 1–19, 2018.
23. Ajami., H. and Mcheick., H., Ontology-Based Model to Support Ubiquitous Healthcare Systems for COPD Patients. *Electronics.*, 7, 371, 1–21, 2018.
24. Uciteli, *et al.*, Ontology-based specification and generation of search queries for post-market surveillance. *J. Biomed. Semant.*, 10, 9, 1–13, 2019.
25. Huang, *et al.*, OmniSearch: a semantic search system based on the Ontology for MIcroRNA Target (OMIT) for microRNA-target gene interaction data. *J. Biomed. Semant.*, 7, 25, 2–17, 2016.
26. Chauhan, R., Goudar, R., Sharma, R., Chauhan, A., Domain ontology based semantic search for efficient information retrieval through automatic query expansion. *Proc. Intelligent Systems and Signal Processing (ISSP)*, pp. 397–402, 2013.
27. Tran, T., Cimiano, P., Rudolph, S., Studer, R., *Ontology-based interpretation of keywords for semantic search*, pp. 523–536, Springer-Verlag Berlin Heidelberg, 2007.
28. Viji Rajendran, V. and Swamynathan, S., MOSS-IR: Multi-Ontology based Search System for Information Retrieval in E-health Domain. *Procedia Comput. Sci.*, V47, 179–187, 2015.
29. Manconi., A., Vargiu., E., Armano., G., Milanesi., L., Literature Retrieval and Mining in Bioinformatics: State of the Art and Challenges. *Adv. Bioinf.*, V2012, 1–10, 2012.
30. Fontaine, J.-F., Barbosa-Silva, A., Schaefer, M., Huska, M.R., Muro, E.M., Andrade-Navarro, M.A., Medline Ranker: Flexible ranking of biomedical literature. *Nucleic Acids Res.*, 37, 141–146, 2009.
31. Fontelo, P., Liu, F., Ackerman, M., ask MEDLINE: A free-text, natural language query tool for MEDLINE/PubMed. *BMC Med. Inf. Decision Making*, 5, 5, 1–6, 2005.
32. Garg, A.X., Iansavichus, A.V., Wilczynski, N.L., Kastner, M., Baier, L.A., Shariff, S.Z., Rehman, F., Weir, M., McKibbon, K.A., Haynes, R.B., Filtering Medline for a clinical discipline: Diagnostic test assessment framework. *BMJ*, v339, 1–5, 2009.

33. Haynes, R.B., McKibbon, K.A., Wilczynski, N.L., Walter, S.D., Werre, S.R., Optimal search strategies for retrieving scientifically strong studies of treatment from Medline: Analytical survey. *BMJ*, 330, 1179–1185, 2005.
34. Shariff., S.Z., Cuerden., M.S., Haynes., R.B., McKibbon., K.A., Wilczynski., N.L., Iansavichus, A.V., Speechley., M.R., Thind, A., Garg., A.X., Evaluating the impact of MEDLINE filters on evidence retrieval: Study protocol. *Implementation Sci.*, 5, 58, 1–28, 2010.
35. Hur, J., Schuyler, A.D., States, D.J., Feldman, E.L., SciMiner: Web-based literature mining tool for target identification and functional enrichment analysis. *Bioinformatics*, 25, 6, 838–840, 2009.
36. Hearst, M.A., Automatic acquisition of hyponyms from large text corpora. *Proceedings of the 14th conference on Computational linguistics*, pp. 268–275, 1992.
37. Bodenreider, O., The unified medical language system (UMLS): Integrating biomedical terminology. *Nucleic Acids Res.*, 32, 1, 267–270, 2004.
38. Embarek, M. and Ferret, O., Learning Patterns for Building Resources about Semantic Relations in the Medical Domain. *Proceedings of the International Conference on Language Resources and Evaluation*, pp. 2006–2012, 2008.
39. Shahi., T.B., Dhamala., T.N., Balami., B., Support Vector Machines based Part of Speech Tagging for Nepali Text. *Int. J. Comput. Appl.*, 70, 24, 38–42, 2013.
40. Blois., M., Escobar., M., Choren., R., Using agents and ontologies for application development on the semantic web. *J. Braz. Comp. Soc.*, 13, 2, 36–44, 2007.
41. Silva, N., Rocha, J., Cardoso, J., E-Business interoperability through ontology semantic mapping. *Proceedings of Processes and Foundations for Virtual Organizations*, pp. 315–322, 2003.
42. Hendler, J.A., Agents and the Semantic Web. *IEEE Intell. Syst.*, 16, 2, 30–37, 2001.
43. El-Sappag., S. and Elmogy., M., A fuzzy ontology modeling for case base knowledge in diabetes mellitus domain. *Eng. Sci. Technol.*, 20, 3, 1025–1040, 2017.
44. Rodríguez, N., Cuéllar, M., Lilius, J., Calvo-Flores, M., A fuzzy ontology for semantic modeling and recognition of human behavior. *Knowl. Based Syst.*, 66, 46–60, 2014.
45. Lee, C., Wang, M., Acampora, G., Loia, V., Hsu., C., Ontology-based intelligent fuzzy agent for diabetes application. *IA'09 IEEE Symposium on Intelligent Agents*, IEEE, pp. 16–22, 2009.

7

Ontology-Based System for Robotic Surgery—A Historical Analysis

Ajay Agarwal* **and Amit Kumar Mishra†**

Department of Computer Science & Engineering, DIT University, Dehradun, India

Abstract

Robotic systems, today, play a vital role in the sustenance of various industries. Today, robotic systems have been granted admission to the medical domain as well. Over time, academic literature has constantly upheld the human consensus regarding the popular vote for reluctance towards an automated medical procedure, even under the pretext of manual and experienced supervision. Whilst the depth of meritorious impact by automation in the field of surgery and medical sciences cannot be ignored, it also stands simultaneously crucial to empathize and analyze the possible roots of fear and the sense of reluctance in sharing trust with a robotic interface, especially in the matters of life-at-hand. In our strive for understanding robotic surgery from an ontological point-of-view, we conduct a succinct and objective meta-analysis to register and annotate the entry of robots in the field of medicine and surgery. We provide our readers with a guided entry toward the historical anthology and document the most significant interventions of robots in medical surgery. Later, we also discuss how the academic field has embraced this new discipline and how inclusive research on a worldwide scale has honed the design and method of robotic procedures, all while maintaining an impeccable metric.

***Keywords*:** Robotic pancreatoduodenectomy, transoral robotic surgery, port placement, da Vinci, minimally invasive surgery, fulcrum effect, probot, assistant port

**Corresponding author*: verslinfiniaudela@gmail.com

†*Corresponding author*: AK.mishra@dituniversity.edu.in

Vishal Jain, Jyotir Moy Chatterjee, Ankita Bansal and Abha Jain (eds.) Semantic Web for Effective Healthcare, (159–174) © 2022 Scrivener Publishing LLC

7.1 Historical Discourse of Surgical Robots

To err is an evolutionary trait of human beings. While it is true that dedicated and single-focused attention towards acquiring a particular skill can significantly reduce the margin of error, the possibility of elimination of all possible errors is a statistical lie. It is important to realize that this lack of guarantee for the elimination of all errors might not hinder or even significantly affect our daily lives and most of the professions, however, fields like surgery and medicine must fail to turn a blind eye to this fact. When the question reduces to saving another person's life, while dealing with a system as convoluted and complicated as the human body, the chances of committing an unforeseen error is increased drastically, significantly hindering possible routes toward focused attention and dilution of error margins. It is to be noted that surgery, in its most simplistic form, is just a set of many instructions that are to be conducted in a step-wise fashion given a particular observation or inference is made regarding the individual's anatomy. This reductionism of the complex nature of 21st-century studies begs to ask us the question that—Can it be automated? [5].

Human beings are creators of machines and machines are the cornerstones of automation. They work on algorithms and are unhindered to the stochastic and transient changes of the environment around them, making them most suitable to conduct activities with the significantly complex instruction set and seemingly high stakes involved. In the context of surgery done with a robotic modality, Puma 560 stands at the entrance of the race. The history of robotic surgery has been of a complex nature. Many significant strides were made from a multi-axial focus to direct the attention of organizations, individuals, and institutions towards the positive aspects and the requited need for implementation of robotic surgery as a new normal in the medical infrastructure.

Being a brainchild of Kwoh *et al.*, Puma 560 was the surgical robot of its time. It was equipped with a state-of-the-art CT scanner, probe guide, and an instruction set of such complicated nature that it allowed Puma 560 to conduct varied surgical invasions—from neurological biopsies by Kwoh to transurethral resection by Davies [10].

The successor of Puma 560 was the extremely non-ubiquitous surgical system of integrated nature developed by the Burgar and Paul, named as—Robodoc. The singular use-case of Robodoc was the conduction of prosthetic hip replacement. Equipped with a visual guiding system, this surgical helped is still in use, however, its distribution stands limited to

Asia and Europe. Robodoc and PUMA 560 had done what the parallel strides in the field could not—they democratized the field of robotic surgery [7–9]. This democratization of research in the field of robotic surgery, as depicted in Figure 7.1 and Figure 7.2, drew the attention of researchers from NASA and Stanford University, which walked into a collaboration (in the early 1990s) to further research and deployment of surgical robots with the unilateral use case. Their focus was more pivoted towards designing and deploying a dexterous telemanipulator that was capable of performing the hand surgery. As their work continued, US Army observed the potential valuation of their research and realized a need for a similar (or same) system for their armed forces. The pain point that stood out the US Army was the possibility of preventing any form of exsanguinating of wounded soldiers with the help of these advancements and mobile surgical robots [1–6].

The intervention of the US Army marked the final stage in the timeline of robotic surgery—academic and industrial commercialization. In the coming decade, robotic surgery became highly commercialized in nature. Academic institutions like MIT and Harvard jumped at the opportunity

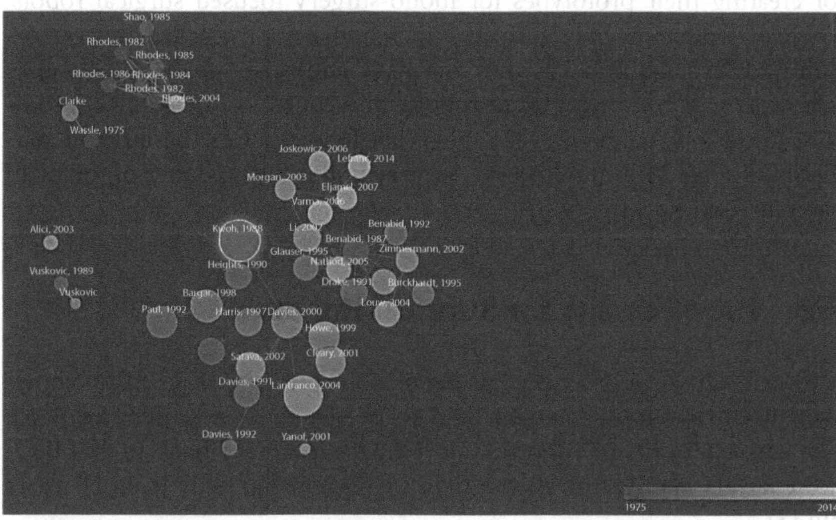

Figure 7.1 The above figure represents a graph-based representation of meta-analysis conducted by the author to depicts how the academic literature in the field of robotic surgery has evolved since the invention of PUMA 560 by Kwoh in 1988 (central node). Research conducted on semantically similar topics is clustered together with strong lines. Each node represents an academic piece of work, with the node size depicting its citation count and its color gradient based on the publication year of the research study.

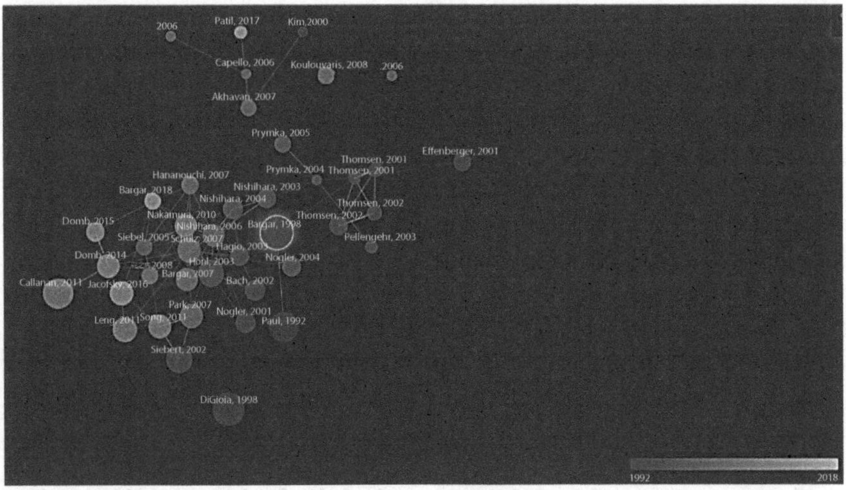

Figure 7.2 The above figure represents a graph-based representation of meta-analysis conducted by the author to depicts how the academic literature in the field of robotic surgery has evolved since the invention of Robodoc by Bargar in 1998 (central node).

for creating their prototypes for mono-surgery focused surgical robots, whereas companies like IBM, da Vinci, and Zeus in cashed this opportunity to leverage pressure over the FDA and other medical regulatory boards to pass the inclusion of robotic procedures in the surgical protocols for various countries [22–25]. What followed was the birth of subdisciplines like Minimal Invasive Surgery under the guidance of the main parent—Robotic Surgery.

7.2 The Necessity for Surgical Robots

Minimally Invasive Surgery has been subjected to various forms, however, Robotic Surgery can be said to be the most advanced of it all. The earliest works of robotics and automation trace back to 400 B.C., however, its application in the field of surgery has only been 20 years old [3].

A major role towards the establishment and development of the field has been a result of the pioneering efforts of surgeons like Archytas of Arentum and visionaries like Vinci, and Jaquet-Droz. They were the first of all to envision the idea of Minimally Invasive Surgery which acted as a founding stone toward the rise of robotic surgery.

Minimally invasive surgery was first performed in 1987. It was a laparoscopic cholecystectomy. As the list of procedures performed laparoscopically grew at an ever-increasing rate, so did the technological advancement and general refinement of the skill of surgeons. Minimally invasive surgery was an idea that the masses immediately bought upon its conception. MIS offered the public and surgeons a great number of advantages. Minimally Invasive Surgery opened a world of smaller incisions, reduced infection risks, and shorter stays in the hospital. It also enables the option to significantly reduce convalescence depending on need.

Though MIS attracted the masses and provided a simplistic system for surgery, it involved a lot of technical and mechanical difficulties. The deficit of haptic feedback, dexterity, and eye-hand coordination posed major difficulties for the surgeons. An example of the above being the movement of laparoscopic instruments in the opposite direction of interest to reach it. This nullified the coordination between hand and eye. This situation is also referred to as the "fulcrum effect."

There are 7 degrees of freedom in the human hand-wrist, this refers to the fact that the hand can independently move and rotate in a total of seven unique directions. However, the current laparoscopic instruments have only 4 degrees of freedom which again posed difficulties to the surgeons. These instruments also lack the sense of touch which makes procedures regarding manipulation of tissue visualization-dependent. Also, the physiologic tremors that were generated in a surgeon's hand while the operation was now transmitted readily across rigid instruments' length.

These limitations accounted for the reason why performing MIS with automated laparoscopic instruments makes the anastomoses and delicate dissections difficult if not impossible. The burning necessity to overcome such limitations laid the founding stones towards the conception of surgical robots.

7.3 Ontological Evolution of Robotic Surgical Procedures in Various Domains

As minimally invasive surgeries open new frontiers for technological advancements, robotic surgeries lead the charge by providing the maximum added advantages, drastically reduced hospital stays, and least counts for intraoperative complications. The surgical procedures have traveled a long way dating with the use of PUMA 560 to insert a needle to the industry being dominated by the two major corporate superpowers - ZEUS and da Vinci.

To provide a slight perspective, the following table represents the counts of complications that were encountered intra- and postoperatively during robotic surgery during a study conducted between February 2015 to July 2018 on 221 robotic surgeries performed at the Erzurum Regional Training and Research Hospital in Turkey. Patient data, such as age, gender, American Society of Anaesthesiologists (ASA) score, underlying disease, smoking habits, type of surgery, invasive procedures (arterial cannulation, or central venous catheter), laparotomy requirement, duration of anesthesia, Trendelenburg, surgery, and discharge times, amount of bleeding, and intra- and post-operative complications were recorded from the digital database system and anesthesia records during monitoring. The three broad categories under which the surgeries are grouped include—Urology, General Surgery, and Gynecology.

7.4 Inferences Drawn From the Table

Two hundred twenty-one robotic surgeries (112 [50.6%] urology, 53 [23.9%] general surgery, 46 [20.8%] gynecology, and 10 [4.5%] ENT department) were performed during the study period. Patients' median age was 61 (17–91) years. The youngest patient was operated on in the ENT department and the oldest in the general surgery department. The majority of patients were male, and most (63.3%) had ASA-II scores. Hypertension was the most frequent underlying disease. The distribution of types of surgical procedures is shown in Table 7.1.

Only 10 (4.7%) patients required laparotomy procedures. The mean duration of anesthesia and surgery was the longest in general surgery department operations. Urology department patients had the longest time to discharge. The Trendelenburg position was used only during urological and gynecological operations.

Hypotension was the most frequent intraoperative complication encountered during robotic surgeries, followed by metabolic acidosis, and bradycardia-lingual or buccal nerve damage was seen in any department. Nausea was the most frequent postoperative complication after robotic surgeries, followed by hypoxia and metabolic acidosis. No cardiac or respiratory arrest, laryngospasm, myocardial ischemia, or visual disturbance was seen in any department postoperatively. Both intra- and post-operative complications were most common in the urology department. Neither any intra- nor any post-operative complications were encountered during the ENT operations.

Table 7.1 The table shows counts of complications that were encountered intra- and postoperatively during robotic surgery during a study conducted between February 2015 and July 2018 on 221 robotic surgeries performed at the Erzurum Regional Training and Research Hospital in Turkey.

	Urology (n = 112)	General surgery (n = 53)	Gynecology (n = 46)	Total
Intra-operative Complications				
Hypotension	11	8	7	26
Hypertension	4	0	0	4
Bleeding	0	1	1	2
Tachycardia	4	0	0	4
Bradycardia	12	0	0	12
Myocardial ischemia	1	0	0	1
Hypoxia	0	1	2	3
Metabolic acidosis	8	3	2	13
Facial edema	9	0	0	9
Conjunctiva edema	11	0	0	11
Lingual edema	3	0	0	3
TOTAL	63	13	12	88
Post-operative complications				
Hypoxia	7	4	2	13
Metabolic acidosis	5	3	2	10
Respiratory acidosis	1	2	1	4
Nausea	18	4	4	26
Vomiting	7	1	1	9
Bradycardia	5	0	0	5
Tachycardia	1	0	0	1

(*Continued*)

Table 7.1 The table shows counts of complications that were encountered intra- and postoperatively during robotic surgery during a study conducted between February 2015 and July 2018 on 221 robotic surgeries performed at the Erzurum Regional Training and Research Hospital in Turkey. (*Continued*)

	Urology (n = 112)	General surgery (n = 53)	Gynecology (n = 46)	Total
Hypotension	2	2	2	6
Hypertension	2	0	0	2
Delirium	2	0	0	2
TOTAL	50	16	12	78

* total number of complications was calculated in 221 patients.

Conclusions for Investigation

This study presents the clinical characteristics of patients undergoing robotic surgeries in the general surgery, urology, gynecology, and ear-nose-throat departments from the anesthesiologist perspective. It appears probable that RAS may develop into a standard procedure as experience increases and concerns decrease. Now, we present a case study where we discuss the applications of robotic surgical procedures in various aspects of surgery. We do not expect the reader to have any medical knowledge for understanding the extent of applications, however, the text might stand to be more informative to a person with little to average medical knowledge of terms. The case study has been done only to portray the extent to which robotic surgery has become a leading commonplace in hospitals. The details regarding the surgery have been presented and the robotic surgical procedures have been contrasted with traditional ones.

7.5 Transoral Robotic Surgery

Robotic automation is now becoming an essentially inclusive part of many fields of surgery. One of the notable examples being tonsillectomy. Recently, a new automatic method has been implemented for the same-TORS Transoral Robotic Surgery Radical tonsillectomy. Developed primarily for the treatment and management of carcinoma of tonsillar nature,

TORS offers the surgeons various advantages. Nonrobotic procedures limit the surgical access and therefore restrict Transoral resections' indications of malignant neoplasms to a restricted area of the tonsillar fossa. TORS, on the other hand, uses the endoscopic optics of high-quality for increased instrument mobility of surgical robot which further facilitates operative and wide-reaching Transoral resection of tonsillar carcinoma. This is done concurrently with decreasing the added indisposition often associated with open surgical processes [13–20]. Today, the use of TORS is not only limited to tonsillectomy. It's also being used in similar arenas of supraglottic partial laryngectomy, canine model of supraglottic laryngectomy, advanced oropharyngeal carcinoma, and head and neck cancer surgery as well.

7.6 Pancreatoduodenectomy

The pancreas is an organ that holds a crucial role in the digestion and regulation of blood sugar. There are mainly three diseases that strike the pancreas—Diabetes, Pancreatitis, and Pancreatic Cancer.

Standing boldly at the fourth position of the foremost root of mortality in the USA is pancreatic cancer [11, 26–30]. The odds of survival further fall low, when its seen statistically that a very small percentage of diagnosed patients (over 50,000 in the year 2019) is operable [12]. These call for the need for automation of the same process and early diagnosis of the same given that pancreatoduodenectomy is itself a challenging procedure for the best of the surgeons. Today as the debate over the advantages between robotic PD and laparoscopic or "open" PD continue, it has been 10 years since surgeons have started using the Da Vinci systems while considering pancreatuoducenomy [2]. A recent study on the literature written about the pancreatoduodenectomy shows that while RPD (Robotic PD) offers theoretical advantages over laparoscopic PD by improved instrument dexterity, better ergonomics, and 3D visualizations practically stand at par with the laparoscopic method [4]. However, this does not deny the fact the advantages it offers weigh out its other aspects.

Currently, it is safe to say that robotic-assisted PD is better suited to patients. This is based on the general observed rate of faster recovery post-operatively alongside the reduced blood loss during the surgery [21]. This also calls the fact that a more comprehensive RCT is badly needed to help us draw more tactful conclusions regarding robotic PD and its manifestations on the patients' signs post-operation.

7.7 Robotic Mitral Valve Surgery

In 1998, a robotic mitral valve to introduced. Due to pervasive excellence in reproducing accurate results with less invasive techniques in conventional sternotomy, it became a great success. As a result, it has become a widely accepted technique to provide anatomic corrections in all categories of prolapse of the mitral valve, irrespective of the complexity of the disease. Various studies have drawn out the benefits of robot-assisted surgery. Lesser interaction of the patient with a mechanical ventilator, reduced hospital stays, fewer bleedings, and superior cosmetic results are some of the advantages.

A study was started in the year 1996, to draw a comparative analysis between the patients undergoing robotic and non-robotic surgery. 129 patients were considered for the study who were suffering from non-ischemic mitral valve disorder. They were then divided into two Groups. Group 1 underwent non-robotic surgical procedures while Group 2 underwent robotic procedures.

The results of the study are summarized in Figures 7.3–7.5 below.

It can be seen through the previous three graphs that the patients falling under Group 2 witness a significant and consistent reduction in the incubation, ICU, Hospitalization time. The patients suffer from lesser pre-operative and postoperative complications. Though certain measures are comparable to the people in Group 1, it can accept as a consensus that the patients who underwent robotic surgery had an overall lesser experience of the complications and stays as compared to the ones with the ones who undergone non-robotic surgery.

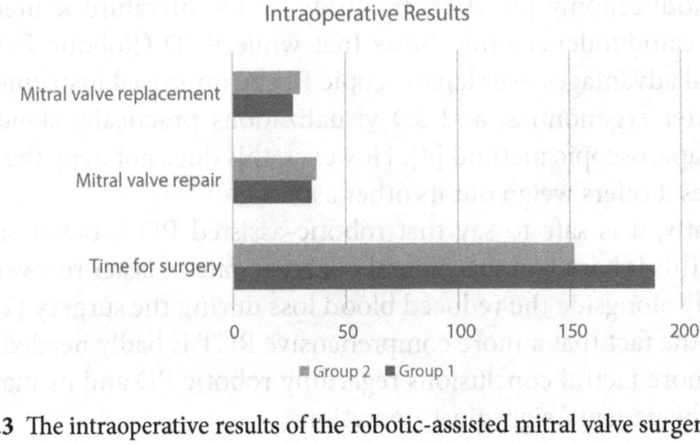

Figure 7.3 The intraoperative results of the robotic-assisted mitral valve surgery are mentioned.

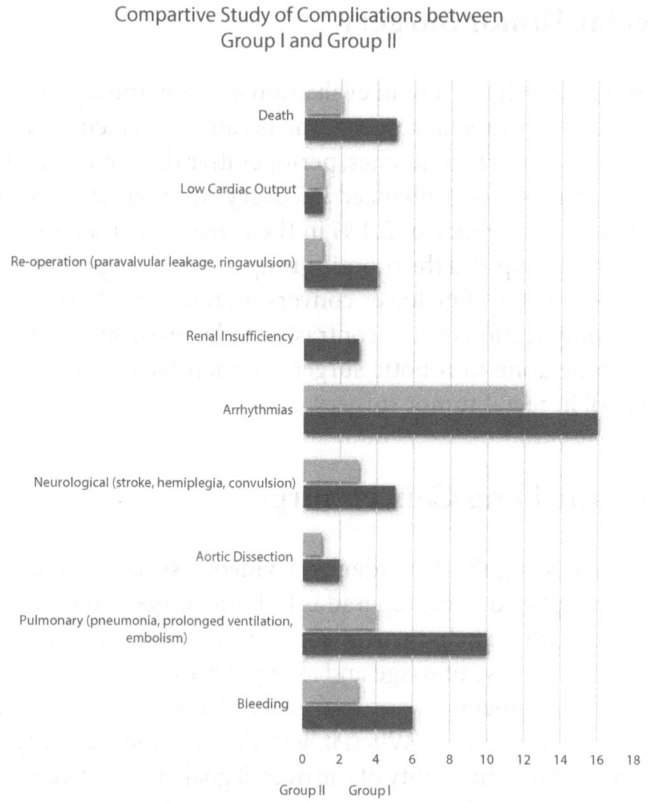

Figure 7.4 The encounters of complications faced during the surgery by both groups are mentioned.

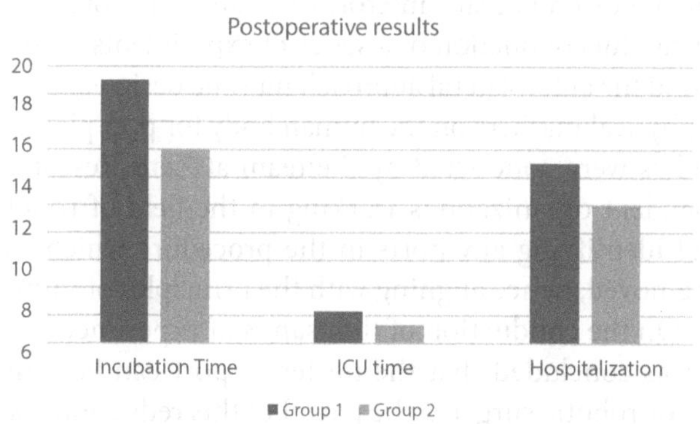

Figure 7.5 The postoperative results depict that the patients in Group II required a lesser stay in comparison to the patients of Group I, which underwent non-robotic assisted surgery.

7.8 Rectal Tumor Surgery

A recent paper published drew an evaluation between the laparoscopic and robotic procedures for rectal surgery. The parameters taken into consideration included short-term outcomes, perioperative data, and extent of compliance to ERAS protocol (Enhanced Recovery After Surgery). Though the paper suggested a difference of 2.4 % in the extent of compliance between the laparoscopic group and the robotic group, robotic surgery was found to responsible for shorter LOS, lower conversion rates, and fewer postoperative surgery complications when contrasted to laparoscopic surgery. There is still a lot to be done in robotic surgery to increase its compliance with ERAS protocol in rectal tumor surgery.

7.9 Robotic Lung Cancer Surgery

For a field that is highly dependent on video-assisted thoracic surgery, robotic surgery placed a big upgrade. Robotic surgery has few features similar to VATS, which help the surgeons easily adapt to the newer system without losing their ease of usage and skill precision.

Proper port placements are crucial when it comes to maximizing the advantages of robotic surgery. When it boils down to the cruciality behind a particular mechanism, the utility of the overall goal often outweighs the cost for minor adjustments. The corporate-giant Zeus, which stands as the front face in the race of robotic surgery, designated a special research team that was assigned the task to chart out the positions and anatomical coordinated for the placement of ports. Various strategies were taken into consideration; these included posterolateral, anterolateral, and mediolateral approach. Finally, after careful conduction of a series of experiments on dummy bodies, it was found the anterolateral approach must be designated for designing and finding physical markers on the human body for port placement.

Later, studies were conducted by the team at Zeus Research Labs and other independent organizations working in the field of robotic surgery, in the lieu of identifying any ports in the procedure which stood excess and can be removed, hence aligning with the principles of minimally invasive surgery. On the conduction of thousands of experiments and years of research, it was concluded that the posterior port can be removed from the protocol for robotic surgery. The payoff of this reduction was the minimalization of the total port count and the optimization of the gap between adjacent robotic arms. However, this payoff is not localized to the reduction of some mathematical quantities.

This inference-based update of the protocols to remove the posterior port resulted in a multi-dimensional impact. This yielded the possibility of the concept to conduct the entire operation with only single manual supervision. The necessity for the assistance of manual nature at any point during the operation for the head surgeon was eliminated. This also impacted and reduced the industrial and production cost and it brought down the count of the total number of required ports to four.

7.10 Robotic Surgery in Gynecology

Currently, the only field in gynecology whose procedures allow the use of robotic surgery is hysterectomy. Up until recently, it was carried out using laparotomy, laparoscopy, or vaginal techniques. The use of robotic-assisted hysterectomy has recently gradually increased, and perioperative complications are generally similar to those in the traditional laparoscopic approach towards benign diseases. RAS has been reported to be faster compared to traditional laparoscopy in patients with endometrial cancer, although surgical outcomes and complication rates are similar. Vaginal cuff hematoma or bleeding has been reported as the most common perioperative complication in hysterectomy and was particularly frequent in this study. Conversion to laparotomy was required in 4.3% of cases in this study, higher than in previous reports of RAS used for both benign diseases and endometrial cancer surgeries.

The surgery time reported by Mäenpää for RAS performed the hysterectomy, bilateral salpingo-oophorectomy, and pelvic lymphadenectomy was shorter than that in the present study. Time to discharge was also shorter than in our study, which was attributed to more experienced surgeons and lower complication rates.

7.11 Robotic Radical Prostatectomy

Robotic radical prostatectomy is the utmost significant and widely performed minimally invasive surgery on the occasion of localized prostate cancer. Today, it is considered to be an acceptable option for men all over the world suffering from prostate cancer. Since its inception in 2001, RARP has continued to be an increasingly popular choice among surgeons and patients alike. In 2005, over 35,000 cases of RARP were recorded. The reduced perioperative complications and favorable long-term oncological outcomes play a significant role in the rising trust toward it.

7.12 Conclusion

From the above comparative study, we can safely conclude that the applications of robotic surgery have spanned to multi-dimensional areas. There stands no doubt that robotic surgery has various key advantages over traditional surgical procedures like VATS, or laparoscopic PD. The traditional approaches might appear a suitable choice in case of severe complications or circumstances arising on an in-depth analysis of the patient's history and conditions on a case-to-case basis. However, the consensus always lies in the favor of robotic automation of surgical procedures.

7.13 Future Work

Medically, robotic surgeries are the favored choice. Given the fact that they provide less blood loss, less postoperative complications, and most importantly for the patients a shortened hospital stay. However, the question arises is that given the advantage that robotic-assisted surgeries have to offer to offer to the patients, there lies a sense of paranoia and skepticism when given the choice to opt for it arises among the patients as well as the surgeons. Is it the underlying failures and faulty cases associated with robotic surgical procedures or the lack of skill to handle the complex system among the surgeons? The further chapters in this series shall deal with the same.

References

1. Ewing, D., Pigazzi, A., Wang, Y., Ballantyne, G., "Robots in the Operating Room The History". *Surg. Innovation*, 11, 2, 63–71, 2004.
2. Giulianotti, P., "Robotics in General Surgery". *Arch. Surgery*, 138, 7, 777, 2003.
3. Kalan, S. *et al.*, "History of robotic surgery". *J. Rob. Surgery*, 4, 3, 141–147, 2010.
4. Kamarajah, S. *et al.*, "Robotic versus conventional laparoscopic pancreaticoduodenectomy a systematic review and meta-analysis". *Eur. J. Surg. Oncol.*, 46, 1, 6–14, 2020.
5. Kwoh, Y., Hou, J., Jonckheere, E., Hayati, S., "A robot with improved absolute positioning accuracy for CT guided stereotactic brain surgery". *IEEE Trans. Biomed. Eng.*, 35, 2, 153–160, 1988.

6. Lanfranco, Castellanos, A., Desai, J., Meyers, W., "Robotic Surgery". *Ann. Surgery*, 239, 1, 14–21, 2004.
7. Cianchetti, M., Laschi, C., Menciassi, A., Dario, P., "Biomedical applications of soft robotics". *Nat. Rev. Mater.*, 3, 6, 143–153, 2018.
8. Dziegielewski, P., Durmus, K., Ozer, E., "Transoral robotic surgery for the excision of base of tongue vascular lesions". *Head Neck*, 37, 8, 1211–1212, 2015.
9. Rashid, O., Mullinax, J., Pimiento, J., Meredith, K., Malafa, M., "Robotic Whipple Procedure for Pancreatic Cancer: The Moffitt Cancer Center Pathway". *Cancer Control*, 22, 3, 340–351, 2015.
10. Saravanan, R., Ramabalan, S., Balamurugan, C., "Evolutionary collision-free optimal trajectory planning for intelligent robots". *Int. J.Adv. Manuf. Technol.*, 36, 11–12, 1234–1251, 2007.
11. Siegel, R., Miller, K., Jemal, A., "Cancer statistics, 2019". *CA: Cancer J. Clin.*, 69, 1, 7–34, 2019.
12. Wecowski, J., Ross, S., Sucandy, I., Rosemurgy, A., "Robotic pancreaticoduodenectomy: A safe minimally invasive option". *Laparoscopic Surgery*, 3, 8–8, 2019.
13. Weinstein, G., O'Malley, B., Snyder, W., Sherman, E., Quon, H., "Transoral Robotic Surgery". *Arch. Otolaryngol. Head Neck Surgery*, 133, 12, 1220, 2007.
14. Malley, B.O., Weinstein, G., Snyder, W., Hockstein, N., "Transoral Robotic Surgery (TORS) for Base of Tongue Neoplasms". *Laryngoscope*, 116, 8, 1465–1472, 2006.
15. Weinstein, G., O'Malley, B., Snyder, W., Hockstein, N., "Transoral Robotic Surgery: Supraglottic Partial Laryngectomy". *Ann. Otol. Rhinol. Laryngol.*, 116, 1, 19–23, 2007.
16. Boudreaux, B. *et al.*, "Robot-Assisted Surgery for Upper Aerodigestive Tract Neoplasms". *Arch. Otolaryngol. Head Neck Surgery*, 135, 4, 397, 2009.
17. Hockstein, N., O'Malley, B., Weinstein, G., "Assessment of Intraoperative Safety in Transoral Robotic Surgery". *Laryngoscope*, 116, 2, 165–168, 2006.
18. Weinstein, G., O'Malley, B., Desai, S., Quon, H., "Transoral robotic surgery: does the ends justify the means?". *Curr. Opin. Otolaryngol. Head Neck Surgery*, 17, 2, 126–131, 2009.
19. Solares, C. and Strome, M., "Transoral Robot-Assisted CO2 Laser Supraglottic Laryngectomy: Experimental and Clinical Data". *Laryngoscope*, 117, 5, 817–820, 2007.
20. Selber, J., Robb, G., Serletti, J., Weinstein, G., Weber, R., Holsinger, F., "Transoral Robotic Free Flap Reconstruction of Oropharyngeal Defects: A Preclinical Investigation". *Plastic Reconstructive Surgery*, 125, 3, 896–900, 2010.
21. Zhou, N. *et al.*, "Outcomes of pancreatoduodenectomy with robotic surgery versus open surgery". *Int. J. Med. Rob. Comput. Assisted Surgery*, 7, 2, 131–137, 2011.

22. Narula, V., Mikami, D., Melvin, W., "Robotic and Laparoscopic Pancreaticoduodenectomy". *Pancreas*, 39, 2, 160–164, 2010.
23. Satava, R., "Robotic surgery: From past to future—A personal journey". *Surg. Clinics North Am.*, 83, 6, 1491–1500, 2003.
24. Lofthouse, M., "Risk factors for gastrointestinal complications after cardiac surgery". *Nat. Clin. Practice Gastroenterol. Hepatol.*, 2, 9, 385–385, 2005.
25. Wang, Y., Butner, S., Darzi, A., "The Developing Market for Medical Robotics". *Proc. IEEE*, 94, 9, 1763–1771, 2006.
26. Siegel, R., Miller, K., Jemal, A., "Cancer statistics, 2016". *CA: Cancer J. Clin.*, 66, 1, 7–30, 2016.
27. Siegel, R., Miller, K., Jemal, A., "Cancer statistics, 2015". *CA: Cancer J. Clin.*, 65, 1, 5–29, 2015.
28. Siegel, R., Naishadham, D., Jemal, A., "Cancer statistics, 2012". *CA: Cancer J. Clin.*, 62, 1, 10–29, 2012.
29. Hanahan, D. and Weinberg, R., "Hallmarks of Cancer: The Next Generation". *Cell*, 144, 5, 646–674, 2011.
30. Islami, F., Siegel, R., Jemal, A., The changing landscape of cancer in the USA — opportunities for advancing prevention and treatment. *Nat. Rev. Clin. Oncol.*, 17, 631–649, 2020.

8

IoT-Enabled Effective Healthcare Monitoring System Using Semantic Web

Sapna Juneja[1*], Abhinav Juneja[2], Annu Dhankhar[2] and Vishal Jain[3]

[1]IMS Engineering College, Ghaziabad, India
[2]KIET Group of Institutions, Ghaziabad, India
[3]Sharda University, Noida, India

Abstract

The growth of the IoT technology is playing a major role in the development of the medical field and healthcare industry as it becomes very easy and economical for the patients to get connected to the doctors and healthcare professionals at any time virtually. Now there is no need to get physical consultation from the doctor all the times and all this has been done only by the development of Internet of Things. In this research work, the applications of IoT in healthcare are defined. Further how these applications can be used with the help of various sensors is also mentioned. The data that has been collected from these sensors is shared on the cloud for the storage purpose. Patients can use various wearable devices and sensors also to get connected with the doctor all the times. Doctors can also suggest treatments to the patients even at the remote locations. This whole system is much beneficial for critically ill patients as when sensor data provides some extraordinary information about the patient, the doctors can immediately send the notification to the patient or his family about what action is needed to be taken immediately.

Keywords: Cloud, healthcare, sensor, Internet of Things

**Corresponding author*: sapnajuneja1983@gmail.com; ORCID:0000-0003-4601-7679

Vishal Jain, Jyotir Moy Chatterjee, Ankita Bansal and Abha Jain (eds.) Semantic Web for Effective Healthcare, (175–190) © 2022 Scrivener Publishing LLC

8.1 Introduction

Smart Health is an on growing technology that has been used in Healthcare Industry for the avoidance, identification, treatment and follows up of the patient anywhere and at any time with the help of connecting IoT devices [1], patients and doctors altogether with each other. Smart Health basically involves the digitalization of healthcare by implementing all time connectivity, using intelligent techniques and applying technology [2]. IoT helps the devices to gather the data and exchange that automatically. Doctors are now capable of providing early diagnosis, preventive methods of care, and better treatment options more efficiently. Patients can get the solution of their problem in real time environment [3]. In this research paper, the major focus is on IoT devices that can be used in healthcare for collection of patient data and communicating that data to healthcare professionals for evaluation. IoT in Healthcare Industry is beneficial for patient, doctor, hospitals, patient's family members, and even healthcare insurance companies also [4].

a) **Patient Care by IoT**—Nowadays, a lot of wearable IoT devices [4] are available and is being used by patients that have been used to monitor vital parameters like Blood Pressure, Heart Rate, etc. These devices can also be used to send regular reminders to patients [5] eg water consumption reminder, calorie counter, variation in parameters if any etc. People's lives has been changed with the invention and usage of IoT in healthcare specially for old age people [6] and patient's living alone are much benefitted with the advent of this technology [4]. Further, these IoT devices also transmit signals to the patient's family members as well if find something different in routine parameter or daily activities [7].

b) **Usage of IoT for Doctors**—Using IoT doctors are now able to keep an eye on the patient's health all the times where a patient can use wearable and other sensors or monitoring devices to get in touch with the doctor [8]. Doctors can check the patient's adhesiveness toward treatment also [9]. IoT capacitate the healthcare workers to be more vigilant and connect with the doctor dynamically in case of any emergency situation. Apart from this, the data collected from IoT, also assist the doctor to find the best possible treatment, which can be given to the patient for the better cure [10].

c) **Usage of IoT for Hospitals**—Not only doctors and patients but hospitals are also get affected by the use of IoT devices. Sensors used in Iot devices can be used to keep track of location of various medical tools and appliances in real time, e.g., Wheelchair, oxygen cylinders, stretcher, etc. [11]. Other than this, hospitals can also decide that where to locate the hospital staff. Resource management of the hospitals resources can also be done using the IoT devices [12], e.g., Drugstore catalog record management, temperature control of the whole or partial area, etc. [13].
d) **Usage of IoT for Insurance Corporations**—Health Insurance Corporations can also get better opportunities of their business activities using IoT devices. These organizations can use the data collected from IoT devices for the verifications of the claims made by the patients [14]. Using the data, company can verify whether the claim is genuine or fraudulence is there [15]. Further, Insurance companies also offer various types of perks to their customers upon usage of IoT devices and sharing data with the company [16]. These companies pay off the customer for using IoT devices in order to monitor the daily activities of the patient. This helps insurance companies to minimize the claims [17].

8.2 Literature Review

IoT along with cloud computing technology can be used in Healthcare for monitoring and providing treatment to patients [18]. The main task of this whole system is to keep an eye on the vital health parameters of the patient with various sensors [19], i.e., wearable body sensors and home installed sensors. This data is further provided to the doctor and after checking that parameters, doctor interact with patient without any physical interaction [20]. The cloud system has been used for storage of this data and hence can be made accessible round the globe. In fact, in the rural areas of the world, it is more beneficial where it becomes quite difficult for the patient to get treatment on time because of the lack of facilities. Here is the list of the research work done by previous researchers in the same field as:

Ref. [21] focused on the healthcare using technology, i.e., IoT based Healthcare and specified that how data that has been transmitted through IoT devices can be kept safe [19] mentioned various Internet of Medical things, their features, uses, and the challenges in this area.

Ref. [22] also discussed about Internet of Medical things in his study and mentioned that IoT is playing a major role in the digital transformation of the healthcare industry. It basically increases the quality of services provided by healthcare professionals. The researchers also mentioned various wearable sensors and devices for patients. Ref. [23] suggested that it is necessary to combine IoT and Healthcare as it is quite useful for the remote patient monitoring, but some fixed conditions and standards should be there for implementing IoT in healthcare. Researcher also mentioned the uses of IoT in healthcare. Ref. [24] suggested IoT based device that is wearable and patient can wear that on his wrist. This device can monitor the body temperature and movement of the patient and it was much useful for elder people suffering with serious diseases [25]. In his work, he used some home based sensors to check the movement rate and falling rate of older people. These wireless sensors were gathering data of the person by verifying the present location of that individual [26]. After analyzing variation in the location, the severity of the patient's problem can be diagnosed. The drawback in their research work was that data security concern was not defined anywhere [27] and represented various applications of IoT based Healthcare. He also elaborated how security of data can be provided to the whole system even by making the system more energy efficient. He defined that permission for the usage of IoT devices will not be kept open for all; instead some authentication mechanism should be applied to every user before accessing the device.

8.3 Phases of IoT-Based Healthcare

The rapid growth of IoT devices in healthcare has opened vast opportunities as the large volume of data gathered by these devices can have the capability of transforming the healthcare [28]. IoT architecture used in Healthcare Industry can be divided into four phases. These phases are connected in such a way that output data of one phase is used as input data to next sub sequential phase and so on [29].

Phase 1. First Phase is composed of various interconnected devices like cameras, sensors, monitors, etc., used to gather the data [16].

Phase 2. Data gathered from these devices is digitalized for processing [30].

Phase 3. After preprocessing, data have been saved to the cloud for storage [31].

Phase 4. At the end, the data are analyzed and based upon this analysis decisions making is to be done.

8.4 IoT-Based Healthcare Architecture

The IoT-based healthcare architecture is easily represented using Figure 8.1. Lowest level is the level that defines the patient's location. Here, various sensors

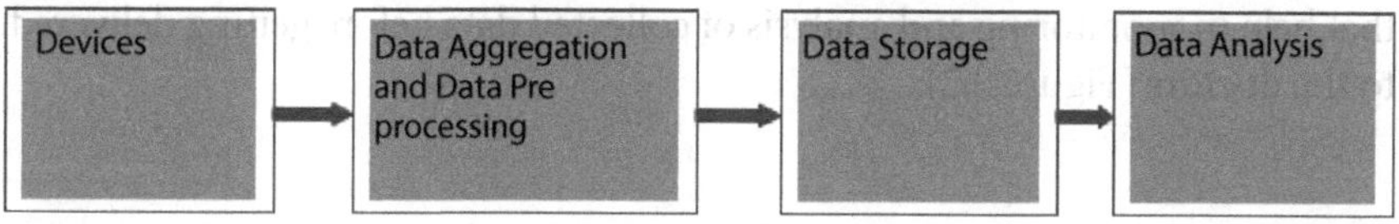

Figure 8.1 Phases of IoT process.

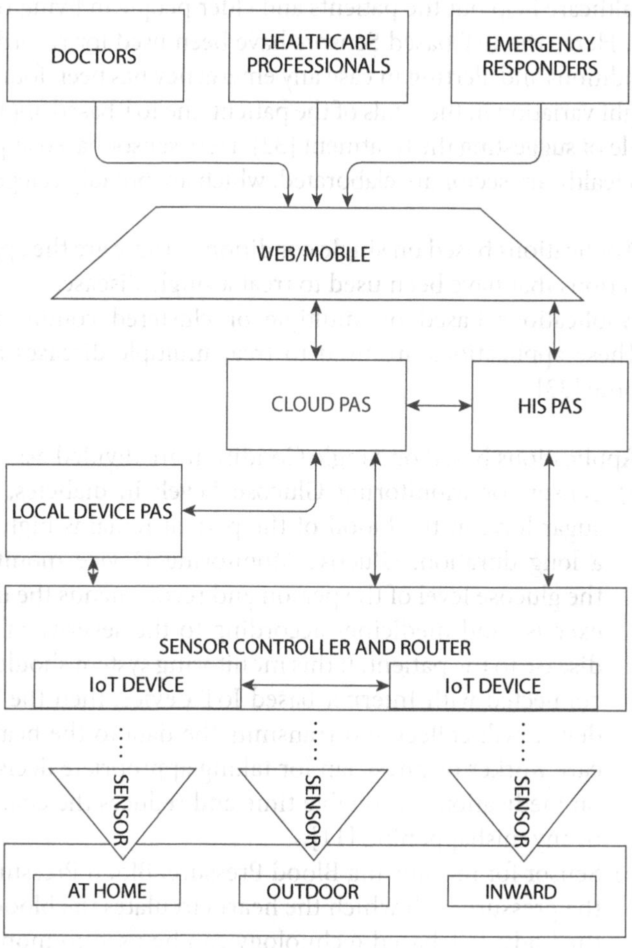

Figure 8.2 IoT-based healthcare architecture.

are attached that has been used to gather the vital data of the patient. If these sensors are based on wireless system, these can be used anywhere like either at home or at some different location when the patient will not be at home. These sensors are further connected to the IoT devices, which transfers this data after analysis, to the healthcare workers with the help of cloud. The cloud stores and processes the data [11]. Application Layer contains various tools that help in monitoring and analysis of collected data before getting delivered to the doctors (Figure 8.2).

8.5 IoT-Based Sensors for Health Monitoring

Smart Healthcare help out the patients and elder people in living the life on their own. Here, The IoT based Sensors have been used for recording their health conditions and alerting in case any emergency has been found. But in case of slight variation in the vitals of the patient, the IoT based application is self-capable of suggesting the treatment [32]. Here sensor based applications of IoT in Healthcare sector are elaborated, which are broadly categorized as:

1. Applications based on single condition—These are the applications that have been used to treat a single disease.
2. Applications based on multiple or clustered condition—These applications are used to treat multiple diseases at a time [33].

   Applications based on Single Condition are divided as:

   a) Sensor for Monitoring Glucose Level: In diabetes, the sugar level in the blood of the patient remains high for a long duration. Glucose Monitoring Device monitors the glucose level of the person and recommends the diet, exercise and medicines according to the severity of the disease to the patient. If this monitoring system should be connected with Internet based IoT device, then the IoT device will collect and transmits the data to the healthcare worker or physician for taking appropriate decision on medication on suitable time and reduces the chances of any mishappening [11].
   b) Sensor for monitoring Blood Pressure: Blood Pressure is the pressure with which the heart circulates the blood in the body. IoT based technology can be used to monitor

the blood pressure and other necessary vitals of the body using various sensors. IoT device checks for the routine BP and sends the signal in case of any variation in the value from the normal value [34]. Sensor for monitoring the temperature of the body: Sensors can be attached with the body to measure the body temperature and then the information has been sent to the IoT device which further collects the data and sends the same to the doctor [35].

c) Monitoring System for measuring the absorption of oxygen in to the body: A device named oximeter has been used by patients as well doctors for monitoring the absorption of the oxygen in to the blood. For improvisation of the services, this oximeter can be used with IoT based technology for providing treatment to the remote patients [36].

d) Monitoring System for measuring the ECG of the body: ECG device has been used to observe the ECG wave pattern of the body, and creates the report based upon these wave patterns to check the functioning of the heart. IOIO-OTG microcontroller.

   Converts ECG signals to digital numbers by using the analog to digital converter, and then the generate binary file is uploaded to the cloud network for analysis and identification of improper health state [13].

Applications based upon Multiple Conditions are:

a) Device Management—As wheel chairs or stretchers are of great use for patients or people with some physical disability, if these devices could be implemented with IoT based sensors, it would become quite easy to keep track of the movement of the patient and to monitor the condition of the patient as well [37].

b) Mobile Phone based Healthcare Solution—In the current scenario; the mobile phones along with the sensors are controlling various electronic devices. In healthcare industry, various mobile base applications have been used to provide service to the patients [38]. Examples of various healthcare solution providers' applications are BP Watch, Pulse Watch, etc.

8.6 IoT Applications in Healthcare

A lot of problems of the healthcare industry can be managed with the usage of IoT. Solutions provided with the IoT devices can help in providing better treatment and better patient monitoring too. Here are some applications of IoT in Healthcare:

1. Remote monitoring of the patient—Although the medical facilities are rapidly increasing, still remote monitoring of the patient is a difficult situation to handle in developing countries. Apart from this many emergency situations can be controlled if medical facility is provided to the patient at the proper time. So with the help of IoT based solution, above problems can be solved and remote monitoring of patient will be done more effectively. Sensor based wearable gadget can be used by the patient for providing timely notification of the health status to the doctor [13].
2. Robot to look after the patient—IoT based robots can be used as assistant in the hospitals as well at homes for the patients living alone for assisting the patient to provide better care. It can monitor the vitals of the patients, help the patient in giving medication on time and can provide timely reminders of routine activities [39].
3. Management of Clinical waste—Management of clinical waste in health sector is a huge problem. If not solved properly, this problem can lead to the infection among the patients or hospital staff. So sensor based bins can be used in order to solve this problem. These sensors work by sending timely alerts when bin is completely filled so that the garbage should be dumped timely at properplace [40].
4. GPS enables shoes for Dementia Patients [41]—Patients suffering from dementia or any other related neural disorder forget their routine activities and even can forget its home location also. GPS enabled shoes can be used to keep track of the patient's location all the time, which further sends an alert to the patient's family via IoT device if patient leaves its home location.
5. Overall Management of Hospitals—IoT devices can be helpful for the overall management of hospitals including booking of appointments, hospital staff management, reduction of the queues of OPD, inventory management, etc. [39].

6. Proactive Treatment of Asthma Patients—The irreversible nature of Asthma makes it a very life critical disease, the only remedy being the use of inhalers throughout the life of patient [27]. The defined symptoms of a patient tentatively getting an attack are visible from half an hour to up to 8 h before the episode occurs. The IoT tools may be very instrumental in providing the aid to the patient. An inhaler that is connected with some smart sensor capable of being actuated from a factor like temperature or air pollen to avoid any such attack of asthma to the patient [7].

8.7 Semantic Web, Ontology, and Its Usage in Healthcare Sector

Semantic Web is an extension of World Wide Web but the main difference is that in this semantic web the information is fabricated not only by machines but also by human beings. The main job of semantic web is to increase the possibility that machines would be able to work with human beings parallel. Semantic web provides the tools that make possible the distribution of information among various systems. Semantic Web is basically a state space where all the knowledge base can be kept collectively in such a way that it represents the meaningful information to the users. Semantic Web is responsible for showing meaningful information on a variety of websites and also helpful for research community for searching the data over various websites. As the main issue in the medical field is production of information and knowledge from a variety of data sources, the semantic web has the ability to provide such information to the healthcare system. The semantic web can escalate the merger of various data sources for the purpose of getting more appropriate results.

Ontology in the field of semantic web can be specified as the file used to represent the relation between various objects. Ontology relationship gives a tree like shape to the semantic web. In some ontology, this tree like structure enhances the features of the ontologies. The main point to be followed before the designing of the ontology is to make it capable to understand and easy to use by the users.

8.8 Semantic Web-Based IoT Healthcare

Semantic Web is the extended web in which data are represented in the form that it provides complete meaning of that data and thus actuates much better association between human and machine. In semantic Web the available information is based upon the real world problems. Using this data or information, compatibility can be generated between human, machines, devices and services. Ontology plays an important role for generating compatibility between various machines. In order to provide complete compatibility between the systems, their semantic web based content should be same. Ontology basically represents the design or structure of information representation of any system. In Healthcare sector, a large amount of information has been used. For utilizing this data for various reasons, this data must be shared among machines. Hence ontology is used as information foundation for a common architecture in Healthcare based system. IoT based devices are much widespread these days as it has the capability of sharing the data universally and precisely. Healthcare sector aims at providing customize service to individual patient. In order to achieve this aim, IoT based system gathers data of remote patients with the help of various sensors and IoT based devices and transfers that data to the healthcare professionals for offering the patient's prompt and good service of treatment. The whole system works by collecting data from healthcare based gadgets like BP Monitor, Sugar Monitor, etc., to smart devices and further data from the smart devices will be transferred over cloud. While transferring these data, the system also takes care of data security and accuracy.

Below is the proposed architecture of semantic web based IoT Healthcare System (Figure 8.3).

This architecture has been generated to provide services to the patients having persistent diseases. This architecture has the ability of examining

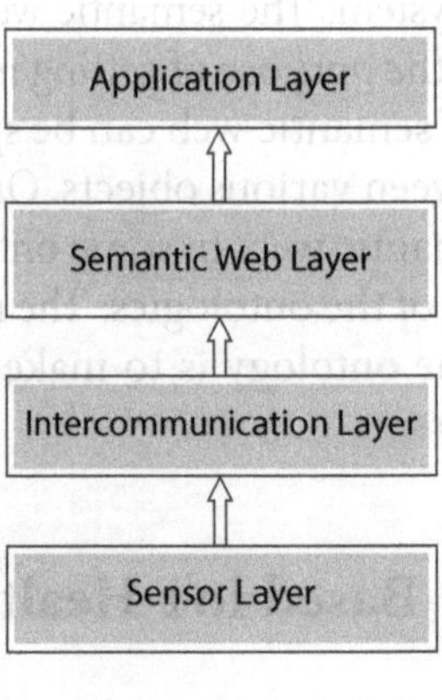

Figure 8.3 Semantic web-based IoT healthcare.

patient's condition on regular basis. The system works by collecting values of different sensors installed at patient' site and then analyze those values to reach to a conclusion about the health condition of the patient.

The main Objective of this system is to serve the patient by taking decisions using the collected information and using a healthcare semantic web to validate the gathered information and knowledge about healthcare system. The above system has four components as: lowest layer is sensor based layer which has various sensors and IoT based devices used to gather the data of the patient. Layer above sensor based layer is intercommunication Layer and its purpose is to provide the communication between sensor based layer and the upper layers. This layer contains various means of networking and communication. Layer above Intercommunication layer is Semantic Web Layer. This layer performs various tasks sequentially. It first gathers data from multiple available sources like sensors and IoT devices and get the detailed information of the patient. After collecting the information, it takes out the data related to the specific disease which the doctor is treating that time. After the extraction of the related data, it has been compared with the available rule based model. By looking at the rule based model, the solution of the problem has been carried out and stored in the database of the patient for future reference. The topmost layer of the system is application layer which acts as an interface between the users of Healthcare sector and the system.

8.9 Challenges of IoT in Healthcare Industry

There are many great benefits that are provided by IoT in the field of healthcare but some problems have to be solved. Without defeating these challenges the implementation of Internet of Things cannot be done.

1. Management of a huge amount of data generated by IoT devices—As millions of devices are connected with each other in healthcare system and these devices generate a large amount of data so it becomes quite difficult to store and manage this massive data [42]. Although Clouds and Artificial Intelligence algorithms can be used to manage these data, still its implementation is very time consuming and complex process [37].
2. Greater chances of vulnerability on IoT devices and associated data—IoT devices are much beneficial for the healthcare

sector but these devices and associated data are more prone to attack [18]. Attackers can attack these devices and can access the information and can change it also. Attackers can also take control over the all associated devices of the hospitals, which is a problematic situation both for patient and hospital as well [43].

3. Universal Healthcare Regulations—The Internet of Things in Medical sector is still needed to be sanctioned by Universal Healthcare Regulations organization in the world [44].
4. Continuous updates in the software are needed—As IoT devices are hardware based and these hardware devices works in collaboration with the software, so these software needed to be updated time to time for proper functioning of the IoT device and routine update of the software is a complex task and consumes much time and effort.

8.10 Conclusion

Healthcare with IoT is an emerging area nowadays and is a major topic of research among researchers. The usage of IoT approach has mechanized the treatment process and patient's care. IoT based devices has established strategies to deal with patient, doctor and hospitals and started providing smarter and faster services. IoT devices makes easy for patient to inform the doctor about their health status anywhere and anytime, for doctor to monitor the patient in real time environment even at the remote location In this research work, we have proposed an IoT based architecture for monitoring the health of remote patients. IoT devices can use sensors to check the status of body vitals like ECG, BP, Blood Sugar, etc. This architecture is very useful for the entire healthcare world and will add on more solutions for monitoring the health.

References

1. Mekonnen, Y., Namuduri, S., Burton, L., Sarwat, A., Bhansali, S., Review—Machine Learning Techniques in Wireless Sensor Network Based Precision Agriculture. *J. Electrochem. Soc.*, 167, 037522, 2020.
2. Information, H. and Records, P.H., Emerging 21st Century Medical Technologies, Mohammad Bajwa, *Pakistan Journal of Medical Sciences,* 30, 1–14, 2014.

3. Archip, A., Botezatu, N., Şerban, E., Herghelegiu, P.C., ZalĂ, A., An IoT based system for remote patient monitoring. *Proc. 2016 17th Int. Carpathian Control Conf. ICCC 2016*, pp. 1–6, 2016.
4. Banka, S., Madan, I., Saranya, S.S., Smart Healthcare Monitoring using IoT. *Int. J. Appl. Eng. Res.*, 13, 11984–11989, 2018.
5. Biswas, J. *et al.*, Sensor based micro context for mild dementia assistance. *ACM Int. Conf. Proceeding Ser*, 2010.
6. Fratiglioni, L. *et al.*, Incidence of dementia and major subtypes in Europe: A collaborative study of population-based cohorts. *Neurology*, 54, 1–10, 2000.
7. Rubí, J.N.S. and Gondim, P.R.L., IoMT platform for pervasive healthcare data aggregation, processing, and sharing based on oneM2M and openEHR. *Sensors (Switzerland)*, 19, 1–25, 2019.
8. Dahiwade, D., Patle, G., Meshram, E., Designing disease prediction model using machine learning approach. *Proc. 3rd Int. Conf. Comput. Methodol. Commun. ICCMC 2019*, pp. 1211–1215, 2019, doi: 10.1109/ICCMC.2019.8819782.
9. Bhat, M. I., Ahmad, S., Amin, A., Ashraf, S., E-Health with Internet of Things. *Int. J. Comput. Sci. Mob. Comput.*, 6, 357–362, 2017.
10. Marques, G., Pitarma, R., Garcia, N.M., Pombo, N., Internet of things architectures, technologies, applications, challenges, and future directions for enhanced living environments and healthcare systems: A review. *Electron.*, 8, 1–27, 2019.
11. Pathinarupothi, R.K., Ramesh, M.V., Rangan, E., Multi-layer architectures for remote health monitoring. *2016 IEEE 18th Int. Conf. e-Health Networking, Appl. Serv. Heal.*, vol. 2016, 2016, doi: 10.1109/HealthCom.2016.7749443.
12. Rojko, A., Industry 4.0 concept: Background and overview. *Int. J. Interact. Mob. Technol.*, 11, 77–90, 2017.
13. Zanjal, S.V. and Talmale, G.R., Medicine Reminder and Monitoring System for Secure Health Using IoT. *Phys. Procedia*, 78, 471–476, 2016.
14. Shinde, G.R. *et al.*, Forecasting Models for Coronavirus Disease (COVID-19): A Survey of the State-of-the-Art. *SN Comput. Sci.*, 1, 1–15, 2020.
15. Almeida, A. *et al.*, An IoT-aware architecture for collecting and managing data related to elderly behavior. *Wirel. Commun. Mob. Comput.*, 2017, 2017.
16. Dhillon, D.K. and Uppal, R.S., Internet of Things - Making Sense of the Next Mega-Trend. *J. Netw. Comput. Appl.*, 67, 19, 2016.
17. Dewangan, K. and Mishra, M., Internet of Things for Healthcare: A Review. *Researchgate. Net*, 8, 526–534, 2018.
18. Hernandez-Penaloza, G., Belmonte-Hernandez, A., Quintana, M., Alvarez, F., A Multi-Sensor Fusion Scheme to Increase Life Autonomy of Elderly People with Cognitive Problems. *IEEE Access*, 6, 12775–12789, 2017.
19. Kadhim, K.T., Alsahlany, A.M., Wadi, S.M., Kadhum, H.T., An Overview of Patient's Health Status Monitoring System Based on Internet of Things (IoT). *Wirel. Pers. Commun.*, 2020, doi: 10.1007/s11277-020-07474-0.

20. Jatav, S. and Sharma, V., An Algorithm for Predictive Data Mining Approach in Medical Diagnosis. *Int. J. Comput. Sci. Inf. Technol.*, 10, 11–20, 2018.
21. Nanayakkara, N., Halgamuge, M.N., Syed, A., Security and Privacy of Internet of Medical Things (IoMT) Based Healthcare Applications: A Review, 2019.
22. Nazir, S., Ali, Y., Ullah, N., García-Magariño, I., Internet of Things for Healthcare Using Effects of Mobile Computing: A Systematic Literature Review. *Wirel. Commun. Mob. Comput.*, 2019, 2019.
23. Chacko, A. and Hayajneh, T., Security and Privacy Issues with IoT in Healthcare. *EAI Endorsed Trans. Pervasive Heal. Technol.*, 4, 1–7, 2018.
24. Evans, J. *et al.*, Remote health monitoring for older adults and those with heart failure: Adherence and system usability. *Telemed. e-Health*, 22, 480–488, 2016.
25. Kearns, W.D., Nams, V.O., Fozard, J.L., Tortuosity in movement paths is related to cognitive impairment wireless fractal Estimation in assisted living facility residents. *Methods Inf. Med.*, 49, 592–598, 2010.
26. Van Os, H.J.A. *et al.*, Concomitant headache in acute ischaemic stroke: Relation with ct angiography and ct perfusion characteristics. *Int. J. Stroke*, 10, 217, 2015.
27. Hamdi, M. and Abie, H., Game-based adaptive security in the Internet of Things for eHealth. *2014 IEEE Int. Conf. Commun. ICC 2014*, pp. 920–925, 2014, doi: 10.1109/ICC.2014.6883437.
28. Death, T.H.E. and Cancer, O.F., Monitor Me! Sensors in Everyday Objects. 19, 2019.
29. Abaker, I. *et al.*, A Machine Learning Solution Framework for Combatting COVID-19 in Smart Cities from Multiple Dimensions. *Medrxiv*, 2020 2020, doi: 10.1101/2020.05.18.20105577. 05.18.20105577.
30. Kumar, A., Kuppusamy, K.S., Aghila, G., A learning model to detect maliciousness of portable executable using integrated feature set. *J. King Saud Univ. - Comput. Inf. Sci.*, 31, 252–265, 2019.
31. Pilloni, V., How data will transform industrial processes: Crowdsensing, crowdsourcing and big data as pillars of industry 4.0. *Futur. Internet*, 10, 2018.
32. Suzuki, S. and Matsui, T., Remote Sensing for Medical and Healthcare Applications. *Remote Sens. - Appl.*, 2012, doi: 10.5772/36924.
33. Dziak, D., Jachimczyk, B., Kulesza, W.J., IoT-based information system for healthcare application: Design methodology approach. *Appl. Sci.*, 7, 2017.
34. Karaolis, M.A., Moutiris, J.A., Hadjipanayi, D., Pattichis, C.S., Assessment of the risk factors of coronary heart events based on data mining with decision trees. *IEEE Trans. Inf. Technol. Biomed.*, 14, 559–566, 2010.
35. Najib, S.M., Hassan, N.B., Shair, N.T.A.B.M., Rahim, N., Wahab, N.A., Intelligent neonatal monitoring system based on android application using multi sensors. *ISCAIE 2019 - 2019 IEEE Symp. Comput. Appl. Ind. Electron*, pp. 131–135, 2019, doi: 10.1109/ISCAIE.2019.8743867.
36. IoT-Based Healthcare Support System for Alzheimer's Patients, Rozita Jamili Oskouei, wireless communication and mobile computing, wiley, Volume 2020 |Article ID 8822598 | https://doi.org/10.1155/2020/8822598, *IoT Support for Dementia Patients*, pp. 41–43, 2015.

37. Kamišalić, A., Fister, I., Turkanović, M., Karakatič, S., Sensors and functionalities of non-invasive wrist-wearable devices: A review. *Sensors (Switzerland)*, 18, 2018.
38. Catarinucci, L. *et al.*, An IoT-Aware Architecture for Smart Healthcare Systems. *IEEE Internet Things J.*, 2, 515–526, 2015.
39. Moosavi, S.R. *et al.*, SEA: A secure and efficient authentication and authorization architecture for IoT-based healthcare using smart gateways. *Procedia Comput. Sci.*, 52, 452–459, 2015.
40. Nilashi, M., Ibrahim, O.B., Ahmadi, H., Shahmoradi, L., An analytical method for diseases prediction using machine learning techniques. *Comput. Chem. Eng.*, 106, 212–223, 2017.
41. Peterson, C.B., Prasad, N.R., Prasad, R., The future of assistive technologies for dementia. *2012 Proc. 29th Int. Symp. Autom. Robot. Constr. ISARC 2012*, 2012, doi: 10.4017/gt.2012.11.02.427.00.
42. Dwivedi, A.K., Performance evaluation of different machine learning techniques for prediction of heart disease. *Neural Comput. Appl.*, 29, 685–693, 2018.
43. Brown, E.L. *et al.*, Smartphone-Based Health Technologies for Dementia Care: Opportunities, Challenges, and Current Practices. *J. Appl. Gerontol.*, 38, 73–91, 2019.
44. Nogueira, V., An Overview of IoT and healthcare. *Actas das 6as Jornadas Informática Univ. Évora*, 2019.

9

Precision Medicine in the Context of Ontology

Rehab A. Rayan[1]* and Imran Zafar[2]

[1]*Department of Epidemiology, High Institute of Public Health, Alexandria University, Alexandria, Egypt*
[2]*Department of Bioinformatics and Computational Biology, Virtual University of Pakistan, Lahore, Pakistan*

Abstract
Data volumes in the field of precision medicine (PM) increase exponentially as biomedical technology develops. The disseminated information contains valuable knowledge about the location of the related biomedical units and their semantic relationships. To this end, a model must be established to represent information as ontology in order to formally reflect the relationships between diseases, phenotypes, genes, mutations, drugs and so on, and to achieve effective integration of heterogeneous data. Ontologies are systematic descriptions of knowledge that can combine and examine substantial quantities of heterogeneous data, enabling accurate analysis of a patient. The application of ontologies in healthcare is largely directed at describing and reorganizing medical terminologies. Health professionals have advanced their technical expressions and vocabulary to support storing and communicating generic medical knowledge and patient-specific information proficiently. These terminologies, optimized for human processing, are marked by a substantial quantity of inherent knowledge. Health information systems should deliver complicated and comprehensive medical concepts without ambiguities, which is a challenging business demanding a thorough investigation of the construction and the concepts of these terminologies. However, it could be realized by building medical domain ontologies for describing these information systems. The principal aim of this chapter is to explain ontologies and their application in computational reasoning to promote an accurate classification of patients' diagnosis and managing care, and for translational research.

***Keywords*:** Precision medicine, personalized healthcare, ontology, classification, machine learning decision support

**Corresponding author*: rayanr@alexu.edu.eg; https://orcid.org/0000-0003-3852-5710

Vishal Jain, Jyotir Moy Chatterjee, Ankita Bansal and Abha Jain (eds.) Semantic Web for Effective Healthcare, (191–214) © 2022 Scrivener Publishing LLC

9.1 Introduction

Precision medicine (PM) is a way to treat and prevent diseases that aims to maximize effectiveness by taking into account variation in genes, environmental factors [1]. The PM network also connects patients, cares, clinical laboratories and prospective investigations [2]. With the rapid expansion of personalized medicine, the amounts of heterogeneous clinical data and scientific information are exponentially growing, where valuable knowledge such as functional biomedical units and their semantine relations are inaccessible. One crucial question is how to know and use the knowledge to assist PM. By incorporating, classifying and standardizing these biomedical tools from different resources and establishing relationships between them, terminologies, classifications and ontologies may provide varying degrees of complexity in computational formats, enabling enormous data collections to be analyzed and a patient to be properly categorized [3]. Construction of these knowledge models is necessary for PM studies, and appropriate.

Ontology is a powerful technique for representing pragmatically and understanding biomedicine. In the same contexts precision or personalized medicine is a novel model in the concept of ontologies that endures the outstanding confidence for individualized patient care with incremental manners. The framework of ontologies is emerging to improve patients' diagnosis and treatment via providing easy tools and methods of medicinal decision support system level for multiple reasoning mechanisms in precision medicines. To deal with this large datasets or data is heterogeneous in nature and collected from individual patients, here we acquired suitable methods to identify the basic knowledge in which every patient potentially different, to handle specifically changing or issues like different signs and symptoms from diseases. The Ontological information has worth to mentioning since the scientific information and clinical data are heterogeneous or hardly to manipulate. Based on classification approaches in the domain of ontologies, it provides the facility for handling disease mechanisms' in several patients correlating top level information [4].

Terminologies have a long history of recalling information, such as searching for documents or database records that meet certain criteria [5]. Many of the most relevant medical knowledge retrieval tools include Medical Subject Headings (MeSH) for PubMed Indexing and Search; RxNorm [6], a standardized and renamed medication terminology; and UMLS (Unified Medical Language System), which contains over 100 clinical terminology and coding systems [7]. These tools, which contain common names and synonyms and cross-reference lists, shape the search and indexing data and are often used in EHRs and public databases. Ontologies differ from vocabulary in that ontologies explain the relationships between concepts in a way that enables rational logical reasoning to draw conclusions from similar statements [8]. For example, if ontology classifies "virus" as an infectious agent and classifies "infectious meningitis" as a form of infectious meningitis, it will conclude that "viral meningitis" is a subclass of "infectious meningitis." Aristotle created a conceptual taxonomy that in some way mimics modern bioontologies [9]. Researchers have recently used the term "ontology" to indicate a computational description that explains the cognitive aspects of comprehension. The ontology contains a set of concepts (terms) and synonyms thereof as well as concise logical definitions that describe the formal relations between concepts.

Using concise syntax in ontology can maintain logical coherence, even with hundreds or thousands of concepts across multiple domains, allowing computational processes to define facts that are implicit but not specifically specified in original data. Therefore, Ontologies can help leverage the latent knowledge of clinical big data by encoding data with "computable" semiconductors, allowing machine learning and other algorithms to meet challenges in the analysis of high-capacity multimodal data by combining it with clinical significance. Ontologies can also be used in conjunction with the use of natural languages in extremely clear textual concepts, such as those found in clinical commentaries [10], and improve knowledge extraction from EHRs and other sources. Ontologies will also enable the integration of basic scientific data such as animal model data and general information like associations between genetic variations and diseases, enabling patient identification based on data collection far beyond the EHR and enabling new clinical understanding [11]. The integration of huge amounts of data and the cheap high-capacity computer offers the ability to gain therapeutic and diagnostic knowledge for excellent interaction analysis, significant descriptive analysis and inferential.

Carl Linné (1707–1778), who classified the diseases into 11 classes, 37 orders, and 325 species, developed the first advanced medical hierarchy that could be known as a real unit of disease (nosology). While the classification of Linnaeus retains certain errors from a scientific perspective, such as the notion that leprosy can be caught by consuming herring worms, its classification lays the foundation for the research that eventually led to the first edition of ICD, 1893. After its development as a cause of death, ICD has developed enormously but it continues to be intended as a guideline for epidemiology, health management and billing, not as a measurement of the patient as a biological substance. Historical reports are statistical classifications that are generally compatible (they do not count twice) and comprehensive (they have a place to put everything). The originality of the ICDs was achieved by a monohierarchy (single parents), where each code has one parent and only one. This eliminates a number of bills but often creates ambiguous connections. In the 10th edition of ICD, for example, malignant neoplasm of the thyroid gland (C73) is a child with malignant neoplasms but is not a child with thyroid disease; it would be a child of both only if the terms in ICD-10 can have several parents; thus, monohierarchies limit artificial crucial elements for analysis and research and hinder the critical assessment of diseases and other environmental factors. The definition of logical illness goes back to Hippocrates because it is still an important area of research today. The phenotype of an individual has historically defined measurable characteristics that are also related to genotype. The concept is increasingly organized by translational researchers working on the boundaries of omics data and clinical records to identify a cluster of patients with the same "diagnosis" based on specific clinical and "omics" functions [12].

In semantic web technologies, the broad deployment of computerized medical records allows accumulating personal and scientific remarks describing demographics, manifestations, examination outcomes, diagnoses, conclusions, interventions, medicines, etc., with case profile ontologies. Recently, substantial quantities of these big data, involving the gained throughout genomics, proteomics, and metabolomics studies, are being applied in medical investigations. The amount, extent, and flow of these data are unique to this mankind's era.

Ontologies provide linkage opportunity for automatic integration of individual patient data or relevant information about clinical research and trials for drug formulation and evaluation. In the same contrast, the already developed ontological system, termed web ontology language (OWL), provides basic discovery for challenges identification of precision medicine, assimilation or interconnection of biological pathways and clinical trial of pharmacogenomics for other life science applications. In next generation Semantic Web technologies, ontologies provide better understanding for research data warehouse systems integrated with the full spectrum of clinical and laboratory research data with efficacy of time, cost and complexity outcomes to analyzing these originated bio-data. With the Advancement of high-throughput technologies in ontology, individual health path may be mapped in several forms with innovative time frame, involving and exploration of different genotypic, phenotypic, and ecosystem characteristics. Medical data coverage described variants in single genes, family history, laboratory results, notes, images, medical equipment, findings, and medications. Nowadays, such characteristics are being paired with the rising powerful big data, which has not yet been fully furnished to sort diseases. Origins of these data incorporate wearable devices, which follow weight, heart rate, physical activity, nutrition, compliance to prescribed medications, geographical location, and hence, accumulated across duration of moments to ages. The whole received data, without sequencing the germline, return a specific time spot in an individual's health path [3].

Despite Electronic Medical Records report many data types, they sometimes hinder examining patient-level, molecular or big data along with medical data; that is because of broken, mistaken, an unidentified origin or missing detailed records. Such issues reflect a framework which is more concerned by invoices than reporting clinically crucial patient's data. Gene-level, wearable devices, behavioral and ecological data are hard to trace and are not consistently gathered or embedded; that is because they are sometimes locked in text files which might be challenging for a computer to analyze in formal research areas. Among these types of challenges, ontologies provide interoperable infrastructure through semantic web technologies to support several statistical aggregations in medical domains.

Advanced contributions of ontologies (UMLS, GO and the EcoCyc Ontology) for biomedical datasets are critical to understand processing of biomedical works. Bioinformatics provides novel insight to deal with upcoming problems using high-level concepts of biology, computer, mathematics and statistical methods to retrieve, analyze, and manage data with effective cost and time frames. Use of bioinformatics tools and applications, with facility of natural language processing, for biomedical data enables managing it according to web semantic analysis for text summarization or document clustering. The patient phenotypic data are sometimes inaccessible or missing details, hence impeding the determination of resemblances and sorting patients into medically relevant categories. These procedures are problematic and crucial in conditions possessing a range of genotypes, biomarkers, signs, and symptoms, which might not be demonstrated in every patient. However, precision medicine aims primarily at applying such data to allocate patients and distinguish resemblances among unique diseases [3]. Therefore, the use of ontologies, with the feature of semantic web technologies, can provide many promising solutions via capturing broad range of concepts in biomedical fields.

9.2 The Rationale Behind Data

The main attributes of ontologies are commonly explored explicit understanding for the novel domain of interconnectedness challenges to enhanced metadata quality within broad ranging fields. The complex nature of separated data takes time to provide depth information for medical entities like pathophysiological progressions, particular genetic assemblies, diseases, knowledge, psychosomatic and therapeutic relationships, etc. Therefore, for confusing nature of data we need specific ontology pathways to deal with medicines, in which we also know to mean the research that try to find what precise entities occur in the world of precision medicine. Now a day's current trend of information accessing is changed via understanding the way of ontologies among manipulation

Table 9.1 Different terms used in computational examination [13].

Term	Description
Terminology	Group of ideal or conventional terms in a field that might be a standard name endorsed by a central body or merely a frequent use originating in a particular practice
Thesaurus	Terminology witch groups equivalent words into classes
Index	A roster of crucial terms picked automatically from a body of the semi-structured or unstructured text. Upon searching, an index can speed up reaching pertinent results
Controlled Vocabulary	Group of ideal terms generated particularly for a body of text or field
Ontology	Controlled terminology using conventional semantic interactions among principles, exhibited as a narrative rationality that is a subclass of FOPL (first-order predicate logic), selected to adapt computing tractability. A popular model is the Web Ontology Language (OWL)
Classification	Controlled vocabulary which thoroughly defines, from a theoretical point of view, a field or subject and is not described exclusively by the body of the text
Statistical Classification	Classification where each principle is reciprocally unique for preventing duplicate calculation. This is usually attained using a mono-hierarchy, whereas every principle has only one parent. Statistical classification is comprehensive since it comprises excess sub-classes like "unspecified"

of natural language processing based on a computational semantic web network such as web ontological languages (OWL). Meaningless manipulation of defined data like data is approved without appreciation can create challenging problems. Intellectual computational techniques like a statistical examination or machine learning (ML) require classifying individuals' characteristics or nature of variables among large connected datasets. However, for generating functional categories of these datasets, we need assumptions, which one entire firm is important to continuous variables with taxonomic classifications difficulties. Classifications in the contexts of medical ontology define groups from relevant fields in matched platforms like phenotypes, exposures, disorders, or medicines for precision levels studies [3]. Progressively definite methods are available for denoting and explaining such interactions from plain terms into ontologies as mentioned in Table 9.1.

9.3 Data Standards for Interoperability

Standards are available for most medical data types, involving signs and symptoms, diagnoses, laboratory findings, imaging medications, adverse events, procedures, and other phenotypical deformities (Table 9.2).

Table 9.2 Examples for interoperability standards and ontologies commonly used in medicine.

Data type	Ontology	Organization
Diagnosis	SNOMED CT	SNOMED Int'l
Laboratory Findings	LOINC	Regenstrief Institute, Inc.
Imaging	DICOM	ACR and NEMA
Medications	RxNorm	National Library of Medicine (NLM)
Adverse Events	OAE	He Group, University of Michigan Medical School
Procedures	CPT	American Medical Association
Phenotypic deformities	HPO	Monarch Initiative

Such standards are only the initiative in classifying patients profoundly and computing data. Incorporating frameworks and layouts from diverse origins to make them interoperable is challenging [3].

Fundamentally data standards could be described by two elements: structure and semantics. Typically, the structure is a data organization, either on a display of a computerized medical record or a back-end database matrix, while semantics denotes principles and interactions among them. Computer systems need affirmations regarding equal terms. For instance, divide equal terms, codes of local laboratory data for a particular laboratory or hospital are challenging when evaluated against comparable data somewhere else. Likewise, diagnoses retrieved by the broad filed known Systematized Nomenclature of Medicine Clinical Terms (SNOMED CT), a group of terms, which define body structures, biological samples, symptoms, organisms, diagnoses, other disorders' triggers, medications, substances, procedures, equipment, and medical outcomes, do not necessarily agree with equally titled conditions in the International Classification of Diseases (ICD). Briefly, tracking medical data over systems is frequently hindered by structure or nomenclature systems' deviation.

Semantics and structure are not linear yet profoundly tangled, such as in a patient's health record, the scope should be considered for an apparently logical term like myocardial infarction. If the stated myocardial infarction was in the family history section of a computerized medical record, the explanation might be that not exactly the patient but one of the family members had a myocardial infarction. The physician would report a problem list that could incorporate one statement merging the diagnosis and the scope, for example, a family history of myocardial infarction. Despite such a case might look insignificant, combining information sources should adapt various semantic bases (classifications and terminologies) along with expecting additional alteration for such semantics based on their local scope. Often there is intensive alteration like in negating cases (no history of myocardial infarction). Therefore, capitalizing the hope of precision medicine relies on adjusting data over patients and systems with coherent and corresponding layouts along with associated implications [3].

9.4 The Evolution of Ontology

Terminologies have been used for long in retrieving information. For example, looking up for text files or database entries entertained meet definite specifications. In medical field, the process of Metathesaurus facilitated by computer is commonly integrated with broad categorized system

The Unified Medical Language System (UMLS), which comprises with approximate 250$^+$ medical terminologies and coding systems; on the other hand, in Medical Subject Headings (MeSH) innovate sorting and inquiring the information form PubMed; RxNorm for the brand and generic medications terminologies; represent some highly crucial repositories for retrieving information. Such repositories incorporating standard names, directories of synonyms, and cross-references to enable looking up and sorting, are frequently adopted in computerized medical records and national databases [3].

Ontologies describe interactions among principles enabling rational computing and reaching decisions from associated claims. For instance, if ontology defines a virus as an infectious agent and defines infectious meningitis as meningitis caused by an infectious agent, ultimately it would infer that viral meningitis is a subset of infectious meningitis. Aristotle formulated theoretical taxonomies, which are analogous to contemporary ontologies. Lately, researchers applied the ontology term to describe a computed illustration defining certain levels of knowledge. Ontology contains a group of principles (words), their thesaurus, and description-logic interpretations, which assign the logical interactions among such principles.

In ontology, using description logics could ensure logical coherence, yet with many principles over many fields, allowing computing resonance to recognize implied findings in the primary data. Hence, ontologies could use the potential knowledge in medical big data by encrypting these data with computable semantics, allowing ML and other algorithms to handle obstacles in examining high-throughput, multi-modal data via combining it with medical interpretation. Ontologies could be combined with natural language processing to explicate principles in text like those shown in medical notes and enhance mining knowledge from computerized medical records and other repositories. Ontologies could incorporate fundamental scientific data (for instance, animal models' data) and general knowledge (for instance, correlations among disorders and genes), allowing sorting patients according to a body of knowledge extending well behind the computerized medical records and enabling novel medical perspective. Integrating the supercomputers and big data permits uncovering relations and, progressively, etiological logic to reach diagnosing and curing realization [3].

9.5 Ontologies and Classifying Disorders

Carl Linnaeus had formulated the initial contemporary clinical classification (nosology), which could be described as an actual disorders' ontology.

He sectioned disorders into wide ranging category consist of classes (11), orders (37), and species (325). From a contemporary view, Linnaeus's classification comprises certain mistakes. However, his classification has founded for the ICD's initial version in 1893. After instituting the ICD as a repository for the causes of death, it has improved tremendously. However, it remains a standard for managing health, invoicing, and epidemiology, not as a computing reflection of the patient as a biological entity. ICD's ancient versions are reciprocally selective statistical classifications which do not enumerate things twice; and comprehensive as they offer input for anything, hence lies the challenge. The ICDs are unique via a mono-hierarchy (one parentage) where every code possesses just a single parent, preventing duplicate numeration through making unwarranted correlations. Therefore, mono-hierarchies deliberately restrict crucial query and description and hinder significant disorders' examination.

Logical classification of disorders dates back to Hippocrates; however, it continues to be a dynamic study domain of today [13]. Typically, phenotype has referred to individual clear features, sometimes related to genes. Gradually, the word is being adopted by translational scientists, dealing with medical records and omics data, to describe patients' population identical diagnosis based on analogous medical and omics characteristics.

The Electronic Medical Records and Genomics (eMERGE) study revealed that algorithms for computing phenotypes are valuable in clinical institutions operating disparate computerized medical records' systems [14]. These consistent and practical techniques apply standardized coding systems for disorders, laboratory results, medications, adverse reactions, phenotypic deformities, and natural language processing of free text. Almost all algorithms are displayed as a group of English commands, guidelines, and filters that are challenging, for every operator, to compute and incorporate with multi-modal, big data. The ICD codes employed in such algorithms are used only for invoicing and not for differential diagnosis. ML and statistical methods that mine-free text and structured data definitions are promising approaches [15].

SNOMED CT could display complicated principles by integrating separate findings and evidence. For example, acute perforated appendicitis may be described by adding appendix structure to perforation (acute inflammation principle). SNOMED CT applies description logic to identify logical equal methods and convey acute perforated appendicitis, hence offering a computerized and coherent model. Thus, SNOMED CT is superior over simplified terminologies where it could be adopted alternatively in diverse settings and systems through various consumers and provides analogous theoretical and computable interpretation. Meanwhile, most of SNOMED CT's content is primordial and not yet described logically.

The growing utilization of bio-monitoring, wearable devices, and progress in digital imaging, predict evolution in the mass of medical data [16]. Ontologies could coordinate and examine immense amounts of data, which are excessively massive to be handled by a single clinician. Patient-reported data has afforded strong conclusions in certain fields like studies on a genome-wide association [17]. Officially coding clinical terms' plain thesaurus in ontology via combining normative clinical terms with patient-reported data might enhance sorting patients into compelling clusters of disorders [18].

9.6 Phenotypic Ontology of Humans in Rare Disorders

Ontologies have contributed considerably to translational studies and the rare disorders' genetic diagnosis. Genome sequencing has facilitated finding several new disorder-related genes [19]. In many subjects, the diagnosis might alter medical management and household counseling [20]. Variant-derived analysis can distinguish a disorder-triggering variant across several variants in a typical genome or exome. Recognizing the entire medical asset for such data necessitates extra information regarding phenotype anomalies and disorders. Ontologies offer a computerized-analyzing model, which reframes the molecular data when assessing phenotype presentation. The Human Phenotype Ontology (HPO) facilitates intense phenotyping whereby computerized phenotype patterns of human disorders connect closely related terminologies in the hierarchy and adjusted against unique phenotype anomalies [21]. There are many terminologies in a subtype hierarchy that encrypts unique terms for differential diagnosis in accordance with the repetition of the term over each disorder in the HPO repository.

The HPO enables a significantly greater comprehensive representation of medical phenotypes [22]. It is configured for computerized examination through connecting to ontologies of biological variables such as gene function, anatomy, biochemistry, and others and computerized disorders' descriptions [21]. For instance, neutropenia is naturally described via three ontologies' terminologies including neutrophil (cell types), blood (anatomy), and reduced count (variable). Using such multi-variable classification enables using a correlating process to each disorder in the repository to get the nearest fit, or locating cases with analogous phenotype aspects for phenotypical-grouping. Using gene sequencing added to HPO-driven phenotype profile matching enabled prioritizing prospect forms of pathogenic genomes [23].

9.7 Annotations and Ontology Integration

HPO is a basic comprehensive domain prototype has been for rare disorders so far, and we have previously provided a large corpus of HPO disease record profiles to OMIM, Orphanet and DECIPHER [24]. With the latest advances in personal medicine, it is becoming increasingly important to create a basis for phenotype-driven genome analysis and other translational research in other medical fields. As a result, we have extended our work to common phenotypes of human disease using a text-breaking strategy [25] to analyze PubMed Corpus 2014, which has enabled us to conclude 132,620 comments on 3145 common diseases [25]. These notes were validated against a manually cured subset of perturbations and the results of experiments showed a total accuracy of 67%. We showed biologically beneficial phenotypic similarity between specific diseases that share one or more associated genetic variants ("Comprehensive Association Study [GWAS] hit"), as well as phenotypic overlaps between a specific and unusual disease linked to the same genes [25]. Some tools have already been incorporated for genotype-phenotype data in the field of complex diseases and via systematic research studies (GWAS), such as GWAS Central [26] and GWASdb [27], which are likely to be adopted throughout the future for phenomenon-wide association studies with electronic health records.

The efficiency of computational search algorithms within and across species may be enhanced if a detailed list of phenotypic functions is recorded. It is fair to say that the individual commenting on the set of comments constitutes a challenge against all existing phenotype profiles. Therefore, the set of phenotypes selected for the document must be as concise as possible and represent the most common and important observable phenotypes. The Monarch strategy developed a reporting demand meter that tests the width and depth of the phenotype annotation profile in conjunction with all selected phenotypes of humans and model organisms using a five-star rating system for a given individual, with the aim of helping the annotator build a comment profile that is specific enough to exclude related diseases and identify model organisms. Monarch reporting potential is seen in PhenoTips [28] and PhenomeCentral [29].

9.8 Precision Annotation and Integration

Implementation and accuracy of successful phenotypes for the identification and support of treatment strategies vary greatly from useful phenotypes for the healthcare industry and evaluation of standard of care. What distinguishes HPO from other ontologies is that it is mainly designed for use in diagnostic and healthcare situations, and is intended to allow comparisons between various species so that non-human data can also be transmitted. Furthermore, HPO also need to provide an incredibly large range of concepts in order to conduct this task. In an assessment of HPO content relative to the other vocabulary incorporated in the Unified Medical Language

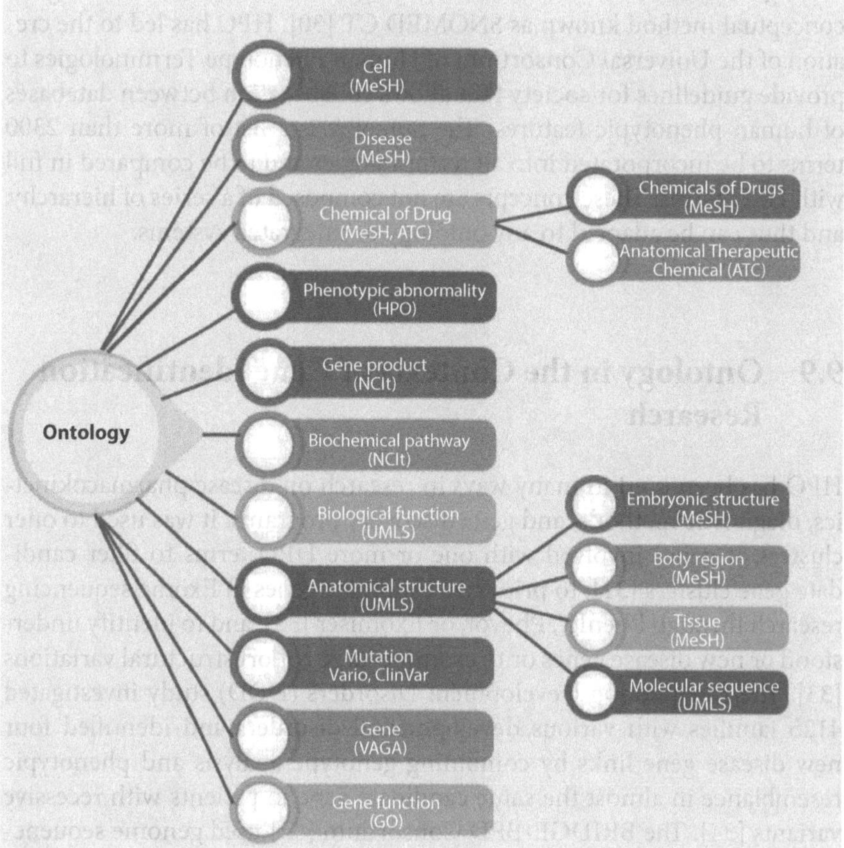

Figure 9.1 Examples of some ontologies.

System (UMLS), Winnenburg and Bodenreider reported 54% range of HPO phenotype terminology in UMLS and just 30% in SNOMED CT. UMLS is a U.S.-developed terminology incorporation framework. The National Medical Library, which contains several traditional biomedical concepts [7]. Some classification systems and terms were used as required in current and well-known biomedical methods, due to the high complexity and diversity of precision medicine and ontology. From well-known biomedical resources such as MeSH, NCIt, UMLS, HPO, Variation Ontology (VariO) and NCBI Gene, we selected and reused the terms and hierarchies according to the different top classes' ontology. These definitions and hierarchies were integrated jointly into a common ontology paradigm as shown in Figure 9.1.

As of the 2015 update, UMLS has now introduced the entire HPO, to expand the reach of phenotype performance. This offers an easy way of finding HPO-coded data into common jargon for healthcare, including the conceptual method known as SNOMED CT [30]. HPO has led to the creation of the Universal Consortium of Human Phenotype Terminologies to provide guidelines for society that allows collaboration between databases of human phenotypic features. The outcome is a list of more than 2300 terms to be incorporated into all terminologies and to be compared in full with HPO terms. These concepts are not composed of a series of hierarchy, and thus can be adapted to any ontology or integrated systems.

9.9 Ontology in the Contexts of Gene Identification Research

HPO has been used in many ways in research on disease pharmacokinetics, diagnostic methods, and gene discovery programs. It was used to offer clusters of genes involved with one or more HPO terms to filter candidate gene clusters [31], to prioritize candidate genes in Exome sequencing research through PhenIX, Phevor, or Exomiser [32], and to identify understood or new disease genes or to examine large cohort structural variations [33]. The Deciphering Development Disorders (DDD) study investigated 4125 families with various developmental disorders and identified four new disease gene links by combining genotype analysis and phenotypic resemblance in almost the same candidate gene in patients with recessive variants [34]. The BRIDGE-BPD Consortium [35] used genome sequencing in conjunction with HPO coding to identify a gain-of-function variant of DIAPH1 into two distinct pedigrees with deafness and macrothrombocytopenia [36]. This result is confirmed by the Phenotype Similarity Regression (SimReg), an algorithm used to identify synthetic phenotypes associated with extreme variation in various genes [38].

HPO-based phenotype analysis also permitted the matching of human phenotypes to mouse phenotypes through crossover testing, thereby helping to discover a dominant enhancement of SRC functional mutation that causes thrombocytopenia, myelofibrosis, bleeding and bone abnormalities [37]. The Matchmaker Exchange Platform (MME) offers a systematic strategy for the discovery of rare gene disease with an integrated phenotype-genotype database network allowing data sharing and data discovery [37] through a robust API [29].

The HPO is the main repository by phenotype for data exchange. Currently, MME connects over 30,000 cases of uncommon diseases to patients through six separate repositories. The HPO is a computational method enabling algorithms to "calculate over" clinical phenotype data through a growing number of HPO Cooperative tools and other classes mentioned in Table 9.3. The tools use the ontological structure of the HPO that allows the connection of individual words to a knowledge content, a specificity metric, or the underlying conceptual meanings of the words, so that HPO terms can be related to other resources such as models.

Table 9.3 Resources and applications in human phenotype ontology contexts.

Resource no.	Resource name and explanations
R1	**A differential diagnosis based tools on phenotypes**
1	Phenomizer
2	BOQA
3	FACE2GENE
4	Phenolyzer
R2	**Analysis of the exomes/genomes by phenotype**
1	Exomiser
2	PhenIX
3	Phevor

(Continued)

Table 9.3 Resources and applications in human phenotype ontology contexts. (*Continued*)

Resource no.	**Resource name and explanations**
4	PhenoVar
5	eXtasy
6	OMIMExplorer
7	Phen-Gen
8	Geno2MP
9	Genomiser
10	SimReg
R3	**Effective tools for network analysis**
1	TopGene/ToppFunn
2	WebGestalt
3	SUPERFAMILY
4	GREAT
R4	**Heterogeneous random walk network analysis**
1	PANDA
2	PREDICT
R5	**Managing and analyzing clinical data**
1	Phenotips
2	Patient Archive
3	GENESIS (GEM.app)
R6	**Cross-species study of the phenotypes**
1	PhenoDigm
2	MouseFinder
3	Monarch

(*Continued*)

Table 9.3 Resources and applications in human phenotype ontology contexts. (*Continued*)

Resource no.	Resource name and explanations
4	PhenomeNet
5	UberPheno
6	MORPHIN
7	PhenogramViz
R7	**Resources and repositories of phenotypic information**
1	Orphanet
2	MalaCards
3	NIH genetic testing registry
4	OMIM
5	dcGO
6	ClinVar
7	GeneSetDB
8	MSeqDR
9	DIDA (digenic diseases database)
10	Genetic and Rare Diseases (GARD) Information Center
R8	**Visualization tool and methods**
1	PhenoStacks
2	PhenoBlocks
3	DECIPHER (phenogram)
4	Phenogrid

9.10 Personalizing Care for Chronic Illness

Chronic patients are complicated medical cases that need harmonious interplay of various professionals. An accurate intervention for these patients necessitates a critical investigation of every patient's conditions individually and compliance with authentication based typical interference schemes to these types of conditions. Various additional experimental incidents in the field of medical science like incorrect diagnosis, non-observed comorbidities, absent information, non-observed relevant complaints, or prevention in which discovery relies on inference capabilities of the concerned professionals. For instance, one personalization method adjusts the ontology content to the observed features in the medical record of a particular patient, rendering a personalized ontology encompassing only the relevant clinical information to handle this patient by the healthcare professionals. Another personalization method employs the modified ontology of an enduring individual patients to change generic medical intervention plans into individual ones. Eventually, for comorbid patients, this method infers with incorporating various personal plans into a unified individualized one. Subsequently, the ontology can also be utilized as the information based, decision supporting computer added tools to assist healthcare providers to identify exceptional incidents like mistaken diagnosis, non-observed comorbidities, absent information, non-observed relevant complaints, or preventive procedures [39].

9.11 Roadblocks Toward Precision Medicine

The greatest dilemma is instituting confidentiality legislation without accounting for the universal big data all around. The confidentiality and privacy of the patient are required to preserve patients' confidence and collaboration. However, a novel ethics model might be needed to match confidentiality legal aspirations' with the community and future patient's demands for disseminating clinical data toward the community wellness.

Another dilemma is the endeavor and price of introducing into and extracting data out of computerized medical records. Submitting hand-operated structured data by healthcare givers is time-consuming and non-adaptable. Growing attempts on standardized application portals with computerized medical records from repositories of data and devices might serve (for example, data gathered and submitted by patients). Consistently extracting medical content from dictated remarks or voice recordings of the patient visits' is growing applicable [39]. Missing interoperability because of insufficient coherence and uniformity of data and information repositories (laboratories, computerized medical record systems, and warehouses),

Standardization could be accomplished via public involvement and robust investment in translational research [21].

9.12 Future Perspectives

The dream on the horizon is optimizing huge quantities of data to find safe and effective therapies. The challenge lies in the multi-axes of patients' features to be inspected. For example, demographics, anthropometrics, family history, signs and symptoms, laboratory findings, radiographic images, diagnoses, or omics measures. The need for readily available data in the individual patient digital record system, the resemblance of the patient's record to the standard patient, and the capacity to analyze such big data in practice either on healthcare facility or population level are challenging. Hence, the rationale for upgrading the learning health system to almost uniform patients' subgroups stage [40].

A precision medicine assembly, chaired by the National Research Council, has submitted a novel biological and medical taxonomy, which would be designed to identify and serve the multi-axes of fundamental science and medical features as a matrix describing disorders endo-types [41]. Ontologies can embed findings from research data and the well-structured medical data, leading to computerize-able fundamental science and medical findings to show current knowledge and enable novel conclusions. Embedding such data allows categorizing disorders over many sorts of data structurally for further potential, powerful, and sophisticated patients' classification.

9.13 Conclusion

Ontologies are expected to create more robust and interoperable healthcare information systems. They also could transfer, reuse, and share patient data. Their most vital advantage might be supporting the assimilation of data and knowledge. Precision medicine can be described as wide-ranging information based along with ontological systems, which executes pattern recognition of individual patient via identifying unique profiles to reduce much of the complexity as a result of presenting a distinct, precise definition of this domain. However, introducing a modern discipline, the case for personalized and precision medicine, generates enthusiasm about its implied applications yet uncertainty regarding its practical achievement for the abundance of the accompanying data which pretends significant hurdles in their analysis.

References

1. Hudson, K., Lifton, R., Patrick-Lake, B., The precision medicine initiative cohort program—Building a Research Foundation for 21st Century Medicine. *Precision Medicine Initiative (PMI) Working Group Rep. Advisory Committee Director, ed.*, 508, 107, 2015.
2. Ginsburg, G.S. and Phillips, K.A., Precision medicine: From science to value. *Health Affairs*, 37, 5, 694–701, 2018.
3. Haendel, M.A., Chute, C.G., Robinson, P.N., Classification, ontology, and precision medicine. *N. Engl. J. Med.*, 379, 15, 1452–1462, 2018.
4. Emmert-Streib, F. and Dehmer, M., A machine learning perspective on Personalized Medicine: An automized, comprehensive knowledge base with ontology for pattern recognition. *Mach. Learn. Knowl. Extr.*, 1, 1, 149–156, 2019.
5. Dennis, J.A., Gittner, L.S., George, A.K., Queen, C.M., Opioid Use Disorder Terminologies and the Role of Public Health in Addressing Stigma. *Alcohol. Treat. Q*, 1–9, 2020.
6. Nelson, S.J., Zeng, K., Kilbourne, J., Powell, T., Moore, R., Normalized names for clinical drugs: RxNorm at 6 years. *J. Am. Med. Inf. Assoc.*, 18, 4, 441–448, 2011.
7. Bodenreider, O., The unified medical language system (UMLS): Integrating biomedical terminology. *Nucleic Acids Res.*, 32, suppl_1, D267–D270, 2004.
8. Chute, C.G., Clinical classification and terminology: Some history and current observations. *J. Am. Med. Inf. Assoc.*, 7, 3, 298–303, 2000.
9. Robinson, P.N. and Bauer, S., *Introduction to bio-ontologies*, CRC Press, Boca Raton, Florida, 2011.
10. Moldovan, D., Leveraging Ontologies for Natural Language Processing in Enterprise Applications, in: *On the Move to Meaningful Internet Systems: OTM 2019 Workshops: Confederated International Workshops: EI2N, FBM, ICSP, Meta4eS and SIAnA 2019*, Rhodes, Greece, October 21–25, 2019, Revised Selected Papers, vol. 11878, Springer Nature, p. 79, 2020.
11. Boyles, R.R., Thessen, A.E., Waldrop, A., Haendel, M.A., Ontology-based data integration for advancing toxicological knowledge. *Curr. Opin. Toxicol.*, 16, 67–74, 2019.
12. Pathak, J., Bailey, K.R., Beebe, C.E., Bethard, S., Carrell, D.S., Chen, P.J., Huff, S.M., Normalization and standardization of electronic health records for high-throughput phenotyping: The SHARPn consortium. *J. Am. Med. Inf. Assoc.*, 20, e2, e341–e348, 2013.
13. Cornet, R. and Chute, C.G., Health concept and knowledge management: Twenty-five years of evolution. *Yearbook Med. Inf.*, Suppl 1, S32, 2016.
14. Newton, K.M., Peissig, P.L., Kho, A.N., Bielinski, S.J., Berg, R.L., Choudhary, V., Pacheco, J.A., Validation of electronic medical record-based phenotyping algorithms: Results and lessons learned from the eMERGE network. *J. Am. Med. Inf. Assoc.*, 20, e1, e147–e154, 2013.

15. Smoller, J.W., The use of electronic health records for psychiatric phenotyping and genomics. *Am. J. Med. Genet. Part B Neuropsychiatr. Genet.*, 177, 7, 601–612, 2018.
16. Pourzanjani, A., Quisel, T., Foschini, L., Adherent use of digital health trackers is associated with weight loss. *PloS One*, 11, 4, e0152504, 2016.
17. Eriksson, N., Macpherson, J.M., Tung, J.Y., Hon, L.S., Naughton, B., Saxonov, S., Mountain, J., Web-based, participant-driven studies yield novel genetic associations for common traits. *PLoS Genet.*, 6, 6, e1000993, 2010.
18. Vasilevsky, N.A., Foster, E.D., Engelstad, M.E., Carmody, L., Might, M., Chambers, C., Boerkoel, C.F., Plain-language medical vocabulary for precision diagnosis. *Nat. Genet.*, 50, 4, 474–476, 2018.
19. Dragojlovic, N., Elliott, A.M., Adam, S., van Karnebeek, C., Lehman, A., Mwenifumbo, J.C., Lynd, L.D., The cost and diagnostic yield of exome sequencing for children with suspected genetic disorders: A benchmarking study. *Genet. Med.*, 20, 9, 1013–1021, 2018.
20. Meng, L., Pammi, M., Saronwala, A., Magoulas, P., Ghazi, A.R., Vetrini, F., Ward, P., Use of exome sequencing for infants in intensive care units: Ascertainment of severe single-gene disorders and effect on medical management. *JAMA Pediatrics*, 171, 12, e173438–e173438, 2017.
21. Köhler, S., Vasilevsky, N.A., Engelstad, M., Foster, E., McMurry, J., Aymé, S., Brudno, M., The human phenotype ontology in 2017. *Nucleic Acids Res.*, 45, D1, D865–D876, 2017.
22. Winnenburg, R. and Bodenreider, O., Coverage of phenotypes in standard terminologies. *Joint Bio-Ontologies BioLINK ISMB*, 41–44, 2014.
23. Smedley, D., Schubach, M., Jacobsen, J.O., Köhler, S., Zemojtel, T., Spielmann, M., Haendel, M.A., A whole-genome analysis framework for effective identification of pathogenic regulatory variants in Mendelian disease. *Am. J. Hum. Genet.*, 99, 3, 595–606, 2016.
24. Köhler, S., Doelken, S.C., Mungall, C.J., Bauer, S., Firth, H.V., Bailleul-Forestier, I., FitzPatrick, D.R., The Human Phenotype Ontology project: Linking molecular biology and disease through phenotype data. *Nucleic Acids Res.*, 42, D1, D966–D974, 2014.
25. Groza, T., Köhler, S., Doelken, S., Collier, N., Oellrich, A., Smedley, D., Robinson, P.N., Automatic concept recognition using the human phenotype ontology reference and test suite corpora. *Database*, 5015bav005, 13, 2015.
26. Beck, T., Hastings, R.K., Gollapudi, S., Free, R.C., Brookes, A.J., GWAS Central: A comprehensive resource for the comparison and interrogation of genome-wide association studies. *Eur. J. Hum. Genet.*, 22, 7, 949–952, 2014.
27. Bush, W.S., Oetjens, M.T., Crawford, D.C., Unravelling the human genome–phenome relationship using phenome-wide association studies. *Nat. Rev. Genet.*, 17, 3, 129, 2016.
28. Girdea, M., Dumitriu, S., Fiume, M., Bowdin, S., Boycott, K.M., Chénier, S., So, J., Pheno Tips: Patient Phenotyping Software for Clinical and Research Use. *Human Mutation*, 34, 8, 1057–1065, 2013.

29. Buske, O.J., Girdea, M., Dumitriu, S., Gallinger, B., Hartley, T., Trang, H., Links, A.E., PhenomeCentral: A portal for phenotypic and genotypic matchmaking of patients with rare genetic diseases. *Human Mutation*, 36, 10, 931–940, 2015.
30. Dhombres, F. and Bodenreider, O., Interoperability between phenotypes in research and healthcare terminologies—Investigating partial mappings between HPO and SNOMED CT. *J. Biomed. Semant.*, 7, 1, 3, 2016.
31. Pinto, D., Delaby, E., Merico, D., Barbosa, M., Merikangas, A., Klei, L., Vorstman, J.A., Convergence of genes and cellular pathways dysregulated in autism spectrum disorders. *Am. J. Hum. Genet.*, 94, 5, 677–694, 2014.
32. Covone, A.E., Fiorillo, C., Acquaviva, M., Trucco, F., Morana, G., Ravazzolo, R., Minetti, C., WES in a family trio suggests involvement of TECPR2 in a complex form of progressive motor neuron disease. *Clin. Genet.*, 90, 2, 182–185, 2016.
33. Singh, T., Kurki, M.I., Curtis, D., Purcell, S.M., Crooks, L., McRae, J., Suvisaari, J. *et al.*, Rare loss-of-function variants in SETD1A are associated with schizophrenia and developmental disorders. *Nat. Neurosci.*, 19, 4, 571–577, 2016.
34. Akawi, N., McRae, J., Ansari, M., Balasubramanian, M., Blyth, M., Brady, A.F., Foulds, N., Discovery of four recessive developmental disorders using probabilistic genotype and phenotype matching among 4,125 families. *Nat. Genet.*, 47, 11, 1363, 2015.
35. Lentaigne, C., Freson, K., Laffan, M.A., Turro, E., Ouwehand, W.H., Inherited platelet disorders: Toward DNA-based diagnosis. *Blood, J. Am. Soc. Hematol.*, 127, 23, 2814–2823, 2016.
36. Philippakis, A.A., Azzariti, D.R., Beltran, S., Brookes, A.J., Brownstein, C.A., Brudno, M., Dumitriu, S., The Matchmaker Exchange: A platform for rare disease gene discovery. *Human Mutation*, 36, 10, 915–921, 2015.
37. Turro, E., Greene, D., Wijgaerts, A., Thys, C., Lentaigne, C., Bariana, T.K., Papadia, S., A dominant gain-of-function mutation in universal tyrosine kinase SRC causes thrombocytopenia, myelofibrosis, bleeding, and bone pathologies. *Sci. Transl. Med.*, 8, 328, 328ra30–328ra30, 2016.
38. Riaño, D., Real, F., López-Vallverdú, J.A., Campana, F., Ercolani, S., Mecocci, P., Caltagirone, C., An ontology-based personalization of healthcare knowledge to support clinical decisions for chronically ill patients. *J. Biomed. Inf.*, 45, 3, 429–446, 2012.
39. Chung, A.E. and Basch, E.M., Incorporating the patient's voice into electronic health records through patient-reported outcomes as the "review of systems". *J. Am. Med. Inf. Assoc.*, 22, 4, 914–916, 2015.

40. Butala, N.M., VanRooyen, M.J., Patel, R.B., Improved health outcomes in urban slums through infrastructure upgrading. *Social Sci. Med.*, 71, 5, 935–940, 2010.
41. Dzau, V., Ginsburg, G.S., Finkelman, E., Balatbat, C., Flott, K., Prestt, J., Precision Medicine A Global Action Plan for Impact, in: *WISH Forums Reports*, Doha, Qatar, World Innovation Summit for Health, 2016.

10

A Knowledgebase Model Using RDF Knowledge Graph for Clinical Decision Support Systems

Ravi Lourdusamy and Xavierlal J. Mattam*

Department of Computer Science, Sacred Heart College (Autonomous), Tirupattur, Tamil Nadu, India

Abstract

Clinical Decision Support Systems are used in healthcare to assist in making life-saving decisions. Therefore, such systems have to be efficient and reliable with relevant knowledge that is periodically updated. With vast knowledge available in medical literature and in websites, the challenge is in curating that knowledge on a knowledgebase to be used by the decision support system. In order to curate knowledge in a knowledgebase system the easiest method is to make use of the already well-developed relational database system. But that does not solve problems specially when it comes to representing knowledge having related concepts. Recently, the use of knowledge graphs has become popular for knowledge representation. The use of RDF triples in storing Knowledge Graphs is a convenient method of knowledgebase curation. With a centralized form of RDF Knowledge Graphs in a clinical decision support system, the required presentation of knowledge will become easier to handle. A model for such a knowledgebase is proposed in the chapter that make use of open information extraction systems to capture relevant knowledge from medical literature and curate that in the knowledgebase of the clinical decision support system.

Keywords: Knowledgebase, knowledge graphs, knowledgebase systems, resources description framework, clinical decision support system

**Corresponding author*: xaviermattam@gmail.com; ORCID ID: 0000-0002-5182-3627

Vishal Jain, Jyotir Moy Chatterjee, Ankita Bansal and Abha Jain (eds.) Semantic Web for Effective Healthcare, (215–248) © 2022 Scrivener Publishing LLC

10.1 Introduction

Knowledgebase systems using relational databases have been popular in recent years especially since the incorporation of artificial intelligence into such a system is an easy task. But the multiple tables and identities linking them have been cumbersome. Even to run artificial intelligence algorithms such as machine learning and deep learning algorithms are found to be difficult on such complicated relational database systems. When it comes to complex decision-making systems such as the clinical decision support systems, relational databases have to be an intricate maze. The information retrieval tasks from the knowledge bases of such a system will be a herculean process beyond the possibility of creating an efficient and reliable system. Graph databases on the other hand make use of the semantic structure of knowledge to link various concepts using its relationship edges. Such a structure is much easier to visualize and so, information retrieval will be more straightforward. It will therefore be less resource-hungry than the relational database systems.

Resource Description Framework or RDF makes use of graph framework to represent information in form of triples. The RDF graphs are directed graphs that consist of the concepts for its nodes and the relationship between the concepts for the edges. RDF graphs make use of semantic networks represented using ontology. The RDF graphs are useful to represent complex information in knowledge bases and the simplicity of its structure makes it highly portable across applications in any system.

Representation of knowledge in any knowledge base is a challenge. The knowledge graphs are pragmatic models of knowledge representation that make use of an ontology to form new knowledge. The interlinking of the entity relationships in a knowledge graph contributes to the search efficiency using knowledge graphs. RDF knowledge graphs are machine-readable and there it can be processed in machines. The RDF knowledge graphs are highly interlinked in a logically consistent form permitting machines to reason using it to search and retrieve relevant information. That is why RDF knowledge graphs can be highly efficient in knowledgebase systems that require robust and reliable information retrieval systems such as the Clinical Decision Support Systems.

The efficiency and reliability of information retrieval depend solely on the query language used. SPARQL with its ability to convert natural language queries into a machine-readable format allows users of the system to retrieve relevant information from the RDF knowledge graph efficiently. Since the natural language queries contain semantic information that can be easily processed on the ontological RDF knowledge graph, the SPARQL interpretation of the queries play the intermediate role. Another advantage of the SPARQL is its portability across multiple programming languages and user interfaces. The difficulty that most knowledgebase systems face is its compatibility with existing systems. With the use of SPARQL on RDF knowledge graph-based systems, the compatibility issue can be reduced to a great extent.

Clinical Decision Support Systems or CDSS are systems that render decision support in healthcare. The knowledgebase CDSS makes use of the knowledge base that is created from multiple sources. The knowledgebase is the backbone of any knowledgebase CDSS. The efficiency, reliability, and robustness of the CDSS depend on the knowledge base. Therefore, the knowledge representation in the knowledge base of the CDSS is the biggest challenge in the creation of a fully functional CDSS. Using RDF knowledge graphs for knowledge representation in the CDSS and using SPARQL for information retrieval has two big advantages over other systems. Firstly, the knowledge representation will be pretty straightforward and visualization of such knowledge will not be difficult. Secondly, such systems will be highly portable. Therefore, the compatibility of such a system with the already existing systems will not become a hindrance to the operation of the systems.

The chapter highlights the use of RDF Knowledge Graph for CDSS and proposes a model of a Knowledgebase CDSS using RDF Knowledge Graph. In the following section, a comparison is made of the traditional relational database and graph database. The section after that will introduce the RDF model of a graph database and elaborate on the technologies associated with it. An elaborate discussion is done in the section following that on knowledgebase systems, Knowledge Graphs, RDF Knowledge Graphs, and SPARQL query language. Methods of information extraction are then discussed together with the proposed knowledge base model and the evaluation measurements generally used. Before the conclusion of the chapter, there is a discussion on the limitations of the knowledge base creation and future possibilities for research and development in knowledgebase systems for CDSS.

10.2 Relational Database to Graph Database

There has been a constant evolution in the storage and use of data ever since computers began to gain popularity in the early 1960s. A lot of study of research has been done to make efficient use of the data available. The relational database model that E.F. Codd formulated in 1970 and was commercialized in the 1980s has developed into a well-evolved system in the later years. It has been traditionally considered for any database application [1]. But with the advent of Big Data precipitated by the universal growth of the internet, the well-developed relational database system is left wanting and newer models have taken its place especially in the field of knowledge management.

10.2.1 Relational Database for Knowledge Representation

In the 1970s when the relational database was a well-developed form of data storage, logic programming in the form of ProLog evolved. The strong affinity between the two could have been the result of the contemporary development of the two [2]. For decades after that, there has been a lot of research on coupling relational databases with ProLog [3–5]. It is effective as far as linked data is utilized for the knowledgebase system. The significant impetus to the growth in the interest in combining logical programming and relational database is the implementation of the Fifth Generation Computer Systems project that began in April 1982 with the formation of the Institute of New Generation Computer Technology (ICOT) [6]. Research and development on knowledge base systems at ICOT envisages the use of logical programming using ProLog integrated into a conventional database system that stores a huge amount of data [7]. Another momentous impulsion that worked in favor of the coalescing of rule-based programming language with a relational database is the growth in the interest in the use of logical queries by the database communities [8].

A database can be considered for logical programming in two fundamental ways. The first is the model-theoretic approach using first-order logic or predictive logic and the second is the proof-theoretic approach which makes use of rule-based propositional logic or production rules [9]. The creation of a knowledge base using the latter approach is convenient since the relational database is similar to production systems in modularity, uniformity, naturalness, and key-connectedness. Using these analogous concepts and the fourth normal form of the relational database to transform IF conditions to relations, the conversion of the production rules to a relational database is achieved. The conversion of production rules to relational database removes barriers of logical programming with regards to knowledge representation, storage, and inferencing [10]. The former approach, on the other hand, allows the representation of incomplete knowledge in the sense that all facts about the knowledge represented need to be in the knowledge base. Therefore, knowledge representation using first-order logic allows the incremental growth of knowledge allowing the system to develop new knowledge by interaction. Although formalism is achieved in the process, the system becomes conceptually and computationally complex requiring a huge database [11].

An intelligent database is one that can not only store data in a perfectly linked relational manner but one that will also be able to produce knowledge for solving various problems. The relational database system has benefits such as being able to share data without compromising data consistency and integrity. Without a tool to extract knowledge from the data, the database cannot be useful for any knowledgebase system. A knowledgebase system is one in which data is stored in the form of knowledge that could be useful to the system. Structured query language (SQL) is a tool that could be utilized to convert data in a relational database system to knowledge. To do that the data is stored in relational database tables and the SQL queries are used to extract knowledge out of the database. So, the system does not operate as a knowledge base system but rather a database system from which knowledge can be extracted [12]. Although the possibility of building an intelligent system using an already existing database system seems to be attractive, their limitations in terms of knowledge and their time and space complexities are far greater than the advantages.

A method of circumventing the problem of using SQL in a programming language is the use of Horn clauses. ProLog is built on Horn clauses and is used to define and query a rational database that is limited to First-Order Logic. The non-terminal relation symbols that restrict first-order formulas could be expressed as sets of Horn clauses by making use of a fix-point operator that is applied to positive existential queries. One drawback of using Horn clauses is that adding a relation tuple to a database using the Horn clause program cannot delete the output of the query. To overcome the deficiency, an extension of the Horn clause to include negated terminal relation symbols could be thought of but universal quantification cannot be express by it. The other possibility is to let arbitrary first-order formulas with non-terminals as programs which are no solution at all [13].

Attempts were also made to infuse taxonomy and semantic interpretation using Horn clauses by making use of the idea of concepts and relations. It was a step towards merging Semantic Networks with logical programming and a relational database to create the knowledge base for a system. These attempts were seen as a stop-gap solution to the problem of constraint satisfaction. The use of domains of concepts greatly helped the reduction of time and space complexities by avoiding redundant computation and backtracking checks through an early deduction of failures [14]. The use of a relational database to store semantic networks has been studied with practical examples of how two-dimensional tables could be used to store nodes that could point to non-structural multidimensional knowledge [15]. Such solutions reduce the time and space complexities of the storage and knowledge query processes but fail in efficiency and robustness that is required of a good knowledge base. When the database reaches the upper limits of its performing capacity, they tend to fail to reduce the efficiency which in the case of any knowledge system is important. Moreover, there is no uniformity in the knowledge representation especially when it comes to the variety of knowledge-sharing activities and therefore relational database storage is insufficient [16]. Another reason why the relational database is bound to fail as the knowledge base is that a complete large-scale knowledge system cannot be effectively represented using a relational database [15].

Although the relational database was a well-developed system and is quite efficient with queries using SQL, it lacks efficiency when it comes to representing and storing knowledge. Knowledge comes from both structured and unstructured sources and so they must be represented in a manner that knowledge acquisition, knowledge base creation, and formation of inferred knowledge is possible without compromising on the time and space complexity.

10.2.2 NoSQL Databases

Relational and SQL databases go beyond data storage and query processing. They offer processing logic with vigorous constructs in declarative language using schemas and metadata and with assured consistency. They are also quick in recovery with logging, allow multiuser operation and synchronization with adequate user roles and security and more importantly, allow indexing for fast searches. All these benefits of the database result in complex processing that makes it quickly reach its limits when dealing with huge data. So the emphasis on data integrity and security compromises its performance, efficiency and flexibility especially when dealing with big data available on the web [17]. Other problems with relational or SQL databases are the slow reading and writing speeds, limited capacity and difficulty in scalability especially when a large amount of data is involved [18].

The term NoSQL was introduced by Carlo Strozzi in 1998 as a modified version of the relational database with open-source, relational, lightweight characteristics without SQL. NoSQL was then standing for "no SQL." It was later converted into a non-relational distributed structured data storage by Johan Oskarsson in early 2009[1]. NoSQL then was updated to mean "not only SQL." The rapid expansion of the internet since the early 2000s assisted the growing popularity of NoSQL especially in the web-scale databases that involve the management of an enormous amount of data [17, 19]. The growth of NoSQL was, heavily influenced by Google's Bigtable and Amazon's Dynamo systems [20].

The obsession with NoSQL among big data users is primarily its non-relational model that avoids the complex join operations of the relational database. Moreover, NoSQL allows data to be distributed in a different location and is managed using metadata. The distributed nature of NoSQL also allows it to be horizontally scalable as necessary. The freedom from schemas in inserting data makes it flexible in adding data. Being open-source software, the possibility for customization and improvement of the model is highly preferred by data users. The data replication is in NoSQL is effortless ensuring high availability of data. The application programming interface (API) provided by NoSQL is simple and is an attractive component for programmers. The ACID (Atomicity, Consistency, Isolation, Durability) properties of the relational database are replaced by BASE (basically available, soft-state, and eventual consistency) property of NoSQL [17–28].

CAP (Consistency, Availability and tolerance to network Partitions) theorem, according to Eric Brewer of University of California, Berkeley, first appeared in 1998 and was published first in 1999 and later in 2000. It is considered midway between the ACID property of relational database and BASE property of NoSQL. According to the theorem only any one of the properties, that is, either consistency or availability or partition tolerance have to be compromised in the database. That is because if network partition is present, then either availability (by replication) or consistency (by holding on to only one set of databases) can be guaranteed as shown in Figure 10.1. If network partitioning is not a requirement, then consistency and availability can co-exist. The consistency spoken of in CAP differs from the consistency in ACID in the sense that consistency in CAP is about the physical consistency of data in all the nodes while the consistency in ACID is the logical consistency or integrity of the data in the database [18, 19, 21, 29].

Network partitions are not easy to come by in a distributed system and therefore, for all practical purposes, the consistency and availability of the database are maintained. In case a partition is present, then the consistency

[1]https://en.wikipedia.org/wiki/NoSQL, Retrieved August 31, 2020.

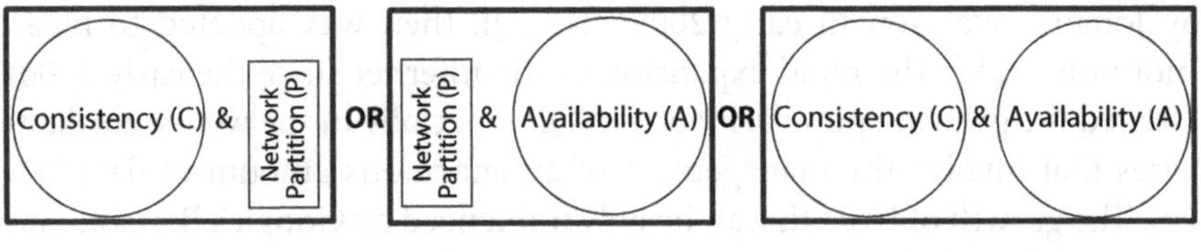

Figure 10.1 CAP. Consistency and tolerance to network partition or availability and tolerance to network partition or consistency and availability.

and availability of the subsystems are taken as an advantage [21, 29]. It is easier to sacrifice partitioning to preserve consistency and availability [30]. There has been criticism against the wide use of CAP theorem in influencing the popularity of distributed data systems like NoSQL especially since there is no clear definition regarding consistency in the literature on CAP [31].

NoSQL is classified according to the different data models that are used in the NoSQL databases. The three common groups of NoSQL are Key-value stores, Document Stores and Column stores. The Key-value stores provide access to the database using a single unique key which may not be from the database and has no specified structure. The key allows modification of data in the fields but is not used to query the data in those fields. Document stores hold data in the form of document which contains an arbitrary set of attributes without any particular structure. The document stores allow indexing and searches based on the indices and query function. Column stores hold data in columns that form tuples which are identified using the column key, row key or the timestamp. The columns could be grouped together to form a column-family [17, 19, 22, 25, 26, 28]. There are other categories like Graph Databases, Multi-model Databases, Object Databases, Grid and Cloud Database Solutions, XML Databases, Multidimensional Databases, Multi-value Databases, Event Sourcing, Time Series Databases, Scientific and Specialized Databases and other related NoSQL Databases [25].

With over 225 NoSQL database management systems available, the evaluation of their performance is important before adapting any model. The performance of the model depends on the type of data that is being used. In general, the evaluation of the NoSQL system is carried out using the following criteria: data access, performance, scalability, availability, multiple data centers, big data integration, administration and mobility. But the use of CAP theorem to evaluate NoSQL system is most convenient. The other criteria for evaluation include cost, requirements, workload and scope of the system. Since there is a variation in the different NoSQL systems, a generalized comparison would be inappropriate even if it is possible. Moreover, with the growth of new versions and systems, a general evaluation cannot be relied on for the choice of the database system. The evaluation of even a single criterion in so many and evolving systems is not easily possible. Therefore, an appropriate system is chosen more of convenience in most cases [32–35].

10.2.3 Graph Database

The outstanding feature of a Graph Database is the Relationship. Relational databases and nearly all models of NoSQL databases have linked data. Linked data expresses the relation between data but does not go deeper. Graph Database on the other hand expresses the relationship between the data. The data in Graph Database is expressed as nodes of a graph and the relationship between the data is expressed as the edge between two nodes. The greatest advantage of establishing a relationship between nodes is that the time complexity of search reduces in comparison with linked data in proposition to the depth between the initial and final nodes [36, 37].

There are some unique characteristics of graphs that make the graph database valuable. A graph can have vector values attached to its nodes or edges that could be used to indicate properties of the nodes or edges and can be critical in influencing an algorithm or analysis of the graphs. Such values, known as attributes, are properties of the nodes or their edges. The relationship between nodes in a graph could also be symmetric or asymmetric depending on the requirement of the problem. If the relation is symmetric, then the graph is directed and the corresponding edges indicate the tail and head node. The tail node is the node from which the edge begins and the head node is where the edge ends. The distinction between directed and undirected graphs are used for measurements such as connectivity or path lengths. In certain graphs, the nodes and edges are labelled to indicate a particular type which could influence the outcome of the algorithm that works on the graph. For example, the nodes or edges may be labeled positive or negative to change the operations on that nodes or edges [38].

Different models of graph databases are in use. A Simple Graph Model is commonly used as a framework for graph processing. They are not commonly used as a database but rather is more often used in designing a more complex model such as the Labelled Property Graph. Hypergraphs, where an edge is connected to any number of nodes and is called hyperedges, is a generalization of a simple graph model. It used mostly to represent networks and rarely used as database storage. Hypernodes are another generalized simple graph model where a hypernode, which is an entity containing a set of nodes and edges, substitute the nodes of a simple graph. In other words, hypernodes are simple graphs nested within graphs. Again, due to the additional complexity involved, the hypernodes, like the hypergraphs, are rarely used as a graph database. The two popularly used graph databases are the Labelled Property Graph Model (LPG) or simply called the property graphs and the Resource Description Framework (RDF), which we will deal with more elaborately in section 2 of the chapter. LPG has additional graph properties or attributes to deal with various complex real-world problems. The labels attached to the nodes or edges of the LPG define different subsets or classes. Every node or edge can have any number of such properties, each containing a key to identify the property and the value associated with the property. The restriction and use of the labels create variants in the LPG [38–40].

Physical storage of the graph database is executed using different methods. Dividing the data into records or smaller units are followed by record-based graph database systems. For the sake of data locality, the records are physically stored in contiguous memory or disk clusters. The records could be of variable or fixed lengths. Each vertex of the graph is stored as one or more records which are sometimes called the vertex or node records and the edges are either stored in the same record that contains their corresponding source and destination vertices or is stored in separate edge records. In these record base systems, the pointers to the connecting memory location are held within each record so that the query concerning the destination vertex can be found faster. To save space, the labels or properties of edges are not stored in the record in some systems. These are the lightweight edges. The lightweight edges contain only the information or the memory address of the destination vertex. Index-based graph database systems store data in index structures that locate data that is stored in different parts and use the location information for faster retrieval. When physical location changes it is enough to update the index rather than to change all the pointers associated with the data locations [39].

Although graph databases have gained a lot of popularity in recent years, they are restricted in certain aspects since they are not yet fully evolved as in the case of the relational database. Functionally they lack query optimization capacity, when partitioned query need access to multiple partitions, unlike NoSQL, graph databases cannot read and write from multiple buffers, graph database has restrictions regarding schema and constraint definitions leading to inconsistencies in the data and finally, graph databases have querying restrictions that do not allow transitive closure. A graph database is meant of the help with Big Data requirements but there are some limitations in that. Extraction of data from non-graphical resources is complex, the complexity and wide distribution of the huge data set lead to high cost in a query, batch processing that is usually carried out in graph database do not work always in real-time processing, graph algorithms are not adequate for Big Data processing, the performance of graph algorithms used for parallel processing are not optimum and heterogeneous, incomplete and inconsistent Big Data sets need to be semantically integrated for effective querying which is not fully functional in any of the present graph database systems. There are many other similar challenges in the use of graph database systems that have to be taken care of in its future evolutions [41].

Graph databases are an ideal solution to the world of Big Data but unlike the relational database systems, the graph database systems are far from a full evolution. Yet, their popularity has not diminished as it can be seen from the increasing number of systems that are developed using a graph database. With further research and development, a system without the present limitations could be developed.

10.3 RDF

Big Data is characterized by five elements, namely, volume, velocity, variety, value and veracity, that intrinsically form the huge and complex datasets that cannot be handled by relational database and the traditional SQL. Big Data, especially in its unstructured form and containing petabytes of data, is analyzed for quick results by leading internet applications like Google, Facebook, Amazon, and the like [42]. In 1995, the Worldwide Web Consortium (W3C) started experimenting with a platform for Internet Content Selection (PICS) that was developed by the Internet Engineering Task Force (IETF) for rating the content of the web pages for the use of various communities that required it specially to monitor the web content. Due to various limitations in PICS, W3C formed the PICS Next Generation (PICSNG) working group to work on the common problem regarding resource description. The specifications worked out by the group could be applied to many applications which were later consolidated by W3C as the RDF working group. Although a lot of contribution was made by PICSNG in the creation of RDF, the RDF as at its present stage of evolution is shaped by the influence of many W3C member companies and several metadata efforts [43–45]. RDF has the five elements of the Big Data and it allows streaming, that is, continuous changes in the data. So even though, RDF might be inconsistent at times, it is popularly used [46].

10.3.1 RDF Model and Technology

The RDF model is based on describing the resources using properties that also the attributes or characteristics. The properties are uniquely identified using the Uniform Resource Identifier (URI) and the resource corresponding to the property are identified using the property type which has its matching values. The property type links a resource to a value that could be another resource or an atomic value or literals like a data value having text strings or integers. A description is a group of properties linked to the same resource. RDF is founded on its capacity to represent a resource and its descriptions using a syntax independent model [43–45, 47].

The resource, its property type and the property value form a triple in which the resource is the subject, its property type is the relationship or predicate and the property value is the object. The RDF model consisting of the triple form the foundation of the RDF technology and is the basis for the integration of data from various heterogeneous data sources. The RDF technology allows the data from varied source to be formatted as a semantic description containing the description of resources and the relationship between the resources. Such liberty in representing data is the reason why RDF technology is popular in knowledge representation for knowledgebase systems and artificial intelligence. The basic requirement for RDF technology is that the resources are identified by the URI and the fundamental conditions for data exchange, that is, the data is represented as a set of triples. Duplication of triples is to be strictly avoided but it does not matter in which position the triple is placed [48, 49].

10.3.2 Metadata and URI

The word metadata was probably first used by Philip Bagley in 1968, in his book "Extension of Programming Language Concepts" in which he describes metadata as a secondary data element like an identifier or an access code that contains information about the contents of the primary data element. He terms such information containing secondary elements as the metadata elements. Earlier to it, the word metadata was used to describe publications, library catalogs, subject indexes, various classifiers, and article abstracts. From the early stages of the development of computer systems, although the word metadata was not specifically mentioned, the features of metadata were visible in the properties of source code, compiler design and file storage. It became more pronounced while in the use of database description and conceptual modelling languages. Later in document retrieval systems, the document indices were provided together with descriptors of the document for quicker retrieval. The Report Program Generator by IBM was used to generate formatted reports that could be metadata. Later with the advent of the world wide web and the use of Hypertext Markup Language, the markup tags became metadata resources. These metadata resources were exploited by the recent semantic web technologies for knowledge representation, data search and logical inferencing. Metadata has now become a necessary element to describe properties associated with a subject domain [50].

Metadata can be categorized into different types based on the function of the metadata. Descriptive metadata describes the content of the resources and the assistance rendered by the metadata in finding or understanding the resources. The administrative metadata contains information regarding the creation or the management of the resources. The preservation metadata is about the long-term support for the metadata or its future migration or about matching the digital files. The technical metadata has information of the digital file that is essential to decrypt and extract them. The technical and preservation metadata could be treated as part of the administrative metadata. Structural metadata consists of information about the relationship between the parts of the resources. The rights metadata has information with regards to licensing, copyrights and the like. Markup languages are also considered as a type of metadata that contains flags or formatting information that help in situating paragraphs, titles, headings, lists, name, date and the so on [51, 52]. There can also be other categories of metadata that could deal with information regarding statistics, references, indices and others.

There is more than one approach to manage metadata. Some metadata management approaches for the structured and semi-structured database are annotations, provenance, quality parameter, schema and mapping, security, super-imposed information and time. Since there is wide heterogeneity in the kinds of metadata that require a high degree of specialization for the management of the metadata, the inter-operability of the metadata is quite a challenging task. Moreover, there was no distinction between data and metadata that can be made while querying. In other words, the system cannot distinguish whether the result of a query is a data or metadata. Many attempts were made to arrive at a clean and simple approach for a uniform model and to query data. The RDF is considered predominantly as the solution to representing interlinked data. RDF was primarily introduced as a means of representing the metadata available on the web. The metadata that is on the web may not be only web domains but could also be other metadata. So, in RDF, the web data is considered as resources and the web domain is represented using unique URI [53].

In 1992 the Internet Engineering Task Force (IETF), which is entrusted with overseeing the required infrastructure for the development of the internet, established the URI working group to solve the issues concerning standardizing Uniform Resource Locator (URL) schemes to avoid causing congestion in servers and reproducing intercontinental traffic. The URI working group came up with a model to standardize the resource identifiers by Uniform Resource Name (URN) and Uniform Resource Characteristics (URC). After a lot of work done on the URN and URC, it was realized that the URL which is part of the URI was the only standard format achieved. So, in July 1995, the IETF disbanded the URI working group and formed the URN working group in July 1996 to work on naming schemes and resolution systems. The URC which describes languages, formats, character sets, version numbers, author names, and so on, has not developed any particular scheme so far [54–56].

URI makes use of the syntax and semantics from the notions presented by the world wide web global information initiative to provide a simple and extendible method of identifying resources. "Functional Recommendations for Internet Resource Locators" [57] and "Functional Requirements for Uniform Resource Names" [58] where the recommendation used in the design of the URI. The URI is characterized by the uniformity that allows the use of different types of resource identifiers even if the methods used to get the identifiers may be different. Moreover, there is uniformity in the use of semantic interpretation of common syntactic resolutions of varied resource identifiers and new types of identifiers might be used without disturbing the existing identifiers. The reuse of the identifiers in various contexts allows newer applications and systems to make use of the large and widely used existing identifiers. The use of the word resource does not limit itself to only for the use of existing resources in the web but rather to anything that might be identified as a resource by the URI. A resource, therefore, need not be only what is in the web but it can be anything from a real-world material like books, reports, surveys and the like or also something belonging to the abstract world like a type of relationship, a mathematical operator and so on. The identifier distinguishes one resource from the other without any emphasis on the identification method. The identifier need not represent the identified resource or the URI will access the identified resource [59].

10.3.3 RDF Stores

Although the already well-developed relational database systems were initially contemplated to store RDF data, it was soon realized that the extensive data of the semantic web that is mostly in semi-structured and unstructured format and which could be referenced by RDF could not be contained in any relational database system. The big challenge arises when conjunctive queries are to made to RDF data which is a triple since most existing query languages will require performing multiple joins and unions that can greatly slow down the scalable query access. But since the relational database systems had the advantage of being highly evolved over decades of usage, some modified versions are still used to store RDF data [60, 61].

RDF Stores are storage systems to hold information in RDF format for faster search and retrieval. It has better capabilities for processing Big Data of the very flexible RDF knowledge and therefore, it has been researched and developed in many different ways. A large number of semantic and knowledge processing applications make use of the RDF stores due to its capacity for devices interoperability. The data model of the RDF stores allows the application user to be presented with ways of viewing the information rather than to present the user with the data itself. Since the information has to be abstracted for such use, there has been a large variation in the data structure used by different RDF Stores. While some RDF Stores rely on the traditional relational database structures many others make use of advanced and complex structures like the RDF specific indexing schema [62].

RDF store models can be classified in three ways. The simplest classification is those in which the RDF resides in the local drive and those in which the RDF is obtained by a federated search in which the RDF is obtained from different web pages. Practically, the federated search boils down to storing the RDF in the local drive for use in the knowledgebase system. A more common classification is one that which identifies RDF store as centralized and distributed storage. Centralized storage makes use of the relational database technology to store data in a centralized system from which it can be queried for search and retrieval. For quicker search and retrieval, the data might be indexed in which case the RDF triples might also include the index value. While the centralized storage can provide efficiency with regards to performance and speed, they are limited by the amount of data that can be handled by such systems. The distributed storage systems on the other hand are scalable. Principally, the distributed storage system has multiple machines running centralized storage that are linked using a conceptual layer to coordinate the distribution of data among them [61, 63–65].

A more generalized classification of the RDF storage systems is by broadly distinguishing them as native and non-native systems. The native storage systems contrive a separate storage backend for the knowledgebase systems. The native systems can be further classified as those that make use of the main memory and those that use disk storages. The main memory storage relies on parsing and loading the RDF files in a portion of the main memory which may be indexed for faster retrieval. The disk storage models make persistent use of indices which causes an operational bottleneck. The non-native RDF stores make use of the existing well-developed database systems to store RDF data. These RDF stores use either a relational database or a NoSQL backend for storage and retrieval of information. The relational database that is used by non-native RDF stores could be a schema-based or a schema-free approach. In comparison, the native approach is more efficient than the non-native approach for a knowledgebase system although it requires a lot of effort in the design and implementation of such systems [60, 62, 66].

10.4 Knowledgebase Systems and Knowledge Graphs

The knowledgebase is a storage of knowledge in a structured form using knowledge representation techniques on which a knowledgebase system can be built [67]. Knowledge can be defined in so many different ways that there is no single definition that encompasses its complete meaning [68–70]. For knowledgebase systems, knowledge can be defined as processed information that is used to solve a given problem. So, the various solutions to the problem for which the system is designed are representatively stored in the in a knowledgebase of the system. The system then retrieves the relevant knowledge from the knowledge base when required.

10.4.1 Knowledgebase Systems

Knowledgebase Systems are systems that hold solutions to problems of a particular domain in their knowledge base. The knowledge-based systems sprouted out of expert systems that were itself an offshoot of Artificial Intelligence [71]. Knowledgebase systems and expert systems were terms interchangeably used because the expert systems that were developed earlier contained knowledge of experts coded in the system, they performed tasks like human experts and were used to solve problems [72]. Later when the term "knowledgebase systems" were used, probably for the first time in 1988 by E. Feigenbaum *et al.* in the book 'The Rise of the Expert Company', it was done interchangeably with expert systems [73]. In later developments, Expert Systems were considered different from Knowledge-based systems in the sense that Expert Systems had knowledge of experts built into the system as a separate entity while Knowledgebase systems could acquire and infer new knowledge. While some consider Expert Systems as a type of Knowledgebase system since they are modelled on human cognitive processes and provide functions of Knowledgebase systems such as decision making [74], some others consider Knowledgebase systems as a category of the Expert Systems since knowledge and knowledge base are part of the Knowledgebase systems similar to Expert Systems [75, 76].

The evolution of the early Expert Systems to the current Knowledgebase systems occurred in different stages. The early Expert Systems that were developed in the late 1970s and the early 1980s, which include systems like MYCIN, a clinical decision support system to diagnose bacterial infection, CASNET, to diagnose glaucoma, PROSPECTOR to identify sites for drilling, and Rt that was used to configure computer systems, used the forward chaining and backward chaining techniques with symbolic logic representation to help in inferences and decision making. These systems were limited in their task because the requirements of complex tasks like planning and design could not be met with the inefficient sophistication and inflexible inferencing of these systems. The next stage of evolution that happened in the late 1980s to the late 1990s saw the commercialization of Knowledgebase systems through various applications that were developed such as predicting and forecasting for commercial planning, assigning work for railway crew members and other job scheduling applications, planning power systems and development of rail routes, finance, design and planning in manufacturing sectors, computer-aided process planning, configuring tools and managing a crisis. The development of the knowledge base in these applications lacked sophistication and so the system was neither efficient nor robust although they were helpful to a great extent. The next generation of Knowledgebase systems had more research and development in the building of the knowledge base. The knowledge base was developed as a generic component that could be attached to any system. Together with the development of a formal theory of knowledge, the methodology for the creation of the knowledge base had a more efficient and reliable knowledge acquisition, representing and inferencing technique [77]. Currently, the Knowledgebase systems have reached a certain degree of maturity to the foundation of Computational Intelligence Systems that are built on intricate theories involving engineering economics, operations research, statistical analysis, and decision theory. These systems make use of various recently evolved techniques such as Knowledge Engineering, Natural Language Processing, Machine Learning, Software Agents, Reasoning Engines and so on for the creation of the knowledge base. Such highly evolved knowledge bases are used in multifaceted applications such as Information Retrieval, Semantic Searches, Information Integration, Decision Support Systems, Information Interoperability, Bioinformatics, Healthcare, Learning tools, Software Engineering, Commerce, Governance, Social Networks, Supply Chain, Blockchain, and the like [78].

10.4.2 Knowledge Graphs

Graph-based knowledge representation has two advantages especially for knowledge engineers and experts who design and build the knowledge base of Knowledgebase system. The visualization of objects in a graph makes it easily understood and comfortable to handle. The reason why semantic networks are a popular form of knowledge representation is precisely due to its graph-like feature. Moreover, the reasoning mechanism in graph structures is understood without much complexity due to the structure-preserving mapping feature of graph or graph homomorphism. The homomorphic feature of the graph allows the graphs to be broken into smaller components for modelling purposes which can be easily visualized. Also, the same graphic form is used in both the computational and interface level circumventing the need for transforming the knowledge base components for the user interface. The other advantage of graph-based knowledge representation is at the level of computation. The homomorphism of graphs allows the basic graphs to be anchored on to the combinatorics. The homomorphism unifies the results of complexity with the algorithm in many domains. The graphic representation used instead of logical formulas can also contribute to newer algorithm ideas. Moreover, labeled graphs are more suitable for knowledge acquisition processes in building a knowledge base [79].

Knowledge graphs can be defined as the knowledge base of a Knowledgebase system in which the knowledge is represented using a graph structure where the different knowledge concepts are the nodes of the graph and its edges are the relationship between the concepts. The building of the knowledge graph involves all the technologies that are used in the creation of the knowledge base since the knowledge graph is itself the knowledge base [80–83]. There are numerous definitions for knowledge graphs ranging from precise technical definition to more generic definitions [84, 85]. There are conceptual and empirical definitions of Knowledge Graphs [86]. The type of the graph of knowledge graphs may vary depending on the model of the knowledge representation. The term "Knowledge Graph" was probably used by E.W. Schneider in 1972 [87] and later in 1982 Cornelis Hoede of the University of Twente and F.N. Stokman of the University of Groningen used it as a discrete mathematical concept [88]. Currently, knowledge graphs are vital to many tech companies especially those that work with Big Data on the internet like Microsoft, Google, Facebook, IBM, eBay, Yahoo, and the like [89, 90].

The generation of a Knowledge Graph involves the process of acquiring knowledge in which the editing, mapping and annotation are done, the storage of the acquired knowledge, the curation of the knowledge by assessment, cleaning and enrichment of the knowledge and the deployment of the knowledge in a Knowledgebase system [80]. The curation or the refinement process is crucial to the deployment of the knowledge base and the efficiency of the system. Knowledge acquisition can be done either by refining existing Knowledge Graphs or by crowd editing or by extracting knowledge from large semi-structured knowledge bases or using information extraction process from unstructured or semi-structured sources. Whichever process of knowledge acquisition is deployed, the result will be imperfect and unreliable unless an effective process of curation is used. Two main aims of the curation process are the graph completion by which the missing knowledge is added to complete the graph and error detection to ensure that the graph is without misinformation and reliable. Although the process of knowledge creation and knowledge refinement may be similar, they are deployed separately since the refinement can work simultaneously on different graphs and the refinement process will give a clearer understanding of the graph that is built [80, 91].

10.4.3 RDF Knowledge Graphs

RDF Stores are usually used to store knowledge graphs and therefore Knowledge Graphs with RDF knowledge model are referred to as RDF Knowledge Graphs. RDF Knowledge Graphs can be defined as Knowledge Graphs in which knowledge is represented in the form of triples consisting subject, predicate and object [92–95]. RDF Knowledge Graph can also be defined as labelled multi-digraph in which the set of nodes could be either URIs or literals, and the corresponding edges are URIs representing the predicates [93–96].

There are several challenges in deploying RDF Knowledge Graphs. Understanding and encapsulating the concepts from a variety of heterogeneous knowledge sources is an important challenge. The users need to understand the entities in the RDF Knowledge Graphs so that the knowledge graph can be deployed directly to user applications. Another challenge is in exploiting the knowledge available in the RDF Knowledge Graph. It requires efficient retrieval techniques. Linking various knowledge bases represented using RDF Knowledge Graph is also a challenge since it requires effectively choosing the right knowledge bases for the solution that is sought by the application. Similarly, efficient and effective retrieval of relevant knowledge from huge knowledge bases for which automatic query generation could give insights is another big challenge in deploying RDF Knowledge Graphs [97].

Some solutions to these challenges have been researched and experimented with. The RDF Mapping Language (RML) is the formalization of specification for mapping various heterogeneous knowledge sources and serialization to the RDF Knowledge Graph. Mapping knowledge from different format to RDF model is a complicated task as it involves uniformity, modularity, interoperability and extensibility. RML is an extension of relational database to RDF (R2RML) which is a W3C recommendation [98–100]. Instance Matching (IM) is another technique used to interlink different knowledge bases to retrieve relevant and reliable knowledge for user applications [96]. RDF Knowledge Graph Visualization during the graph compilation process can help extract relevant knowledge while textual document processing and is an effective tool for efficient and effective retrieval [101]. A solution proposed for faster discoverability and efficient integration of knowledge is content-based union and complement metrics from among the knowledge subsets [102]. Centralized storage architectures are also seen as efficient knowledge bases that are cost-effective while being robust [93]. More recent research has been in the use of Artificial Intelligence techniques like Machine Learning for the predictive analysis of the knowledge bases. RDF Frames is a proposal to connect RDF Knowledge Graphs with Machine Learning algorithms [92].

10.4.4 Information Retrieval Using SPARQL

SPARQL (Simple Protocol and RDF Query Language[2]) is a formalized specification to query RDF data to retrieve and manipulate knowledge. It is deployed by Knowledgebase systems to process and produce relevant knowledge from the knowledge base. After the standardization of RDF, many query languages came up as personal, academic and commercial endeavors. In early 2004, W3C established the RDF Data Access Working Group and in late 2004, the working group came up with a draft of the SPARQL specification. Although the SPARQL specification became operational by then, the official W3C specification of the standard SPARQL 1.0 was announced only in 2008. After the expiration of the RDF Data Access Working Group, the SPARQL Working Group was formed 2009 and in late 2009 they came up Drafts of the SPARQL 1.1, which, after many revisions and improvisations became official W3C Recommendations in March of 2013 [103].

[2]SPARQL. (n.d.) TheFreeDictionary.com. (2020). Retrieved September 21 2020 from https://acronyms.thefreedictionary.com/SPARQL.

Although SPARQL adopts various structures of SQL, SPARQL uses the navigation-based approach on an RDF graph unlike the joins between tables used by SQL implementation. While certain keywords like SELECT, FROM, and WHERE and arguments such as LIMIT, DISTINCT, OFFSET, ORDER BY, GROUP BY, and HAVING are adopted from the SQL and implemented with modification in SPARQL, keywords such as OPTIONAL, FILTER, and UNION are unique of SPARQL. Additionally, since SPARQL deals with graph datasets, the keyword FROM NAMED is used to identify the specific sets of triples under a common identifier. SPARQL also allows query of remote datasets using the SERVICE keyword [104].

SPARQL queries can be broadly classified into belonging to two frameworks. The centralized RDF query processing systems work on the efficiency and scalability of the SPARQL queries. While these systems greatly reduce communication overhead, they are limited to the power and memory of a single system [105, 106]. The distributed or federated RDF query processing involves combined access to decentralized knowledge bases spread among multiple clusters. The key benchmarking components of such clusters are data storage capacity, indexing capability, language support and generation of optimized queries [106]. The federated query models or the federated information systems can be of multi-database query languages, federated knowledge bases or mediator based information systems [107]. A subclassification that can be used in both the centralized and distributed query processing models is the link traversal framework that is based on the principle of linked data to dynamically discover knowledge from a distributed knowledge base. The link traversal can effectively reduce the size and cost of query searches [108].

10.5 Knowledge Base for CDSS

CDSS are computer systems that help in the decision making of healthcare workers and patients. Knowledgebase CDSS is a category of CDSS that has a knowledge base and interface systems. The inference engine or the reasoner is a part of the knowledge base help in processing the data that comes from the interface systems. CDSS has several functional advantages such as diagnostics, alarm systems, disease management, prescription, drug control, retrenchment predictions and so on. The effectiveness of the CDSS depends on the comfortable retrieval of relevant, accurate, reliable and expedient knowledge available for decision making [109, 110]. A CDSS, apart from its conceptual architecture, consist of modular tasks and responsibilities that function independently of the application environment and therefore they are designed to be portable, reusable and maintainable on its own [111].

10.5.1 Curation of Knowledge Base for CDSS

The process of selecting, organizing, and managing entities of a knowledge base is a complex task. The data has to be extracted from structured and unstructured sources and integrated into the existing knowledge base accurately and efficiently capable of creating visualized reports. A manual curation process has the efficiency of producing validated and timely knowledge [112], but the cost and scalability of the manually populated knowledge base make it inefficient. Collaborative curation can mitigate the shortcoming to some extent but it does not solve the problem [113]. Due to the scarcity of human resources for the manual curation process, it is estimated that it takes an average of 1 year to translate the knowledge from the source to the knowledge base [114]. The exiting computational population and curation methods have scalability limitation when it comes to harnessing a huge volume of knowledge available. The computational complexity involved in the deductive process results in proportionally very small knowledge bases [115]. There are studies conducted on the application of RDF Knowledge Graphs for information retrieval from literature or more with other huge sources of clinical data like the Electronic Health Records [116]. There has been a lot of research in building a knowledge base from semi-structured and unstructured data. The traditional ontology-based information extraction tries to populate the existing knowledge base using the canonical identifiers already found in the knowledge base. Information extraction does not include new entities or relationships. The open information extraction includes new entities and relationships that are discovered in the literature. For CDSS, the categorization of information extraction as targeted and non-targeted is more relevant since, the knowledge base is meant only for clinical decision support. Therefore, the method of information retrieval from medical journal only and using only medical jargoned entities is a targeted or focused information extraction, while those that apply to all documents without any distinction is non-targeted or unfocussed [114].

10.5.2 Proposed Model for Curation

RDF Knowledge Graph that works as the knowledge base of a CDSS is build using knowledge extraction from medical literature. The earlier methods of knowledge extraction were rule-based and its result was found to be too noisy leading to unreliable knowledge. Moreover, the rules need to be constantly broken to get sufficient knowledge from unstructured text. Later the statistical method based on algorithms of artificial intelligence was used for a more accurate knowledge extraction but due to a lack of cost and time efficiency, the newer rule-based techniques are preferred for knowledge extraction The hybrid system comprising of both the rule-based and the artificial intelligence algorithms are considered better than using just the either of them [117, 118]. Open Information Extraction (OpenIE) systems published by Stanford University, Freiburg University and the University of Washington among others are very promising knowledge extraction techniques [118, 119].

OpenIE can be used to construct RDF Knowledge Graphs from texts [120–124] from which relevant knowledge can be queried using SPARQL for the curation of the CDSS knowledge base. The URI of the texts that have been already referred to is held in a table to avoid repetition of information extraction from the same text. The RDF Knowledge Graph that is constructed from the text is only stored temporarily until the SPARQL query results are added to the knowledge base to reduce the space complexity of the system. In the proposed model, as shown in Algorithm 10.1, the system will query the RDF Knowledge Graph that is temporarily constructed using SPARQL with the keywords that are used in the CDSS. If any RDF triples are returned, they are added to the knowledge base of the CDSS. Otherwise, the system checks for any new document that is to be considered and which is not in the URI table of already checked documents.

Algorithm 10.1 Curating the CDSS knowledge base using RDF knowledge graph.

URI table U = $\{u_1, u_2, \ldots, u_n\}$
RDF Knowledge Graph G ={V,E} where V ∈ {v1,v2,....,vn} and E ∈ {e1,e2,...,en}
RDF triple S = {s, p, o} (*subject*(s), *predicate*(p), *object*(o))
CDSS Keyword K = $\{k_1, k_2, \ldots k_n\}$
1 **Read** u_i (*URI of a new document*)
2 **If** $u_i \in U$ GOTO Step 9
3   **Else** use OpenIE to create G
4   **For** every K
5   use SPARQL query to find k_i in G
6   **For** every S found
7   **If** S not in CDSS knowledge base
8   **Append** S to CDSS knowledge base
9 **If** another document exists **GOTO** Step 1
10 **Else STOP**

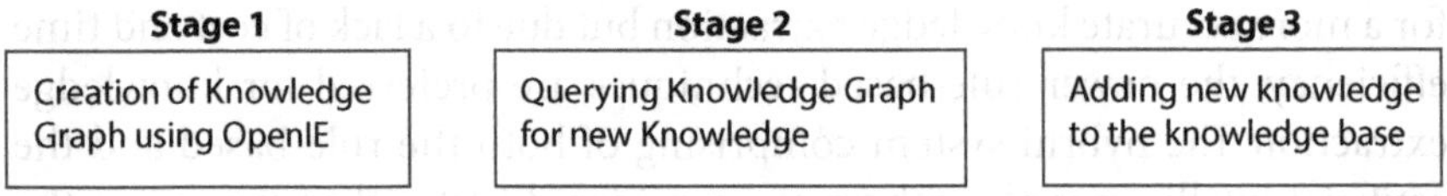

Figure 10.2 Stages in the proposed model.

The model will have three stages as shown in Figure 10.2. In the first stage, the knowledge graph is created. In the second stage, the Knowledge Graph is queried. In the third stage, new RDF triples are added to the knowledge base.

10.5.3 Evaluation Methodology

There are many measures that are used to evaluate the knowledge base. These measures are based on whether the RDF triple is relevant or irrelevant to the particular knowledge base. Accordingly, a contingency matrix of positives and negatives can be formed as shown in Table 10.1. If the RDF triple that is retrieved by the query is relevant it is true positive otherwise it is a false positive. Similarly, if a relevant triple is not retrieved then it is a false negative and if it is not relevant and not retrieved, it is a true negative. For the knowledge bases curation, measures such as precision, recall, accuracy, F-measure, G-measure, error rate, miss rate, fallout and so on could be used on the RDF triples that are retrieved from the relevant RDF triples in the document [125, 126].

Evaluation of the queried result is done also using community benchmarking campaigns such as the Text Retrieval Conference (TREC), Initiative for the Evaluation of XML Retrieval (INEX), DBpedia-Entity Test Collection and so on which makes use of text collections consisting of a dataset, a set of information needs and the corresponding relevance assessments [127].

Table 10.1 Contingency matrix of positives and negatives.

	Relevant	**Irrelevant**
RDF triple retrieved	True positive	False positive
RDF triple not retrieved	False negative	True negative

10.6 Discussion for Further Research and Development

A fully automated knowledge base curation may not be currently possible because of certain connected issues. First of all, the Intellectual Property Rights (IPR) does not allow full literature to be freely obtained from the web sources for use in the system. Secondly, there are contradictory literature available that could undermine the reliability of the knowledge base even if it is automatically populated. The third reason is that the literature need not be complete that could cause problems in curating the knowledge base. So, an expert is required to monitor the curation process of the knowledge base if the application has to be robust. Any possible method of a fully automatic curation process will be of great use to create an independent system.

Another possible research and development will be on effectively making use of extended RDF Knowledge Graph to rank the knowledge in the knowledge base. It could help remove the obliterated knowledge from the knowledgebase and also help in the rank-based evaluation. There are some studies already done in adding weights to RDF Triples [94] but further study and research will be useful.

10.7 Conclusion

RDF Knowledge Graphs have several benefits when it comes to making a reliable and efficient knowledgebase that is of utmost importance to systems like the CDSS. It provides a concise and intuitive abstraction of the knowledge from structured, semi-structured and even unstructured sources. For a system such as the knowledgebase CDSS, the accurate and recent knowledge has to be in the knowledgebase for the system to be useful for any healthcare personal. At the same time, the knowledgebase, although scalable, has a limitation in its space complexity. To provide a budgeted space requirement, the proposed model of using RDF Knowledge Graph to build the knowledgebase of a system such as a CDSS is advantages since the entire graph of an unstructured source is not held within the system permanently. Moreover, the ability of the model to abstract knowledge from unstructured sources such as medical literature that hold the recent and relevant knowledge makes the proposed model important.

References

1. Berg, K.L., Seymour, T., Goel, R., History of Databases. *Int. J. Manag. Inf. Syst.*, 17, 29, 2012.
2. Parsaye, K., Database Management, Knowledge Base Management, and Expert System Development in PROLOG. *Databases Bus. Off. Appl. Database Week*, 159–178, 1983.
3. Vardi, M., Database logic programming. *J. Log. Program.*, 10, 179, 1991.
4. Ceri, S., Gottlob, G., Tanca, L., Logic Programming and Databases: An Overview, in: *Logic Programming and Databases. Surveys in Computer Science*, pp. 1–15, Springer: Berlin Heidelberg, 1990.
5. Gallaire, H., Minker, J., Nicolas, J.M., Logic and Databases: A Deductive Approach. *ACM Comput. Surv.*, 16, 153, 1984.
6. Morgan, M.G., Feigenbaum, E.A., McCorduck, P., The Fifth Generation: Artificial Intelligence and Japan's Computer Challenge to the World. *J. Policy Anal. Manag.*, 3, 156, 1983.
7. Itoh, H., Research and Development on Knowledge Bases Systems at ICOT. *VLDB '86 Proc. 12th Int. Conf. Very Large Data Bases*, vol. 437, 1986.
8. Ullman, J.D., Implementation of logical query languages for databases. *ACM Trans. Database Syst.*, 10, 289, 1985.
9. Bibel, W. and Nicolas, J.-M., The Role of Logic for Data and Knowledge Bases: A Brief Survey, in: *Foundations of Knowledge Base Management. Topics in Information Systems*, J.W. Schmidt and C. Thanos (Eds.), pp. 3–22, Springer: Berlin, Heidelberg, 1989.
10. Li, H., To Develop A Data-Knowledge Base Management System By Utilizing Relational Database Management Systems. Proceedings of SPIE, 657, 82–94. 82, 1987.
11. Levesque, H.J. and Lakemeyer, G., *The Logic of Knowledge Bases*, pp. 3–18, The MIT Press: London, England, 2001.
12. Adams, T.M., Knowledge Representation and Processing in Relational Data Base. *J. Comput. Civ. Eng.*, 7, 238, 1993.
13. Chandra, A.K. and Harel, D., Horn clause queries and generalizations. *J. Log. Program.*, 2, 1, 1985.
14. Popescu, I., A relational model for knowledge representation in expert systems. *J. Syst. Softw.*, 18, 147, 1992.
15. Li, Y. and Xiao, R., A Relational Model Based Semantic Network Knowledge Representation Technology and Its Application, in: *2014 Int. Conf. Identification, Inf. Knowl. Internet Things*, vol. 100, 2014.
16. Gruber, T.R., Toward principles for the design of ontologies used for knowledge sharing? *Int. J. Hum. Comput. Stud.*, 43, 907, 1995.
17. Meier, A. and Kaufmann, M., *SQL & NoSQL Databases*, pp. 201–218, Association for Computing Machinery: New York, NY, USA, 2019.
18. Han, J., Haihong, E., Le, G., Du, J., Survey on NoSQL database. *2011 6th Int. Conf. Pervasive Comput. Appl*, vol. 363, 2011.

19. Kuznetsov, S.D. and Poskonin, A.V., NoSQL data management systems. *Program. Comput. Softw.*, 40, 323, 2014.
20. Schram, A. and Anderson, K.M., MySQL to NoSQL. *Proc. 3rd Annu. Conf. Syst. Program. Appl. Softw. Humanit. - SPLASH '12*, vol. 191, 2012.
21. Lourenço, J.R., Cabral, B., Carreiro, P., Vieira, M., Bernardino, J., Choosing the right NoSQL database for the job: a quality attribute evaluation. *J. Big Data*, 2, 18, 2015.
22. Li, Z., NoSQL Databases. *Geogr. Inf. Sci. Technol. Body Knowl.*, (2nd Quarter 2018 Edition), John P. Wilson (Ed). DOI: 10.22224/gistbok/2018.2.10, 2018.
23. Stonebraker, M., SQL databases v. NoSQL databases. *Commun. ACM*, 53, 10, 2010.
24. Pokorny, J., NoSQL databases: A step to database scalability in web environment. *Int. J. Web Inf. Syst.*, 9, 69, 2013.
25. Chen, J.-K. and Lee, W.-Z., An Introduction of NoSQL Databases Based on Their Categories and Application Industries. *Algorithms*, 12, 106, 2019. open access - https://www.mdpi.com/1999-4893/12/5/106
26. Pereira, D.A., Ourique de Morais, W., Pignaton de Freitas, E., NoSQL real-time database performance comparison. *Int. J. Parallel, Emergent Distrib. Syst.*, 33, 144, 2018.
27. Cattell, R., Scalable SQL and NoSQL data stores. *ACM SIGMOD Rec.*, 39, 12, 2011.
28. Huang, Y. and Luo, T., NoSQL Database: A Scalable, Availability, High Performance Storage for Big Data, in: *Pervasive Computing and the Networked World, ICPCA/SWS 2013. Lecture Notes in Computer Science*, vol. 8351, Q. Zu, M. Vargas-Vera, B. Hu (Eds.), pp. 172–183, Springer: Cham, 2014.
29. Brewer, E., CAP twelve years later: How the "rules" have changed. *Computer (Long. Beach. Calif).*, 45, 23, 2012.
30. Stonebraker, M., In search of database consistency. *Commun. ACM*, 53, 8, 2010.
31. Kleppmann, M., A Critique of the CAP Theorem. *arXiv preprint arXiv*, 2015. 1509.05393. open access: http://arxiv.org/abs/1509.05393
32. Gandini, A., Gribaudo, M., Knottenbelt, W.J., Osman, R., Piazzolla, P., Performance Evaluation of NoSQL Databases. *Comput. Performance Eng. EPEW*, 2014, pp. 16–29, Springer: Cham, 2014.
33. Klein, J., Gorton, I., Ernst, N., Donohoe, P., Pham, K., Matser, C., Performance Evaluation of NoSQL Databases. *Proc. 1st Work. Perform. Anal. Big Data Syst. - PABS '15*, vol. 5, 2015.
34. Abramova, V., Bernardino, J., Furtado, P., Experimental Evaluation of NoSQL Databases. *Int. J. Database Manag. Syst.*, 6, 1, 2014.
35. Schulz, W.L., Nelson, B.G., Felker, D.K., Durant, T.J.S., Torres, R., Evaluation of relational and NoSQL database architectures to manage genomic annotations. *J. Biomed. Inform.*, 64, 288, 2016.
36. Robinson, I., Webber, J., Eifrem, E., *Graph Databases: New Opportunities for Connected Data*, pp. 11–24, O'Reilly, Media: Sebastopol, CA, 2015.

37. Celko, J., *Joe Celko's Complete Guide to NoSQL*, pp. 27–46, Elsevier: Boston, 2014.
38. Larriba-Pey, J.L., Martínez-Bazán, N., Domínguez-Sal, D. *et al.*, Introduction to Graph Databases, in: *Reasoning Web. Reasoning on the Web in the Big Data Era, Reasoning Web 2014, Lecture Notes in Computer Science*, vol. 8714, M. Koubarakis (Ed.), pp. 171–194, Springer: Cham, 2014.
39. Besta, M. *et al.*, Demystifying graph databases: Analysis and taxonomy of data organization, system designs, and graph queries. *arXiv preprint arXiv*, 2019. 1910.09017. open access: http://arxiv.org/abs/1910.09017
40. Angles, R. and Gutierrez, C., Survey of graph database models. *ACM Comput. Surv.*, 40, 1–39, 2008.
41. Pokorný, J., Graph Databases: Their Power and Limitations, in: *Computer Information Systems and Industrial Management. CISIM 2015. Lecture Notes in Computer Science*, vol. 9339, K. Saeed and W. Homenda (Eds.), pp. 58–69, Springer: Cham, 2015.
42. Ishwarappa, and Anuradha, J., A Brief Introduction on Big Data 5Vs Characteristics and Hadoop Technology. *Procedia Comput. Sci.*, 48, 319, 2015.
43. Needleman, M.H., Rdf: The resource description framework. *Ser. Rev.*, 27, 58, 2001.
44. Miller, E., An Introduction to the Resource Description Framework. *D-Lib Mag.*, 4, 15–19, 1998.
45. Bizer, C., Vidal, M.-E., Weiss, M., Resource Description Framework, in: *Encyclopedia of Database Systems*, pp. 3221–3224, Springer: New York, 2018.
46. Özsu, M.T., A survey of RDF data management systems. *Front. Comput. Sci.*, 10, 418, 2016.
47. Pan, J.Z., Resource Description Framework, in: *Handbook on Ontologies*, S. Staab and R. Studer (Eds.), pp. 71–90, Springer: Berlin, Heidelberg, 2009.
48. Bizer, C., Vidal, M.-E., Weiss, M., RDF Technology, in: *Encyclopedia of Database Systems*, L. Liu and M.T. Özsu (Eds.), pp. 3106–3109, Springer: New York, 2018.
49. Iannella, R., An idiot's guide to the Resource Description Framework. *New Rev. Inf. Netw.*, 4, 181, 1998.
50. Kogalovsky, M.R., Metadata in computer systems. *Program. Comput. Softw.*, 39, 182–193, 2013.
51. Riley, J., Understanding Metadata—What Is Metadata? *Nat. Inf. Standards Organiz. (NISO)*, open access: http://www. niso. org/publications/press/ UnderstandingMetadata. pdf, 2017.
52. Gilliland, A.J., Setting the Stage, in: *Introduction to Metadata*, M. Baca (Ed.), pp. 1–19, Getty Research Institute, Los Angeles, 2008.
53. Bretherton, F.P. and Singley, P.T., Metadata: a User's View. *Seventh Int. Work. Conf. Sci. Stat. Database Manag*, vol. 166, 1994.

54. Schwartz, R., Uniform Resource Identifiers and the Effort to Bring "Bibliographic Control" to the Web: An Overview of Current Progress. *Bull. Am. Soc. Inf. Sci. Technol.*, 24, 12, 2005.
55. Daigle, L., Daniel, R., Preston, C., Uniform Resource Identifiers and Online Serials. *Ser. Libr.*, 33, 325, 1998.
56. Duranceau, E.F., Naming and describing networked electronic resources: The role of uniform resource identifiers. *Ser. Rev.*, 20, 31, 1994.
57. Kunze, J., Functional Recommendations for Internet Resource Locators. *RFC series*, 1, 1995, 1736.
58. Sollins, K. and Masinter, L., Functional Requirements for Uniform Resource Names. *RFC series*, 1, 1994, 1737.
59. Berners-Lee, T., Fielding, R., Masinter, L., Uniform Resource Identifier (URI): Generic Syntax. *RFC series*, 3986, 1, 2005.
60. Faye, D.C., Curé, O., Blin, G., A survey of RDF storage approaches. *Rev. Africaine la Rech. en Inform. Mathématiques Appliquées*, 15, 11, 2012.
61. Hose, K. and Schenkel, R., RDF Stores, in: *Encyclopedia of Database Systems*, L. Liu and M.T. Özsu (Eds.), pp. 3100–3106, Springer: New York, 2017.
62. Karvinen, P., Díaz-Rodríguez, N., Grönroos, S., Lilius, J., RDF Stores for Enhanced Living Environments: An Overview, in: *Enhanced Living Environments. Lecture Notes in Computer Science*, vol. 11369, I. Ganchev, N. Garcia, C. Dobre, C. Mavromoustakis, R. Goleva (Eds.), pp. 19–52, Springer: Cham, 2019.
63. Hose, K., Schenkel, R., Theobald, M., Weikum, G., Database Foundations for Scalable RDF Processing, in: *Reasoning Web. Semantic Technologies for the Web of Data*, A. Polleres, C. D'Amato, M. Arenas, S. Handschuh, P. Kroner, S. Ossowski, P. Patel-Schneider (Eds.), pp. 202–249, Springer: Berlin, Heidelberg, 2011.
64. Harth, A., Hose, K., Schenkel, R., Database techniques for linked data management. *Proc. 2012 Int. Conf. Manag. Data - SIGMOD '12*, vol. 597, 2012.
65. Nitta, K. and Savnik, I., Survey of RDF Storage Managers. *DBKDA 2014, Sixth Int. Conf. Adv. Databases, Knowledge, Data Appl.*, pp. 148–153, 2014.
66. Curé, O. and Blin, G. (Eds.), Storage and Indexing of RDF Data, in: *RDF Database Systems*, pp. 105–144, Elsevier: Boston, 2015.
67. Swain, M., Knowledge Base, in: *Encyclopedia of Systems Biology*, W. Dubitzky, O. Wolkenhauer, H. Yokota, K.-H. Cho (Eds.), pp. 1073–1074, Springer: New York , 2013.
68. Partridge, D., Representation of Knowledge, in: *Artificial Intelligence*, M.A. Boden (Ed.), pp. 55–87, Academic Press: San Diego, 1996.
69. Zins, C., Conceptual Approaches for Defining Data, Information, and Knowledge. *J. Am. Soc. Inf. Sci. Technol.*, 58, 479, 2007.
70. Kakabadse, N.K., Kakabadse, A., Kouzmin, A., Reviewing the knowledge management literature: towards a taxonomy. *J. Knowl. Manag.*, 7, 75, 2003.
71. Mainzer, K., Knowledge-based systems. *J. Gen. Philos. Sci.*, 21, 47, 1990.
72. Buchanan, B.G., Bobrow, D., Davis, R., McDermott, J., Shortliffe, E.H., Knowledge-Based Systems. *Annu. Rev. Comput. Sci.*, 4, 395, 1990.

73. Feigenbaum, E.A., McCorduck, P., Nii, H.P., *The rise of the expert company*, pp. 1–348, Times Books: New York, 1988.
74. Kendal, S. and Creen, M., An Introduction to Knowledge Engineering, in: *An Introduction to Knowledge Engineering*, pp. 1–25, Springer: London, 2007.
75. Liao, S.-H., Expert system methodologies and applications—A decade review from 1995 to 2004. *Expert Syst. Appl.*, 28, pp. 93–103, 2005.
76. Sajja, P.S. and Akerkar, R., Knowledge-Based Systems for Development, in: *Advanced Knowledge Based Systems: Model, Applications & Research*, P.S. Sajja and R. Akerkar (Eds.), pp. 1–11, Technomathematics Research Foundation (TMRF): Kolhapur, India, 2010.
77. Fox, J., Expert Systems and Theories of Knowledge, in: *Artificial Intelligence*, M.A. Boden (Ed.), pp. 157–181, Academic Press: San Diego, 1996.
78. Alor-Hernández, G. and Valencia-García, R., *Current Trends on Knowledge-Based Systems*, vol. 120, pp. iii–ix, Springer: Cham, 2017.
79. Michel, C. and Marie-Laure, M., *Graph-based Knowledge Representation*, pp. 1–17, Springer: London, 2009.
80. Fensel, D., Şimşek, U., Angele, K., Huaman, E., Kärle, E., Panasiuk, O., Toma, I., Umbrich, J., Wahler, A., *Knowledge Graphs*, pp. 11–68, Springer: Cham, 2020.
81. Gomez-Perez, J.M., Pan, J.Z., Vetere, G., Wu, H., Enterprise Knowledge Graph: An Introduction, in: *Exploiting Linked Data and Knowledge Graphs in Large Organisations*, J.Z. Pan, G. Vetere, J.M. Gomez-Perez, H. Wu (Eds.), pp. 1–14, Springer: Cham, 2017.
82. Yan, J., Wang, C., Cheng, W., Gao, M., Zhou, A., A retrospective of knowledge graphs. *Front. Comput. Sci.*, 12, 55, 2018.
83. Balog, K., *Entity-Oriented Search*, pp. 25–53, Springer: Cham, 2018.
84. Ehrlinger, L. and Wöß, W., Towards a Definition of Knowledge Graphs. *Jt. Proc. Postersand Demos Track 12th Int. Conf. Semant. Syst. - Semant. 1st Int. Semant. Chang. Evol. Semant. co-located with 12th Int. Conf*, 2016.
85. Hogan, A., Blomqvist, E. *et al.*, Knowledge Graphs. *arXiv preprint arXiv*, 2020. 2003.02320v3, open access: http://arxiv.org/abs/2003.02320
86. Fensel, D., Şimşek, U., Angele, K., Huaman, E., Kärle, E., Panasiuk, O., Toma, I., Umbrich, J., Wahler, A., *Knowledge Graphs*, pp. 1–10, Springer: Cham, 2020.
87. Schneider, E.W., *Course Modularization Applied: The Interface System and its Implications for Sequence Control and Data Analysis*, Human Resources Research Organization (HumRRO): Virginia, 1973.
88. Nurdiati, S.N.S. and Hoede, C., 25 years development of knowledge graph theory: the results and the challenge. *Memorandum 1876*, 2, 2008 open access - https://core.ac.uk/download/pdf/11468596.pdf
89. Noy, N., Gao, Y., Jain, A., Narayanan, A., Patterson, A., Taylor, J., Industry-scale knowledge graphs. *Commun. ACM*, 62, 36, 2019.
90. Guha, R.V., Brickley, D., MacBeth, S., Schema.org: Evolution of Structured Data on the Web. *Queue*, 13, 10, 2015.
91. Paulheim, H., Knowledge graph refinement: A survey of approaches and evaluation methods. *Semant. Web*, 8, 2017 open access - http://www.

semantic-web-journal.net/content/knowledge-graph-refinement-survey-approaches-and-evaluation-methods

92. Mohamed, A., Abuoda, G., Ghanem, A., Kaoudi, Z., Aboulnaga, A., RDFFrames: Knowledge Graph Access for Machine Learning Tools. *Proc. VLDB Endow.*, 13, 2889, 2020.
93. Urbani, J. and Jacobs, C., Adaptive Low-level Storage of Very Large Knowledge Graphs. *arXiv preprint arXiv*, 2020. 2001.09078v1. open access: http://arxiv.org/abs/2001.09078
94. Arnaout, H. and Elbassuoni, S., Effective searching of RDF knowledge graphs. *J. Web Semant.*, 48, 66, 2018.
95. Zheng, W., Zou, L., Peng, W., Yan, X., Song, S., Zhao, D., Semantic SPARQL Similarity Search over RDF Knowledge Graphs. *Proc. VLDB Endow.*, 9, 840, 2016.
96. Assi, A., Mcheick, H., Dhifli, W., Data linking over RDF knowledge graphs: A survey. *Concurr. Comput. Pract. Exp*, 32, 19, p.e5746, 2020.
97. Wu, H., Denaux, R., Alexopoulos, P., Ren, Y., Pan, J.Z., Understanding Knowledge Graphs, in: *Exploiting Linked Data and Knowledge Graphs in Large Organisations*, J.Z. Pan, G. Vetere, J.M. Gomez-Perez, H. Wu (Eds.), pp. 147–180, Springer: Cham, 2017.
98. Dimou, A., Sande, M., Colpaert, P., Verborgh, R., Mannens, E., Van de, R., RML: A Generic Language for Integrated RDF Mappings of Heterogeneous Data. *CEUR Workshop Proceedings (CEUR-WS.org)*, 2014. open access: http://ceur-ws.org/Vol-1184/ldow2014_paper_01.pdf
99. Iglesias, E., Jozashoori, S., Chaves-Fraga, D., Collarana, D., Vidal, M.-E., SDM-RDFizer: An RML Interpreter for the Efficient Creation of RDF Knowledge Graphs. *arXiv preprint arXiv*, 2020. 2008.07176v1. open access: http://arxiv.org/abs/2008.07176
100. Heyvaert, P., Chaves-Fraga, D., Priyatna, F., Corcho, O., Mannens, E., Verborgh, R., Dimou, A., Conformance Test Cases for the RDF Mapping Language (RML), in: *Knowledge Graphs and Semantic Web*, B. Villazón-Terrazas and Y. Hidalgo-Delgado (Eds.), pp. 162–173, Springer: Cham, 2019.
101. Kerdjoudj, F. and Curé, O., RDF Knowledge Graph Visualization From a Knowledge Extraction System. *CoRR*, 2015. abs/1510.0. open access: http://arxiv.org/abs/1510.00244
102. Mountantonakis, M. and Tzitzikas, Y., Content-based Union and Complement Metrics for Dataset Search over RDF Knowledge Graphs. *J. Data Inf. Qual.*, 12, 1, 2020.
103. DuCharme, B., *Learning SPARQL*, pp. 19–45, O'Reilly Media: Sebastopol, CA, 2013.
104. Curé, O. and Blin, G., RDF and the Semantic Web Stack, in: *RDF Database Systems*, O. Curé and G. Blin (Eds.), pp. 41–80, Elsevier: Waltham, MA, 2015.
105. Sakr, S., Wylot, M., Mutharaju, R., Le Phuoc, D., Fundulaki, I., *Linked Data*, pp. 33–49, Springer: Cham, 2018.

106. Ali, W., Saleem, M., Yao, B., Hogan, A., Ngomo, A.-C.N., Storage, Indexing, Query Processing, and Benchmarking in Centralized and Distributed RDF Engines: A Survey. *arXiv preprint arXiv*, 2020. 2009.10331v2 open access: https://www.preprints.org/manuscript/202005.0360/v2#
107. Quilitz, B. and Leser, U., Querying Distributed RDF Data Sources with SPARQL, in: *The Semantic Web: Research and Applications*, Y. Sure and J. Domingue (Eds.), pp. 524–538, Springer: Berlin, Heidelberg, 2008.
108. Fafalios, P. and Tzitzikas, Y., How many and what types of SPARQL queries can be answered through zero-knowledge link traversal? *Proc. 34th ACM/SIGAPP Symp. Appl. Comput*, vol. 2267, 2019.
109. Berner, E.S. and La Lande, T.J., Overview of Clinical Decision Support Systems, in: *Clinical decision support systems*, E.S. Berner (Ed.), pp. 1–17, Springer: Cham, 2016.
110. Sutton, R.T., Pincock, D., Baumgart, D.C., Sadowski, D.C., Fedorak, R.N., Kroeker, K.I., An Overview of Clinical Decision Support Systems: Benefits, Risks, and Strategies for Success. *npj Digit. Med.*, 3, 17, 2020.
111. Greenes, R.A., *Clinical Decision Support*, pp. 111–144, Academic Press: Oxford, 2014.
112. Bauch, A., Pellet, J., Schleicher, T., Yu, X., Gelemanović, A., Cristella, C., Fraaij, P.L., Polasek, O., Auffray, C., Maier, D., Koopmans, M., de Jong, M.D., Informing epidemic (research) responses in a timely fashion by knowledge management—A Zika virus use case. *bioRxiv*, 2020. 2020.04.17.044743. open access: https://www.biorxiv.org/content/10.1101/2020.04.17.044743v1.full.pdf
113. Baumgartner, W.A., Cohen, K.B., Fox, L.M., Acquaah-Mensah, G., Hunter, L., Manual curation is not sufficient for annotation of genomic databases. *Bioinformatics*, 23, 141, 2007.
114. Balog, K., *Entity-Oriented Search*, pp. 189–222, Springer: Cham, 2018.
115. Hunter, L.E., Knowledge-based biomedical Data Science. *Data Sci.*, 1, 19, 2017.
116. Callahan, T.J., Tripodi, I.J., Pielke-Lombardo, H., Hunter, L.E., Knowledge-Based Biomedical Data Science. *Annu. Rev. Biomed. Data Sci.*, 3, 23, 2020.
117. Sarawagi, S., Information Extraction. *Found. Trends Databases*, 1, 261, 2007.
118. Jiang, J., *Mining Text Data*, pp. 11–41, Springer: Boston, MA, 2012.
119. Etzioni, O., Banko, M., Soderland, S., Weld, D.S., Open Information Extraction from the Web. *Commun. ACM*, 51, 68, 2008.
120. Martinez-Rodriguez, J.L., Lopez-Arevalo, I., Rios-Alvarado, A.B., OpenIE-based approach for Knowledge Graph construction from text. *Expert Syst. Appl.*, 113, 339, 2018.
121. Wang, C., Ma, X., Chen, J., Chen, J., Information extraction and knowledge graph construction from geoscience literature. *Comput. Geosci.*, 112, 112, 2018.

122. Muhammad, I., Kearney, A., Gamble, C., Coenen, F., Williamson, P., Open Information Extraction for Knowledge Graph Construction. *Database Expert Syst. Appl.*, pp. 103–113, 2020.
123. Clancy, R., Ilyas, I.F., Lin, J., Scalable Knowledge Graph Construction from Text Collections. *Proc. Second Work. Fact Extr. Verif.*, pp. 39–46, 2019.
124. Martinez-Rodriguez, J.L., Lopez-Arevalo, I., Rios-Alvarado, A.B., Hernandez, J., Aldana-Bobadilla, E., Extraction of RDF Statements from Text. *Knowl. Graphs Semant. Web*, pp. 87–101, 2019.
125. Latha, K., *Experiment and Evaluation in Information Retrieval Models*, pp. 39–46, Chapman and Hall/CRC: Boca Raton, FL, 2017.
126. Manning, C.D., Raghavan, P., Schütze, H., *Introduction to Information Retrieval*, pp. 139–161, Cambridge University Press: Cambridge, 2008.
127. Balog, K., *Entity-Oriented Search*, pp. 57–99, Springer: Cham, 2018.

11

Medical Data Supervised Learning Ontologies for Accurate Data Analysis

B. Tarakeswara Rao[1], R. S. M. Lakshmi Patibandla[2*], V. Lakshman Narayana[3] and Arepalli Peda Gopi[4]

[1]Department of CSE, Kallam Haranadha Reddy Institute of Technology, Guntur, Andhra Pradesh, India
[2]Department of IT, Vignan's Foundation for Science Technology and Research, Guntur, Andhra Pradesh, India
[3]Department of IT, Vignan's Nirula Institute of Technology & Science for Women, Guntur, Andhra Pradesh, India
[4]Department of CSE, Vignan's Nirula Institute of Technology & Science for Women, Guntur, Andhra Pradesh, India

Abstract

Ontologies and AI develop into two movements for space express information extraction effectively used in information-based frameworks. Ontologies are a postponed outcome of the information elicitation measure from a genius by information planners, and information is not commonly included during this cycle. The motivation behind the two movements is regularly equal to the extraction of steady information. Clinical ontologies offer data to PC helped clinical choice assistance. PC helped clinical choice earnestly consistent associations could in like way be deterministic. For example, a standard-based framework makes clinicians aware of medication drug collaboration. The standards are settled really from the clinical cosmology. Man-made knowledge assessments are applied to kill significant information in a few issue spaces by looking at enchanting models (conditions) in colossal volumes of information. The fundamental objective inside the inferred information certifiable similarity measures is on making a changed segment work for each specific part, and not, generally speaking, full-scale division. Ontologies are the quality systems for expressive genuine variables in clinical and flourishing fields. Incredibly, miserable AI ways to deal with oversee assent for debilitating ontologies to watch adjusting way. This part gives the custom of

**Corresponding author*: patibandla.lakshmi@gmail.com

Vishal Jain, Jyotir Moy Chatterjee, Ankita Bansal and Abha Jain (eds.) Semantic Web for Effective Healthcare, (249–268) © 2022 Scrivener Publishing LLC

information semantics and ontologies in success and clinical jobs of free learning and all things considered depicts how the Unified Medical framework (UMLS) is used inside AQ21 rule getting programming.

Keywords: Machine learning, knowledge, techniques, learning, semantic

11.1 Introduction

Ongoing headways of Machine Learning (ML) made it appropriate to a wide scope of issues, incorporating those in clinical, medical services, and wellbeing areas. These techniques can make exact forecasts in dubious conditions, by discovering designs dispersed over enormous measures of information.

Quality of a considerable lot of the most up to date techniques comes likewise in the capacity to join Natural Language Processing (NLP) instruments with gaining from organized information [1]. Most of the novel techniques are measurable and center around the examination of numeric information. Area information for such strategies is restricted to the impromptu encoding of credits in the information or earlier boundaries of the model being found out as in case of profound learning of neural organizations. Shockingly, not many AI techniques take into consideration displaying area information so as to direct the learning cycle.

The introduced research investigates the utilization of ontologies and information semantics, to direct learning measure, by giving data extra to those effectively present in the information. The exploration is spurred by the presence of rich biomedical ontologies made to be utilized by information mix strategies, NLP calculations, and the Semantic Web. This presence of area information gives an ideal occasion to supplement unadulterated information for AI, with connections that length over the information.

This segment introduces biomedical ontologies easily, AI guided, presents a way to tackle semantonic data management and dissuade ontology in regulated learning. Indeed, cosmology was used to portray part of ancient Greece's theory, which worried about the investigation of the nature and of the relationships of being [1]. In the current software engineering, the word was used to make reference to a standard, controlled portrait of information designed to help information sharing and the use of computers for a particular field. Currently, the Web Ontology (OWL) Web Consortium (W3C) is the most widely used language in metaphysics.

Ontologies may be distinguished from the point of view of usage of three kinds. The big kind is high-level metaphysics, a standard system that characterizes and organizes concepts and relations in a particular domain [2]. The third is application metaphysics produced for a particular situation/application and provides an insignificant phrasing structure to meet restricted needs [3–12]. Cosmology has been used in the biomedical area in many years to understand the issue of information heterogeneity, leading to advanced research, information partnership, and more.

Search Database Solution
The creator used accompanying criteria or methods to recuperate matching written material:

(i) An overall hunt has been carried out for progress in metaphysics somewhere between 2000 and 2019, primarily using Google Scholar and NCBI Information Basis and Google worker and zeroing into the improvement of philosophy and application.
(ii) The use of "cosmology" and "biomedical" catchphrases, "clinical" to limit inclusion in discovering cosmology used in the biomedical field, has been used and has an initial understanding of biomedical philosophy.
(iii) The result was screened with additional terms "asset" and "vault" to locate certain incorporated metaphysical gateways to have an overview of biomedical collections of philosophy and networks.
(iv) Correspondingly, in the home-grown scholastic search for writing by the Baidu worker and several connected data sets in China were also applied to discover related assets of homemade assembled philosophy.

11.2 Ontology of Biomedicine

An ontology officially talks about the field knowledge as a community of ideas and relations between these definitions. The thesaurus, wording, arrangements and coding systems are commonly used. Ontologies play a major role in biomedical exams across a broad variety of applications, including reconciliation of facts, information and choice aid. Systematized Nomenclature in Medicine—SNOMED CT, International Classification of Disasters (ICD), Names and Codes for Conceptual Observation (LOINC),

Gene Ontology (GO), Medical Topic Headings (MeSH), RxNorm, Foundational Model of Anatomy (FMA), and Medical Dictionary for regulatory practices are the most popular biomedical ontologies in the field of pharmacy (MedDRA). Each ontology has its own personal cause and scope. Correspondence obstructions between numerous data thus occur.

Frameworks or applications where varied words are used by multiple clients and frameworks. In 1986, the National Library of Medicine (NLM) developed the UMLS to settle these borders, and is constantly being refreshed. There are three sources of information: Metathesaurus, Semantic Network and Professional Lexicon. The UMLS (2016AA) includes more than 3.25 million CUIs, 22 million links and 12 million interesting ideas (AUIs) from over 150 outlets. A major objective of the UMLS is to establish maps between different bio-ontologies. It is done by relegating an interesting identificator (CUI) to words from various ontologies of source that are of similar significance in the metathesaurus. The mapping of these vocabularies helps PC frameworks to view details among the various data frames. In addition, the rich ties in the UMLS offer a good base for thinking about clinical knowledge [8]. Different UMLS implementations include the provision of ontology, common language control, and useful collections of clinical quality controls (CQMs). Since US researchers Michael Cox and David Ellsworth, the National Aeronautics & Space Administration, initially suggested the imminent test for enormous information in 1997 [13], the possibility that vast amounts of information might be collected rapidly all over the world has had an impact in all fields of characteristic technology, sociology, and engineering [14]. Exactness drug is another therapeutic concept and clinical paradigm that relies on the inclusion of knowledge from multiple sources [16], including multiomics, electronic wellbeing reports, and even portable devices, which is otherwise regarded as "personal drug."

The heterogeneity of these organic details has significantly impeded the harmonization of knowledge and synchronization of the accuracy medicines. A persuasive and productive clinical choice system thus includes advanced study, knowledge association, portrayal, and thinking. Ontology plays a vital role in associating and applying consistency clinical knowledge. To begin with, ontology offers a phrasing mechanism for reducing the heterogeneity of knowledge and makes interoperable information within biomedical data structures. Via the loop of biomedical ontology details and metadata representation, an exceptional ID with its comparative label was encrypted. For example, the HPO terms may be used to normalize the symptoms and symptoms of a patient. DOID can be used to express the results of the results. Regarding metadata standardization, Ontology for Biomedical Science (OBI) [17] provides an accurate portrait of the metadata forms substance. Thus it simply illustrates the concepts of metadata, but also reveals the similarities between them. The semanthe heterogeneity of biomedical data systems can therefore be reduced to include interoperability and the programmed reconciliation of knowledge, the examination pipeline and certain extensible reasoning centered on information inquiry strategy can be recognized without any problems.

Ontology may help to form the precise and useful arrangement necessary for particular medications. Arrangements depict elements from spaces of interest, for example, sicknesses, aggregates, drugs, and introductions, by naming the elements in every area and giving computational determinations of assorted levels of advancement [18]. The key link in ontology is the "is a" association used to construct a fundamental progressive system. Past that, ontology additionally indicates other rationale connections between substances, for example, the "has aggregate" (RO_0002200) relationship, which is mostly used to portray an infection inhering in a creature, at that point the life form has an aggregate. The disorders of tyrosinemia type II is clearly indicated in Figure 11.1.

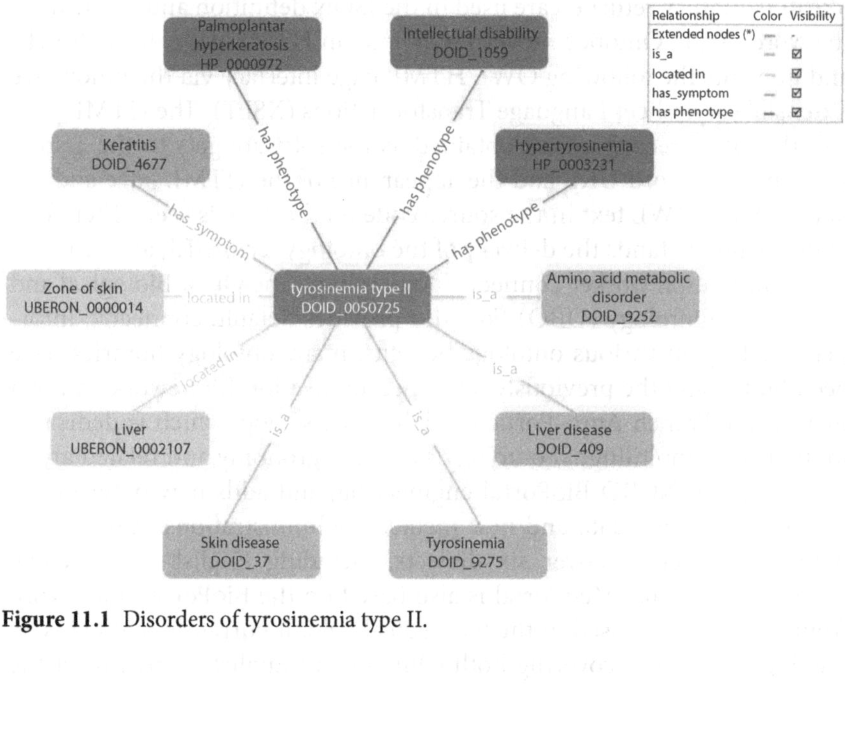

Figure 11.1 Disorders of tyrosinemia type II.

11.2.1 Ontology Resource Open Sharing

In the last 20 years, the complexity and spectrum of ontologies have greatly increased. The interest in ontology reuse, integration of knowledge and descriptions as well as ontology arrangements contributed to the creation of some ontological vaults [19–25]. These ontology repositories provide ontology with various apparatuses. For example, Ontology Lookup Service OxO and NCBO BioPortal Annotator are information commenting instruments that clarify ordinary language using ontology terms. Linked information administrations is a continuous test hotspot even though there are difficulties in online ontology. One of the significant standards of connected information is to give the Standardized Resource Identifier (URI) substantial information if specified, especially to display the meaning of a solitary word through the ontology term's URI.

In fact, however the customer cannot legitimately use the term URI to derefer to a genuine website page and to obtain a related Resource Description Framework document. The group has produced a wording dereference model in Ontobee to achieve the transformation to associated information that is not quite identical to different strategies. Both ontology increases are seen in the Virtuoso triple store in this model, SPARQL queries are sent by PHP to the triple store, and the findings of the SPARQL inquiry returned are used in the JSON definition and as a text for the word OWL. Ontobee moves JSON into an HTML page through PHP and implants the following OWL HTML page interface via the innovative Extensible Stylesheet Language Transformations (XSLT). The HTML page and the OWL record are all obtained as the software gets to the associated ontology word URI, and the appearance of the HTML page and the output of the OWL text in the source code on the page is seen. Therefore, Ontobee understands the delivery of the ontology term URI, and is a genuine information worker connected to ontology. The Open Biological and Biomedical Ontology (OBO) Foundry provides default, connected information. To gain various ontology benefits, many ontology libraries have been built using the previously described innovation framework. Among them is the French Agro-Portal ontology assets shop, which is dedicated to improving multilingual ontology assets in agronomy and related areas, in the light of NCBO BioPortal engineering, and adds new outer ontology term planning data and new metadata administrations. AgroPortal's ontology properties cover six dialects, including English and French. Produced in China, MedPortal is also based on the BioPortal framework from NCBO and is used in the biomedical field. It currently maintains 55 ontology properties covering both Chinese and English, which meet the needs of homemade Chinese customers for worldwide main ontological terms and Chinese understanding ontology terms. In addition, ontological assets and system mirrors, for example, in China, Ontobee and Ontofox are also used to address the needs of homegrown ontology improvement and implementation.

Community-Based Development of Ontology
With the proliferation of ontology, heterogeneity and abundance have become big challenges in the development of ontology. A typical approach to resolve these concerns is to create synonymous relationship-dependent evaluation preparation. However, this methodology learns new errors and chaos with ontology. Thus the OBO Foundry, as a generally accepted network of Ontology builders, promotes a separate method of constructing a network of biomedical ontologies focused on unique criteria.

11.3 Supervised Learning

While AI is an expansive field, the work introduced focuses on tailored learning and even more specifically on research. It can very well be extended to yield open, ordinary or structured ideas. The methods presented here can also be applied to relapse learning much like various forms of AI, such as solo techniques.

The problem is to learn competence with the model M X à Y as a capability that allocates classes from Y to objects from X. A variety of such methods have been developed in the field, among them representative learning approaches, for example, the Vector Machines Help [9] Logistic Regression or non-Negative Matrix Factorization. Despite the previous approach, the ultimate goal is to assemble models that improve the calculation of quality (or limit misfortune work). A problem under consideration is how strategies can be enhanced once an external framework is known, i.e., as different level connections between qualities assessments or non-IS-A connections among attributes.

It can be seen that continuing work on neural organizations, identified with deep learning can be used as an encoding type of problem in the model structure. In deep learning, diverse hierarchical models are thought of, and can be based on progressions. Early and subsequent studies on learning systems and use of fundamental knowledge involved sophisticated inductive logical programming (ILP) and different level learning techniques.

11.4 AQ21 Rule in Machine Learning

AQ21 is the latest guidance system developed by the Ryszard Michalski group at the University of George Mason and previously at the University of Illinois. AQ21 is actually being approached by methods that discourage difficult knowledge, i.e., expected information into ontologies, information of several kinds, as well as points of health and well-being information interest. The rule behind this work is that a standard learning system with semantics should reason in a way that is better than one which only receives knowledge, much like links between characteristics or values. For example, understanding that Diabetes type I and Type II are also diabetes, decreases the various facets and considers the knowledgeable picture to be wider. By semantics of information we understand property classes, meta-values, gathered versus specific data, and relations between components of information. Value kinds are used to show which thought techniques can be used in learning, including knowledge shifts. The basic property types perceived are ostensible, ordinary, cyclical, ordered, diagram, fixed, specified, range, proportional, cyclic, and supreme. Complete knowledge refers to information in which models provided the learning system, rather than a single article for which the framework reasons. The cumulative knowledge is usually shown using the average and standard deviation of properties measured for model selection or recurrence of representative characteristics. Meta-values apply to exceptional quality, the name black, trivial and insignificant (Michalski furthermore, [16]). These meta-values are related to likely purposes for which normal qualities are lacking: they are unknown, do not bode well or are eliminated according to the master opinion. The accompanying segments illustrate the primary focal point of this paper, which is how different levels of connections are removed from UMLS to be used for AQ21, and then how progressive and normal models are found by AQ21, the current possibility of speculation with orders as reflected in AQ21 provides a technology for learning with non-IS-A connectors.

The system has been expanded late to include explicit highlights in the preparation of biomedical information [17, 18]. AQ21 is a kind of characteristic list frame to recognize designs that have been mentioned as attribution decisions [19], which can be interpreted effectively by end-clients. CONSEQUENT <= PREMISE is the main kind of attribution rule where both CONSEQUENT and PREMISE are combined with attribution conditions. Each attribution condition includes credits contained or developed by the program in the information. The AQ21 system will also contend with information anomalies. The framework learns standard guidelines and produces exemptions that refer to negative covered models. The case may be either an attributive conjunctive representation or a rundown of models with exemptions to the standard. Exemptions are reliably pessimistic models of clinical databases such as malignant development repeats and disease movement. Min *et al.* Min. Biomedical Semantics Diary (2017) 8:39 Page 2 of 8 AQ21 learning rules are a few steps to delegate input, rule age and rule improvement. The means are usually performed in a certain order, despite the fact that the learning cycle of AQ21 is iterative in some ways. Pre-handling of information includes reworking information in classes, eliminating misleading models and changing depictory space through basic pre-preparation strategies (e.g., discretization, choice of quality) or developed policies which use useful acceptability calculations [20]. At its core, rule learning modifies the rearranged rendition of the ideal semi calculation (Aq) for developing standards, which represents a notable consecutive calculation of the calculations [21]. The calculation starts with a haphazardly chosen positive, seed-referred model that creates all conceivable (top notch) decisions covering the seed and not covering (or not covering) the negative models. The best quality guidelines are then selected and submitted. Other arbitrary seeds are selected and activity is renewed among positive models not covered by these rules. This cycle produces several general concepts that should be upgraded and organized for yield (usually more than needed). Improvement of laws requires their administration, the over-simplification by ordering, option and property planning. The general objective of AQ21 is to make choices that increase customer characterized quality models, which regularly compromise the accuracy (exactitude/revision) and its simplicity and simplicity. Finally, the Program uses several strategies designed to achieve results in human-oriented structures, including age of guidelines in a typical language representation (layman terms) [22]. AQ21 is the most recent advance of students who decide AQ progression dating back to the 1970s [23]. Various remarkable guidelines were developed in recent years [24], but many are not currently being used in standard exploration. In the last few years, the ML field has been overwhelmed by factual strategies which essentially focused on providing extremely precise models. In any case, the network has begun to gradually change the understanding and simplicity of the provided models, which are particularly important in biomedical applications. AQ21-OG (Ontology-oriented AQ21-OG) is an increase in the learning framework for the AQ21 rule. It implements progressive thought strategies [25] in which UMLS and different ontologies are integrated while information is broken down. Currently, the software calls IS-A link preparation. The AQ21-OG execution includes step 1: Mapping UMLS CUI information. This advancement is used to recognize the basic CUIs. Consequently, the competition CUIs (SQL) were recognized and subsequently checked by specialists for hazardous mappings. Step 2: Extracting total command subchains by using base CUIs to follow IS-A connections. This is completed by following IS-A connections in the UMLS for every idea, until the entire parent, youth and family subchain is divided. The complete sub-pecking order is specified as the direction from the base CUI (the farthest child(ren) in the control chain) to the root ("super parent" for instance a parent who is also not a kid). This extraction is why the info record (in Phase 4) is used by AQ21 to locate the most common precursors for base CUIs (in Step 5). Step 3: Settlement in the order of anomalies. Due to the concept of the UMLS, different anomalies (e.g. loops, copies) can arise as they have been produced from multiple source textures. Cycles in AQ21 are not permitted, so they are decided by shattering connections which bind the spirit to ideas that are higher in order, as estimated by good root ways. The last chain of command excludes different forms of anomalies. Step 4: Encoding eliminated essential chains into a cohesive organization of ML programming. AQ21 involves the reworking of parent-younger sets across all relations structuring the command chain. The information is read from text records which incorporate all the semantic data required to effectively dominate the information. In the AQ21 in particular, progressive connections are important for the sense of the spaces of qualities (set of potential qualities), which reflect knowledge. Stage 5: Optimization of the values by using phase 2's independent UMLS pecking orders. In the progressive method AQ21-OG is seeking the highest degree of speculation, which is either predictable by knowledge or extends the normal quality metrics. This is highly important where coded clinical knowledge is dissected with a possible wide amount of double credits.

For example, ICD-9-CM analytical codes can make nearly 10,000 double subscriptions necessary. The need to summarize these codes to decrease the number of highlights is also important. Information from SEER-MHOS (monitoring, epidemiology and end-results—Medicare Health Outcomes Survey) from 1998 to 2011 (1,849,311 records) was used as malignant growth attributes to separate daily co-morbidities and daily life exercises (ADLs). This data set includes two huge populace-based data that provide nitty sticky data about disease recipients of Medicare. The information on SEER separated from the malignant library includes clinical, segment and death data for disease patients while MHOS information is removed from reactions and provided by Min *et al.* Diary of Biomedical Semantics (2017) personal satisfaction related well-being (HRQOL) data of Medicare

Advantage Organization (MAO). Various advances have been followed to make the data set for the examination population. Initially, the population of the investigation was limited to those who had, at any rate, completed a review before their malignancy and a study about a year after the conclusion. If a patient has completed numerous studies, the nearest studies have been utilized before the malignant growth analysis and the 1-year development. These extremely serious standards essentially reduced the size of the example and led to 829 malignant patients. Subordinate/Output Variables: six ADLs (strolling, dressing, washing, seating, toileting, and eating) showed the essential results in a patient overview that took one year after the disease. Autonomous/Input Variables: the potential indicators have been selected depending on the previous examination and are as follows:

(1) Socio-economics for patients: age, race, and marital status.
(2) Six ADLs detailed before the malignancy determination in a patient study.
(3) Thirteen self-reported comorbidities removed from patient studies performed prior to the malignancy analysis: angina pectoris/coronary artery disease.
(4) In total, six malignant characteristics of assessment, organization, tumor size, histology, tumor increase, and behavior excluded from the SEER library.
(5) Radiation from tumors and markers of medical procedures excluded from SEER library.

11.5 Unified Medical Systems

The Metathesaurus, a storehouse between biomedical concepts, is the main part of UMLS. The Semantic Network offers two other source points of information for each Metathesaurus idea. It also provides high-level classes and lexical assets including the SPECIALIST wording and lexical variations in biomedical term development projects. Metathesaurus was the primary asset rendered in depth in this research The version shown here is 2003AB, except if decided in any case (July 2003). The UMLS sources of knowledge are updated quarterly.

11.5.1 Note of Relevance to Bioinformatic Experts

Although the UMLS is not specifically developed for the needs of bioinformaticians, the wording in bioinformatics is incorporated. For example,

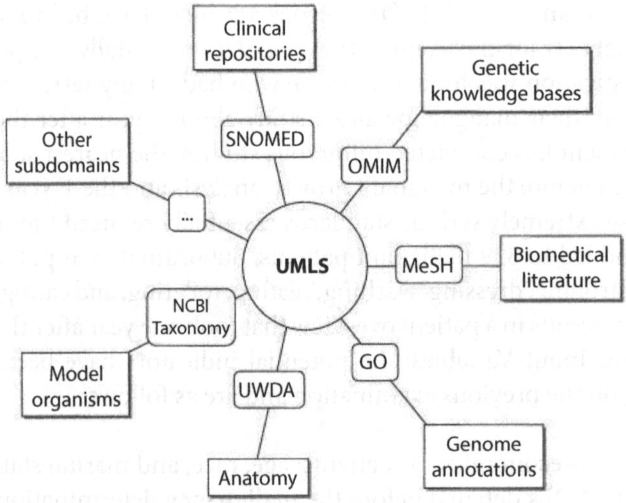

Figure 11.2 UMLS metathesaurus relations.

the NCBI, a scientific classification used for the identification of creatures and Gene Ontology, used for explained quality things between various model life beings, are included as late organized phrases. In addition, the Metathesaurus covers biomedical writing with the MeSH, regulated jargon for documenting MEDLINE. In addition, in the Interactive Anatomist Symbolic Knowledgebase, center subdomains, for example, life systems used in a wide variety of biomedical applications, are discussed. The clinical segment of biomedicine was finally most prominently addressed, with some explanations to be given in general terms such as SNOMED® International (and soon SNOMED-CT®), version 3 of Clinical Terms and the international disease classification. Medical genetic properties The on-line heritage for manTM (OMIMTM) and multiple congenital anomaly/mental retardation syndromes (MCA/MR)© is recalled by assets of clinical heritage qualities. Have basic controls (e.g., nursing, psychiatry) and clinical data structure segments in various text classification in the metathesaurus (for example, illnesses, drugs, methods, unfavorable impacts). Figure 11.2 shows how the UMLS metathesaurus can fill in the relation between the language and the subdomains of which it communicates by arranging these phrases.

11.5.2 Terminological Incorporation Principles

Knowledge in the UMLS is sorted by concept (e.g., which means) (8). Interchangeable concepts are joined together to construct an idea and ideas by methods for different types of relations are linked to various ideas and generate a rich diagram. Between concepts, the arrangement of the original vocabularies or the editors of the Metathesaurus directly acquired relations. Emblematic linkages can be different levels (e.g., "is a" or "part of or cooperative" (e.g., "region of" or "brought on by")). Additionally, there are actual connections between MeSH jargon views obtained from the MeSH co-event in MEDLINE. Last of all, every term from Metathesaurus is thoroughly sorted by semantic methods (for example the 135 essential classifications that the Semantic Network has found), relegated to the editors of Metathesaurus. This makes it easier for consumers, for example, to perform work tasks.

(i) The various words used to name an idea are collected;
(ii) Eliminating associations, progressive or acquainted, representative or observable, from one concept to another;
(iii) Creating a community of ideas for the sort category, using an overview of ideas appointed to a category of week.

The lexical relation used for grouping biomedical concepts into ideas is more formally synonymous. The progressive basis on which the ideas are composed is the hyponymy ("is a") and meronia ("a piece of") relationships. Affiliated connections, like co-event relationships, are expanding this structure to various subdomains. With part of the different leveled connections, the arrangement can be called repetitive by semantic form. By and by, since the structure is independent of the organization of the source terms, this provides a simple and steady theoretical course in the Metathesaurus.

11.5.3 Cross-References External

Biomedical formulations also contain more details than basic terms and relationships. In addition to descriptions, additional details can provide cross-references, either within or outside (e.g., See as well in MeSH, treated as cooperative relationships) (for example cross-references to different wordings or information bases). In the Metathesaurus, this data is also spoken to. MeSH advantageous ideas documents, for example, contain multiple proteins that are marked with a GenBank recognition. Moreover, in any case when the OMIM concept is not in the metathesaurus, ideas from Online MCA/MR syndromes highlight related infections in both MeSH and OMIM. Cases of these cross-references are given below.

11.5.4 UMLS Data Access

The access to UMLS information sources does not require any expenses. However, UMLS clients are expected to agree to a licensing agreement before the information is obtained. Under this arrangement, all vocabulary may be used within a base for research purposes, although some vocabularies for different purposes may be limited in use. UMLS sources are both CD-ROM and FTP available.

The social documents of the UMLS can be stacked and accessed via SQL requests. On the contrary, an item-situated UMLS model has been late developed that allows customers to assemble Java applications against the NLM archive through an API, much like XML queries. The Knowledge Source Server is an online tool for the collection and dissemination of UMLS data. These three components expect UMLS licensees to be customers.

11.6 Performance Analysis

The data set was separated randomly for the planning (75%) and testing (25%). The set was used to create high-performance models and the set were used to analyze the segregation of the product. First models were produced to find the indicator or set of indicators to anticipate the outcome (the six ADLs post disease determination). To make models, two ML techniques have been used: AQ21 and AQ21-OG, which have previously been described. The nature and nature of both techniques were examined using the positive (p) amounts, negative (n) cases covered by the rules and guidelines Q (w). Standard R quality is established by using the accompanying recipes depicted by Michalski and Kaufman, Q(R,w) with weight w or just Q(w) (signified by Q in standard). P and N show all the positive and negative models in the information (here, impaired versus practically autonomous as far as ADLs).

$$Q(R,w) = \text{compl}(R)w \times \text{consign}(R)1 - w$$

where

$$\text{compl}(R) = p/P$$

$$\text{consig}(R) = ((p/(p+n)) - (P/(P+N))) \times (P+N)/N$$

The w is a weight (0 to 1), which speaks to the compromise in the range of continuity and culmination. The lower the w, the more accurate the

Table 11.1 Patients characteristics in the final dataset (n = 829).

	Number	**%**
Age		
<65	26	3.14%
65-74	398	48%
75-84	364	44%
>=85	41	5%
Top 5 Comorbidities		
Hypertension	486	59%
Arthritis of Hip	298	36%
Arthritis of Hand	263	32%
Other Heart	152	18.4%
Sciatic	187	23%
Cancer Type		
Bladder	59	7%
Breast	209	25%
Colorectal	112	14%
Head Neck	28	4%
Lung	94	11%
Melanoma	62	8%
Pancreas	17	21%
Prostate	178	22%
Stomach	24	29%
Uterus	36	43%

Table 11.2 ADL disabilities patients before and after cancer diagnosis.

ADLs	**No. of patients before cancer diagnosis**	**%**	**No. of patients after cancer diagnosis**	**%**
Dressing	29	35%	83	10%
Chairing	15	2%	67	81%
Bathing	39	47%	87	11%
Toileting	87	11%	124	15%
Walking	99	12%	152	18%
Eating	27	33%	56	68%

Table 11.3 Q (R, w*), rule for ADL.

ADL	AQ21 Q (R, w)	AQ21-OG Q (R, w)	AQ21 precision	AQ21OG precision	AQ21 recall	AQ21-OG recall	AQ21 F1-score	AQ21-OG F1-score
Dressing	0.498	0.664	0.87	1.13	0.3	0.32	0.23	0.38
Chairing	0.472	0.536	0.93	1.02	0.13	0.15	0.25	0.26
Bathing	0.654	0.645	0.97	0.98	0.32	0.37	0.45	0.47
Toileting	0.592	0.595	1.03	1.04	0.19	0.19	0.34	0.35
Walking	0.463	0.497	1.04	1.03	0.23	0.32	0.33	0.47
Eating	0.626	0.687	1.05	1.07	0.24	0.35	0.34	0.48

rules are (less negative models covered). Table 11.1 indicates the patients characteristics in the final dataset and Table 11.2 indicates ADL disabilities patients before and after cancer diagnosis and Table 11.3 represents rules for ADL. The greater the w the more the instructions are the more complete the (more sure models covered). In light of the theory test evaluation, we have chosen w = 0.3 to demonstrate a slightly greater load for better predictability. In the two instances, with and without ontology, this value was used. Completion is referred to as an AI analysis as much as possible. The increase in consistency can be seen as standard accuracy that tests the exactness of an irregular theory.

11.7 Conclusion

This chapter indicates that ML calculations can be discussed by bio-ontologies to provide clinical knowledge. The technique introduced shows that encoding various types of explicit levels to monitor rules can be conceived and different types of semantical relations in biomedical ontologies can be accessed. The ontology-guided ML strategy was preferential to the ontology-free approach. The technique adopted can also be used to enhance ML's efficacy and efficiency in medical care, where the use of basic knowledge and continuity with established clinical capacity are basic.

References

1. Narula, G.S., Yadav, U., Duhan, N., Jain, V., Evolution of FOAF and SIOC in Semantic Web: A Survey. *CSI-2015; 50th Golden Jubilee Annual Convention on "Digital Life*, at New Delhi, held on 02nd to 05th December, 2015, published by the Springer under Big Data Analytics, Advances in Intelligent Systems and Computing.
2. Min, H., Mobahi, H., Irvin, K., Avramovic, S., Wojtusiak, J., Predicting activities of daily living for cancer patients using an ontology-guided machine learning methodology. *J. Biomed. Semant.*, 8, 2017.
3. Yadav, U., Murthy, B.K., Narula, G.S., Duhan, N., Jain, V., EasyOnto: A Collaborative Semi Formal Ontology Development Platform. *CSI-2015; 50th Golden Jubilee Annual Convention on "Digital Life"*, at New Delhi, held on 02nd to 05th December, 2015, published by the Springer under Nature Inspired Computing, Advances in Intelligent Systems and Computing.
4. Patibandla, R.S.M.L. and Narayana, V.L., Computational Intelligence Approach for Prediction of COVID-19 Using Particle Swarm Optimization,

in: *Computational Intelligence Methods in COVID-19: Surveillance, Prevention, Prediction and Diagnosis. Studies in Computational Intelligence*, vol. 923, K. Raza (Ed.), Springer, Singapore, 2021, https://doi.org/10.1007/978-981-15-8534-0_9.
5. Yadav, U., Narula, G.S., Duhan, N., Jain, V., Murthy, B.K., Development and Visualization of Domain Specific Ontology using Protege. *Indian J. Sci. Technol.*, 9, 16, 1–7, April, 2016.
6. Jain, V. and Singh, Dr. M, Ontology Development and Query Retrieval using Protégé Tool. *Int. J. Intell. Syst. Appl. (IJISA), Hongkong*, 5, 9, 67–75, August 2013.
7. Sandhya Krishna, P., Ummadi, J.R., Lakshmi Patibandla, R.S.M., Reshmi Khadherbhi, S.K., Identification of lung cancer stages using efficient machine learning framework. *J. Crit. Rev.*, 7, 6, 385–390, 2020.
8. Jain, V. and Singh, Dr. M, Ontology Based Information Retrieval in Semantic Web: A Survey. *Int. J. Inf. Technol. Comput. Sci. (IJITCS), Hongkong*, 5, 10, 62–69, September 2013.
9. PRSML *et al.*, Prediction of pneumonia disease by using deep convolutioanl neural networks. *J. Eng. Sci.*, 9, 4, 393–399, May 2020.
10. PRSML *et al.*, Seer cancer prediction using machine learning. *J. Eng. Sci.*, 9, 4, 387–392, May 2020.
11. Singh, G. and Jain, V., Information Retrieval through Semantic Web: An Overview. *Confluence 2012, held on 27th and 28th September*, at Amity School of Engineering & Technology, Amity University, Noida, pp. 114–118, 2012.
12. Jain, V., Singh, G., Singh, Dr. M, Ontology Development Using Hozo and Semantic Analysis for Information Retrieval in Semantic Web. *2013 IEEE Second International Conference on Image Information Processing (ICIIP-2013)*, held on December 9 - 11, 2013.
13. *Precision Medicine*, Available from: https://www.nih.gov/precision-medicineinitiative-cohort-program. Accessed 16 Sept 2017.
14. Wojtusiak, J., Min, H., Elashkar, E., Mobahi, H., Vukomanovic, S., *Ontologies in Supervised Learning from Medical Data*, 2016.
15. Lakshmi Patibandla, R.S.M. *et al.*, Medical data clustering using particle swarm optimization method. *J. Crit. Rev.*, 7, 6, 363–367, 2020 2020.
16. Wojtusiak, J., Recent advances in AQ21 rule learning system for healthcare data. *American Medical Informatics Annual Symposium*, 2012.
17. Briganti, A. *et al.*, Impact of age and comorbidities on long-term survival of patients with high-risk prostate cancer treated with radical prostatectomy: A multi-institutional competing-risks analysis. *Eur. Urol.*, 63, 4, 693–701, 2013.
18. Agborsangaya, C.B. *et al.*, Health-related quality of life and healthcare utilization in multimorbidity: Results of a cross-sectional survey. *Qual Life Res.*, 22, 4, 791–9, 2013.

19. Maier, A., Syben, C., Lasser, T., Riess, C., A gentle introduction to deep learning in medical image processing. *Z. Med. Phys.*, 29, 2, 86–101, 2019, https://doi.org/10.1016/j.zemedi.2018.12.003.
20. Wernick, M.N., Yang, Y., Brankov, J.G., Yourganov, G., Strother, S.C., Machine Learning in Medical Imaging. *IEEE Signal Process. Mag.*, 27, 4, 25–38, 2010. https://doi.org/10.1109/MSP.2010.936730.
21. Khan, A., Doucette, J.A., Cohen, R., Lizotte, D.J., Integrating Machine Learning Into a Medical Decision Support System to Address the Problem of Missing Patient Data. *2012 11th International Conference on Machine Learning and Applications*, Boca Raton, FL, pp. 454–457, 2012.
22. Dou, D., Wang, H., Liu, H., Semantic data mining: A survey of ontology-based approaches. *Proceedings of the 2015 IEEE 9th International Conference on Semantic Computing (IEEE ICSC 2015)*, Anaheim, CA, pp. 244–251, 2015.
23. Silachan, K. and Tantatsanawong, P., Domain Ontology Health Informatics Service from Text Medical Data Classification. *2011 Annual SRII Global Conference*, San Jose, CA, pp. 357–362, 2011.
24. Asim, M.N., Wasim, M., Khan, M., Mahmood, W., Abbasi, H.M., A survey of ontology learning techniques and applications. *Database J. Biol. Databases Curation 2018*, 2018. bay101. https://doi.org/10.1093/database/bay101.
25. Muhlbacher, T., Linhardt, L., Möller, T., Piringer, H., TreePOD: Sensitivity-aware selection of pareto-optimal decision trees. *IEEE Trans. Visual. Comput. Graphics*, 24, 1, 174–183, 2018.

12

Rare Disease Diagnosis as Information Retrieval Task

Jaya Lakkakula, Rutuja Phate, Alfiya Korbu and Sagar Barage*

Amity Institute of Biotechnology, Amity University, Mumbai, Maharashtra, India

Abstract

Rare diseases are defined as a condition which affects a small percentage of the population. It is also known as orphan diseases due to lack of attention, support, and resources available from the government as well as the private sector to develop therapeutics. The purpose of this chapter is to provide information on rare diseases. It explores the relationship between rare diseases, diagnosis, and information retrieval. In particular, it illustrates the history, characteristics, types, and classification along with databases of rare disease information. We also explore challenges faced by researchers in rare disease information retrieval and how they can resolve by optimizing search query. Specifically, the section with rare disease information database and information retrieval through Google/semantic web search gives a wealth of useful information to clinicians and medical practitioners for rare disease diagnosis. Moreover, a rare disease research institute is useful to a young researcher for career development. Finally, the information on the rare disease is available under a single umbrella useful for academicians, researchers, and medical practitioners.

Keywords: Rare disease, rare disease database, rare disease diagnosis, information retrieval

**Corresponding author*: sagarbarage@gmail.com

Vishal Jain, Jyotir Moy Chatterjee, Ankita Bansal and Abha Jain (eds.) Semantic Web for Effective Healthcare, (269–292) © 2022 Scrivener Publishing LLC

12.1 Introduction

Rare diseases are disorders that are found in an extremely small population of people. This can also be referred to as a disorder. The rareness of the disease varies in different regions and countries. Generally, a disease found in fewer than five people in a population of 10,000 people is termed as a rare disease [1]. It is also called "orphan diseases" and affects a very scarce population worldwide numbering hardly tens to hundreds of a community [1]. They are being studied and regulated worldwide promoting various aids for research and development with around 6000–8000 rare diseases, with mostly 250–280 added annually [2]. However, most of them are less frequent and cannot even be treated competently. Recognition of these rare diseases is a prevailing challenge for global healthcare. For an approximation, 6% to 8% of the population internationally, is suffering from rare diseases. In India, 72 to 96 million people suffering from rare diseases [3]. Up till now, about 450 rare diseases have been documented from tertiary care hospitals in India [3]. Rare diseases can be caused due to inherited mutations, de novo dominant mutations, or mosaic mutations. Some of the examples of rare diseases are cystic fibrosis, IgA nephropathy, rare forms of cancer, X-linked severe combined immunodeficiency, Gaucher disease, etc. [1, 4, 5].

Being affected by a "rare" disease eventually states the fact that it is rare to find the disease as no ancestral records of the disease are found. The whole family is affected somehow relating to each other but the source is unexplained or unknown [5]. Rare diseases often result in impairment of health conditions and abnormal functioning. It is a pathological condition where infections, genetic defects, or other environmental stresses are observed in any part or organ of the body. These symptoms can be grouped as a basis for observation of characterization, mostly identified by its low prevalence [5]. These uncommon diseases tend to create a lot of difficulties and challenges for the affected individuals for proper diagnosis and treatment. The insufficiency of constructive treatment for a maximum of rare diseases and when diagnosed, its expensive treatment, and other scientific interrogations make these cases difficult to settle [2]. Like most, these diseases are asymptomatic or may not show symptoms immediately as they may be genetic or appear in early life, their diagnosis becomes difficult. The majority of the rare diseases are genetic and there exists a wide heterogeneity.

There are various diagnostic web tools, biochemical and genetic tests for diagnosing the atypical symptoms of rare diseases [6]. As these are solely the common laboratory tests, they might fail to cover all the specific symptoms. Hence, this can lead to a delayed and improper correct diagnosis of rare diseases [6]. Physicians currently are increasingly using the web and internet-based tools for diagnosing and treating rare diseases effectively. Due to the rarity of these disorders, it has been challenging to ensure proper diagnosis until there were initiatives taken towards the use of web bases tools [6]. Advancements in technology opened possibilities to find resources of correct information. Web search engines, semantic web tools, databases, general medical literature platforms, etc. have turned up to be the most popular interfaces for rare diseases diagnosis [6]. These interfaces help us obtain a list of rare diseases, their symptoms, known diagnosis, other specialized and general search about rare diseases, medical repositories, etc. FindZebra, Google, PubMed are some of the widely used search engines [6].

The main objective of this paper is to emphasize web designed systems to ensure proper treatment and diagnosis of these rare diseases. Internet and other web tools which are widely used nowadays can prove a very efficient and excellent means to provide the diagnostic capabilities to medical professionals, clinicians, and non-professionals too. These initiatives can prove useful as a means of knowledge and potential enough for accurate diagnostic aids.

12.2 Definition

There is no such specific definition for rare diseases that would be accepted universally. More or less, few of these definitions place reliance on the population size of affected individuals whereas others are focused on other factors like treatments available or severity of the disease [4]. Overall, 1109 organizations or agencies have been searched from around 32 jurisdictions that resulted in identifying 296 rare disease definitions. The most repeatedly defined term was "rare diseases" resulting in 112 definitions. This term was included in about 38% of all identified definitions and has been defined more frequently than "orphan diseases." Seventy-nine definitions included the term "orphan drug(s)" among those identified [7].

There is currently no standard definition for rare diseases in India [3]. ORDI has suggested a disease to be defined as a rare disease if it is found to affect1 in every 5000 people roughly, taking into consideration the huge population of India. As there is no data available on an epidemiological basis, there are no figures based on rare diseases or any kind of mortality or morbidity associated with them [3]. Some of the common rare diseases usually found are Thalassemia, Hemophilia, Sickle-cell Anemia and autoimmune diseases, Primary Immuno Deficiency in children, Lysosomal storage disorders such as Pompe disease, Gaucher's disease, Hirschsprung disease, Cystic Fibrosis, Hemangiomas, and some forms of muscular dystrophies [3].

In the United States, the Rare Diseases Act of the year 2002 defines a rare disease firmly according to its occurrence frequency, as "any disease or condition that affects fewer than 200,000 people in the United States," usually 1 in every 1500 people. This definition is principally similar to that of the Orphan Drug Act, 1983, which was a federal law written to inspire and encourage research into rare diseases and probable cures [4]. In Japan, the legally accepted definition of a rare disease is one that affects less than 50,000 patients in Japan or having a frequency of about 1 in every 2,500 people [4].

On the other hand, the European Commission on Public Health has defined rare diseases as "life-threatening or chronically debilitating diseases which are of such low prevalence that special combined efforts are needed to address them" [4]. The term *low prevalence* has later been defined as usually meaning less than 1 in every 2,000 people. Statistically, the diseases which are rare, but not life-threatening, frequently debilitating, or ineffectively treated, have been excluded from their definition [4]. The World Health Organization defines a rare disease as all pathological conditions affecting 0.65–1 out of every 1000 inhabitants. These figures clearly relate to the size of the population of these countries, but even modifying for that, the definitions differ from about one to eight in 10,000 [8].

12.3 Characteristics of Rare Diseases (RDs)

Rare diseases are very challenging within the scope of diagnosis. Due to a lack of proper information, early detection of rare diseases becomes a major challenge. To avoid any sort of complications, proper information and characteristics of rare diseases have become a top priority. Characterization helps to identify the types of rare diseases and its classification becomes easier. This would ease the physician to diagnose and proceed relatively smoothly.

Following are some of the common characteristics of rare diseases [5]:

1. Among various anticipation, RDs may result from a genetic disorder, pathogen agents, toxic agents, allergies, or due to

other possible causes. Rare diseases can be acute or chronic and can affect anyone at any age [10].

2. Though there are numerous causes for rare diseases many of them are thought to be genetic, which either can be passed from generation to generation or can randomly occur in a person which can become first to be diagnosed in the family.
3. The symptoms might range from severe to very severe or may be chronic and degenerative leading to lethal conditions.
4. Some rare diseases prove to be inevitably fatal given currently available treatments.
5. The diseases are not easy to manage; both patients and families undergo struggles for a treatment. Therefore, can be extremely painful resulting in psychological stress. As there is no proper cure and treatment, there is no hope of getting over the disease and living a normal healthy life.
6. It risks the quality of life and as most of them are incurable, they increase the mortality chances being unusual for treatment [5].

The characteristics of rare diseases depend on distinct factors. Several factors such as disease history, clinical research, available disease monitoring, treatment evaluation, etc. are often considered for the characterization of rare diseases. Moreover, geographical factors (geographic area, geographic, country, geographic international, etc.) also plays a major role [9, 10]. There might be diseases rare in one part of the world but common in the other part. For example, tuberculosis, a rare disease, is common in less economically developed countries but rare in developed countries. Thus the range of rarity may change from rare to extremely rare or rare to common, and vice versa.

12.4 Types of Rare Diseases

Generally, types of rare diseases are studied based on their cause genetic, non-genetic, pathogenic, toxic, or other factors. There are still some rare diseases with not known, unspecified, or insufficient facts. There are few rare diseases with obscure causes such as Gorham's disease. It is a very rare disease that is named and characterized for decades but now under idiopathic diseases. Likewise, some rare diseases have more than one cause like hepatitis or herpes virus with multiple causes. Hepatitis can be inherited or caused by sexual contact or contact with the virus through food or drinks. Based on causes some types of rare diseases listed below.

12.4.1 Genetic Causes

Rare diseases can be caused by alterations in single or multiple genes. According to experts, the rarest of diseases are genetic in origin, almost more than 80 percent [10]. Generally, a genetic disease is classified into two types: single gene disorder (monogenic) where a specific gene is mutated or permanently altered, and multiple gene disorders where more than one gene is altered. This mutation can be due to failure of repair mechanism, environmental factors, or other reasons. These are inherited depending on their inheritance pattern i.e. autosomal dominant or recessive, X linked or Y linked. Depending on this pattern, rare diseases can be inherited by two carriers (both affected parent) or by a single carrier (single affected parent) from generation to generation. Following are some examples of inherited rare diseases listed below:

I) Von Hipple–Lindau syndrome (VHL) [11, 12] affects numerous organ systems in the body by the formation of cysts and benign tumors with potency to transform into malignant form affecting various body parts like kidneys, uterus, pancreas, and nervous system. It is caused by a mutation in a specific tumor suppressor gene (chromosome 3) and is inherited in an autosomal dominant manner. Studies show that 80% of patients are due to heredity and the rest are due to different mutations [12].

II) Chronic granulomatous disease (CGD), [11] is a genetic disease inherited by an autosomal recessive X-linked pattern. The affected person loses resistance to various infectious diseases. According to reports, this is a mutation on the X chromosome and defect on chromosome 7 (CYBG gene) and chromosome 16 (NCFI gene). Mutations can interfere with the WBC's ability to produce oxygen compounds that are essential to kill harmful pathogens. On the contrary, the immune system can produce granulomas in various parts of the body, thereby isolating bacteria [12].

Some metabolic disorders caused by a specific enzyme due to malfunction or enzyme deficiency are monogenic. For example, lysosome storage disorder results in numerous enzymes efficiency causing metabolic disorders like Hurler syndrome (alpha-L iduronidase deficiency), Tay–Sachs disease (Hex-A deficiency), Fabry disease (alpha-galactosidase A deficiency), Gaucher disease, etc. These are caused as a result of an alteration in a specific gene [11, 13, 14].

12.4.2 Non-Genetic Causes

Some diseases are a result of genetic mutations but not inherited. Mutations in the genes can be due to environmental factors, for example, toxic substances due to smoking. Klippel–Trenaunay syndrome [14] is a rare disease that is a result of genetic mutation in the PIK3CA gene but is nonhereditary. These mutations are responsible for developing tissues overgrowth in the body [16].

12.4.3 Pathogenic Causes (Infectious Agents)

Numerous pathogens like bacteria, viruses, fungi, and parasites cause disease more often. Among the estimated statistics, there are several rare diseases caused by infectious agents. As these diseases are rare, many public health experts and non-profit organizations have encouraged people to raise awareness through intensive campaigns and the development of affordable treatments [9]. Many diseases caused by pathogens can also be fatal due to insufficient information and unaffordable treatments. Rocky Mountain Spotted Fever (Rickettsia bacterium), Whipple disease (*Tropheryma whipplei* or *Tropheryma whippelii*), Legionnaires' disease (bacteria Legionella), Hansen's disease (also known as leprosy) (*Mycobacterium leprae*) are some fatal diseases caused by pathogenic agents. Likewise, some viral diseases are Hantavirus pulmonary syndrome, Rabies, Zika virus infection, and monkeypox virus infection [13, 14].

12.4.4 Toxic Agents

Some of the existing rare diseases are caused by environmental or man-made substances. Long exposure to such substances is harmful, sometimes lethal. Many studies on the physical and chemical properties of toxic substances determining their chemical structure help to understand their properties, disposition, and their reactivity in the human body. The source of these substances can be infectious vectors that produce toxic substances, animal venom, feces, phytotoxins, and natural substances from the earth. These substances enter the food chain in a variety of ways like substance abuse, drugs, domestic use, occupational exposure, animal bites, environmental exposure, or natural (UV) [14, 15]. The entry of these agents can be through the skin, lungs, GI tract, eyes, suppositories, intravenous, implants, radiation, etc. Thus, it is important to study the entry mechanisms as toxicity may vary through various modes [14, 15]. Heavy metal poisoning diseases are caused due to excessive exposure to heavy metals like lead, mercury, arsenic, cadmium, and chromium that affects the body's homeostasis [14, 15].

12.4.5 Other Causes

Several other causes such as nutritional deficiencies, drug toxicity, etc. are also responsible for rare diseases. For example, beriberi caused due to thiamine deficiency that adversely affects the other treatments mostly because of drug toxicity. Superbugs, radiation-induced meningioma are some of these diseases [9].

12.5 A Brief Classification

Taking into consideration the importance of rare disease worldwide, the proper classification of rare diseases is immensely significant. Proper classification can help healthcare experts and researchers in preventing, diagnosing, and treating rare diseases. However, there is not any specific classification system but there are various databases, organizations, and machinery tools. These contain information about all the discovered rare diseases. Nowadays, there are many non-profit organizations engaged in rare disease research. Each of these organizations has its classification criteria. For example, the Orphanet classification system is a multi-level classification divided into three levels: barrier group, barrier, and barrier subtype. It helps to diagnose the diseases in a specific manner and is included in the nomenclature of Orphanet data [11], whereas the ICD 10 International Classification of Diseases that uses a codifying arrangement for the classification. Taking into account all the studied available data, codes are assigned to each rare disease. As some rare diseases in ICD 10 were misclassified using the same coding system, improved version ICD 11 was enforced.

Every classification system is comprised of rare diseases occurrence. However, in broader classification, there are many heterogeneities, such as diseases occurring from birth, age-wise, etc. Together with all these factors, rare diseases can be classified into three groups:

1. Characterized by a genetic disorder, diseases including genetic bases, extreme rarity, occurrence from birth, prevalence rate lower than 1/10,000, etc.
2. Based on known infectious diseases and frequency of occurrence.
3. Based on typical heterogeneity like diseases occurring with age, whether widespread, etc.

This classification being undefined is to cover all possible rare diseases and the existing heterogeneity.

12.6 Rare Disease Databases and Online Resources

Here are some reference databases by Orphanet that would help to enable the correlation between different information systems and its retrieval.

12.6.1 European Reference Network: ERN

The European Reference Network is a virtually developed that includes the healthcare suppliers all over Europe. It is a network for rare diseases to manage access to the required knowledge and information about the rare disease which generally is not available in any health center due to the rarity of the disease. Its main objective is to conduct discussions regarding the complexity of rare diseases and its highly specialized treatment, information, and diagnostic resources. This virtual platform is collaborative in its terms with access given to restricted ERN users only [16]. It does not work as a platform for the exchange of personal or clinical patient data. The main purpose of this network is to deal with the complex rare diseases that require highly specialized treatment and diagnosis. It provides users with all the necessary knowledge and resources [17].

The database has a total of 24 networks where the first ERN was launched in March 2017. It includes over 900 specialized healthcare units from more than 300 hospitals in 26 countries across the European Union [16]. The framework with 18 indicators for monitoring systems will help build an improved system with excellent outcomes to identify the potential limitations and demonstrate its success [17]. It includes video clips consisting of information, stories, and presentations of ERNs, information flyers, and brochures [17].

Following are its characteristics [11]:

I. To make sure that the treatment facilities are available wherever necessary.
II. Proper and systematic application of European Union criteria to deal with these rare diseases requiring special care.
III. Serve as a tool for knowledge, research, and information and a center for treating patients from all countries in Europe [11].
IV. The ERN network is also classified according to ERN members per network and per country.
V. The Network subheading on the database page has a "Search tool," which presents information in a way that contains the ERN names, clinical centers, and details.

12.6.2 Genetic and Rare Diseases Information Center: GARD

The Genetic and Rare Diseases Information Center is a program which has been initiated and funded by the National Center for Advancing Translational Sciences (NCATS) and the National Human Genome Research Institute (NHGRI) in 2002, which are the parts of the National Institute of Health (NIH) [13]. GARD provides the people to access the latest and easily understood information round the clock regarding rare or genetic diseases in either English or Spanish [13]. This database sums up information from the NIH resources, journals, websites, medical textbooks, and databases. Scientists and researchers studying rare or genetic diseases can access information through this database. Even doctors, nurses, and other healthcare providers can obtain the necessary information from this [13].

The GARD webpage has the following components [13]:

I. The questions are being answered by GARD Information Specialists.
II. Links to resources have also been provided where you can find more information.
III. It also contains information about genetic testing and services.
IV. Contains information about all the scientific conferences that have been sponsored by NIH.
V. Information about organizations that provide information, support, and research studies and clinical trials.
VI. Also lists down the FDA-approved medications for rare diseases.

12.6.3 International Classification of Diseases, 10th Revision: ICD-10

The new National Center for Health Statistics ICD-10-CM Browser tool is an easily accessible web-based query application that permits the users to search for codes from the *International Classification of Diseases, 10th Revision, Clinical Modification* (ICD-10-CM) and provides information required to apprehend the usage of ICD-10-CM codes [18]. This application offers access to several fiscal year version sets which are available with real-time wide-ranging results via the search abilities [18]. The International Classification of Diseases (ICD) has been designed to collect, process, classify, and present the mortality statistics and compare them at an international level. It has a specified format that includes death certificates and its cause. The conditions are then reported and decrypted into medical codes by using the standardized grouping system and the rules for selection-modification contained in the valid revision of the ICD, published by the World Health Organization (WHO) [18]. These coding rules are useful to develop the mortality statistics by giving a certain preference to certain categories by selecting the death cause and its sequence [18].

The database consists of the following components [18]:

I. A tabular list which consists of the codes and the cause of death
II. Inclusion and exclusion terms for the death cause titles

III. Diseases and its nature in alphabetical order, drugs, and chemicals
IV. Other rules, guidelines, and coding information.
V. Cause of injury index
VI. Any external causes

12.6.4 Orphanet-INSERM (Institut National de la Santé et de la Recherche Médicale)

Orphanet is a very distinctive information portal for collecting the resources and improving the knowledge about rare diseases to develop its diagnosis and treatment of the affected patients. It also maintains its nomenclature called ORPHAcode, which helps in improving the perceptibility of rare diseases in the healthcare and research information retrieval systems [19]. Orphanet has been established in 1997 by the INSERM i.e. French National Institute for Health and Medical Research in France. But since 2000, it gained much importance by the European Union, and the initiative was supported by a grant from the European Commission and was eventually grown to a Consortium of 40 countries all over the world [19].

It has a platform called "Orphadata" that provides scientific professionals with high-quality data sets regarding rare diseases, also the drugs that are in a reusable form [19].

The webpage of orphaned INSERM consists of the following features:

I. It gives permission to access the classification, inventory, and encyclopedia of rare diseases along with its genes involved.
II. It has an inventory of all the orphan drugs.
III. It consists of a directory of patient organizations.
IV. It has a directory of professionals and institutions.
V. It also consists of a directory of expert cultures and medical laboratories providing diagnostic tests.
VI. It gives access to the collection of thematic reports and the directory of currently ongoing research projects, registries, clinical trials, and biobanks.

12.6.5 Medical Dictionary for Regulatory Activities: MedDRA

MedDRA is a multilingual platform that allows users to access and retrieve information in their native language. This terminology is extensively used for use of data entry, analysis, retrieval, and display regarding stages of drug development and devices [20]. It has a very straightforward and sophisticated analysis used to analyze and detect different medical issues by using its hierarchical structure. MedDRA was developed by ICH partners including the WHO. ICH provides a standardized and international terminology MedDRA which can be used to pertain and access all the medically important data and evaluate the same [20]. This platform proves the best for continuously developing and maintaining the MedDRA database for effective and transparent regulation of product which contributes to the global public health [20].

MedDRA contains the following tools under the "Tools" section of the webpage [20].

I. MedDRA users can access powerful computer tools after subscribing and it helps to get all the information about the database along with the training available on the implementation of the database.
II. It gives access to commercial software tools like Coding and browsing tools, SMQs (Standardized MedDRA Queries), APIs (application program interfaces), Mapping tools, MVAT (MedDRA Version Analysis Tool).
III. There are other tools too including clinical data management systems, autoencoders, and safety systems that have applied MedDRA.
IV. MedDRA allows the users to access the required information through a wide range of options available on the webpage, which are MedDRA hierarchy, Multilingual MedDRA, Standardized MedDRA Queries, Multiaxiality, and Electronic Communication.

12.6.6 Medical Subject Headings: MeSH

MeSH is a precise vocabulary by the US National Library of Medicine (NLM) used to organize the database. It is also used for searching the required data on PubMed, and also some other databases where information is fitted into a hierarchy. The MeSH is available on PubMed's homepage and it allows the users to locate the information for any disease and find its position in the MeSH hierarchy. Some of the subheadings found on the homepage for rare diseases are analysis, classification, metabolism, statistics and numerical data, etc. [21].

12.6.7 Online Mendelian Inheritance in Man: OMIM

OMIM is a wide-ranging database consisting of human genes and genetic phenotypes which is available freely. OMIM consists of information about all the known Mendelian disorders and around 15,000 genes [22]. OMIM concerns the relationship between phenotype and genotype. This database was introduced in the 1960s by Dr. Victor A. McKusick as a catalog which consisted of Mendelian traits and disorders, entitled Mendelian Inheritance in Man (MIM). Now it is a project by the National Center for Biotechnology Information (NCBI) at Johns Hopkins University (USA) [22].

12.6.8 Orphanet Rare Disease Ontology: ORDO

Orphanet has its terminology platform called "ORDO" (Orphanet Rare Disease Ontology) for collecting information about rare diseases obtained from the Orphanet Database and find the relationship between the diseases, genes, and other relevant characteristics. These data are reusable for computational analysis [19]. It is mutually developed by Orphanet and EBI as a multilingual system dedicated to validation and literature of the resources. It resulted from the Orphanet database (www.orpha.net), which is a multilingual database that is inclined toward rare diseases that have been derived from literature and confirmed by the international experts. It incorporates a nosology, i.e., classification of rare diseases, the relationships (epidemiological data, gene–disease relations) and its connections with other terminologies (SNOMED CT, MeSH, UMLS, MedDRA), databases (UniProtKB, OMIM, HGNC, Ensembl, IUPHAR, Reactome, Geantlas), or categorizations (ICD-10).

The ontology will be kept up by Orphanet and will further be added with new data. Orphanet classifications can be browsed in the OLS view. The Orphanet Rare Disease Ontology is updated every six months and it strictly follows the OBO guidelines on disapproval of the terms. It consists of the official ontology of various rare diseases which is produced and kept by Orphanet (INSERM, US14).

12.6.9 UMLS: Unified Medical Language System

The Unified Medical Language System (UMLS) is a software that is a collection of many health and biomedical vocabularies and standards to enable access to the required knowledge by a computer system. The three knowledge sources are Metathesaurus, Semantic network, and Specialist

Lexicon and Lexical tools. It contains its hierarchy that helps to find out the relationships and attributes of these rare diseases [23].

UMLS provides users with the following features [23]:

I. Link codes and terms between the pharmacy, doctor, and the insurance company
II. Coordination of patient care among the various departments in a healthcare facility or hospital
III. Processing the texts to extract concepts, relationships, or knowledge
IV. Facilitation of mapping between the terminologies
V. Develop a system for information retrieval
VI. Extraction of specific terminologies from the Metathesaurus
VII. Creation and maintenance of a local terminology
VIII. Development of a terminology service
IX. Research terminologies or ontologies [23]

12.6.10 SNOMED-CT: Systematized Nomenclature of Human and Veterinary Medicine—Clinical Terms

SNOMED CT is a designated system of electronic exchange of information by the US Federal government. It is used for obtaining the clinical health information and also generates specifications of the US Healthcare Information Standards Panel. SNOMED CT is a very comprehensive and multilingual healthcare database used for rare diseases with scientific validated clinical data. It is used in more than 80 countries and is mapped according to international standards [24]. SNOMED CT is a growing and upcoming platform that supports the development of quality clinical data in electronic form and allows its interpretation.

SNOMED CT supports the following tools and software on its webpage

I. Change or add to SNOMED CT
II. SNOMED CT tooling
III. Software development
IV. SNOMED CT browser
V. SNOMED International Managed Service

The webpage also explains Concepts, Descriptions, and Relationships, how to use the tool, and the benefits of the tool to the individuals and population [24].

12.7 Information Retrieval of Rare Diseases Through a Web Search and Other Methods

12.7.1 What Is Information Retrieval (IR)?

Information retrieval is a task where the clinicians or researchers use symptoms as queries for diagnosing the disease correctly. Several features define the standard web information retrieval which consists of all the developing approaches for the rare disease domain. Lately, the IR systems have gained much importance for all the clinicians and researchers that allow them to work on the difficult rare diseases in a highly comprehensive manner. There can be both offline retrieval and Google web search ways. Offline retrieval can be achieved from a specialized collection of rare diseases [6, 25].

The main objective of IR systems is to acquaint with the challenges and characteristics of the diagnosis of rare diseases.

12.7.2 Listed Below Are Some of the Methods for Information Retrieval

12.7.2.1 Web Search for a Diagnosis

Recently, the use of the web for retrieving information has been a very important tool for studying various rare diseases. Google Search, PubMed, and Semantic Web are the most widely used interfaces. Other highly specialized interfaces, e.g., FindZebra, Omim.org, etc. have also been used. But PubMed proves to be the major database of all the medical abstracts in the world. These search engines not just help in compiling the differential diagnosis but also provides the list of most likely rare diseases [6–25]. FindZebra is a specified search engine for rare diseases powered by open-source search technology. It uses freely available online medicated data and information. The FindZebra search engine is available at http://www.findzebra.com/ [25]. It emphasizes authoritative resources and that can improve the performance for searching the required information. It is a very straightforward and open-source experimental IR system providing functionalities for rare diseases diagnosis. The limitations occur in constructing the appropriate queries based upon the descriptions of the symptoms of the disease. The collection of the queries also proves to be a very challenging task. Initiatives are being undertaken for efficient data acquisition and improving the IR system's performance [6, 25]. The increasing number of patient registries for diseases proves to be a major challenge because of its closed data, its model, and the mechanism for sharing data. Semantic Web-based solutions have been developed to connect the different registries, integrate access, and querying. The Semantic web interconnections between registries allow us to query single or even multiple instances as required. It also helps us improvise the way we share knowledge, publish, access, and express across the web, and federate the data from various registries [26].

12.7.2.2 Cause of Diagnostic Errors in Web-Based Tools

Researchers have identified insufficient knowledge as the main cause of an error in diagnosis or effective medications provided. Graber *et al.* classified the most common 3 errors as follows [6]:

I. Context errors: The prospects for diagnosis are very restrictive. For example, gastrointestinal causes are not considered for chest pain symptoms.
II. Premature closure: As soon as a probable diagnosis is identified other possibilities are no longer considered.
III. Availability errors: A more familiar or common diagnosis is preferred.

Thus, the web-based approaches need to be developed to confront such mistakes and offer fast access to the available information [6].

12.7.2.3 Nonprofessional Use of Web Tool for Diagnosis

Clinicians not only use the web but also the internet for diagnosis. 77% of online diagnoses tend to use search engines like Google, Yahoo, or Bing [6]. Others rely on health websites and places like Wikipedia or Facebook. Non-professionals nowadays are also using these tools to search results for diagnostic conclusions, which may help overcome unnecessary anxiety about the disease [6].

12.7.2.4 Performance of Web Search Tools

Studies have shown that the various search tools had a great influence on the quality of results obtained. Google, PubMed, and FindZebra provided with all the necessary information like the list of most of the rare diseases along with their symptoms and known diagnosis [6]. The versions of these search engines were timely updated.

FindZebra turned out to be the highest performing with better results and mostly widely search tools followed by Google, Pubmed, and OMIM [6].

Following are the different diagnostic tools used recently:

I. FindZebra
II. London Dysmorphology Database
III. OMIM
IV. Phenomizer
V. POSSUM
VI. PubMed
VII. SimulConsult
VIII. Watson
IX. WebMD, etc.

12.7.2.5 Design of Watson

The purpose of Watson was to build a computer-based system that would consist of the codes and questionnaires that would help the medical professionals to diagnose the disease. The design of this model was overall simple and can be broken down into five different stages as follows [6]:

I. Question and topic analysis: Here, language processing is carried out to identify the type of question to construct a structured search query.
II. Hypotheses generation: The search query then generates a list of all the possible hypotheses, e.g., "The disease is beta-thalassemia."
III. Evidence and hypotheses scoring: For each hypothesis, different dimensions are scored as evidence (e.g., gender, symptoms, demographics), and the evidence scores are then collected together to score the hypothesis:
IV. Ranking: The hypotheses are then together combined. A ranking list of hypotheses is created which is based on these hypothesis scores.
V. Answer and confidence: In the last stage, a ranked list of all answers is generated and a level of each hypothesis is calculated [6].

Other methods for information is the use of social media for diagnosing as collective intelligence and expert's authority. Data mining of the information available etc.

12.8 Tips and Tricks for Information Retrieval

Rare diseases are a particularly challenging area in the healthcare system. The limited understanding of rare diseases often leads to delays and mistakes in diagnosis as a result of restricted data availability [9]. There are profuse cases of a general physician not being familiar with the medical cases or dealing with such cases for the first time. Many experts and non-professionals have collaborated to study the number of the population using web-based tools to retrieve disease information. It has been found that not only professionals but also the general public users have been progressively using web Information Retrieval (IR) systems effectively. IR systems help them to find answers to their medical queries. Google is one of the tools used largely by the general public to get their required health-related information. It is also referred by doctors in certain difficult cases.

According to statistics, Google search for diagnosis proves to be less efficient by patients as compares to doctors. PubMed, the second widely used platform amongst search engines for rare diseases and it answers the questions using well-known resources. Users use different words to search, such as "rare," "orphan," "specialization," "ignored," "syndrome," "disability," etc. Therefore, Google and PubMed have their strategies to provide users with accurate information. More often, as these rare diseases are uncertain, diversity in symptoms and restricted available resources were responsible for improper data provided so far. It was important to introduce an efficient search engine especially for rare diseases that would solve all the medical queries of its users. As a result, specialized tools are required for rare disease diagnoses while searching the web.

FindZebra is one such widely used search engine that is used for the diagnosis of rare diseases on basis of possible symptoms. It is also known as a Symptom checker [26]. The interface of FindZebra is very easy to use as it is like other web searches. FindZebra was initially established for doctors and experts involved in the diagnosis of rare diseases. But now, even non-professionals can refer it for diagnosis. However, if misapprehended FindZebra cannot be held accountable [26]. It uses a simple ranking algorithm that ranks the document on the frequency of its counts. It has attracted many experts and professionals because of its easy interface. FindZebra uses a ranking algorithm like all other wide-reaching web search engines. The only characterizing feature that differentiates FindZebra was its specification towards rare diseases only.

Research has been constantly carried out to improve efficiency and use more advanced information retrieval models for collecting data from

Table 12.1 List of various diagnostic tools with their webpages [6].

	Diagnostic tool	**Webpage**
1.	FindZebra	www.findzebra.com
2.	OMIM	www.omim.org
3.	PubMed	www.ncbi.nlm.nih.gov/pubmed
4.	WebMD	www.webmd.com
5.	POSSUM	www.possum.net.au
6.	Phenomizer	compbio.charite.de/phenomizer

additional authoritative sources. While FindZebra is a leading tool, there are distinct semantic webs that are used for the same purpose, as mentioned in Table 12.1. Although building a semantic web is a tricky job, lately, Artificial Intelligence (AI) is a tremendously helpful tool. Through Machine Learning, AI is extensively providing algorithms capable of learning data in this "big data" era. And hence, the AI mediated technology is increasing the efficiency not only in the field of diagnosis but also in research. The Semantic Web is henceforth the future of the web search tools. Its development and dissemination will surely create meaningful content. The semantic web is an excellent technology that promotes all the necessary information and required data management. In the healthcare system, the Semantic Web provides services, applications, and personnel that helps from "syntax" to "semantic" levels. It exclusively helps the clinicians, researchers, and healthcare providers to share useful and sufficient data [27].

Similarly, it also provides great benefits in the rare disease research area. Semantic Web helps users in every possible aspect also contributes as a novel portal for RD. It provides easy and quick access to rare disease resources directly from various sources [27]. In this way, the advancements in web search tools can solely simplify the diagnostic processes.

12.9 Research on Rare Disease Throughout the World

Due to several reasons, rare disease research is facing a great challenge. As for any plant, the availability of germinated seeds is crucial, so is the funding for research. The research on rare diseases is still considered complicated. As these diseases affect a small number of the population, they are neglected from funding and government support. However, the last decade had auspicious awareness because many experts and enthusiasts of health organizations have conducted many surveys and research. It revealed that it had a serious impact on the population. These surveys and awareness programs led to breakthroughs in research of rare diseases. Although the complexity of these diseases still exists, this disease can be caused by multiple factors and reasons (genetic, non-genetic, infectious agents, toxic agents, etc.). The research of any disease is carried out through developments in the field of science. For example, cancer treatment research has achieved success after advances in the field of biochemistry [9]. Hence, progresses into various fields relative to genetic, non-genetic, toxic wastewater, pathogens, etc., is key for the research.

Today the list of an organization working on rare diseases is pretty wide [9]. Some non-profit organization that works on rare disease research are Orphanet, Rare Disease International (RDI), International Classification of Diseases (ICD), etc. Also, there is a regional independent organization such as Europe, Asia, the USA that has its organizations some linked with international some not. India has a Centre of Excellence for Rare Disease (COERD) organization for the rare diseases.

All these organizations have been working on research, diagnosis, and cure of rare disease. The main objective of all these organizations is to study the natural history of the disease, its cause, and ways for improving the quality of life of patients. Even after the correct diagnosis, 95% of these rare diseases still lack FDA approved treatments. Some organization like NORD (NORD's Rare Disease Research Grant Program), ORD, GeRaD, Rare Disease Fund, Every Life Foundation for rare diseases, etc. encourages physicians and researchers worldwide to study and grant funding. The rate of problems faced by rare diseases, increasing diagnostic odysseys, and prevailing for long decades, thousands of rare diseases led to an insight of global cooperation and collaboration, to capitalize and maximize the efforts on research of Rare Disease around the world.

Researchers are now focusing on supporting web-based networks that work on classification, gathering information, and research the infrastructure of these diseases. For example, information including the patient experience, family history, etc. Fundamental research on rare diseases would thereby increase understanding of people enabling them to assess, adapted, and boost therapeutics development. There is still a need for innovative methods for early detection and diagnosis, awareness of prevention strategies, available treatments, infrastructure, and implementation guidelines for both physical and mental health.

Artificial Intelligence has astonished the world by developing technologies to analyze the vast spectrum of data from an individual's health record to multi-parametric cohort activities [27]. Its ability to perform a mutation, prediction, detection, and classification has improved diagnosis to a great extent. Moreover, the algorithms can uncover any new disease mechanism and its therapeutic targets efficiently. Despite all these advancements in AI, there is still room for more improvements. With AI mediated technologies, biomedical systems have been experiencing progress with simple algorithms for rare diseases.

12.10 Conclusion

The rare diseases are neglected due to less number of population affected by the individual disease. Furthermore, the overall population of rare diseases is a large but individual disease with fewer patients and scattered across countries. Thus, information about the disease is very sparse, and rare medical expertise leads to misdiagnosis and delay treatment. In this respect, information on the rare disease will be act as an imperative guide to researchers and clinicians for the development and treatment of disease. In the present chapter, we have collected information about rare disease characteristics, types, causes, and databases. This information will act as a starting point for researchers and medical practitioners for research and diagnosis of rare diseases. Moreover, we incorporated tips and tricks regarding information retrieval helpful to collect and extract information about the disease. The present information offers useful insights about rare diseases and challenges in rare disease diagnosis and information retrieval.

References

1. Hilgers., R.D., König, F., Molenberghs, G., Senn, S., Design and analysis ofclinical trials for small rare disease populations. *J. Rare Dis. Res. Treat.*, 1, 3, 53–60, 2016
2. Dawkins, H., Draghia-Akli, R., Lasko, P., Lau, L., Jonker, A.H., Cutillo, C.M., Rath, A., Boycott, K.M., Baynam, G., Lochmüller, H., Kaufmann, P., Le Cam, Y., Hivert, V., Austin, C.P., International Rare Diseases Research Consortium (IRDiRC), Progress in Rare Diseases Research 2010–2016: An IRDiRC Perspective. *Clin. Trans. Sci.*, 1, 11–20, 2018.
3. National Policy for treatment of Rare Diseases, Ministry of Health and Family Welfare, Government of India, New-Delhi, 2020.
4. Rare disease, From Wikipedia, the Free Encyclopedia, https://en.wikipedia.org/w/index.php?title=Rare_disease&oldid=960745659, 2020.
5. Rare Diseases: Understanding this Public Health Priority, Eurordis, https://www.eurordis.org/, 2020.

6. Svenstrup, D., Jørgensen, H.L., Winther, O., Rare disease diagnosis: A review of web search, social media and large-scale data-mining approaches. *Rare Diseases (Austin, Tex.)*, 3, 1, e1083145, 2015
7. Richter, T., Nestler-Parr, S., Babela, R., Khan, Z.M., Tesoro, T., Molsen, E., Hughes, D.A., International Society for Pharmacoeconomics and Outcomes Research Rare Disease Special Interest Group. Rare Disease Terminology and Definitions-A Systematic Global Review: Report of the ISPOR Rare Disease Special Interest Group. *Value Health*, 6, 906, 2015.
8. Zhao, H., Cui, Y., Zhou, X., Pang, J., Zhang, X., Xu, S., & Han, J. Study and analysis of the state of rare disease research in Shandong Province, China. *Intractable Rare Dis. Res.*, 1, 4, 161–166, 2012.
9. Institute of Medicine of the National Academies, *Rare Diseases and Orphan Products: Accelerating Research and Development* Field, M. J. and Boat, T. F. (eds.),The National Academies Press, Washington, DC, 2010.
10. Coi, A., Santoro, M., Lipucci, M., Bianucci, A. M., Gainotti, S., Mollo, E., ... Bianchi, F., Characterization and classification of Rare Disease Registries by using exploratory data analyses. *Orphanet J. Rare Dis.*, 9, 1, 1–2, 2014.
11. Orphanet-The Portal for Rare Diseases and Orphan Drugs, https://www.orpha.net/consor/cgi-bin/index.php, 2020.
12. RankRed Science|Technology|Knowledge, 13 Rare Genetic Disorders And How They Are Inherited, https://www.rankred.com/rare-genetic-disorders, 2020.
13. NIH – About GARD, https://rarediseases.info.nih.gov/about-gard/pages/23/about-gard, 2020.
14. NORD, National Organization for Rare Disorders, https://rarediseases.org/, 2020.
15. Clevaland Clinic, Klippel-Trenaunay syndrome (KTS), https://my.clevelandclinic.org/health/diseases/17152-klippel-trenaunay-syndrome-kts#:~:text=Klippel%2DTrenaunay%20syndrome%20(KTS)%20is%20a%20rare%20congenital%20vascular,The%20cause%20is%20unknown, 2020.
16. ERN Collaborative Platform-About the European Reference Networks for Rare and Low Prevalence Complex Diseases, https://webgate.ec.europa.eu/ern/, 2020.
17. European Reference Network-Overview, https://ec.europa.eu/health/ern_en, 2020.
18. Centers for Disease Control and Prevention—NCHS—International Classification of Diseases, Tenth Revision (ICD-10), https://www.cdc.gov/nchs/icd/icd10.htm, 2020.
19. Orphanet-Portal for Rare Diseses and Orphan drugs—Access our Services, https://www.orpha.net/consor/cgi-bin/index.php, 2020.
20. MedDRA, Medical Dictionary for Regular Activities, Vision for MedDRA, https://www.meddra.org/about-meddra/vision, 2020.
21. NCBI Resources, MeSH, https://www.ncbi.nlm.nih.gov/mesh/, 2020.

22. Rare Commons, OMIM-Information, https://www.rarecommons.org/en/recurso/omim, 2020.
23. National Library of Medicine, Unified Medical Language System (UMLS), https://www.nlm.nih.gov/research/umls/index.html, 2020.
24. SNOMED International, http://www.snomed.org/snomed-ct/five-step-briefing, 2020.
25. Dragusin, R., Petcu, P., Lioma, C., Larsen, B., Jørgensen, H. L., Cox, I. J., ... Winther, O., FindZebra: a search engine for rare diseases. *Int. J. Med. Inf.*, 82, 6, 528–538, 2013.
26. FindZebra Rare Disease Search, https://www.findzebra.com/, 2020.
27. Karami, M., and Rahimi, A., Semantic web technologies for sharing clinical information in healthcare systems. *Acta Informatica Medica*, 27, 1, 4–7, 2019.

13

Atypical Point of View on Semantic Computing in Healthcare

L. Mayuri[1]* and K. M. Mehata[2†]

[1]Health Informaticist, Chennai, India
[2]Director (Sponsored Research), VIT-AP University, Andhra Pradesh, India

Abstract
Medical information systems are built using good engineering concepts. It outperforms its competitors when it comes to recording detailed and sophisticated data. This chapter examines recent improvements in medical terminology tools and its application methodologies for semantic reasoning and healthcare interoperability.

Health information is multifaceted, sensitive, and siloed. Medical terminology systems are designed to promote semantic interoperability across different healthcare information systems. Due to data granularity requirements, current reference terminology mapping solutions that enable semantic interoperability of data between health systems are heavyweight. They are difficult to use and maintain for health professionals. They are not fit for usage by non-clinical or non-experts. Patients who were once passive are now active consumers. Understanding and integrating consumer health languages can help healthcare consumers and professionals better communicate.

The rapidly growing interdisciplinary field of healthcare analytics attempts to provide semantically standardized language to help clinical decision support systems and related technology make positive advances. Despite recent advances, a comprehensive terminology system that accommodates all clinical and administrative data according to local needs will remain a distant dream for the foreseeable future. Different stakeholders will need to work together to examine present fragmented upstream, midstream, and downstream care protocols.

**Corresponding author*: mayuril@gmail.com; orcid.org/0000-0001-6857-0104
†*Corresponding author*: mehatakm@gmail.com; orcid.org/0000-0003-4968-1356

Vishal Jain, Jyotir Moy Chatterjee, Ankita Bansal and Abha Jain (eds.) Semantic Web for Effective Healthcare, (293–308) © 2022 Scrivener Publishing LLC

***Keywords*:** Healthcare, health data, linked data, clinical data, semantic interoperability, clinical text, data integration, semantic data

13.1 Introduction

Usage of paper to record detailed facts and figures about illnesses began in the early twentieth century. As medical practices evolved, so did the pile of paperwork. Swollen case files of individual patients became difficult for medical practitioners to process mentally and for the medical record department to store and maintain in medical record libraries. By the mid-twentieth century, myriads of other problems clouded the inherent efficiencies of paper-based medical records and founded the use of computers to address the "information explosion" in medical practices. Computers came in use to complement conventional paper records by capturing and organizing key data in medical records [1–3].

In its nascent stages, the pace of adoption of information technology (IT) within health for supporting care protocols was decades behind other fields such as finance, owing to uncertainty in general, and high costs of procurement and operations in specific. Improvements in IT in the late twentieth century pushed forward the adoption of computers to some extent. The Institute of Medicine in the United States (U.S.) reported that electronic patient records is essential standard for all medical records. The U.S. General Accounting Office reported that medical records offer great potential to bring improvements in patient care, by increasing efficiency, and reducing costs. The report also called for development of standards to ensure uniform electronic recording and transmission of medical information [4–6].

By the end of the twentieth century, healthcare systems of many countries, such as Canada and Australia, revolved around the electronic health records (EHRs). As IT systems started generating and aggregating health data, methods to analyze data, and infer knowledge lead to defining systems to aid decision support in clinical settings. The full spectrum of health data used for medical knowledge representation comes from varied sources like problem and medication lists, procedure and treatment notes, social determinants of health, and genomics and proteomics data. Improved networking technologies allowed connecting computers to share patient information for continuity of care, sprouting the need for data exchange standards and interface terminologies [7–10].

By the dawn of the twenty-first century, the practice of medicine had undergone many economic transformations on the backbone of IT. Medical information systems use sound engineering principles for their construction. It is second to none of its peer systems in recording detailed and complex data. In parallel, advancements in IT came to be available in scales and costs unreachable in the last century. In the current IT era, there is no dearth of tools and techniques for mining undecipherable knowledge from the piles of EHR data aggregated in medical record system libraries. Yet, health data remains a double-edged sword because of its inherent, unique, and multi-faceted characteristics. In theory, EHR systems are able to collect, store, analyze, and exchange near-infinite amounts of health information. In reality, IT system barriers such as lack of interoperability and incomplete data standards hinder health data collection, sharing, and usability across the care continuum.

Healthcare delivery system's fragmented legacy structure needs major transformation. The quest to find the delicate and elusive balance between healthcare delivery cost and quality remains unconquered. Disparities among the different health data source repositories pose bizarre challenges to exploit the structured and unstructured data for its true and complete value [11, 12]. In a special publication [13], the National Academy of Medicine reports on the current and near-term AI solutions; highlighting the challenges, limitations, and best practices for AI development, adoption, and maintenance. The report further emphasizes the need for thoughtful, inclusive healthcare AI while balancing the further exacerbation of existing health- and technology-driven disparities.

13.2 Mind the Language

Ever-evolving medical practices make it challenging to baseline a clinical technology landscape. Health data is primarily heterogeneous, highly sensitive, and usually siloed. Sourcing and handling such transactional data is not a straightforward task. Medical terminology systems aim to provide semantic interoperability among disparate healthcare information systems. Common terminology standards used in health information and technology are SNOMED-CT, RxNORM, LOINC, ICD-x-CM, and UMLS. These standard vocabularies and code sets have specific usage. Current reference terminology mapping solutions that enable semantic interoperability of data between health systems are heavyweight because of data granularity constraints. Health professionals find them difficult to use and costly to maintain. They are unsuited for non-clinical or non-expert use. Passive patients of yesteryears are active consumers of health information today. Understanding and integrating consumer health vocabularies will improve health dialog between healthcare consumers and health professionals.

This section summarizes the problem of semantics in healthcare and general solution trends adopted in use.

13.2.1 Why Words Matter

From time immemorial, physicians have used free text narrative formats to document findings from health assessments and outcomes from care protocols. Using natural language for narratives should enable understanding the meaning of words (semantics) and the meaning of the intent of words (pragmatics), the two essential elements in communication. In fact, free text narratives lack structure, and heavily depend on the user's communication style, making them ambiguous to other users. With computers, it became possible to enter data in a highly structured format. However, this took away the expressiveness and flexibility of narrative format from physicians. Also, interpretation and reconstruction of the (semantic) meaning from structured data is usually difficult because of the loss of contextual (pragmatic) information [14–17].

13.2.2 What Words Matter

Clinical information systems capture multimodal data. In contrast, medical terminology systems, such as vocabularies, taxonomies, and ontologies, support converting human-readable clinical terms to computer-processable formats. Thus, while medical terminologies define context-independent meanings of domain terms, clinical information models define the situational contexts using domain terms, and together, they provide the standards for the exchange of meaningful clinical information. In practice, multiple domain or subject-specific terminologies and overlapping information models at different levels of abstraction and detail represent clinical data [18]. Various industry-specific associations, standards organizations, and vendors build individual terminologies or ontologies for the systematic recording of clinical data for specific use cases [19] as there is no single universally accepted standard for representing clinical concepts [20–22].

13.2.3 How Words Matter

Ivo *et al.* [23] survey literature for a global way to develop taxonomy as the lack of a proven method to design a domain-specific industry taxonomy hinders development of a complete, encompassing, and error-free domain-specific industry taxonomy. They present a method called the Industry Taxonomy Engineering Method (ITAXEM), to design Industry Taxonomies in a structured manner. In this method, the team borrows from existing methods, and adds the missing on top of it taking into account stakeholder viewpoints. This approach makes the ITAXEM method applicable to any industry.

Because of the complexities of medical terminologies and the fact that a medical term can meaning differently in different contexts, lay people easily misunderstand terms commonly used by physicians. Cosic *et al.* [24] tested how well patients understand terminology commonly used with them in inpatient and emergency settings of an orthopedic department. Two key findings from this study are that patients (1) do not completely understand healthcare terms commonly used by the professionals, and (2) were ignorant of this fact that they have a poor understanding of orthopedic terms. The findings of this study highlight the seriousness of having clear terminology in use to enable (a) effective communication between healthcare professionals and patients, (b) transparent and informed dialog with patient to get consent to care, and (c) patient satisfaction regarding health outcomes.

13.3 Semantic Analytics and Cognitive Computing: Recent Trends

From the early nineteenth century, statistical techniques have contributed in bringing about notable transformations to healthcare. The advances in design, engineering, and analytics in recent decades offer much improved capabilities and disruptive solutions to age-old problems. "Data Normalization," "Semantic Analytics," "Cognitive Computing," "eHealth Literacy" are recent industry buzzwords for the evolving interdisciplinary field in healthcare big data analytics to bring positive shifts in clinical decision support systems and related technologies using semantically normalized medical terminology.

Although there is much progress in knowledge and NLP techniques, the results are not yet significantly satisfactory to use free text without any constraints in clinical documentation. This section presents select research trends from this growing interdisciplinary field to draw the attention of the reader to the complexities of the underlying research problems that makes finding a practical solution difficult and elusive.

13.3.1 Semantic Data Analysis

Since the late twentieth century, informaticists and data scientists are tirelessly exploring novel solutions to extract, standardize, and analyze health data locked as narrative free-text in health data repositories. Advances in cognitive computing tools offer exciting opportunities in integrating NLP techniques with everyday clinical care.

For the medical informatics generalist, Nadkarni *et al.* [25] offer an overview and tutorial of NLP and design of modern NLP systems. Starting with the historical evolution of NLP, the authors describe key NLP subproblems and draw attention of the reader to selected medical NLP efforts. Velupillai *et al.* [26] review advances in clinical NLP used to analyze clinical texts semantically. The review focuses on three thematic areas: (1) corpus creation, (2) semantic building blocks, and (3) clinical utility. Nenadic *et al.* [27] investigate suitability of different types of NLP tasks and their applications when supported by machine learning algorithms. They also explore the needed properties that must be present in the text data used for training the model. They show how data annotation is one of the key impediments in wide spread adoption of clinical machine learning. Deng *et al.* [28] show a way of addressing the annotation obstacle in medical procedure classification by building a neural network-based processing pipeline for query matching. In particular, they show how adding related concepts to the original input of the semantic network improves semantic matching.

Recognizing the relations between patient problems, clinical treatments, and medical tests is one of the most important capabilities required for cognitive processing of clinical texts. To find the relation between medical concepts and to assign them semantic types, Rink *et al.* [29] use a single support vector machine classifier. This technique got the highest F1 score for the relation extraction task when tested in the 2010 i2b2 Challenge. It remains to be seen if use of medical ontologies such as Unified Medical

Language System (UMLS) for knowledge mining will alter the high F1 scores.

To enable automated knowledge extraction from texts, it is essential to compute the semantic relatedness between concepts or their textual representation using highly specialized knowledge-rich resources. Spasic *et al.* [30] explore the current state of sentiment analysis in health and well-being. The study focuses on spontaneously generated narratives on social networking and Web-based platforms. The study finds that there any not many domain-specific corpora and lexica shared publicly for research purposes and thus the domain of health and well-being is resource poor. In cases where there is either no known knowledge base, or the available knowledge base is huge, or the knowledge base is subject to frequent changes, instead of creating a knowledge base or synchronizing the changes, Rybinski *et al.* [31] present a generic and flexible method for calculating semantic relatedness. Their solution offers an alternative to the costly construction of specialized knowledge-rich resources using a simple resource-efficient method in such knowledge-poor environments.

13.3.2 Semantic Data Integration

What follows are some novel approaches to integrate data from heterogeneous data sources addressing large-scale data integrations.

Employing the best practices in ontology engineering, Hansi Zhang and Yi Guo [32] create the Ontology for Cancer Research Variables (OCRV) to adapt existing semantic resources like the National Cancer Institute (NCI) Thesaurus. To standardize the definitions of data variables, they use an ontology-based data integration method in conjunction with common and controlled vocabulary. This approach makes the semantic relationships from the original source variables unambiguous to all users of the datasets and resolves the ambiguity in variable selection, extraction, and integration processes. Like medical and clinical practices, various scientific disciplines of biomedical research generate data in heterogeneous formats. "Translational Bioinformatics" supports the joint semantic exploitation of biological and medical data from heterogeneous sources. Fernández *et al.* [33] present a solution to create biomedical datasets in open, semantic formats, and transform data by ontology-driven and Semantic Web principles to support data integration.

Though semantics is key to interoperability and integration of health-related data, assessing semantic heterogeneity in domain-associated data elements is very challenging. Brown *et al.* [34] use an expert-based method that complements a data-driven method to assess semantic heterogeneity for empirically generated data elements in HIV-associated data dictionaries. Integrating biodiversity data from distributed heterogeneous sources for research is challenging because of the variety of terms, vocabularies, and languages used to record data. Laurenne *et al.* [35] contrast using a traditional relational database with Linked Data approach for expressing taxonomic information within the checklists of species being studied. Being compatible with Linked Data, semantic web technologies nicely describe species checklists. As an added advantage, Linked Data prevents formation of silos in absence of inter-linkable distributed information.

Without semantic interoperability, integrating data trapped inside various clinical registries designed on vendor-specific custom information models is a humongous task. Lu *et al.* [36] propose a solution based on openEHR for the problem of semantic interoperability of clinical data registries. They verify the feasibility of the proposed approach using a Coronary Computed Tomography Angiography registry. Similarly, to open access to rich sources of health data for secondary data usage, full interoperability within and between population-based patient-registry domains needs to be enabled. Nicholson *et al.* [37] discuss an implementation that is based on the concept of federated semantic metadata registries.

Like health IT applications, the Internet of Things (IoT) enabled smart home devices and wearable health devices record vast amounts of data in silos. Unavailability of easy to adopt common standards hinder integration of health data from the heterogeneous eHealth and IoT data models. Peng *et al.* [38] present a method to incorporate health data with data from home environment using heterogeneous implementation of health services and Web of Things services. Zhengru *et al.* [39] propose a lightweight, extensible, and configurable framework for building clinical NLP systems with external NLP APIs. Their solution is programming language independent, fast to develop, cost-efficient and flexible. Also, users have the freedom to choose an NLP API vendor and integrate with multiple APIs for unfamiliar NLP tasks for better results.

13.3.3 Semantic Applications

Clinical models (CMs) drive documentation of clinical examinations, screenings or measurements in primary care settings and are defined locally to suit various clinical workflows. Gøeg *et al.* [40] hierarchically cluster CMs based on SNOMED-CT and semantic similarity estimation with average and best-match-average aggregation techniques. Dendrograms enable visualization of the hierarchical clusters and comparison of the results of the two aggregation techniques. In secondary care settings, care plans in clinical pathways (CPs) are of greater use when adapted to personalize the treatment experience. A care plan is too generic to provide value in its standardized form. Wang *et al.* [41] customize CPs using a data-driven approach for semantic analysis and reasoning of historical clinical data in the hospital. The authors represent hospital-specific terms by adding local ontologies to the CPs. Hospital-specific clinical data undergoes semantic transformation for storage in a semantic data model and disease-specific treatment procedures include physicians' frequently used medical interventions. "To standardize, or not to standardize" remains an elusive question in clinical practices where the care needs of patients vary by the healthcare environment. The challenge is to take local customizations and reach the summit point where information models and terminologies are globally standardized using semantic interoperability.

Decision making requires actionable information, synthesized from smart data. Panahiazar *et al.* [42] use semantic web technology for integrating and re-using heterogeneous resources for knowledge discovery. They standardize data by annotating unstructured and semi-structured data with the ontology concepts. Web agents use the annotated data to interpret knowledge from resources such as images, text, and XML files. Highlighting the challenges in using big data, the authors present practical use cases to emphasize the need for a semantic data-driven environment. Jovanovik *et al.* [43] develop a set of reusable methods and tools to transform heterogeneous dataset of drug products available from independent and distributed sources into a comprehensive Linked Drug Data dataset. Drug data is collected from the official national drug registries of twenty-three countries using an automated system which then cleans the data, aligning it for transformation into 5-star Linked Data. The consolidated Linked Data dataset is then published on the Web for common use.

Extraction of temporal information available in clinical narratives and normalizing their representation for reasoning and constructing the clinical timeline is yet another challenging task. Madkour *et al.* [44] study the problem of constructing a clinical timeline at the point of care. They consolidate solution trends in representation of time and time related concepts in the clinical domain; medical NLP methods for time reasoning and processing temporal information of clinical narratives. Real-time surveillance is one of the missing characteristics of public health surveillance systems. Current research on automated surveillance methods involves extracting structured information from clinical narratives using NLP pipelines that can deal with synonyms but not similar terms. The challenge here is not the technology per se but the data. Automated surveillance algorithms are blind to data related to emerging diseases such as influenza H1N1 which broke out in 2009. Lin *et al.* [45] develop a real-time surveillance pipeline for disease statistics by combining word embedding with a convolutional neural network instead of traditional NLP-based approaches.

13.4 Semantics-Powered Healthcare SOS Engineering

Systems-of-Systems (SOS) Engineering is one of the sub-fields of Systems Engineering. SOS is a composition of systems consisting of independent, distributed and evolving constituent systems acting jointly toward a common goal by exploiting the synergies between them. Power grid technology, transportation, production and military enterprises are some areas where examples of working SOS systems are available. Nielsen *et al.* [46] review the current state in model-based techniques in SOS engineering.

A breakout session [47] held at the National Center for Research Resources Conference on the Future of Telehealth recognized telehealth as a SOS based on scale and complexity. The session participants identified key topics on telehealth and discussed the known barriers from the points of view of (1) the patient, (2) the system, and (3) the data. From the perspective of data, barriers identified hindering data collection, compilation, and transmission between healthcare providers, and accessibility of data for research purposes were (a) lack of data standards, and (b) issues around data security, privacy, and trust.

Application of semantic technologies to resource-constrained IoT-based systems is difficult because of the distributed and heterogeneous nature of resources. Ryu *et al.* [48] present an integrated semantic service platform (ISSP) to create ontological models in various IoT-based service domains of a smart city. This ISSP method attempts to address problem areas in providing integrated semantic services in IoT systems such as semantic discovery, dynamic semantic representation, and semantic data repository. Smart home environments come with many heterogeneous sensors for monitoring health and environmental parameters in users with special needs at home. Alirezaie *et al.* [49] present an IoT infrastructure system, E-care@home, which gathers measurements from heterogeneous sources using ontologies and integrates the data to enable semantic interpretation of activity-based and event-based context recognition in home environment. Huang *et al.* [50] present a semantic approach based on ontology for risk recognition and rule reasoning for the expression of context for decision support to provide safety services in a smart homes neighborhood.

The realm of digital epidemiology offers methods for application of IT in digital disease detection for supporting infectious disease monitoring and surveillance or for understanding attitudes and concerns about infectious diseases. In their supplement paper, McClure *et al.* [51] set out to examine the transformations brought by advances in Information and Communications Technology. They draw attention to functional and technical challenges posed by internet-based research and social media usage in epidemiology and healthcare. In his paper [52], Denecke highlights the ethical issues for consideration during integration of digital epidemiology with existing practices. Ioppolo *et al.* [53] question the readiness of the society to host smart technologies for remote connectedness to allow continuous monitoring and gathering of data for deriving actionable outcomes. After a brief discussion of the links between technological innovation and the healthcare sector, they discuss viewpoints of change needed to drive future research.

13.5 Conclusion

Healthcare does not have a universally accepted, clinically fit for purpose, semantically inter-operable standard language. The need of the hour to advance semantic computing in healthcare is not yet another approach to merge medical vocabularies. Merging existing terminologies into a common vocabulary will have inherent clinically significant differences. Despite all recent advances in ML/AI, NLP, and automated data processing technologies, a comprehensive vocabulary system that provides for all clinical and administrative data as per local health needs, at the same time engaging with consumers, will remain a dream for the foreseeable future.

Different stakeholders must come together to revisit existing fragmented upstream, midstream, and downstream care protocols. As care becomes more holistic and encompassing, redundancies, and idiosyncrasies in individual-level "health needs" and community-level "health determinants" will ease. This will pave the way for lightweight data exchange solutions that will make it possible to exchange data in a meaningful way by creating a shared vocabulary for the interplay between pertinent clinical and administrative data along the health continuum.

The direction this era of data economy will take for healthcare depends on how raw data and products associated with data are shared. For the data economy to succeed in the current and future environments, we need to harness data from all known sources in all its sizes and forms. In their viewpoint paper, Tang *et al.* [54] drive home this exact fact and envision emergence of economic cluster effects within the health data economy, whose potential is maximized by the sharing of data products. Legal and ethical restrictions will continue to limit sharing of sensitive data across organizational boundaries. National and International regulations such as the EU's GDPR levy strict requirements to protect sensitive personal data. Novel emergent approaches to use data residing in their original repositories, such as the Personal Health Train initiative [55], brings immense potential to circumvent the need to transfer data.

To put it succinctly, standards for data and data interoperability are no longer necessary and sufficient. The primary focus is the development of necessary and sufficient standards for knowledge and knowledge interoperability.

References

1. Moroney, M.C., The Doctor's Paper Work: A Medical Record Librarian's View. *Can. Med. Assoc. J.*, 91, 12, 655–658, 1964.
2. Johnson, O.G., Nature and purpose of local health unit record and report systems. *Public Health Rep.*, 68, 11, 1078–1082, 1953.
3. Mitchell, J.H., Relevance of the electronic computer to hospital medical records. *Br. Med. J.*, 4, 5676, 157–159, 1969.
4. Institute of Medicine, *Computer-Based Patient Record: An Essential Technology for Healthcare*, The National Academies Press, Washington, DC, 1991, https://doi.org/10.17226/18459.
5. Institute of Medicine, *The Computer-Based Patient Record: An Essential Technology for Healthcare, Revised Edition*, The National Academies Press, Washington, DC, 1997, https://doi.org/10.17226/5306.
6. U.S. General Accounting Office, *Automated Medical Records: Leadership Needed to Expedite Standards Development*, U.S. General Accounting Office, GAO/IMTEC-93-17. Washington, DC, 1993.
7. Ambinder, E.P., A history of the shift toward full computerization of medicine. *J. Oncol. Pract.*, 1, 2, 54–56, 2005. https://doi.org/10.1200/JOP.2005.1.2.54.

8. Middleton, B., Sittig, D.F., Wright, A., Clinical Decision Support: a 25 Year Retrospective and a 25 Year Vision. *Yearb Med. Inform.*, Suppl 1, Suppl 1, S103–S116, 2016.
9. Rosenbloom, S.T., Miller, R.A., Johnson, K.B., Elkin, P.L., Brown, S.H., Interface terminologies: facilitating direct entry of clinical data into electronic health record systems. *J. Am. Med. Inform. Assoc.*, 13, 3, 277–288, 2006.
10. González Bernaldo de Quirós, F., Otero, C., Luna, D., Terminology Services: Standard Terminologies to Control Health Vocabulary. *Yearbook Med. Inform.*, 27,1, 227–233, 2018. https://doi.org/10.1055/s-0038-1641200.
11. Evans, R.S., Electronic Health Records: Then, Now, and in the Future. *Yearb Med. Inform.*, Suppl 1, Suppl 1, S48–S61, 2016, doi: 10.15265/IYS-2016-s006. Published 2016 May 20.
12. Feeley, T., Zachary, L., Porter, M., The Agenda for the Next Generation of Healthcare Information Technology. NEJM Catalyst Innovations in Care Delivery 2020; 03 https://doi.org/10.1056/CAT.20.0132
13. *Artificial Intelligence in Healthcare: The Hope, the Hype, the Promise, the Peril*, (2019) A Special Publication from the National Academy of Medicine, https://nam.edu/wp-content/uploads/2019/12/AI-in-Health-Care-PREPUB-FINAL.pdf.
14. Nessa, J., From a medical consultation to a written text: 2. Pragmatics and text linguistics applied to medicine. *Scand. J. Primary Healthcare*, 13, 2, 89–92, 1995.
15. Rosenbloom, S.T., Denny, J.C., Xu, H., Lorenzi, N., Stead, W.W., Johnson, K.B., Data from clinical notes: a perspective on the tension between structure and flexible documentation. *J. Am. Med. Inform. Assoc.*, 18, 2, 181–186, 2011.
16. Luna, D., Otero, C., Gambarte, M., Frangella, M., Terminology Services: Standard Terminologies to Control Medical Vocabulary. "Words are Not What they Say but What they Mean", In book: eHealth - Making Healthcare Smarter, 2018, 10.5772/intechopen.75781.
17. Burrows, E.K., Razzaghi, H., Utidjian, L., Bailey, L.C., Standardizing Clinical Diagnoses: Evaluating Alternate Terminology Selection. *AMIA Jt Summits Transl. Sci. Proc.*, 2020, 71–79, 2020. Published 2020 May 30.
18. Keloth, V.K., He, Z., Elhanan, G., Geller, J., Alternative classification of identical concepts in different terminologies: Different ways to view the world. *J. Biomed. Inform.*, 94, 103193, 2019.
19. He, Y., Yu, H., Ong, E. *et al.*, CIDO, a community-based ontology for coronavirus disease knowledge and data integration, sharing, and analysis. *Sci. Data.*, 7, 1, 181, 2020. Published 2020 Jun 12.
20. Harald, K. *et al.*, Standardization of terminology in dermoscopy/dermatoscopy: Results of the third consensus conference of the International Society of Dermoscopy. *J. Am. Acad. Dermatol.*, 74, 6, 1093–106, 2016.
21. Vuitton, D.A., McManus, D.P., Rogan, M.T. *et al.*, International consensus on terminology to be used in the field of echinococcoses. *Parasite.*, 27, 41, 2020.

22. Smoktunowicz, E., Barak, A., Andersson, G. *et al.*, Consensus statement on the problem of terminology in psychological interventions using the internet or digital components. *Internet Interv.*, 21, 100331, 2020. Published 2020 Jun 2.
23. Hunink, I., van Erk, R., Jansen, S., Brinkkemper, S., Industry taxonomy engineering: the case of the European software ecosystem. *Proceedings of the Fourth European Conference on Software Architecture: Companion Volume (ECSA '10)*, Association for Computing Machinery, New York, NY, USA, pp. 111–118, 2010, https://doi.org/10.1145/1842752.1842779.
24. Cosic, F., Kimmel, L., Edwards, E., Patient Comprehension of Common Orthopedic Terminology. *Health Literacy Res. Pract.*, 3, 3, e187–e193, 2019. https://doi.org/10.3928/24748307-20190624-04.
25. Nadkarni, P.M., Ohno-Machado, L., Chapman, W.W., Natural language processing: an introduction. *J. Am. Med. Inform. Assoc.*, 18, 5, 544–551, 2011.
26. Velupillai, S., Mowery, D., South, B.R., Kvist, M., Dalianis, H., Recent Advances in Clinical Natural Language Processing in Support of Semantic Analysis. *Yearb Med. Inform.*, 10, 1, 183–193, 2015.
27. Spasic, I. and Nenadic, G., Clinical Text Data in Machine Learning: Systematic Review. *JMIR Med. Inform.*, 8, 3, e17984, 2020. Published 2020 Mar 31.
28. Deng, Y., Sander, A., Faulstich, L., Denecke, K., Towards automatic encoding of medical procedures using convolutional neural networks and autoencoders. *Artif. Intell. Med.*, 93, 2018. 10.1016/j.artmed.2018.10.001.
29. Rink, B., Harabagiu, S., Roberts, K., Automatic extraction of relations between medical concepts in clinical texts. *J. Am. Med. Inform. Assoc.*, 18, 5, 594–600, 2011.
30. Zunic, A., Corcoran, P., Spasic, I., Sentiment Analysis in Health and Well-Being: Systematic Review. *JMIR Med. Inform.*, 8, 1, e16023, 2020.
31. Rybinski, M. and Aldana-Montes, J., Calculating semantic relatedness for biomedical use in a knowledge-poor environment. *BMC Bioinf.*, 15 Suppl 14, Suppl 14, S2, 2014.
32. Zhang, H., Guo, Y., Li, Q. *et al.*, An ontology-guided semantic data integration framework to support integrative data analysis of cancer survival. *BMC Med. Inform. Decis. Mak.*, 18, 41, 2018. https://doi.org/10.1186/s12911-018-0636-4.
33. Carmen Legaz-García, M.D., Miñarro-Giménez, J.A., Menárguez-Tortosa, M., Fernández-Breis, J.T., Generation of open biomedical datasets through ontology-driven transformation and integration processes. *J. Biomed. Semant.*, 7, 32, 2016. Published 2016 Jun 3.
34. Brown, W 3rd, Weng, C., Vawdrey, D.K., Carballo-Diéguez, A., Bakken, S., SMASH: A Data-driven Informatics Method to Assist Experts in Characterizing Semantic Heterogeneity among Data Elements. *AMIA Annu. Symp, Proc.*, 2016, 1717–1726, 2017. Published 2017 Feb 10.
35. Laurenne, N., Tuominen, J., Saarenmaa, H., Hyvönen, E., Making species checklists understandable to machines—a shift from relational databases to ontologies. *J. Biomed. Semant.*, 5, 40, 2014. Published 2014 Sep 8.

36. Min, L., Tian, Q., Lu, X., An, J., Duan, H., An openEHR based approach to improve the semantic interoperability of clinical data registry. *BMC Med. Inform. Decis. Mak.*, 18, Suppl 1, 15, 2018. Published 2018 Mar 22.
37. Nicholson, N. and Perego, A., Interoperability of population-based patient registries. *J. Biomed. Inform. X.*, 6, 100074, 2020.
38. Peng, C. and Goswami, P., Meaningful Integration of Data from Heterogeneous Health Services and Home Environment Based on Ontology. *Sensors (Basel).*, 19, 8, 1747, 2019. Published 2019 Apr 12.
39. Shen, Z., van Krimpen, H., Spruit, M., A Lightweight API-Based Approach for Building Flexible Clinical NLP Systems. *J. Healthc. Eng.*, 2019, 3435609, 2019. Published 2019 Aug 15.
40. Gøeg, K.R., Cornet, R., Andersen, S.K., Clustering clinical models from local electronic health records based on semantic similarity. *J. Biomed. Inform.*, 54, 294–304, 2015.
41. Wang, H.Q., Zhou, T.S., Tian, L.L., Qian, Y.M., Li, J.S., Creating hospital-specific customized clinical pathways by applying semantic reasoning to clinical data. *J. Biomed. Inform.*, 52, 354–363, 2014.
42. Panahiazar, M., Taslimitehrani, V., Jadhav, A., Pathak, J., Empowering Personalized Medicine with Big Data and Semantic Web Technology: Promises, Challenges, and Use Cases. *Proc. IEEE Int. Conf. Big Data*, 2014, 790–795, 2014.
43. Jovanovik, M. and Trajanov, D., Consolidating drug data on a global scale using Linked Data. *J. Biomed. Semant.*, 8, 1, 3, 2017. Published 2017 Jan 21.
44. Madkour, M., Benhaddou, D., Tao, C., Temporal data representation, normalization, extraction, and reasoning: A review from clinical domain. *Comput. Methods Programs Biomed.*, 128, 52–68, 2016.
45. Lin, C., Hsu, C.J., Lou, Y.S. *et al.*, Artificial Intelligence Learning Semantics via External Resources for Classifying Diagnosis Codes in Discharge Notes. *J. Med. Int. Res.*, 19, 11, e380, 2017. Published 2017 Nov 6.
46. Nielsen, C., Larsen, P., Fitzgerald, J., Woodcock, J., Peleska, J., Systems of Systems Engineering. *ACM Comput. Surv.*, 48, 1–41, 2015.
47. Ackerman, M.J., Filart, R., Burgess, L.P., Lee, I., Poropatich, R.K., Developing next-generation telehealth tools and technologies: patients, systems, and data perspectives. *Telemed. J. E Health.*, 16, 1, 93–95, 2010.
48. Ryu, M., Kim, J., Yun, J., Integrated semantics service platform for the Internet of Things: a case study of a smart office. *Sensors (Basel).*, 15, 1, 2137–2160, 2015. Published 2015 Jan 19.
49. Alirezaie, M., Renoux, J., Köckemann, U. *et al.*, An Ontology-based Context-aware System for Smart Homes: E-care@home. *Sensors (Basel).*, 17, 7, 1586, 2017. Published 2017 Jul 6.
50. Huang, X., Yi, J., Zhu, X., Chen, S., A Semantic Approach with Decision Support for Safety Service in Smart Home Management. *Sensors (Basel).*, 16, 8, 1224, 2016. Published 2016 Aug 3.

51. McClure, R.J. and Mack, K., Injury surveillance as a distributed system of systems. *Inj. Prev.*, 22 Suppl 1, Suppl 1, i1–i2, 2016.
52. Denecke, K., An ethical assessment model for digital disease detection technologies. *Life Sci. Soc. Policy*, 13, 1, 16, 2017. Published 2017 Sep 20.
53. Ioppolo, G., Vazquez, F., Hennerici, M., Andrès, E., Medicine 4.0: New Technologies as Tools for a Society 5.0. *J. Clin. Med.*, 9, 2198, 2020.
54. Tang, C., Plasek, J.M., Bates, D.W., Rethinking Data Sharing at the Dawn of a Health Data Economy: A Viewpoint. *J. Med. Int. Res.*, 20, 11, e11519, 2018. Published 2018 Nov 22.
55. Gleim, L.C., Karim, M.R., Zimmermann, L. *et al.*, Enabling ad-hoc reuse of private data repositories through schema extraction. *J. Biomed. Semant.*, 11, 1, 6, 2020. Published 2020 Jul 8.

14

Using Artificial Intelligence to Help COVID-19 Patients

Ayush Hans

Department of Computer Engineering, Indian Institute of Information Technology, Sonepat, Kurukshetra, Haryana, India

Abstract

COVID-19 is an infectious disease caused by the SARS-CoV-2 virus. SARS CoV-2 infection is spreading similar to wildfire across the globe. In March 20, it was declared a global pandemic by the World Health Organization (WHO). At the time of writing, more than 14 million people have tested positive. Infections have been growing rapidly across the globe and tremendous efforts are being made to fight this disease. The major challenge that the COVID-19 outbreak has brought is for effective management of the healthcare industry. The supervision of COVID-19 patients in an effective way so as to reduce the threat of further spread has to be the most challenging job for the healthcare industry. This study has its' main focus on discovering new and build upon the existing AI based model so as to improve the healthcare facilities for better recovery of the COVID-19 patients.

After selective studying through the resources, many AI related solutions for the healthcare industry have been proposed. This includes a three stage model of AI application in critical cares which includes input, process and output stage. The Input stage includes data for pre-processing. The Process stage includes various Artificial Intelligence techniques, Machine Learning algorithms, Deep Learning Algorithms for creating a model. The output stage includes the decision making part. This involves treatment of patients, diagnosis of disease, risks analysis, estimation, and management. All the efforts put in defeating COVID-19 by the healthcare industry could be supported by AI-based solutions, which would enhance the process of curing COVID-19 patients, especially those with critical symptoms in ICU's.

Keywords: Artificial intelligence (AI), COVID-19, critical care, pandemic, healthcare

Email: ayushhans2011@gmail.com

Vishal Jain, Jyotir Moy Chatterjee, Ankita Bansal and Abha Jain (eds.) Semantic Web for Effective Healthcare, (309–324) © 2022 Scrivener Publishing LLC

14.1 Introduction

Since the beginning of the mankind, humans have faced a large number of pandemics. Pandemic is the term which is used for an epidemic which occurs worldwide or has its effect on a greater part of the world population. According to the World Health Organization, a pandemic is the one which involves the worldwide spread of a new disease whereas an epidemic is the one which remains limited to one region, city or country. A pandemic is said to spreads beyond national borders and possibly worldwide. The main causes of such pandemics can be the introduction of some new bacteria or virus strain or its subtype which easily transmits into the human body and even between them. Some of the deadliest pandemics in the history of mankind have been caused by a single bacterium which is known by Yersinia pestis, and commonly called Plague.

We have recorded many pandemics in the past. Some of the known ones include:

- Plague of Justinian (540 AD): estimated to have killed over 40 million (approximately half of the world's population) [1].
- Black Death (1347 AD): same Plague resurfaced after around 800 years killing around 200 million in a span of 3–4 years [2].
- Small pox (15th century): it was a constant source of error for almost 3 centuries and was believed to be the cause of death of every third person at its peak. It wiped out 90% of the indigenous population of North American countries like USA and Mexico. Later in 1980, the World Health Organization announced the complete eradication of small pox [3].
- Cholera (early 19th century): It is a water borne disease, which is believed to have originated in India and traveled across the world killing countless people over the century [4].
- Influenza (early to mid-19th century): This appeared nearly simultaneously across the globe and was the cause of over 70 million deaths.

All these pandemics had a huge impact on world population due to the lack of adequate healthcare facilities. The late diagnosis was one of the main reasons that these diseases were very lethal and also became pandemics. But with the advent of new technologies and better healthcare facilities over the years, it seemed like mankind had proclaimed the victory over microbes as seen in Graph 14.1. This was in sight of the vaccines, medicines, antibodies, better treatments, and advance technology, which were developed over the past few decades.

This was a very dangerous complacency, as the microbes never went away, they were just out of sight and have now resurfaced again. Since the start of 21st century, we have witnessed many such pathogens which have had an impact on the public health. Some notable ones include the Ebola virus, HIV, Zika virus, and many others, which were either new and less harmful viruses or were just the ones which we have already encountered in the past.

In 2019 an old virus known by the name corona virus resurfaced. This is a type of virus which impacts the respiratory tracts in humans. Coronaviruses are known to cause different diseases some of which include the SARS (severe acute respiratory syndrome), MERS (Middle East respiratory syndrome), and the most recent, coronavirus disease 2019 (COVID-19).

COVID-19 (shorthand of Corona Virus) was first identified in Wuhan, China in December 2019. It was later declared a global pandemic by the World Health Organization (WHO) on 11 March 2020. At the time of writing, there are 21,450,473 confirmed cases, 805,587 deaths, and 12,34,808 recovered cases. The distribution of these cases across the world can be seen in Figure 14.1. The mortality rate (MR) and the number of cases of this virus is mainly dependent on a few important factors [5]. But the most important of them is the care of the critically affected patients. As the research suggests that nasal cavity is the initial entry point of COVID virus.

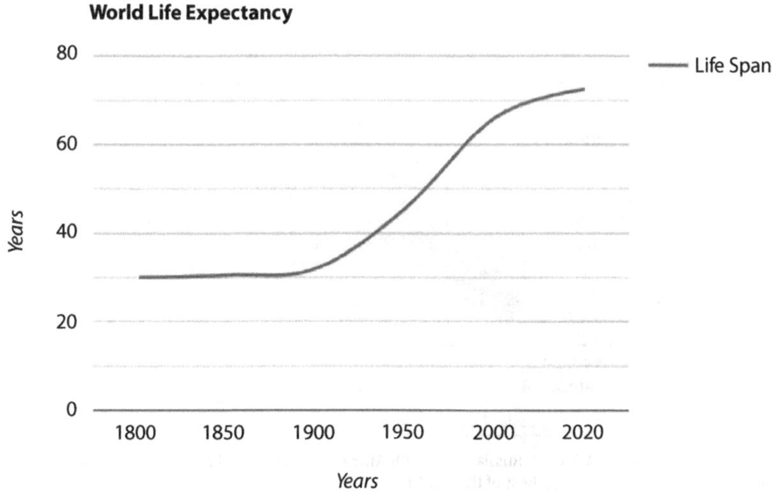

Graph 14.1 Increase in life expectancy with the advancement in healthcare sector.

Therefore, one of the most prominent challenge of this virus is the proper treatment of COVID-19 patients who need acute or critical respiratory care and have had a number of medical records in the past [6, 7].

These types of treatments have become possible because of the advancement in technology which has occurred in this century. Advent of computers was a major boost in the healthcare sector. Next huge boost that started a new face in the healthcare sector was the introduction of World Wide Web. This was due to www, that high level of expertise reached to even the smallest of areas, and now the computers or electronic devices have become essential parts of the healthcare industry.

But even with this type of advancement, healthcare facilities have been overburdened during these times due to the rapid increase in the number of cases as depicted in Figure 14.2. So the main question that arises is that how can the critical care of the COVID-19 patients using AI be managed by the healthcare institutes around the world?

Over the past few years, AI (Artificial Intelligence) has become a necessity in healthcare. This is due to the benefits it brings to the table like automated clinical workflows, reduction in diagnostic errors, early detection of a disease and many more [8]. But in these situations where doctors need to work long shifts and also with immense precision, the role of AI needs to be an innovative one. A slight disturbance in the process of patients' critical care and clinical decision making of these healthcare institutes would make all the people involved vulnerable to COVID [9].

The main aim of this paper was to evaluate the role of Machine Learning (ML) and Artificial Intelligence (AI) techniques in the treatment and

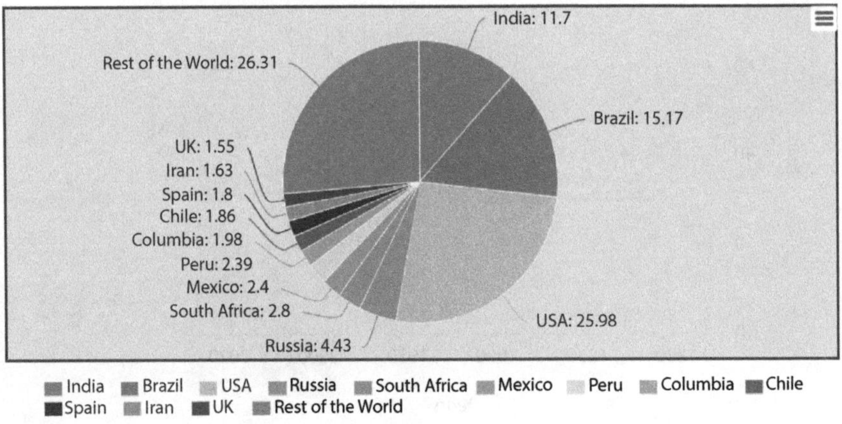

Figure 14.1 Distribution of COVID cases across the world.

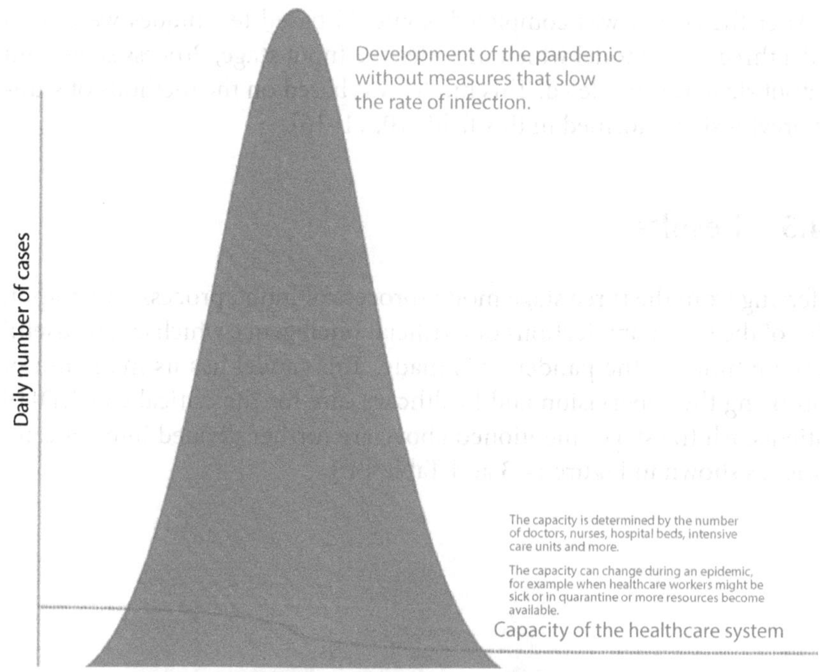

Figure 14.2 Projections of the healthcare facilities present VS that we require.

supervision of COVID positive patients. This study was performed to propose some AI based techniques to improve the condition of healthcare for the COVID-19 patients.

14.2 Method

The Search strategy which was adopted for making this paper was paved on following path:

Search Topic was "History of pandemics," "How can Artificial Intelligence help the healthcare sector during COVID times," "Use of AI in respiratory disease detection," and "Use of AI for critical care patients."

Search Engines used were Google, Scholar Google, PubMed and other useful databases.

Search Terms were AI, COVID 19, pandemics, healthcare sector and respiratory diseases.

After the search was completed, some AI based techniques were used and a three stage model which includes the Input stage, Process stage, and Output stage was modeled. This model was based on the methods of studies previously performed in this field [10, 11–16].

14.3 Results

Inferring from the three stage model/process of input, process and output, a list of the major applications of Artificial Intelligence which can be useful in these times of the pandemic is made. This model has its main aim of improving the supervision and healthcare care for the critical COVID-19 patients. All the stages mentioned above are further divided into subcategories as shown in Figure 14.3 and Table 14.1.

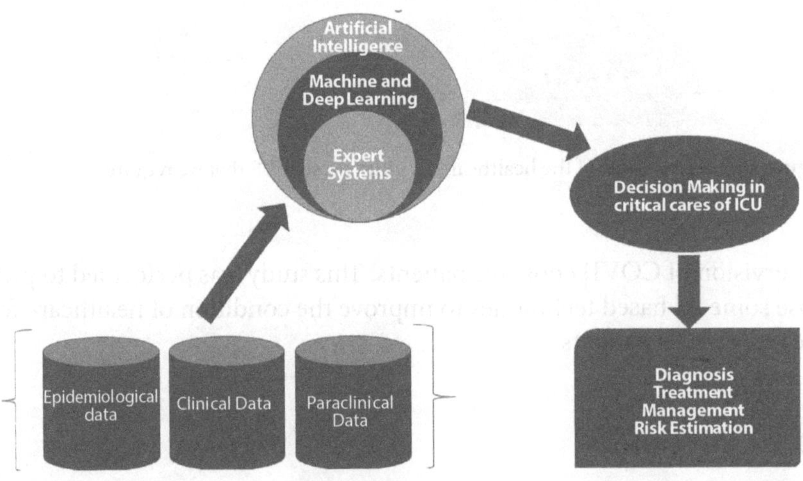

Figure 14.3 Three-stage model for critical care patients.

Table 14.1 Three-stage model of application of AI for patients in critical care.

Input	Process	Output
o Paraclinical Data o Clinical data o Epidemiological data	o Machine Learning o Artificial Intelligence o Deep Learning o Expert Systems	o Decision Making o Diagnosis o Risk Estimate o Treatment o Management

Furthermore, some major advancements/innovations which can be seen in the healthcare industry post COVID-19 have also been mentioned at the end.

14.4 Discussion

14.4.1 What is the Use of AI in Healthcare?

For Healthcare, AI is considered to be a set of computerized applications that imitates human cognition for complex medical information and data with the help of various algorithms and software. AI's main objective is to perform a detailed analysis of the connections between the techniques used for prevention, diagnosis or treatment of diseases and present those results [17]. Application of these Artificial intelligence (AI) programs can be seen during medical procedures such as treatment protocol development, diagnosis processes, patient monitoring, drug development, and various others.

14.4.2 How to Use AI for Critical Care Units

Seeing the above advancements which have been made in Healthcare industry with the help of Artificial Intelligence, we can say that, it is very well possible to develop an Artificial Intelligence model to predict if a patient has a higher risk of having a health issue or not based on their past health records [18]. Also, providing software services, which possess the ability to automate the process of categorizing the risks involved in pandemics such as that of COVID on different patients around the world, is considered as a possible solution to this issue [19]. Furthermore, reduction in the frequency of lab testing due to increasing cases is an important issue.

With the help of AI, we can predict the tests performed in laboratories worldwide with even higher accuracy and precisely estimate the probable causes. Also, various surveillance systems have been developed which can monitor the emergence of respiratory tract infections [20].

14.4.2.1 Input Stage

All the items that could be classified under Input stage are briefly summarized here. Almost all the symptomatic patients could be flagged based on their signs and symptoms of COVID even before clinical testing. This is an early alarming system, which can be created with the help of AI. In fact, the detection of COVID Positive patients in clinical testing will take considerable time and also visiting facilities will put the patient under higher risk because of being in the vicinity of other high-risk patients due to the lack of space available to each facility. Also, data mining approaches can be used for the prediction of epidemiological data.

Building on this method, pandemics could be flagged even before healthcare industries discover them. This would be a beneficial option as it can save many other people who might come in contact with them. In addition to the above method, hotspots can be defined (places with high number of cases) along with some other places which will be the emerging epicenters in the near future with the help of mobile phone contacts, like the ones used in Arogya setu app in India, data mining approaches, social media data, air traffic maps and many other such possible ways.

Another kind of approach which can be made useful is that of having AI assisted techniques for defining the patterns by which the virus can spread across in the community along with telling the most probable effects on the health of patients beforehand on the upcoming steps of the outbreak. Setting an example, COVID-19 outbreak in China was effectively controlled by finding active cases through mobile phones [21]. This was an AI-based method which was used to a community's effect. AI could also boost personalized medicine by identifying potential and most susceptible people based on each persons' genetics and physiological characteristics. All these approaches will lead to the discovery of therapeutics and diagnostics; which are also, part of the output.

14.4.2.2 Process Stage

All the items that could be classified under Process stage are briefly summarized here. Deep learning can be a very useful tool in differential diagnosis of COVID-19 from various different diseases. Along with this, variations in genetic of severe, mild or even asymptomatic patients of COVID-19 can be used and machine learning analysis can be performed on them to predict potential patients in the future.

This approach would be performed based keeping in mind how well these patients resist to the potential COVID-19 infection. Studies have shown that critically ill patients can be monitored with the help of AI with especial focus on deep learning and pervasive sensing. Alternative approaches include, the use of AI for the improvement in the risk communication strategies in patients who are affected by COVID based on their location and timing.

14.4.2.3 Output Stage

All the items that could be classified under Output stage are briefly summarized here. Regarding output stage, the following items could be briefed as follows. COVID-19 being a systemic disease, affects the lungs with its most lethal complications. However, a confirmatory diagnosis of the patient is mandatory, before starting treatment. This relies on patients' past records, physical examination records and other clinical data. One of the most sensitive items still remains the Chest CT scans [22, 23].

Adding to the above, we can include CRISPR roles for detection of COVID-19 and enhance the speed of diagnosis and also the accuracy of the tests. An AI based system for patients that require critical care can also analyze the efficacy of lab tests for diagnosis of COVID and other related diseases and therefore, enhance its efficiency. Based on past experiences, AI based methods would help improve therapeutic approaches for COVID-19 patients.

One of the challenges that critical patients may face is the absence of proper methods and models for early detection and better management of critically ill patients undergoing perpetuated tracheostomy and mechanical ventilation. Here, a probable solution is brought forward with the use of AI. Along with the above Artificial Intelligence has paved out approaches which build upon algorithms like the Random Forest to manage and predict difficult airway for patients.

During the current times, production of COVID-19 vaccine is a challenge for the healthcare systems all over the world. In these times, Artificial Intelligence has come to the rescue and a new vaccinology tool has been proposed which integrates the healthcare with machine learning; this has come out as one of the major candidate in the field. Another mode of vaccine production which is influenced by silico models have also been claimed useful in this field. These are the ones which again rely on Artificial Intelligence, databases and also on silico tools.

The difficulties in the decision-making processes has been the major aspect, which appears whenever we have discussions about COVID patients. Artificial Intelligence along with its related models and algorithms could prove very effective in enabling better decision making. This process starts with estimation of the risks involved. This is followed by diagnosis of dataset, forecasting of medical and survival trends, then, the risks involved are classified and according to various categories specified followed by predicting the risk on the dataset provided. Finally, we predict the survival percentage according to the model formed.

During this pandemic, another important issue is the management for bed allocation; AI could be of help to us in deciding a cost-effective manner to do the task. Along with the above mentioned importance, AI can be useful for the protection of personal healthcare issues. This can be done by using various Artificial Intelligence algorithms and models, which include silico screening, mobile based surveys in quarantined areas and many more [24].

Management of COVID positive patients admitted in hospitals/healthcare centers is not a new challenge as it is just a new model for an old problem which occurred even before this pandemic. Usually, several therapies are taken concurrently by patients who have been admitted in healthcare centers, which is probably due to their health conditions. Sometimes, fixed guidelines are absent and this encourages the doctors/healthcare practitioners to make some decisions from his/her acquired knowledge, common belief and mostly experience. But, all this can be resolved whit the advent of Artificial Intelligence due to the fact that it has the potential to compute large volumes of data, make models on it and analyze the right choices so that no wrong practice is done.

Finally, AI and AI based methods will make the answering of difficult questions with good validity and reliability for each individual patient more probable. This has been the main reason why focus of studies has shifted to Artificial Intelligence in the fields of respiratory problems and also in managing of COVID patients. This is mainly done as AI can assist in creating an effective approach for these problems. Large datasets of heterogeneous and complex data are used for decision making by many healthcare professionals. If Artificial Intelligence is used effectively and efficiently in this sector, it can significantly reduce the complexity of the datasets by conversion of this data into more useful and relevant information [25–27].

Besides, AI is well known for having a defining role in determination of respiratory infectious diseases along with the determination of some serious obstructive lung disease. Still, we require studies at a higher scale with hard proofs for validating the AI findings. Also, we need proof for increasing the acceptance of AI by the healthcare sector as even the slightest of mistakes in these approaches can prove to be very fatal in such an industry.

Looking alternatively, making slight errors in medicine are always very costly and can be largely and more efficiently prevented with the help of Artificial Intelligence, Big Data, and various Machine Learning algorithms and models. The role of AI in decision making can be of great interest especially when sufficient data or physical evidence is unavailable.

According to a study, AI has the potential to reduce medical treatment expenses by approximately 50% and also medical errors by around 35% [28]. According to WHO, the two factors, which are, faulty diagnosis and medical errors are among the top causes of fatalities around the globe and around 10% of hospital admissions can lead to a medical error and around 0.3% admissions result in death as a result of these medical errors. So given this current scenario, AI is unarguably the most efficient way forward for healthcare institutions to eliminate these errors and make healthcare more safe and efficient [29].

Deep learning algorithms and models are now being used extensively in bioinformatics and classification. This is also being considered as a very impactful tool for analysis of infectious diseases. Considering another case which has provided some brilliant results is the use of ANN (artificial neural networks) for creation of models for classifying patients with respect to their respiratory problems [30].

This technology can further be utilized for the monitoring of the various trends in the healthcare sector, this will make the following aspects plausible in day-to-day practice:

- facial recognition
- facial detection
- facial action unit detection
- posture recognition
- sound pressure level detection
- visitation frequency detection
- light level detection

The use of Artificial Intelligence based decision making engines to efficiently manage patients with COVID-19 admitted in the healthcare institutes will provide assistance to the healthcare practitioners. The availability of accurate and comprehensive data is required for the design of this argument engine. This means that collection and storage of records on COVID prone patients has been seen as being of utmost importance for the making of models. Furthermore, disease registry systems need to be present for patients dealing with COVID.

As of now, healthcare sectors of most of the countries' are focused on controlling the pandemic along with properly treating the affected patients. Another concern is the production and manufacturing of the right vaccine and that too as quickly as possible. Along with the above, focus should also be on having quicker implementation of a complete and faster system for registry of the infected people. These efforts done by the whole world in defeating COVID-19 could be effectively aided with the introduction of decision-making system which use AI models. This would help in easier and better management of COVID patients.

COVID-19 will not only effect the lifestyle of people for a short term, but, will have a long and persistent impact on the society both mentally as well as economically. Each country has taken an economic hit, due to COVID-19, in a different way. This can be seen with respect to the GDP (Gross Domestic Product) of each country which has declined drastically over the first quarter of 2020 [31]. It will take years if not decades to recover these losses.

Nevertheless, COVID-19 has had its own positives also. This pandemic has led to a public which is more willing to accept and act on public health messages. Sources have also claimed a significant reduction in air pollution (20–30%) in many major cities around the world [32].

Also the enhancements made in the healthcare industry across the world during these times would help in the betterment of healthcare facilities in the longer run. Perhaps the most prominent change, which has been encountered is the widespread adoption of telehealth services and technologies which require the use of video calling to connect patients with both urgent and preventive care centers without their having to leave home. These Telehealth services has the potential to drastically expand healthcare to patients in remote areas where the access might be limited or extinct. It also has the potential to let other doctors or healthcare workers to handle patient screening and post-care follow-ups when a local facility is overloaded.

Also, the pandemic has emphasized on the importance of looking ahead and preparing for a crisis for the healthcare providers. If the spikes in COVID-19 cases was not controlled, it had the potential to overwhelm and overburden the hospitals and at the same time creating drug and equipment shortages. That's the reason these healthcare professionals maneuvered new and innovative ways for predicting the location and severity of future rise in COVID-19 cases. This technological advancement in the healthcare industry can be of utmost importance in predicting and restricting any pandemic beforehand in the future.

14.5 Conclusion

All the efforts that the healthcare industry all around the world is putting in to defeat this COVID-19 could have a real benefit with the inclusion of an AI-based decision-making system. This would not only help in increasing the rate of COVID-19 testing but also help in creating a system which manages the patients with ease and a higher efficiency and especially the ones in critical care during this pandemic.

Acknowledgment

The author would like to acknowledge the efforts of Mr. Saddam in making this possible, and also, National Institute of Technology, Kurukshetra, India for their help and support.

References

1. Paules, C.I., Marston, H.D., Fauci, A.S., Coronavirus Infections-More Than Just the Common Cold. *JAMA*, 323, 8, 707–708, 2020.
2. Zhu, N., Zhang, D., Wang, W., Li, X., Yang, B., Song, J. *et al.*, A Novel Coronavirus from Patients with Pneumonia in China, 2019. *N. Engl. J. Med.*, 382, 8, 727–33, 2020.
3. Wu, F., Zhao, S., Yu, B., Chen, Y.M., Wang, W., Song, Z.G. *et al.*, A new coronavirus associated with human respiratory disease in China. *Nature*, 579, 7798, 265–9, 2020.
4. Hui, D.S., IA, E., Madani, T.A., Ntoumi, F., Kock, R., Dar, O. *et al.*, The continuing 2019-nCoV epidemic threat of novel coronaviruses to global health—The latest 2019 novel coronavirus outbreak in Wuhan, China. *Int. J. Infect. Dis.*, 91, 264–6, 2020.
5. Takian, A., Raoofi, A., Kazempour-Ardebili, S., COVID-19 battle during the toughest sanctions against Iran. *Lancet*, 1035–1036, 1, 2020.
6. Namendys-Silva, S.A., Respiratory support for patients with COVID-19 infection. *Lancet Respir. Med.*, 8, 4, 18, 2020.
7. Zhang, D.H., Wu, K.L., Zhang, X., Deng, S.Q., Peng, B., In silico screening of Chinese herbal medicines with the potential to directly inhibit 2019 novel coronavirus. *J. Integr. Med.*, 18, 2, 152–8, 2020.
8. Alimadadi, A., Aryal, S., Manandhar, I., Munroe, P.B., Joe, B., Cheng, X., Artificial Intelligence and Machine Learning to Fight COVID-19. *Physiol. Genomics*, 52, 4, 200–202, 2020.
9. Keuning, B.E., Kaufmann, T., Wiersema, R., Granholm, A., Pettilä, V., Møller, M. *et al.*, Mortality prediction models in the adult critically ill: A scoping review. *Acta Anaesthesiol. Scand.*, 64, 4, 424–42, 2020.
10. Rao, A. and Vazquez, J., Identification of COVID-19 Can be Quicker through Artificial Intelligence framework using a Mobile PhoneBased Survey in the Populations when Cities/Towns Are Under Quarantine. *Infect. Control Hosp. Epidemiol.*, 41, 7, 826–830, 2020.
11. Alexis Ruiz, A., Wyszynska, P.K., Laudanski, K., Narrative Review of Decision-Making Processes in Critical Care. *Anesth. Analg.*, 128, 5, 962–70, 2019.
12. Gutierrez, G., Artificial Intelligence in the Intensive Care Unit. *Crit. Care*, 24, 1, 101, 2020.

13. Chapalain, X. and Huet, O., Is artificial intelligence (AI) at the doorstep of Intensive Care Units (ICU) and operating room (OR)? *Anaesth. Crit. Care Pain Med.*, 38, 4, 337–8, 2019.
14. Mathur, P. and Burns, M.L., Artificial Intelligence in Critical Care. *Int. Anesthesiol. Clin.*, 57, 2, 89–102, 2019.
15. Mupparapu, M., Wu, C.W., Chen, Y.C., Artificial intelligence, machine learning, neural networks, and deep learning: Futuristic concepts for new dental diagnosis. *Quintessence Int.*, 49, 9, 687–8, 2018.
16. Bini, S.A., Artificial Intelligence, Machine Learning, Deep Learning, and Cognitive Computing: What Do These Terms Mean and How Will They Impact Healthcare? *J. Arthroplasty*, 33, 8, 2358–61, 2018.
17. Lin, E. and Tsai, S.J., Machine Learning in Neural Networks. *Adv. Exp. Med. Biol.*, 1192, 127–37, 2019.
18. Cosgriff, C.V., Celi, L.A., Stone, D.J., Critical Care, Critical Data. *Biomed. Eng. Comput. Biol.*, 10, 1179597219856564, 2019.
19. Ghassemi, M., Celi, L.A., Stone, D.J., State of the art review: the data revolution in critical care. *Crit. Care*, 19, 118, 2015.
20. Hashimoto, D.A., Witkowski, E., Gao, L., Meireles, O., Rosman, G., Artificial Intelligence in Anesthesiology: Current Techniques, Clinical Applications, and Limitations. *Anesthesiology*, 132, 2, 379–94, 2020.
21. Pino Pena, I., Cheplygina, V., Paschaloudi, S., Vuust, M., Carl, J., Weinreich, U.M. *et al.*, Automatic emphysema detection using weakly labeled HRCT lung images. *PLoS One*, 13, 10, e0205397.4, 2018.
22. Badnjevic, A., Gurbeta, L., Custovic, E., An Expert Diagnostic System to Automatically Identify Asthma and Chronic Obstructive Pulmonary Disease in Clinical Settings. *Sci. Rep.*, 8, 1, 11645, 2018.
23. Tuite, A.R., Bogoch, I.I., Sherbo, R., Watts, A., Fisman, D., Khan, K., Estimation of Coronavirus Disease 2019 (COVID-19) Burden and Potential for International Dissemination of Infection From Iran. *Ann. Intern. Med.*, 172, 10, 699–701, 2020.
24. Robson, B., Computers and viral diseases. Preliminary bioinformatics studies on the design of a synthetic vaccine and a preventative peptidomimetic antagonist against the SARS-CoV-2 (2019-nCoV, COVID-19) coronavirus. *Comput. Biol. Med.*, 119, 103670, 2020.
25. Cismondi, F., Celi, L.A., Fialho, A.S., Vieira, S.M., Reti, S.R., Sousa, J.M. *et al.*, Reducing unnecessary lab testing in the ICU with artificial intelligence. *Int. J. Med. Inform.*, 82, 5, 345–58, 2013.
26. Bogoch, I.I., Watts, A., Thomas-Bachli, A., Huber, C., Kraemer, M.U.G., Khan, K., Potential for global spread of a novel coronavirus from China. *J. Travel. Med.*, 27, 2, 1195–1982, 2020.
27. Husnayain, A., Fuad, A., Su, E.C., Applications of google search trends for risk communication in infectious disease management: A case study of COVID-19 outbreak in Taiwan. *Int J. Infect. Dis.*, 95, 221–223, 2020.

28. Santosh, K.C., AI-Driven Tools for Coronavirus Outbreak: Need of Active Learning and Cross-Population Train/Test Models on Multitudinal/ Multimodal Data. *J. Med. Syst.*, 44, 5, 93, 2020.
29. Fraser, C., Donnelly, C.A., Cauchemez, S., Hanage, W.P., Van Kerkhove, M.D., Hollingsworth, T.D. *et al.*, Pandemic potential of a strain of influenza A (H1N1): Early findings. *Science*, 324, 5934, 1557–61, 2009.
30. Tarnok, A., Machine Learning, COVID-19 (2019-nCoV), and multi-OMICS. *Cytometry A*, 97, 3, 215–6, 2020.
31. Alan, C., Lee, COVID-19 and the Advancement of Digital Physical Therapist Practice and Telehealth, *Phys. Therapy,* 100, 7, 1054–1057, 2020.
32. Nelson, B., The Positive Effects of COVID-19, *BMJ (Clinical research ed.),* 369, m1775, 2020.

Index